Five Years of an Enlarged EU

Filip Keereman • Istvan Szekely
Editors

Five Years of an Enlarged EU

A Positive Sum Game

Springer

Editors
Filip Keereman
European Commission
ECFIN.E.2
BU1 -1/10
1049 Brussels
Belgium
filip.keereman@ec.europa.eu

Istvan Szekely
European Commission
ECFIN.A
BU-1 03/209
1049 Brussels
Belgium
istvan-pal.szekely@ec.europa.eu

The information and views set out in this book are those of the authors and do not necessarily reflect those of the Commission of the European Communities.

ISBN 978-3-642-12515-7 e-ISBN 978-3-642-12516-4
DOI 10.1007/978-3-642-12516-4
Springer Heidelberg Dordrecht London New York

Library of Congress Control Number: 2010931435

Cover design: WMXDesign GmbH, Heidelberg, Germany

Printed on acid-free paper

Springer is part of Springer Science+Business Media (www.springer.com)

Foreword

The Fifth Enlargement that took place in 2004 and 2007 was a milestone in the history of the European Union. Not only because of the large number of acceding countries but also because of their recent political and economic experience. Ten of them had undergone a profound transition from a totalitarian regime to democracy, and from a centrally planned economy to a market-based system. Most of them had income levels significantly below those of the then EU-15. Now, 6 years later, we can clearly see that the process of European integration, both before and after 2004, was what enabled Europe to overcome the gaps between various parts of the continent. The enlargement made Europe a better and wealthier place and strengthened its position in the world.

Integration into the European Union has always been one of the strongest incentives for reform in the new Member States. Particularly important in my view have been the development of financial markets through foreign direct investment and capital inflows, and the opening of labour markets – which was a two-way phenomenon, with markets being opened up in acceding as well as the incumbent Member States. The Fifth Enlargement was thus an exercise of globalisation in miniature, a practice run for the Union to tackle the challenges of the ever smaller world.

This book brings together a number of papers by academic researchers and colleagues in other international institutions and critically assesses the first 5 years of the enlarged European Union. Despite the setback which the economic and financial crisis undoubtedly represents, I am convinced that the path followed was the right one and that the foundations of European integration are sound and robust. This book supports this view. But we cannot rest on our laurels in times of economic hardship. We need to carefully analyse and critically assess the factors of growth and the role of the EU in enhancing welfare and accelerating convergence. This book is an excellent contribution to the ongoing debate on these issues.

Olli Rehn
Commissioner for Economic and Financial Affairs

Acknowledgements and Disclaimer

The 2004 and 2007 enlargements of the European Union were unprecedented in many ways. While the political dimension cannot be overestimated, the economic significance is equally important. In order to make a contribution to the understanding of the process of market integration and income convergence, the Directorate General Economic and Financial Affairs of the European Commission launched a series of studies ahead of the fifth anniversary of the latest enlargement on 1 May 2009. The academic studies prepared by researchers at universities and think-tanks were presented at a workshop organised in Brussels on 13 and 14 November 2008 and an edited version of their papers can be found in this book, as well as the discussants' comments.

We would like to thank all those who contributed to make the workshop a success and broaden our knowledge on economic growth and catching-up in Europe. The insights provided helped us drafting the Commission report on the matter including a Communication released on 20 February 2009. Further to authors and discussants, we acknowledge the chairpersons of the various sessions at the workshop. Last but not least the technical assistance by Rajko Vodovnik and Martine Maebe in preparing this manuscript was greatly appreciated as well as Anita Ivan's contribution to the index list and Robert Gangl's work as publication manager.

The views expressed are the authors', discussants' and editors' alone and do not necessarily correspond to those of the European Commission or the institutions to which some of the contributors mentioned in this book are affiliated.

Filip Keereman and Istvan F. Szekely
The editors

Contents

Authors

Jan Babecký Jan Babecký obtained a Master in economics at the University of the State of New York and CERGE-EI, Prague (2000) and holds a PhD. from the University of Paris-1 Sorbonne and CERGE-EI, Prague (2005) with a thesis on transition and EU enlargement. He joined the Czech National Bank in 2003 and is since 2007 Senior Economist in the Economic Research and Financial Stability Department. His academic activities include various teaching and research assignments at universities and international institutions as well as being a member of the editorial board of the Czech Economic Review. He published on international monetary issues, exchange rates, labour markets and wage flexibility.

Jean-Claude Berthélemy Jean-Claude Berthélemy is Professor of Economics at Paris 1 Pantheon Sorbonne University since 1993. He is also affiliated with the French Academy of Social Sciences. He has spent part of his career at the Organization for Economic Co-operation and Development (OECD), where he was director of research at the Development Centre from 1994 to 1997. He has published extensively on various aspects of development economics and his recent research papers are focused on health, poverty and economic development, with a particular attention to Africa. Besides his academic activities, he is regularly consulted on development policies by international organizations such as the World Bank and the European Commission and by governments.

Fritz Breuss Fritz Breuss is emeritus professor of international economics at the Vienna University of Economics and Business. Since 1995, professor Breuss is also Jean Monnet Professor for Economics of European Integration. Prof. Breuss was a visiting scholar at the University of Cambridge in 1980 and at University of California (Berkeley) in 1985. At the beginning of his career, Prof. Breuss was an economist at the Austrian Institute of Economic Research in Vienna. Key areas of interest are international economics and European integration with special focus on monetary integration and EU enlargement. He published extensively on these topics.

Aleš Bulíř Aleš Bulíř works since 1993 at the International Monetary Fund and prior to that appointment he was Associate Professor at the Prague University of Economics and Advisor to the Czech National Bank. He holds a MSc (Economics) from the London School of Economics and Political Science and a PhD from the Prague University of Economics. He is associate editor of the Czech Journal of Economics and Finance. Aleš Bulíř published on development aid, monetary policy, economic convergence and exchange rates.

Stefania Fabrizio Stefania Fabrizio is Deputy Division Chief in the IMF's Strategy, Policy and Review Department. Prior to the current position, she was in the European Department, where she was mission head for Cyprus and was involved in several Article IV consultation missions to Hungary, Lithuania and Italy. She also did extensive country-specific work on low-income countries when she was at the IMF's African Department. Before joining the IMF, Ms. Fabrizio was a visit professor at the University of Salamanca, Spain. She published on topics related to the politics of public finances, public debt sustainability and external competitiveness.

Sabine Hermann Sabine Hermann is currently employed in the Economics department as well as in the economic research centre of the Deutsche Bundesbank. She also worked for 6 month in the European Neighbouring Region Division of the European Central Bank as a national central bank expert. Mrs. Hermann has a Master of Arts from the University of Basel and obtained an MBA at the University of Munich. She holds a PhD in economics from the Faculty of Applied Macroeconomics at the University of Basel. She is a lecturer at the Frankfurt School of Finance and a referee for several economic Journals. Mrs. Hermann has published extensively on issues related to monetary and financial integration, current account developments in Central and Eastern Europe and real convergence in Eastern Europe.

Martin Kahanec Martin Kahanec is Assistant Professor at the Central European University in Budapest and Senior Research Associate, Deputy Program Director "Migration", and former Deputy Director of Research at the Institute for the Study of Labour (IZA) in Bonn. He has a PhD in Economics from Tilburg University, a Master of Arts degree in Economics from the Central European University and a Master degree in Management from Comenius University in Bratislava. He has held several advisory positions and participated in and coordinated a number of scientific and policy projects with the World Bank, European Commission, OECD, and other international and national institutions. Dr. Kahanec is a member of several professional associations. His topics of interest include labour markets, ethnicity and migration, on which he has published extensively over the last few years.

Elzbieta Kawecka-Wyrzykowska Elzbieta Kawecka-Wyrzykowska is professor of Economics (Ad personam Jean Monnet Chairholder), Head of the Jean Monnet Chair of European Integration at the Warsaw School of Economics since

1998 and Vice Rector of the Warsaw School of Economics (for International Cooperation) since 2008. Ms. Kawecka-Wyrzykowska has published widely on European economic integration and the GATT/WTO system. She was a representative of the Polish government at trade negotiations during the GATT Uruguay Round and served as an economic adviser to the President of Poland in the period 2002–2005. She coordinated several international research projects and prepared a number of expertises for OECD and Economic Commission for Europe on implications of the Uruguay Round for countries in transition.

Filip Keereman Filip Keereman studied economics at the Catholic University of Leuven (Belgium), obtained an MBA at the University of Chicago (USA) and holds a PhD. from the European University Institute in Florence (Italy). He joined the research department of Kredietbank (now KBC) in 1984. As an official of the European Commission since 1986, he has dealt with the liberalisation of capital movements, monetary integration, economic forecasts, fiscal policy and EU enlargement. Currently, he is head of the unit responsible for monitoring national financial developments and external funding in the Directorate General for Economic and Financial Affairs. He published on financial integration, forecast accuracy and the new EU Member States.

Daniel Leigh Daniel Leigh is an Economist at the Research Department of the IMF. He also served on the IMF teams of number of emerging market economies, including Hungary, Lithuania, Gabon, Colombia, and Peru. His research interests fall in the general field of international macroeconomics. He has publications in *Economic Policy*, the *Journal of Money, Credit and Banking*, and the *Journal of Economic Dynamics and Control*. In addition, he has written several chapters of the IMF's *World Economic Outlook*. He holds a PhD in Economics from Johns Hopkins University, and a MSc in Economics from the London School of Economics.

Mathilde Maurel Mathilde Maurel is currently researcher at the CNRS (Centre National de la Recherche Scientifique) and Deputy Director of the CES (Centre d'économie de la Sorbonne). She holds a PhD in Applied Economics from the Ecole des Hautes Etudes en Sciences Sociales. She has published extensively on transition economics and her recent research papers are focused on European integration, economies of Central and Eastern Europe, exchange rates and migration. Besides her academic activities, she is consulted on development policies by international organizations such as the World Bank, the European Commission and by Consulting Agencies. She is a member in several professional associations and a referee in editorial boards of international economics and comparative economics journals.

Ashoka Mody Ashoka Mody is Assistant Director in the IMF's European Department. He headed the IMF's 2008 Article IV consultation mission to Germany. He has led missions to Switzerland and Hungary, and is currently also mission head for Ireland. Prior to this country-specific work, he held managerial positions in the IMF's Research Department and at the World Bank. He has held teaching positions at the University of Pennsylvania's Wharton School. He has published widely on international finance, especially emerging markets' access to foreign capital, domestic political economy, and the politics of reforming the financial sector and public finances.

Karl Pichelmann Karl Pichelmann is currently Research Adviser in the Directorate General for Economic and Financial Affairs and Associate Professor at the Universite Libre de Bruxelles. Mr. Pichelmann earned his PhD from the University of Vienna in 1983. Before joining the European Commission, he was a senior economist at the Institute for Advanced Studies in Vienna. He held various consultancy positions in the past, including a stint at the OECD in the context of the Jobs Study. Current research interests focus on globalisation and European economic and monetary integration and its impact on labour markets and social models in Europe.

Ryszard Rapacki Ryszard Rapacki is professor of economics and head of the department of economics at the Warsaw School of Economics. Since 2000, he is also an Associate Professor at the Carlson School of Management, University of Minnesota. Previously, he was a Fulbright scholar at Michigan State University and a visiting scholar at the University of Minnesota. His main areas of research are macroeconomic theory, economic policy, systemic transformation in Eastern Europe, public finances as well as economic growth and real convergence. Professor Rapacki published extensively in Poland, UK, Germany and the US.

Sandor Richter Since 1990, Sandor Richter is senior economist at the Vienna Institute for International Economic Studies. At the beginning of his career, Mr. Richter was a research economist at the Institute of Economics of the Hungarian Academy of Sciences. He pursued undergraduate and doctoral studies at the Budapest University of Economic Sciences. His topics of research cover regional integration, international trade and the Hungarian economy. He has published extensively on these topics.

Katerina Smidkova Katerina Smidkova is currently an Executive Director in the Economic Research and Financial Stability Department of the Czech National Bank and an Associate Professor at the Faculty of Social Sciences of the Charles University in Prague. She has a PhD. in economics from the Faculty of Social Sciences of the Charles University. Mrs. Smidkova is a member of several professional associations in the Czech Republic and a member of the Steering committee of the ECB-CFS Network on Capital Markets and Financial Integration in Europe. Current research focuses on issues related to exchange rates, FDI and the transmission mechanism of monetary policy.

Juraj Stančík Juraj Stančík is currently a scientific fellow in the Institute for Prospective Technological Studies of the European Commission in Seville. He has a PhD in economics from the Center for Economic Research and Graduate Education in Prague. In 2007, he was a visiting scholar at the School of Arts and Sciences of the University of Pennsylvania. His areas of interests cover international economics and econometrics.

Istvan Szekely He has a PhD in economics from the University of Cambridge. He is also on the faculty of the Corvinus University in Budapest as an honorary professor. Before joining the European Commission in 2007, he worked at the International Monetary Fund (1999–2007) as a mission chief and in the National Bank of Hungary (1996–1999) as a general manager and advisor the governor. His research focuses on financial market and macroeconomic policy issues and on Central and Eastern European economies. He has published several books and articles in these areas.

Corina Weidinger Sosdean Corina Weidinger Sosdean is an economist in the Directorate General for Economic and Financial Affairs (Macrofinancial stability). Before joining the European Commission, she worked in the field of financial market supervision, as expert at the Austrian Financial Market Authority in Vienna. She has a PhD. in economics from the University of Timisoara (Romania) and a Master of Arts in international relations from the University of Vienna and Vienna Institute of International Studies. Topics of interests: financial markets, banking and insurance supervision, emerging economies.

Adalbert Winkler Adalbert Winkler holds a PhD from Trier University and a post-doc ("Habilitation") from the Bayerische Julius-Maximilians University of Würzburg. Mr. Winkler held lectureships at Frankfurt's Goethe University, at Chemnitz University of Technology (Commerzbank Visiting Professor) and served for more than 10 years as (senior) lecturer at the Bayerische Julius-Maximilians University of Würzburg. In 2001 Mr. Winkler joined the European Central Bank (ECB) in the ECB's Directorate General International and European Relations and from 2004 to 2007 he was Deputy Head of Division. In the first half of 2008 he served as an advisor at the International Department of Deutsche Bundesbank. Mr. Winkler research interests and publications have been focusing on financial development and growth, development and microfinance as well as monetary policy and financial stability challenges in emerging markets, the international role of currencies and developments in the global monetary system.

Klaus F. Zimmermann Klaus F. Zimmermann is Director of the Institute for the Study of Labor (IZA) in Bonn, President of DIW Berlin and Professor of Economics at Bonn University. He received his doctoral degree and habilitation from the University of Mannheim. His current professional interests cover issues of migration, labour, financial markets and the macro economy. Prof. Zimmermann has served as an adviser to the President of the EU Commission as a Member of the Group of Economic Analysis and he is currently a Member of the "Group of Societal Policy Analysis." He has held numerous other advisory and consulting positions for senior policy makers, opinion leaders in Germany, and international organisations. Prof. Zimmermann is a member of many international organisations and has co-ordinated a wide range of academic projects and organised many professional conferences.

Abbreviations

Member States

AT	Austria
BE	Belgium
BG	Bulgaria
CY	Cyprus
CZ	Czech Republic
DE	Germany
DK	Denmark
EE	Estonia
EL	Greece
ES	Spain
FI	Finland
FR	France
HU	Hungary
IE	Ireland
IT	Italy
LT	Lithuania
LU	Luxembourg
LV	Latvia
MT	Malta
NL	The Netherlands
PL	Poland
PT	Portugal
RO	Romania
SE	Sweden
SI	Slovenia
SK	Slovakia
UK	United Kingdom

Other Countries

AL	Albania
BA	Bosnia Herzegovina
BR	Brunei
EA	Euro area
EU	European Union
EU-2	RO, BG
EU-8	EU-10 minus Cyprus and Malta (Central and Eastern European countries)
EU-10	European Union, Member States that joined the EU on 1 May 2004 (CZ, EE, CY, LT, LV, HU, MT, PL, SI and SK)
EU-12	EU-10 plus Member States that joined the EU on 1 January 2007 (BG, RO)
EU-15	European Union, 15 Member States before 1 May 2004 (BE, DK, DE, EL, ES, FR, IE, IT, LU, NL, AT, PT, FI, SE and UK)
EU-25	European Union, 25 Member States before 1 January 2007
EU-27	European Union, 27 Member States
HK	Hong-Kong
HR	Croatia
ID	Indonesia
KR	South Korea
KS	Kosovo
MK	FYR Macedonia
MY	Malaysia
PH	The Philippines
RS	Serbia
SG	Singapore
TH	Thailand
TR	Turkey
TW	Taiwan

Currencies

BGN	New Bulgarian lev
CZK	Czech koruna
DKK	Danish krone
EEK	Estonian kroon
EUR	Euro
GBP	Pound sterling
HUF	Hungarian forint
JPY	Japanese yen
LTL	Lithuanian litas

LVL	Latvian lats
PLN	New Polish złoty
RON	New Romanian leu
SEK	Swedish krona
SKK	Slovak koruna
USD	US dollar

Other Abbreviations

AMECO	Annual Macro ECOnomic database (Directorate General Economic and Financial Affairs, European Commission)
BIS	Bank for International Settlements
Bn.	Billion
CAP	Common Agricultural Policy
CARDS	Community Assistance for Reconstruction, Development and Stabilisation
CEE	Central and Eastern European
CEECs	Central and Eastern European Countries
CET	Common external tariff
CF	Cohesion fund
CGE	Computable general equilibrium
CIS	Commonwealth of independent states
CUs	Custom unions
DCR	Domestically captured rent
DG ECFIN	Directorate General Economic and Financial Affairs (European Commission)
EAFRD	European Agricultural Fund for Rural Development
EAGF	European Agricultural Guarantee Fund
EAs	Europe Agreements
EBRD	European Bank for Reconstruction and Development
ECB	European Central Bank
EDP	Excessive deficit procedure
EFF	European Fisheries Fund
EFTA	European Free Trade Association
EMBI	Emerging Markets Bond Index
EMU	Economic and Monetary Union
ERDF	European Regional Development Fund
ERM II	Exchange Rate Mechanism, mark II
ESCB	European System of Central Banks
ESF	European Social Fund
Eurostat	Statistical Office of the European Communities
FDI	Foreign direct investment
FTAs	Free trade agreements

GDP	Gross domestic product
GNI	Gross national income
GTAP	Global Trade Analysis Project
GUT	Grand Unified Theory
HICP	Harmonised index of consumer prices
HIIT	Horizontal Intra-Industry Trade
ICRG	International Country Risk Guide
ICT	Information and communications technology
IIT	Intra-Industry Trade
IMF	International Monetary Fund
IP	Industrial Production
IPA	Instrument for Pre-Accession Assistance
ISPA	Instrument for Structural Policies for Pre-Accession
lhs	Left hand side
M&A	Mergers and Acquisitions
MENA	Middle East and Northern Africa
MFN	Most favored nations
Mio.	Million
NAFTA	North American Free Trade Agreement
NiGEM	National Institute of Economic & Social Research Global Econometric Model (UK)
NMS	New Member States
NTB	Non-tariff barrier
NUTS	Nomenclature of Territorial Units for Statistics
OCA	Optimum currency area
OMS	Old Member States
p.p.	Percentage point
PHARE	Poland and Hungary: Assistance for Restructuring their Economies
PPS	Purchasing Power Standard
R&D	Research and development
REER	Real effective exchange rate
rhs	Right hand side
RIAs	Regional Integration Agreements
RoE	Return on equity
RoW	Rest of the World
RTAs	Regional Trade agreements
SAPARD	Special Accession Programme for Agriculture and Rural Development
SE Asia	Southeast Asia
SF	Structural Fund
SGP	Stability and Growth Pact
SITC	Standard International Trade Classification
SM	Single Market

SRER	Sustainable real exchange rates
Tacis	Technical Assistance to the Commonwealth of Independent States
TFP	Total factor productivity
ULC	Unit labour costs
UN	United Nations
USSR	Union of Soviet Socialist Republics
VA	Value added
VAT	Value added tax
VER	Voluntary export restraints
VIIT	Vertical Intra-Industry Trade
WTO	World Trade Organisation

Legend to Tables

:	Figures are negligible
na	Not available

List of Figures

List of Tables

List of Boxes

Chapter 1
Overview

Filip Keereman and István P. Székely

Abstract As an input to its own report on the impact of the 2004–2007 enlargement on the European Union (European Commission 2009), the Directorate General Economic and Financial Affairs (DG ECFIN) of the European Commission invited lead experts in the area to provide their assessment of the key aspects of EU enlargement. This volume contains these contributions presented at a workshop on "Five years of an enlarged EU – a positive sum-game", organized by DG ECFIN in Brussels on 13–14 November 2008.

1.1 Enlargement Is a Positive Sum Game, but Strong Domestic Policies Are Essential to Fully Realize Benefits

The biggest enlargement in the history of the EU took place more than 5 years ago. While it may be too soon to draw final conclusions, the main findings of the contributions to this volume, and those of a comprehensive report by the European Commission (2009), suggest that the first 5 years of the enlargement were a major success. The present severe downturn and the financial crisis do not put this assessment into doubt, but it highlights many of the future challenges. Key is to set in place the appropriate policy framework to make real income convergence and integration a lasting process.

In particular, the new Member States benefited from faster growth that enabled them to increase their per capita GDP (at purchasing power parity) from 40% of the EU-15 average prior to enlargement to 52% by 2008. The EU made a difference in this regard. Based on a growth regression analysis, it is estimated that each year during the period 2000–2008 accession helped the new Member States raise growth

F. Keereman and I.P. Székely
European Commission, Directorate General Economic and Financial Affairs, Brussels, Belgium
e-mail: filip.keereman@ec.europa.eu

F. Keereman and I. Szekely (eds.), *Five Years of an Enlarged EU*,
DOI 10.1007/978-3-642-12516-4_1, © Springer-Verlag Berlin Heidelberg 2010

by $1\frac{3}{4}$% points on average. This compares favourably with the Commission services' *ex ante* estimate in 2001 of 1¼% points additional growth in a central scenario. The most important factor explaining this growth premium was the productivity improvements that FDI and the associated transfer of technology brought about.

Financial integration also played an important role in accelerating real convergence. Model simulations suggest that the narrowing of the interest rate spread was important in this regard. Estimations suggest that new Member States enjoyed a 50–100 basis point advantage relative to other emerging countries with comparable fundamentals, in fact starting prior to accession. This contributed some 0.3% point of additional growth. With the outbreak of the financial crisis in 2007, risk premia have risen, but it seems the new Member States continue to benefit in this regard, certainly those under the protective umbrella of the euro and those with sound macroeconomic policies.

Old Member States gained from enlargement as well. Firstly, they benefited from a larger export market. It is estimated that in the 5 years after enlargement exports to the new Member States contributed 1% point per year on average to an overall annual export growth of 6% in the old Member States. Partly as a result, most of them realised a comfortable trade surplus with the new Member States.

Secondly, the private sector responded to the challenges enlargement brought about by restructuring production networks and locating plants to maximise efficiency. This helped maintain global competitiveness, boost growth all across the EU and ultimately safeguard jobs in the old Member States. Sizable short-term adjustment costs arose in some sectors (e.g. food, clothing, publishing, communication equipment, office machinery, motor vehicles) as employment in the old Member States was negatively correlated with the rise in employment in the new Member States. However, as the Commission's report points out (European Commission 2009), in several sectors (machinery, furniture, medical instruments, chemicals, wood) investment in new Member States went hand-in-hand with employment creation in the old members.

Finally, enlargement did not lead to a flood of migrant workers "stealing" jobs in the old Member States. Since 2004, about 1.6 million people migrated from new to old Member States, bringing the total to 3.6 million. This is less than 1% of the working age population in the old Member States, except in Ireland where it reached a much higher level (about 5%). According to simulations with DG ECFIN's QUEST model (D'Auria et al. 2008), this migration adds some 0.4% to GDP in the medium term as bottlenecks in labour markets ease and the skill composition of the migrants is favourable, albeit not optimally used in the short term.

In short, global competitiveness, and thus the growth potential, of the EU economy as a whole strengthened through deepening financial intermediation and integration, accelerated knowledge transfer, and increasing cross-border employment. Particularly, increased FDI, cross-border holding of financial assets, and remittances of migrant workers improved allocative efficiency and risk sharing, promoting a higher degree of specialisation and raising productivity all across the enlarged EU. But benefits do not come automatically. Strong domestic policies, both at the macroeconomic and structural levels, are necessary to ensure that the possibilities offered through the opening of the borders are well used and, thus, the benefits of integration are fully reaped. In a catching-up context, particular attention has to be paid to maintain macrofinancial stability, improve competitiveness and enhance the productive potential of the economy.

1.2 The EU Made a Difference, but Not Every Country Took Full Advantage

EU policies and institutions, including the Stability and Growth Pact, the Lisbon agenda, the Single Market rules and the EU transfer system, played an important role, explaining why the benefits of EU enlargement went beyond the classical benefits of economic integration. Structural and cohesion funds provided sizable new resources to lower-income Member States, focused efforts on growth-enhancing investments in infrastructure and human capital, and increased the quality of public spending in general. Model-based calculations suggest that the transfers new Member States will receive through 2013 from structural and cohesion funds will increase their income level by about 4% permanently (Varga and in 't Veld 2009).

However, not every country has fully exploited the potential benefits of EU enlargement, and some of the processes involved in economic and financial integration have also created vulnerabilities, mostly because of poor domestic policies. History shows that catching-up cannot be taken for granted, and that it is not a linear process (Fig. 1), pointing at the responsibility of policy makers in this regard. Moreover, the current crisis will no doubt stress test the development model the new members have followed so far. This model was based on easy access to relatively cheap foreign capital (made possible by rapid financial integration) and led to rapid financial deepening in these countries. Thus, these countries could not only exploit investment opportunities in productive sectors but also significantly raise consumption and increase housing investment, in a way bringing forward the benefits of EU enlargement.

1.3 Main Messages from the Workshop

The findings of the papers presented in this volume corroborate this overall assessment, albeit with important nuances regarding some of the key aspects.

Regarding trade and FDI discussed in Chap. 2, E. Kawecka-Wyrzykowska (Warsaw School of Economics, Poland) analyses the quality of the trade between the new and old Member States, and documents that intra-industry trade increased. She sees this as evidence of catching up by the recently acceded countries, driven by the modernization of the product structure of exports which became more similar

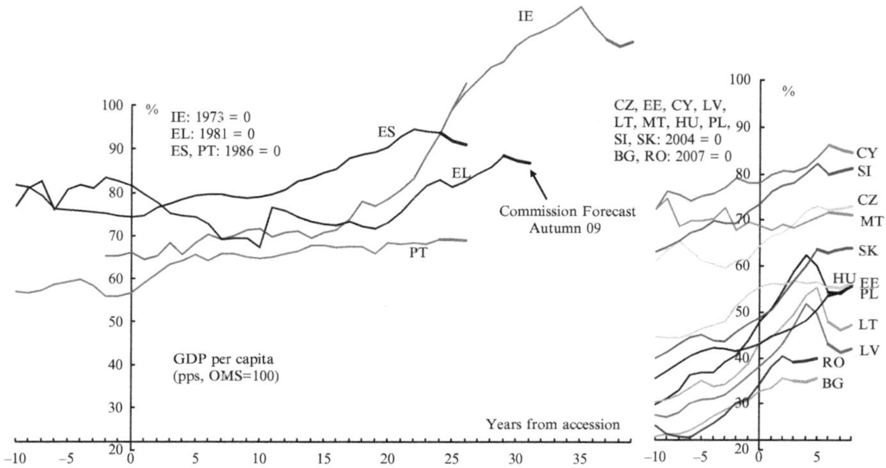

Fig. 1.1 Catching up, member states now and before

to that of the old Member States. J. Stančik (Center for Economic Research and Graduate Education and the Economics Institute, Czech Republic) is more critical on the role of foreign direct investment than most observers. His econometric research on the Czech Republic suggests that the hoped-for positive spillovers to domestic firms do not always materialize. In his comments on these papers, S. Richter (Vienna Institute for International Economic Studies, Austria) emphasizes that most of the changes in trade and investment in the EU occurred before enlargement. He also underlines the limitations of using intra-industry trade as an indicator of the quality upgrade of trade, and argues that the full advantages of foreign direct investment will be seen only later when necessary adjustment takes place.

In Chap. 5 on labor migration, M. Kahanec and K. Zimmermann (Institute for the Study of Labour, Bonn University, respectively; Germany) find that the feared disturbances associated with cross border movements of people did not happen following the 2004–2007 enlargement of the EU. Wage differentials are found to be the most important motive for leaving the country, while there is no evidence that migrants are primarily attracted by access to welfare payments. In the second contribution to this chapter, J.-C. Berthélemy and M. Maurel (University of Paris, France) defend a non-linear relationship between migration and income. Up to a certain threshold, the prospect of higher earnings will stimulate migration because it can help alleviate the family budget constraint, while above a certain threshold, rising incomes will start slowing down or even reversing this process. With this hump-shaped curve the authors rationalize a restrictive migration policy towards poor countries, while they find such a policy inconsistent for countries beyond a critical threshold. As to the EU, they argue that most new Member States have already passed this threshold. In their comments K. Pichelmann and F. Keereman (Directorate General Economic and Financial Affairs of the European Commission) broadly agree with Kahanec and Zimmermann and present further evidence of the positive impact on both receiving and sending countries. However, they question that existence of a hump-shaped relationship between income and migration.

Regarding financial integration and stability in an enlarged EU, discussed in Chap. 8, S. Hermann and A. Winkler (Deutsche Bundesbank and European Central Bank, respectively) test for the relevance of financial characteristics in explaining the apparent differences between the catching up processes in Europe and Asia. Based on an elaborate empirical analysis, they argue that developed and more integrated financial markets increase emerging market economies' ability to borrow abroad. Moreover, they also find that the degree of financial integration within convergence clubs (the EU, on the one hand, and the US and Emerging Asia on the other) and the extent of reserve accumulation are significant factors in explaining the divergent patterns of real convergence and the current account in these regions. In the other contribution, J. Babecký, A. Bulíř and K. Šmídková (Czech National Bank, International Monetary Fund, Czech National Bank, respectively) call the attention to the importance of allocative efficiency regarding FDI. They find that the real appreciation brought about by FDI in most NMS is moderate enough to allow for smooth nominal convergence required for euro adoption. In some case, however, mostly when the initial net external debt is low and the FDI inflow is massive, and/or when FDI is channeled mostly into housing construction and other non-tradables, meeting the Maastricht criteria poses a major challenge to policy makers. In the latter countries, increasing net external debt does not seem to lead to improving trade balance in a later phase. In her comments, C. Weidinger (Directorate General Economic and Financial Affairs of the European Commission) points out that while the EU-15 countries are clearly the core for European convergence club, this issue is more complex in the case of emerging Asia, which has important ties to Japan. She also argues for using price-based indicators of financial integration in the empirical analysis. On FDI inflows, she points out that they accelerated already prior to EU enlargement, mostly as a result of capital account liberalization in the Central and Eastern European countries in the early 1990s after the start of economic transition. She also calls the attention to the impact of other types of capital flows, including from EU structural funds, on real exchange rate dynamics.

In Chap. 11 on integration, growth and openness, S. Fabrizio, D. Leigh, and A. Mody (International Monetary Fund) discuss the characteristics of two remarkable transitions Eastern European countries achieved in the past two decades: from plan to market and, then, in the run-up to and entry into the European Union. Focusing on the second transition, they also compare East Europe and East Asia and find that the growth performances of these two regions have been about on par since the mid-1990s. But they point out that the mechanisms of growth in East Europe and East Asia have been very different. East Europe has relied on financial integration, with structural change to compensate for appreciating real exchange rates. In contrast, East Asia has contained further financial integration and maintained steady or depreciating real exchange rates. Regarding the ongoing financial crisis, they find no obvious differentiation among emerging market regions: rather, the hot spots in each region seem to reflect individual country vulnerabilities. In the other contribution, F. Breuss (Vienna University of Economics and Business) focuses on the impact of the 2007 enlargement when Bulgaria and Romania joined the EU. Using a simple macro-economic integration model, he finds that the direct integration effects spill-over to the old Member States and the ten new Member States of the 2004 EU enlargement. The pattern of the integration effects is qualitatively similar to those of the 2004 enlargement. In the medium-run up to 2020, Bulgaria and Romania can expect a sizable overall integration gain, amounting to an additional ½% point real GDP growth per annum. Among the incumbent EU Member States, Austria will gain somewhat more (+0.05%) than the average of EU-15 (+0.02%) and the ten new EU Member States (+0.01%). In his comments on development models, R Rapacki (Warsaw School of Economics), calls the attention to de Soto's (2002) work on development and the importance of trust emphasized by Fukuyama (1996). He also points out the significant role EU accession played as an external anchor by promoting important growth-enhancing institutional and structural reforms. Regarding the second paper, he argues that by following the golden rule, fiscal restraint, and more generally, the tradeoff between the real and nominal convergence, becomes a much less difficult issue to handle.

1.4 A Three-Pronged Strategy by the EU to Safeguard Achievements

The contributions to this volume, as well as the Commission's report on the EU enlargement (European Commission 2009), were mostly written and reflect developments prior to the current crisis. The EU, however, is now facing the most severe global economic crisis since its creation. This crisis may have strong longer-term effects on potential growth, as the relative price of risk is likely to have increased significantly and the pace of financial integration and deepening could slow down as a result of the necessary re-regulation of the financial system. As the new Member states were particularly affected, real convergence may be hindered in the longer run. To preserve cohesion in the EU, it is essential to ensure that the setback is only temporary (Buti et al. 2009).

The new Member states, however, are not left on their own in this difficult situation. The European Commission is implementing a three-pronged strategy to respond to the crisis. First, it is crucial to enhance multilateral surveillance with a view to reducing external vulnerabilities. A significant part of foreign capital has been allocated to non-productive uses and foreign exchange risk has not been allocated optimally in the system, leaving households and firms in the non-tradable sector with too much currency risk. Private markets have also created sizable maturity mismatches, mostly in the financial system and in foreign exchange. Maintaining fiscal sustainability will be critical to keeping interest rates low and avoiding the crowding out of private business. While the Stability and Growth Pact will most certainly play a central role in this regard, strong national fiscal frameworks are equally important. The structural reform agenda of the EU (EU2020) is more relevant than ever, as the reforms identified in this process are crucial to counterbalance the negative impact of the crisis on potential growth and to increase the resilience of European economies.

Second, more financial resources have been made available on a case-by-case basis. The EU Balance of Payments facility was increased significantly, and, as part of a multilateral rescue effort, three countries (Hungary, Latvia and Romania) have so far tapped this facility. The European Investment Bank and the European Bank for Reconstruction and Development have also stepped up their efforts to provide co-ordinated financial assistance mainly for the private sector. The EU also contributed significantly to the increase of financial resources of the IMF, and through advance payments, front-loaded EU transfers to the new Member states.

Finally, given the importance of strengthening financial markets, the third element of the strategy is to foster co-operation between home and host supervisors and to get parent banks from the old Member States on board in the multilateral support programmes.

Summing up, the 2004/2007 enlargement made the EU more competitive, and it is therefore better positioned to face the new challenges that the current crisis has created. By eliminating trade barriers, gradually allowing higher cross-border labour mobility, promoting financial integration, strengthening institutions, and significantly reducing political risk in the new Member States, enlargement brought about major benefits for both old and new Member States. Notwithstanding these achievements, the financial crisis has revealed major vulnerabilities that are not limited to the new Member States because of the increased interdependencies within the enlarged EU. These vulnerabilities need to be addressed and adequate measures should be taken to limit the setback to real convergence within the EU.

References

Buti, M., Keereman, F., & Szekely, I. P. (2009). *Five years after the enlargement of the EU*. http://www.VoxEU.org, June.

D'Auria, F., Morrow, K. Mc., & Pichelmann, K. (2008, November). *Economic impact of migration flows following the 2004 EU enlargement process: A model based analysis*. European Economy Economic Papers, No. 349.

De Soto, H. (2002). *The mystery of capital. Why capitalism triumphs in the West and fails everywhere else*. Polish ed., Wydawnictwo: Fijorr Publishing

European Commission (2009). Five years of an enlarged EU: Economic achievements and challenges. *European economy*, vol. 1.

Fukuyama, F. (1996). *Trust. The social virtues and the creation of prosperity*. London: Penguin Books.

Varga, J. & in 't Veld, J. (2009, March). *A model-based assessment of the macroeconomic impact of EU structural funds on the new member states*. European Economy Economic Papers, No. 371.

Part I
Trade and Foreign Direct Investment in an Enlarged EU: Opportunities and Challenges

Chapter 2
Evolving Pattern of Intra-industry Trade Specialization of the New Member States of the EU: The Case of the Automotive Industry

Elżbieta Kawecka-Wyrzykowska

Abstract The paper investigates the development of intra-industry trade of the new Member States with major partners between 2000 and 2007. Intra-industry trade is separated into horizontal and vertical components on the basis of differences in unit values. We have found that although inter-industry trade still accounts for almost 50% of the trade of the countries that joined the EU in 2004, its share has been declining to the benefit of intra-industry trade (except for Malta). Intra-industry trade accelerated in the post-accession period and in 2007 Slovenia and the Czech Republic recorded the highest shares. Intra-industry trade of the new Member States has been dominated by the vertical component, usually low-quality goods. However, in almost all new Member States, the share of high-quality vertical intra-industry trade, as well as the horizontal component increased. Thus, the pattern of trade specialization in the new Member States has improved. Growing shares of intra-industry trade, particularly the horizontal component, reflect increasing similarities between new and old Member States and a favourable convergence process between the two groups of countries. In the automotive sector, intra-industry trade is generally larger than in total trade, meaning deeper specialization. This phenomenon can be largely attributed to the high volume of foreign direct investment in the sector.

2.1 Introduction

Statistics reveal high growth of foreign trade of the new EU Member States in recent years, including the post-accession period.[1] In this paper we want to see whether the impressive quantitative changes of new Member States' trade are

E. Kawecka-Wyrzykowska
Jean Monnet Chair of European Integration, Warsaw School of Economics, Warsaw, Poland
e-mail: ekawec@sgh.waw.pl

[1]The average exports of the EU-10 countries in the period 2000–2003 developed at 15.2% per year while in the after-accession period (2004–2007) at 19.4%. The respective average rates of growth of exports from the EU-15 amounted to 5.7 and 7.8%, respectively.

F. Keereman and I. Szekely (eds.), *Five Years of an Enlarged EU*,
DOI 10.1007/978-3-642-12516-4_2, © Springer-Verlag Berlin Heidelberg 2010

associated with changes in the pattern of trade specialization of those countries. The objective of the paper is to address the issue of accession effects on changes in intra-industry trade (IIT, called also two-way trade) which shows the extent to which bilateral imports and exports are matched within sectors.

Apart from total intra-industry trade changes of new Member States of the EU, we present indices of IIT developments in the automotive sector and try to identify the interrelations between IIT and FDI flows.

The main reason behind the interest in intra-industry trade is that closer analysis of changes of this type of trade allows for an insight into the changing patterns of specialization and scope of benefits from foreign trade. Increasing IIT implies structural convergence of economies. The higher the IIT, the more similar and higher developed are the trading partners. This, in turn, is an important consideration for the convergence process of the new Member States vis-à-vis the EU-15 countries.

The main research hypothesis is that two-way trade has been an important engine of trade growth of the new Member States with their trading partners, reflecting their catching up with the EU-15 countries.

Theory and empirical research on international trade show that an important part of intra-industry trade flows is driven by foreign direct investment as fragmentation of production and trade specialization proceeds – in particular, in more sophisticated industries – inside activities of transnational corporations. As new Member States have attracted relatively much FDI (in terms of their shares in total investments in the industries, shares in jobs, etc.) we ask whether those foreign investments stimulated intra-industry trade growth of those countries (taking as an example the automotive industry). In that section of the study we test the hypothesis that FDI has positively impacted trade changes in the automotive sector, due to increase of intra-industry trade.

The analysis is structured as follows. After the introduction, the Sects. 2.2 and 2.3 inform on data sources, coverage of the study and methodology. Sections 2.4 and 2.5 briefly summarize the theoretical framework of IIT and review the literature. In the main Sect. 2.6, the results of various types of IIT indices are discussed. Sect. 2.7 focuses on interrelations between IIT and FDI in five Central European countries. Finally, concluding remarks are provided.

2.2 Data Sources and the Coverage of the Analysis

The study is based on EUROSTAT data (COMEXT trade data, SITC Rev. 3), at five-digit level.

The analysis focuses on the ten new Member States that joined the EU on 1 May 2004. Bulgaria and Romania were also included, but they were treated separately as they joined the EU only in 2007 and many of the accession-related effects have not been identified in those countries yet. In some cases it was necessary to underline that the analysis was valid only for new Member States originating from the Central and Eastern European countries (Cyprus and Malta have been market economies for many years and did not experience radical transformation); then the abbreviation

"CEECs" was used for "Central and Eastern European countries". The research on IIT in the automotive industry covers five countries highly penetrated by FDI flows (the Czech Republic, Hungary, Poland, Slovakia and Slovenia).

The analysis covers the period 2000–2007, i.e. four years of the accession period of the EU-10 and 4 years preceding accession.

The analysis is conducted in the nominal values (in euro). The impact of variations in the exchange rates is not taken into account, while it has to be recognised that such changes affected trade trends (see e.g. Przystupa 2006).

2.3 Methodology

The importance of IIT in the process of enlargement was analysed by calculating various IIT indices in the new Member States and comparing them with the pre-accession period as well as with respective indices for the old EU Member States. The impact of FDI in the automotive industry on IIT growth is assessed by examining the shares of FDI and of IIT in the car sector.

A standard Grubel–Lloyd index was calculated to obtain a measure of IIT (Box 2.1). This index is very sensitive to the level of aggregation (Finger 1975). The more products are grouped together into an "industry", i.e. the more aggregated the level of analysis, the higher the probability of overlap between exports and imports of that industry and the higher the IIT intensity, without necessarily implying trade in similar products. Therefore, the same approach was applied to all analyzed countries and sectors, thus reducing that bias. All indices were computed for each analyzed EU-12 country in its trade with major groups of trading partners (EU-15, EU-10, other and all partners) for each five-digit SITC. Later they were aggregated into total trade (all groups of SITC products) with those partners. The Grubel–Lloyd index takes a minimum value of zero when there are no products in the same class that are both imported and exported, and a maximum value of 1 (or 100%) when all trade is intra-industry.[2]

Box 2.1 Measuring Intra-industry Trade

A standard Grubel–Lloyd index (*GL*) measures IIT according to the following ratio:

$$GL = \sum_{i=1}^{n} w_i GL_i = \sum_{i=1}^{n} \frac{X_i + M_i}{\sum_{i=1}^{n}(X_i + M_i)} GL_i = \frac{\sum_{i=1}^{n}(X_i + M_i) - \sum_{i=1}^{n}|X_i - M_i|}{\sum_{i=1}^{n}(X_i + M_i)}$$

(continued)

[2]The Grubel-Lloyd index is useful for comparisons across products and over time, but it can overstate the size of IIT trade and can mask different levels of IIT within a given group of products. (see: *European Competitiveness Report 2004*. Commission Staff Working Document SEC(2004) 1397. European Commission. Brussels. 2004, p. 91).

where GL_i is the intra-industry trade index for commodity class i (5-digit SITC level); w_i: share of trade in product i in the total trade; X_i (M_i): exports (imports) of product i from (to) a given country or group of countries to (from) a given country of group of countries; n is the number of commodity classes (industries). Source: Grubel and Lloyd (1975).

Next, IIT was separated into vertical and horizontal intra-industry trade (VIIT and HIIT). The first type of specialization involves the exchange of final goods with different qualities or an exchange of final goods and intermediate products manufactured in the same industry. Horizontal IIT is an exchange of differentiated goods with similar qualities and various other features that are important for consumers (it is motivated mainly by consumers' preference for varieties of goods, e.g. cars of similar class and price range).

Horizontal and vertical IIT of the analyzed countries was measured by using the Hine et al. (1998) methodology. According to this approach, the distinction between HIIT and VIIT is based on the assessment of product quality. To assess different qualities, unit values were used. The underlying assumption is that relative prices are likely to reflect relative qualities of goods. While this approach is commonly adopted in the literature, it has to be noted that it does not guarantee a clear distinction between trade flows (Box 2.2).

Box 2.2 The Distinction Between Vertical and Horizontal Intra-industry Trade

Typically, trade flows are defined as horizontally differentiated when the unit value ratio (*UV*) is inside the ±15% range. When relative unit values are outside this range, products are considered as vertically differentiated. In other words, HIIT takes place when unit values of exports and imports are in the range of 0.85 and 1.15.

The unit value approach is usually criticized for at least two reasons. First, it may be difficult to distinguish correctly between products as unit values of two groups of products may also differ because of the composition of the groups. Second, consumers may buy a more expensive product for reasons other than quality. In addition, the 15% threshold can be considered arbitrary.

Intra-industry trade is considered to be horizontal if the following criteria are met:

$$1-\alpha \leqslant \frac{UV_i^x}{UV_i^m} \leqslant 1+\alpha$$

Intra-industry trade is vertical trade when:

$\frac{UV_i^x}{UV_i^m} \leqslant 1-\alpha$ or $\frac{UV_i^x}{UV_i^m} \geqslant 1+\alpha$

(continued)

UV_i^x: unit value of exports for a product from industry i (5-digit level of SITC)

UV_i^m: unit value of imports for a product from industry i (5-digit level of SITC)

α :deviation of relative unit values of exports $\left(\frac{UV_i^x}{UV_i^m}\right)$; $\alpha = 15\%$.

When the unit value index is below the 0.85 threshold, it is considered to characterize low quality products (sold at a lower average price); when this index is above 1.15, it is treated as an indicator of high quality products (sold at a higher average price).

Source: Hine et al. 1998.

2.4 Theoretical Framework

Standard trade theory (based on comparative advantage) involves trade in homogeneous products. With perfect competition there is only inter-industry trade. This theory deals with various factors of international trade that are generated by the differences among countries.

For many years, more and more trade has been taking place between similar countries (mainly highly developed countries with similar patterns of economic structures). It includes often parallel export and import of products that belong to the same industry, which is intra-industry trade. Such trade cannot be explained by traditional trade theory.

The phenomenon of IIT was initially noticed in trade among the members of the EEC. The first papers covering the issue of parallel export and import of products that belonged to the same industry were presented by Verdoorn (1960) and Balassa (1966). Later research revealed IIT in relations between various other countries.

The important publication of Grubel and Lloyd on the concept and measurement of intra-industry trade in 1975 stimulated enormous interest in this type of trade specialization and was followed by many theoretical and empirical studies on IIT.

The first models of IIT basing on monopolistic competition and product differentiation (as developed by Krugman 1979, 1980, Lancaster 1980, and Helpman 1981) assumed that goods are horizontally differentiated and IIT develops in monopolistically competitive markets. On the supply side, it is driven by increasing returns to scale and on the demand side, it is driven by diverse consumer preferences. Helpman and Krugman (1985) added factor endowment differences that explain the co-existence of inter- and intra-industry trade.

The other group of theories deals with vertical IIT. The theoretical model of IIT in vertically differentiated products was developed mainly by Falvey (1981), Falvey and Kierzkowski (1987) and Flam and Helpman (1987). These studies showed the significance of differences in technology, income levels and income distribution and also the role of factor endowments as factors affecting VIIT.

The studies of Abd-el-Rahman (1991) and Greenaway et al. (1994) established a method to separate vertical from horizontal IIT and suggested that the exchange of vertically differentiated products is the dominant form of IIT, even in trade among developed countries.

Let's stress that the theoretical literature argues that HIIT and VIIT depend on different determinants, although some of them (e.g. factor endowments) can explain both, inter-industry and intra-industry trade (Box 2.3). The role of different determinants of IIT was broadly presented, among others, by R. Loertscher and F. Wolter (1980). Apart from the IIT determinants mentioned above, other factors were also taken into account (e.g. geographical proximity, elimination of trade barriers).

Box 2.3 Inter- and Intra-industry Trade
Inter-industry trade (one-way trade) reflects different factor (labour and capital) endowments and technology. It is explained by a standard trade theory involving the exchange of homogeneous products where perfect competition exists. It is dealt with mainly by the theory of comparative advantages.

Intra-industry trade (two-way trade) usually is not based on comparative advantage, although some elements of comparative advantage may be also involved (especially, in the case of vertical IIT). To a large extent intra-industry trade is explained by factors such as economies of scale, income levels, innovations and demand for differentiated products as well as, in some cases, by comparative advantages.

From the point of view of this analysis, of crucial importance is the separation of IIT into HIIT and VIIT, as suggested by Hine et al. (1998) who also presented the methodology of such separation of IIT. It also allows to better assess the catching up process. HIIT is typical for countries with similar and highly developed patterns of economic structures. Such countries are able to produce differentiated goods, offered usually by well developed manufacturing sectors. Also, developed countries create the biggest demand for such products.

In particular, theory explains that horizontal intra-industry trade consists of exchange of varieties of goods with similar qualities and various other features that are important for consumers, and is driven mainly by economies of scale and consumers' preferences for variety (e.g. cars of a similar class and price range). Vertical IIT is an exchange of final goods with different qualities and prices (e.g. Italy exports high-quality clothing and imports low-quality clothing) or an exchange of final and intermediate goods produced in the same industry, driven mainly by different factor endowments, i.e. by comparative advantages (e.g. exchange of seats of the car for engines, thus reflecting exchange of cheap unskilled labour for highly qualified personnel).

Consequently we expect vertical IIT to be more pronounced between developing and developed economies than among developed countries. Less developed countries specialize usually in those stages of production in which they possess comparative advantage, e.g. cheap, unskilled labour. Thus, much of IIT in those countries results from FDI and is conducted in the framework of global activities of transnational corporations. It has also been the case in the EU-12 countries. The inward foreign direct investments to those countries have increased rapidly over the recent years. As a result, we can expect IIT of those countries to have expanded.

With regard to HIIT, theoretical models suggest that the more similar countries are in terms of their factor endowments and incomes, the higher the share of this type of trade. Thus, we should expect HIIT to be higher between developed countries than less developed countries. As HIIT is usually correlated with economic similarities, increasing HIIT implies structural convergence of economies. For the new Member States, which are catching up countries and trying to reduce their economic distance vis-à-vis highly developed countries, one may expect increasing IIT (in particular HIIT) and a decreasing inter-industry type of specialization.

Let us stress, that increasing role of both types of IIT in total trade should be assessed explicitly positively as IIT allows for more trade benefits than inter-industry trade. The reason is that with IIT, producers concentrate on a limited number of products which leads to an increase in output because of savings on fixed costs. IIT also stimulates innovations because producing a greater variety and number of goods reduces the costs of knowledge accumulation (Ruffin 1999).

Another important positive aspect of IIT as compared to inter-industry trade is that it is less disruptive than inter-industry trade as the adjustments in production to ongoing competition and reallocation of resources take place within the same industry. This aspect of IIT is important for all countries, but in particular for catching up economies which face more adjustment challenges than highly developed countries. In other words, increasing IIT reduces adjustment costs.

2.5 Review of the Literature

Numerous studies have been conducted since the beginning of transformation of the CEECs to analyse changes and determinants of IIT. The focus has been usually on CEECs' trade with the EU Members States because the EU is the main trading partner, but other factors played also a role like the economic weight of the EU, geographical proximity, deep liberalization and integration of the CEECs with the EU and EU accession.

Before transformation started, the share of IIT was very low and horizontal IIT was almost non-existent (di Simone 2007). The rapid growth of IIT between the CEECs and the EU was observed already in the early years of transition. Gacs (1994) noted that the share of IIT in Hungarian trade with the EU, measured according to NACE 3-digit level, increased from 40% in 1980 to 47% in 1988 and jumped to 53% in 1992. According to Kaminski (2001), the share of IIT increased between 1993 and 1998 for all CEECs except Bulgaria, Lithuania and Latvia. The largest increase in the value of the Grubel–Lloyd index in that period was registered in Estonia, followed by Slovakia, the Czech Republic, Romania and Poland.

Around the middle of the 1990s, an increasing number of authors have found that an important part of the dynamic development of trade between the CEECs and the EU was IIT, predominantly of the vertical type. A statistically significant positive association between horizontal intra-industry trade, foreign direct investment, product differentiation and industry concentration was detected (Aturupane et al. 1999) as well as a significant negative relationship for economies of scale and labour intensity.

Fidrmuc et al. (1997) showed that a reduction of trade barriers among CEECs and the EU resulted in increased IIT indices. They observed, however, that "the increase of intra-industry trade is not uniform, but reflects different patterns of integration and progress of industrial restructuring". The authors found that "Hungary and Slovenia showed the largest growth of intra-industry trade that became very similar to intra-industry trade within the European Union". However, "the Czech Republic had the highest share of intra-industry trade reaching 68% in the trade with the five selected EU-countries[3]."

The relative importance of vertical and horizontal IIT was analyzed by Aturupane et al. (1999) who concluded that "the magnitude of IIT is relatively high in bilateral trade between the CEECs and the EU. Levels of total IIT are comparable to those observed for countries such as Canada, Israel, Korea or Portugal. Most of the IIT is vertical in nature .... Horizontal IIT has been static over the 1990–1995 period for the majority of countries. However, for some countries such as the Czech Republic and Slovenia it has been growing rapidly and has attained levels that exceed those reported for countries such as Greece, Finland and Israel". Similar conclusions have been reached by Ferto and Soos (2006).

Quite recently, details of HIIT and VIIT between the former Central European Free Trade Agreement countries and the EU were analyzed by Černoša (2007). He concentrated on production pattern (IIT specialization) of the Czech Republic, Hungary, Poland, Slovakia and Slovenia in foreign trade with EU Member States in 1995–2001 (across countries and twenty manufacturing activities: divisions 17–36 of the ISIC). This analysis revealed "the predominance of IIT specialization of the majority of the chosen manufacturing activities in the production of lower quality products". It also found, however, "a few activities in each of the five observed former Central European Free Trade Agreement countries, which, by contrast, showed predominant specialization in the production of higher quality products".

A study on Poland's IIT by Czarny and Śledziewska (2008) concluded that "in 2000–2006, the structure of Poland's trade with the EU-15 improved. The share of vertical IIT in which Poland exported high-quality products grew consistently.... Poland is no longer just a supplier of non-processed or low-quality goods and intermediates. It increasingly exports high-quality and technologically advanced

[3]Austria, the Netherlands, Germany, Italy and Sweden.

products. This change is a result of modernization in the Polish economy thanks to an inflow of FDI, free trade and adjustments to EU standards after Poland's entry to the single market".

Many studies concentrated on the role of FDI in trade changes. Kaminski (2001) found that countries which received relatively big inflows of FDI in the 1990s experienced also an expansion of IIT. For an earlier period, a similar conclusion was presented by Aturupane et al. (1999): "After controlling for country-specific factors, we find a positive and significant relationship between FDI and product differentiation and both vertical and horizontal IIT". Contrary to the majority of the studies, a very low interrelationship between FDI and IIT was found in Polish foreign trade by A. Cieślik (2008): "It was found that although the activity of multinational firms is positively related to the volume of bilateral trade between Poland and EU-15 countries, at the same time these firms do not seem to contribute to the development of the intra-industry-trade".

2.6 Results for the New Member States

2.6.1 Changes in the Intensity of Total Intra-industry Trade in the New Member States

Although inter-industry trade (exchange of goods coming from different industries) still accounts for almost 50% (on average) for the EU-10 group of countries, its share has been declining in all those countries (except for Malta) in recent years and, the other side of the same coin, intra-industry trade became more important. For the whole EU-10 group, the IIT share in their total trade increased from 42% in 2000 to 51% in 2007 (Table 2.1).

In 2007, in most recently acceded countries, the IIT share ranged from about 41% (Slovakia) to 58% (Slovenia and the Czech Republic). In Malta and Cyprus the IIT shares were much lower: 16–17%, lower even than in Bulgaria (32%) and Romania (33%). In general, countries with relatively high IIT shares in 2000 did not progress much. Starting from low levels, the biggest increases took place in the Baltic countries with a doubling of the IIT share in Latvia, in the period studied. In Malta, a large fall was recorded.

The rapid increase of IIT trade specialization took place already in the 1990s, in the period of fast legal and real transformation-related adjustments and integration into the EU-15. At that time it was predominantly the growth of vertical IIT, driven mainly by FDI. The reason behind this development of FDI and VIIT was first of all the need of Central European companies to obtain access to know-how, capital and distribution channels. These developments allowed for successful restructuring of many industries in the CEECs. As a result of accession, FDI flows and deepening of trade specialization have continued and accelerated. In all EU-10 countries, except

Table 2.1 The importance of various types of specialization in new Member States' total trade in 2000 and 2007

% of total trade	Year	Total	Type of specialization					
			Inter-industry	Intra-industry total	Vertical intra-industry trade			HIIT
					Total	Low quality	High quality	
		(1=2+3)	(2)	(3=4+7)	(4=5+6)	(5)	(6)	(7)
Czech Republic	2000	100	49.2	50.8	38.5	27.7	10.8	12.3
	2007	100	42.8	57.2	39.8	18.8	21.0	17.4
Estonia	2000	100	66.8	33.2	26.0	17.4	8.6	7.2
	2007	100	49.6	50.4	33.2	15.5	17.7	17.2
Cyprus	2000	100	84.8	15.2	12.4	10.8	1.6	2.8
	2007	100	84.1	15.9	14.3	6.7	7.6	1.6
Latvia	2000	100	78.0	22.0	14.9	9.5	5.4	7.1
	2007	100	56.0	44.0	35.0	21.6	13.4	9.0
Lithuania	2000	100	73.3	26.7	19.3	10.7	8.6	7.4
	2007	100	54.9	45.1	28.5	17.0	11.5	16.6
Hungary	2000	100	55.9	44.1	34.1	17.2	16.9	10.0
	2007	100	48.2	51.8	37.6	19.9	17.7	14.2
Malta	2000	100	42.8	57.2	54.4	53.3	1.1	2.8
	2007	100	83.2	16.8	15.7	3.5	12.2	1.1
Poland	2000	100	60.7	39.3	31.2	19.3	11.8	8.1
	2007	100	49.1	50.9	28.1	15.7	12.4	22.8
Slovenia	2000	100	55.8	44.2	29.9	17.3	12.6	14.3
	2007	100	42.5	57.5	31.7	17.2	14.5	25.8
Slovakia	2000	100	65.9	34.1	26.5	16.8	9.7	7.6
	2007	100	59.3	40.7	31.9	12.4	19.4	8.8
EU-10	2000	100	58.1	41.9	32.3	20.4	6.9	9.6
	2007	100	49.3	50.7	33.3	16.9	9.5	17.4
Bulgaria	2000	100	73.0	27.0	21.9	15.0	7.6	5.1
	2007	100	67.7	32.3	23.5	14.1	10.6	8.8
Romania	2000	100	78.1	21.9	19.1	11.5	11.9	2.8
	2007	100	67.2	32.8	25.3	14.7	16.4	7.5

Source: Eurostat (COMEXT) Database

for Malta, IIT shares in total trade (also in trade with major groups of partners) increased after accession faster than before 2004.

Let's us notice, that despite a relatively high increase, IIT is still lower in the new Member States than in the old EU countries. The average share of IIT in EU-10 trade with the EU-15 was 44% in 2007 (in intra-EU-10 trade it amounted to 49%) while IIT among EU-15 countries amounted to 59% of trade (Table 2.2). It is also interesting to note that, in 2007, the IIT share was in several EU-10 countries higher than in some EU-15 countries. In countries as the Czech Republic, Estonia, Hungary, Poland and Slovenia the IIT share was above 50% while it was below 50% in Finland, Greece, Ireland, Luxembourg and Portugal. Thus, the share of intra-industry trade in total trade of many of the EU-10 countries is already at the level of some industrially advanced countries, such as Italy and Sweden (Table 2.3).

Table 2.2 Importance of intra-industry trade of the EU-12 countries with major trading partners in 2000 and 2007

% of trade	Year	Intra-industry trade					Intra-industry trade vertical (low quality)					Intra-industry trade vertical (high quality)					Intra-industry trade horizontal				
		World	EU-25	EU-15	EU-10	Other	World	EU-25	EU-15	EU-10	Other	World	EU-25	EU-15	EU-10	Other	World	EU-25	EU-15	EU-10	Other
Czech	00	50.8	53.2	49.2	41.7	24.6	27.7	29.6	28.7	11.4	11.5	10.8	10.5	10.0	11.9	9.0	12.3	13.1	10.5	18.4	4.1
Republic	07	57.3	58.8	52.7	55.0	34.3	18.8	29.5	27.7	21.3	9.8	21.0	14.0	11.6	13.1	16.6	17.4	15.2	13.5	20.6	7.8
Cyprus	00	15.2	13.2	12.9	3.3	10.3	10.8	9.3	9.0	1.8	6.9	1.6	1.7	1.8	1.5	1.5	2.8	2.1	2.1	0.0	1.9
	07	15.9	14.2	13.9	4.1	10.1	6.7	7.8	7.9	1.2	4.4	7.6	5.8	5.4	1.7	5.3	1.6	0.6	0.6	1.2	0.5
Estonia	00	33.2	29.5	24.1	34.4	16.9	17.4	12.6	10.2	6.7	6.4	8.6	11.6	10.2	14.5	9.5	7.2	5.2	3.8	13.2	1.0
	07	50.4	42.6	33.6	44.0	45.9	15.5	18.7	18.0	17.7	5.5	17.7	15.7	10.0	19.1	11.1	17.2	8.2	5.5	7.3	29.2
Latvia	00	22.0	18.9	9.7	31.7	19.4	9.5	9.6	6.5	10.0	8.1	5.4	4.3	2.2	15.3	6.6	7.1	5.1	1.0	6.5	4.7
	07	44.0	35.8	18.2	46.4	33.4	21.6	25.3	12.9	34.4	8.6	13.4	5.1	2.5	6.5	18.9	9.0	5.4	2.8	5.5	5.9
Lithuania	00	26.7	23.3	17.7	24.8	20.4	10.7	11.1	8.9	10.2	9.6	8.6	6.1	4.7	8.5	7.6	7.4	6.1	4.1	6.1	3.2
	07	45.1	32.5	19.4	44.5	34.1	17.0	14.3	10.9	15.2	9.0	11.5	9.4	5.2	15.4	12.2	16.6	8.8	3.3	13.9	12.9
Hungary	00	44.1	40.7	38.4	33.7	22.4	17.2	17.2	17.8	7.8	10.3	16.9	14.4	14.4	12.8	8.3	10.0	9.1	6.2	13.1	3.9
	07	51.9	49.4	45.5	47.5	37.7	19.9	21.1	20.2	17.9	16.6	17.7	17.4	12.0	18.8	14.0	14.2	10.8	13.4	10.8	7.2
Malta	00	57.1	28.2	27.6	4.6	55.4	53.3	26.7	26.1	3.7	53.6	1.1	1.1	1.1	0.0	0.5	2.8	0.4	0.4	0.9	1.3
	07	16.9	16.3	16.1	8.6	10.5	3.5	2.9	2.6	0.5	2.8	12.2	12.8	12.6	7.2	6.6	1.1	0.5	1.0	0.9	1.2
Poland	00	39.2	41.0	37.4	39.7	21.6	19.3	22.4	20.8	11.0	10.1	11.8	12.0	11.4	14.1	7.1	8.1	6.6	5.2	14.6	4.3
	07	50.8	49.9	44.9	48.8	34.8	15.7	16.7	16.2	12.1	9.9	12.4	11.7	9.9	18.4	14.2	22.8	21.4	18.8	18.3	10.7
Slovenia	00	44.2	43.2	41.4	22.3	26.4	17.3	16.7	17.5	4.0	9.5	12.6	12.0	10.7	6.1	8.4	14.3	14.6	13.3	12.2	8.4
	07	57.5	47.6	44.0	33.7	35.9	17.2	23.6	17.1	16.3	14.9	14.5	9.8	9.5	7.3	16.1	25.8	14.2	17.5	10.1	4.9
Slovakia	00	34.1	35.8	29.7	35.4	14.6	16.8	18.9	15.8	11.4	4.9	9.7	9.5	7.1	13.4	6.6	7.6	7.4	6.8	10.5	3.1
	07	40.7	42.9	35.2	48.8	17.5	12.4	14.8	15.0	20.5	5.2	19.4	20.1	14.7	20.2	9.1	8.8	8.0	5.4	8.1	3.3
EU-10	00	41.9	41.8	38.3	36.6	23.1	20.4	21.4	20.4	10.3	11.6	11.9	11.3	10.8	12.5	7.4	9.6	9.1	7.1	13.8	4.1
	07	50.8	49.4	44.0	49.0	33.4	16.9	20.9	19.4	18.6	10.9	16.4	14.0	10.9	16.3	13.9	17.4	14.5	13.7	14.1	8.5
Bulgaria	00	27.0	19.3	18.7	12.2	26.4	15.0	9.1	8.4	5.9	14.7	6.9	8.2	8.4	4.4	5.1	5.1	2.0	1.9	2.0	6.6
	07	32.3	28.5	28.3	17.6	26.9	14.1	13.7	14.6	9.6	7.4	9.5	8.0	7.7	4.9	6.9	8.8	6.8	6.1	3.1	12.6
Romania	00	21.9	20.8	20.0	14.6	13.9	11.5	11.2	9.7	8.0	7.3	7.6	7.9	7.8	3.0	3.4	2.8	1.7	2.5	3.6	3.2
	07	32.8	32.5	31.0	25.7	24.0	14.7	15.9	16.7	14.6	8.4	10.6	9.9	9.6	5.8	7.5	7.5	6.8	4.7	5.3	8.2

Source: Eurostat Database

Table 2.3 Importance of intra-industry trade of EU-15 countries in their mutual trade

% of intra EU trade	2000	2001	2002	2003	2004	2005	2006	2007
Austria	55.1	54.6	56.2	56.7	60.6	59.7	59.3	58.1
Belgium	63.1	62.9	64.8	65.3	65.6	65.3	65.1	65.5
Germany	63.8	64.6	65.7	66.2	65.6	64.7	65.1	64.9
Denmark	48.0	47.8	49.9	50.1	49.3	49.5	48.6	48.2
Spain	56.8	58.4	58.6	58.6	59.2	59.3	58.4	59.4
Finland	29.1	31.3	30.1	30.3	29.9	30.6	31.0	32.6
France	69.8	70.6	68.9	69.1	68.6	66.4	66.7	66.9
United Kingdom	60.8	56.7	55.1	57.3	58.5	57.0	54.0	58.8
Greece	15.2	15.5	16.2	17.2	18.3	19.4	19.3	19.5
Ireland	39.0	42.9	41.1	33.1	31.9	34.7	34.1	32.6
Italy	50.2	50.3	50.2	50.7	50.3	50.4	51.3	51.4
Luxembourg	33.3	37.9	37.9	37.0	32.6	29.9	33.9	32.9
Netherlands	58.9	57.0	60.5	60.4	58.5	54.4	55.6	58.7
Portugal	40.0	41.7	42.6	42.7	43.5	44.0	44.9	44.6
Sweden	48.6	49.1	50.1	50.7	51.3	51.3	52.9	54.3

Source: Eurostat Database

2.6.2 Changes in Intensity of Vertical and Horizontal Intra-industry Trade of the EU-12 Countries in Total Trade and in Trade with the EU-15

In all EU-12 countries, intra-industry trade has been dominated by the vertical type (column 4 of Table 2.1). In order to have a better insight into the type of specialization VIIT specialization can be distinguished in low and high quality products (Box 2.2).

Over the years 2000–2007, VIIT was mainly dominated by specialization in production of low quality products (countries exported mainly low-quality products and imported high-quality ones). This was the situation in Hungary, Lithuania, Latvia, Poland and Slovenia. In some of those countries (Hungary, Latvia and Lithuania) the share of low quality VIIT even increased in 2007 as compared to 2000. Shares of low quality VIIT were higher than those of high quality VIIT in trade with all groups of countries, except for trade with non-EU countries (Table 2.2).

At the same time, the share of high quality VIIT has increased in all EU-12 countries and in some countries very much: in Cyprus, the Czech Republic, Estonia Latvia, Malta, Slovakia the intensity of this type of trade more than doubled with respect to total trade. Intensity of low quality VIIT usually also increased, but at a much slower pace. As a result, in all six countries, except Latvia, the share of high quality VIIT has become higher than the share of low quality VIIT.

Thus, over the years 2000–2007, the pattern of VIIT has improved in all EU-12 countries. Albeit low quality VIIT still dominates trade of many EU-12 countries, the share of high quality VITT has increased and the distance between both types of vertical specialization was in 2007 much lower than in 2000 (respectively 7.4 p.p. and 13.5 p.p.).

Another positive trend has been a significant rise of HIIT with its average share doubling in the EU-10 countries from 7% to almost 14% in the period 2000–2007. This improvement has resulted mainly from a significant increase of HIIT in Poland, Estonia and Slovenia. Bulgaria and Romania followed this trend, albeit from much lower initial levels. Only Cyprus and Malta recorded a decrease of the HIIT share in their total trade.

Summing up so far, while VIIT of low quality products decelerated over the years 2000–2007, vertical IIT of high quality products as well as horizontal IIT developed faster in the same period. These different rates of growth of various types of IIT reflect positive changes of trade and production specialization in the EU-10 countries, involving specialization in more advanced products. Such positive changes in the pattern of trade specialization have taken place over 2000–2007 in almost all new Member States.

Trade of the new Member States with their main trading partner, the EU-15 countries, is somewhat different. First, the intensity of high quality VIIT increased in most EU-12 countries, the exceptions being Estonia, Hungary, Poland, Slovenia and Bulgaria. The increase of this type of trade was, however, much lower than in the case of total trade of the EU-10 group (respectively by 0.1 p.p. and 2.6 p.p., Tables 2.4 and 2.1). Second, changes relating to low quality VIIT with EU-15 countries were in opposite direction in individual EU-10 countries, while in total trade of the EU-10 countries the intensity of low quality VIIT has been steadily decreasing (except for Malta).

With regard to HIIT, the share of this type of trade almost doubled, both in total trade of the EU-10 group (from 9.6% in 2000 to 17.4% in 2007) and in their trade with the EU-15 countries (from 7.1% in 2000 to 13.7% in 2007). This very positive upward trend of HIIT resulted mainly from the expansion in Poland, the biggest country of the analyzed group of new Member States. In Poland's trade with the EU-15 the HIIT share increased from 5.2% in 2000 to 18.8% in 2007, and in total trade, respectively from 8.1% to 22.8%. As a result, HIIT intensity in total Poland's trade has become in 2007 not much lower than the intensity of VIIT: 22.8% and 28.1%. Also in Hungary, the HIIT share in trade with the EU-15 increased impressively from 6.2% in 2000 to 13.4% in 2007 (Table 2.1 and 2.4). In several countries an opposite trend was registered: the share of HIIT has decreased over the period 2000–2007 in Cyprus, Lithuania and Slovakia in their trade with the EU-15.

Despite impressive growth of HIIT intensity and a very stable share of VIIT, the absolute level of VIIT indices was in 2007 still much higher than the level of HIIT. This observation applies both, to EU-10 countries' trade with the EU-15 and to their total trade. At the same time, the role of VIIT increased much in intra EU-10 countries' trade, while the increase of HIIT has been almost negligible (Fig. 2.1). Still, in 2007, the average index of HIIT for intra-EU-10 countries' trade was slightly higher than HIIT index in the EU-10 countries with the old EU-15 Member States'.

Thus, changes in the pattern of intra-industry specialization were of different character in the case of intra-EU-10 countries' trade and their trade with the EU-15. The increase of intra-industry trade among the EU-10 countries was mainly of

Table 2.4 The importance of various types of specialization in new Member States' trade with the EU-15 in 2000 and 2007

% of total	Year	Total trade	Type of specialization					
			Inter-industry	Intra-industry total	Vertical intra-industry trade			HIIT
					Total	Low quality	High quality	
		(1=2+3)	(2)	(3=4+7)	(4=5+6)	(5)	(6)	(7)
Czech Republic	2000	100	50.8	49.2	38.7	28.7	10.0	10.5
	2007	100	47.3	52.7	39.2	27.7	11.6	13.5
Estonia	2000	100	75.9	24.1	20.3	10.2	10.2	3.8
	2007	100	66.5	33.5	28.0	18.0	10.0	5.5
Cyprus	2000	100	87.1	12.9	10.8	9.0	1.8	2.1
	2007	100	86.1	13.9	13.3	7.9	5.4	0.6
Latvia	2000	100	90.3	9.7	8.7	6.5	2.2	1.0
	2007	100	81.7	18.3	15.5	12.9	2.5	2.8
Lithuania	2000	100	82.3	17.7	13.6	8.9	4.7	4.1
	2007	100	80.6	19.4	16.1	10.9	5.2	3.3
Hungary	2000	100	61.6	38.4	32.2	17.8	14.4	6.2
	2007	100	54.5	45.5	32.1	20.2	12.0	13.4
Malta	2000	100	72.4	27.6	27.2	26.1	1.1	0.4
	2007	100	83.9	16.1	15.1	2.6	12.6	1.0
Poland	2000	100	62.6	37.4	32.2	20.8	11.4	5.2
	2007	100	55.1	44.9	26.1	16.2	9.9	18.8
Slovenia	2000	100	58.6	41.4	28.1	17.5	10.7	13.3
	2007	100	56.0	44.0	26.5	17.1	9.5	17.5
Slovakia	2000	100	70.3	29.7	22.9	15.8	7.1	6.8
	2007	100	64.9	35.1	29.7	15.0	14.7	5.4
EU-10	2000	100	61.7	38.3	31.2	20.4	10.8	7.1
	2007	100	56.0	44.0	30.3	19.4	10.9	13.7
Bulgaria	2000	100	81.3	18.7	16.8	8.4	8.4	1.9
	2007	100	71.7	28.3	22.2	14.6	7.7	6.1
Romania	2000	100	80.0	20.0	17.5	9.7	7.8	2.5
	2007	100	69.0	31.0	26.3	16.7	9.6	4.7

Source: Eurostat (COMEXT) Database

vertical character while the levels of intra-industry trade of those countries with their major trading partners (i.e. EU-15) grew first of all in horizontally differentiated products.

As already mentioned, theoretical models suggest that horizontal specialization takes place first of all among countries with high level of incomes and similar economic patterns. As disparities between the EU-12 countries and the EU-15 are getting lower, the new Member States are becoming more similar with the old EU Members. Thus, increasing shares of HIIT with the EU-15 countries confirm the convergence process of the EU-12 vis-à-vis the EU-15 group. HIIT is a more advanced type of trade, allowing for bigger trade benefits and lower adjustment costs. The relatively fast increase of this type of specialization in EU-10 trade with the EU-15 allowed for a smooth adjustment to the internal market of the EU.

At the same time, HIIT for many EU-10 countries was higher in the analyzed period in their trade with other EU-10 countries than in trade with EU-15 partners

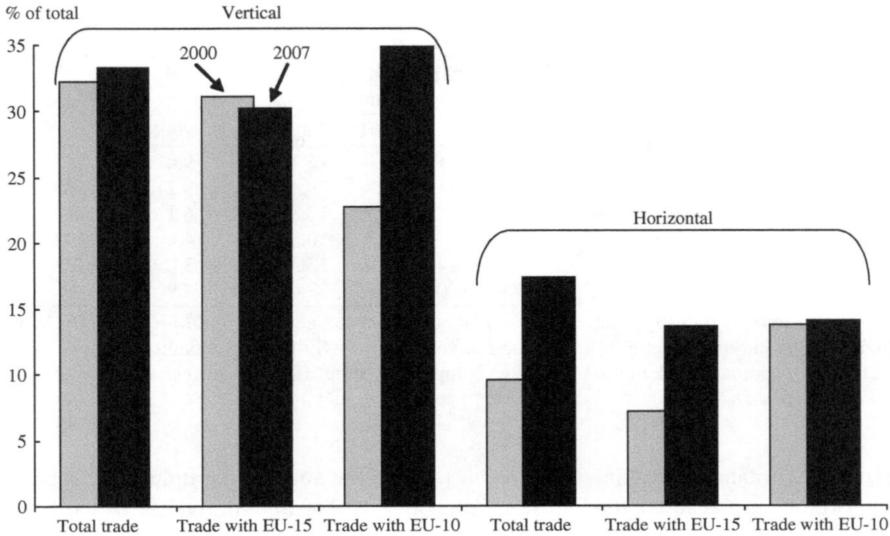

Fig. 2.1 Vertical and horizontal intra-industry trade of the EU-10 countries in 2000 and 2007
Source: Data of Table 2.2

(Table 2.2). This observation is also in line with the theory as the EU-10 countries – on average - are more similar between each other than as compared with the EU-15. Exceptions are Malta and Slovenia with higher HIIT shares in their trade with the EU-15 than in trade with the EU-10. One possible interpretation is that both countries are more similar with the EU-15 than with the EU-10 countries.

2.7 Intra-Industry Trade in the Automotive Industry and the Role of FDI

Intra-industry trade (in particular VIIT) in more sophisticated manufactured products is often correlated with inflows of FDI as these products rely on many components and/or processes and benefit more readily from splitting up production across countries. The EU-12 countries have been recording for many years big inflows of FDI.[4] In this context we analyze statistical data in order to identify the relationship between FDI and IIT in the automotive sector. The underlying assumption is that IIT (especially VIIT) in this sector is driven by transnational corporations. We concentrate on data for five new Member States (the Czech Republic,

[4]Taking into account that FDI flows towards the new Member States are dominated by financial services, the FDI impact on trade is lower than it might result from the size of total FDI flows. In this study we take into account only FDI in manufacturing sector.

Table 2.5 The FDI stock in the in automotive industry in 2001 and 2006

	Mio. EUR		% of total		% of				Inward FDI stock per capita (EUR, 2006)
	2001	2006	2001	2006	FDI in manufacturing		Total FDI		
					2001	2006	2001	2006	
Czech Republic	2,192.0	5,700.3	28.5	31.3	19.0	26.1	7.1	9.4	557
Hungary	2,833.1	5,683.1	36.7	31.2	24.4	29.1	9.1	9.2	563
Poland	2,421.7	5,692.1	31.4	31.2	14.7	17.8	5.2	6.1	149
Slovenia	127.6	271.2	1.6	1.5	9.5	10.8	4.3	4.0	135
Slovakia	141.3	879.0	1.8	4.8	5.9	16.3	2.2	3.0	163
Total	7,715.7	18,226.7	100	100	17.8	22.4	6.4	7.9	–

Notes: Automotive industry: Motor vehicles and other transport equipment (DM NACE, NACE 34 and 35). The importance of FDI in the automotive industry in Slovakia is underestimated because of not fully comparable definition of FDI as compared to other EU-5 countries
Source: WIIW Database

Hungary, Poland, Slovakia and Slovenia) where the automotive industry has been important in trade and in the FDI stock[5] (Table 2.5). The automotive sector has been selected as a case study for four reasons: (1) it has attracted relatively big inflows of FDI to new Member States as compared to other sectors; (2) in developed countries this sector has been one of the engines of IIT growth; (3) it is one of the mostly internationalized industries; (4) this sector can be relatively easily identified for statistical comparisons.

2.7.1 The Importance of FDI in the Automotive Industry

The automotive industry plays a very important role in Europe as an engine for employment, growth and innovation which is based on many linkages it has within the domestic and international economy. For example, this sector creates demand for inputs from other industrial sectors (steel and metal products, high-tech manufacturing etc.). It also stimulates new types of activities, thus creating new jobs and incomes (e.g. car repair services, fuel stations, car wash facilities). The high level of competition in the industry is forcing car producers to optimise costs optimization and is also a key factor of ongoing innovations, resulting in positive spillovers for the whole economies (Tirpak 2006).

Enlargement has become a very important development for many EU-15 automotive industry firms (Kaminski 2001). Assembly plants and production of cars and their components in the region have clustered, mainly through FDI, in a relatively small area spanning West Slovakia, Eastern and Central Czech Republic, Southern Poland and Northern Hungary. The automotive industry had accumulated around

[5]Automotive goods are relatively important also in industrial trade of Estonia, Lithuania and Latvia but the share of FDI in automotive sectors is here relatively low.

7.9% of the total inward FDI stock in the five countries we study and 22.4% of FDI in the manufacturing sector (Table 2.5).

The automotive sector is highly penetrated by foreign capital. Data for 2001 (the latest year available) shows that in Slovakia and Hungary 98% of total investments in this industry is foreign, while the penetration ratio is about 95% in Poland and the Czech Republic. Slovenia is the only country with a relatively significant automotive industry, but lower FDI in this sector. Also, foreign investors accounted for more than 90% of sales and export sales in the analyzed countries, except for Slovenia, where these indicators were lower (77 and 86%). In three countries, the Czech Republic, Hungary and Poland, the automotive industry ranked first in total manufacturing FDI.

2.7.2 The Intensity of Intra-industry Trade in the Automotive Industry

In Table 2.6 we compare the intensity of total IIT and IIT in the automotive industry with the shares of the automotive industry in industrial trade and in FDI in 2000 and 2007.

Four countries with the highest indices of IIT in total trade in 2007, i.e. Slovenia, the Czech Republic, Hungary and Poland also recorded the highest indices of IIT in automotive products (columns 1 and 4 of Table 2.6). At the same time, in three of those countries: Hungary, Poland and Slovenia, indices of IIT in the automotive sector outpaced the overall IIT indices (by more than 20 p.p.), meaning deeper specialization in automotive trade than in total trade. Intra-industry trade accounted for more than 70% of the automotive trade of those countries (Fig. 2.2). Also, in all those countries the automotive goods were important in total industrial trade and have increased over the years 2000–2007 (columns 5 and 6 of Table 2.6).

In the Czech Republic, Hungary and Slovakia, intra-industry trade in the automotive sector was mainly of vertical character. This type of trade results often from intra-firm trade and is usually evidence of transnational corporations being active. In particular, in Hungary the role of IIT, totally of vertical character in 2007, substantially increased. The Czech Republic and Poland recorded decreasing VIIT intensity over the period 2000–2007, while HIIT increased. This was notably the case in Poland (Fig. 2.2), reflecting the parallel export and import of similar cars.[6] Poland has exported in recent years many cars originating in FDI-based firms, while at the same time, importing used, but relatively new cars. The unit values of exported and imported cars are in the range of ±15% leading to relatively high HIIT shares. In addition, Poland increased its production and exports of car engines

[6]In the first half of 2008, around 94% of cars produced in Poland were exported. At the same time, almost all cars sold on the Polish market were of foreign origin, a big part of them being used cars (about 40% in 2002–2003).

Table 2.6 Indices of total IIT and IIT in automotive industry as compared to the share of automotive industry in industrial trade and in FDI in 2000 and 2007

% of total trade	Total IIT	Intra-industry automotive trade			Share of automotive goods in industrial trade		Share of automotive FDI in total FDI stock (manufacturing)[a]
		HIIT	VIIT	Total IIT in automotive products	Exports	Imports	
	1	2	3	4 = 2 + 3	5	6	7
Czech Republic							
2000	50.8	8.6	47.8	56.4	16.8	8.1	19.0
2007	57.3	22.8	31.6	54.4	17.7	9.6	26.1
Hungary							
2000	44.1	12.9	36.5	49.4	9.2	8.1	24.4
2007	51.9	0.3	73.6	73.9	11.6	9.5	29.1
Poland							
2000	39.2	0.4	81.4	81.8	10.7	9.6	14.7
2007	50.8	68.2	9.3	77.5	15.0	11.2	17.8
Slovakia							
2000	34.1	5.4	33.5	38.9	23.6	14.6	5.9
2007	40.7	2.1	33.5	35.6	26.5	16.5	16.3
Slovenia							
2000	44.2	57.8	11.3	69.1	11.9	13.0	9.5
2007	57.5	67.7	12.1	79.8	19.1	18.9	10.8
EU-5							
2000	43.1	10.8	49.7	60.5	13.4	9.5	17.8
2007	51.9	32.5	30.3	62.8	16.8	11.6	22.4

[a]2001 instead of 2000 and 2006 instead of 2007
Source: Eurostat and WIIW Database

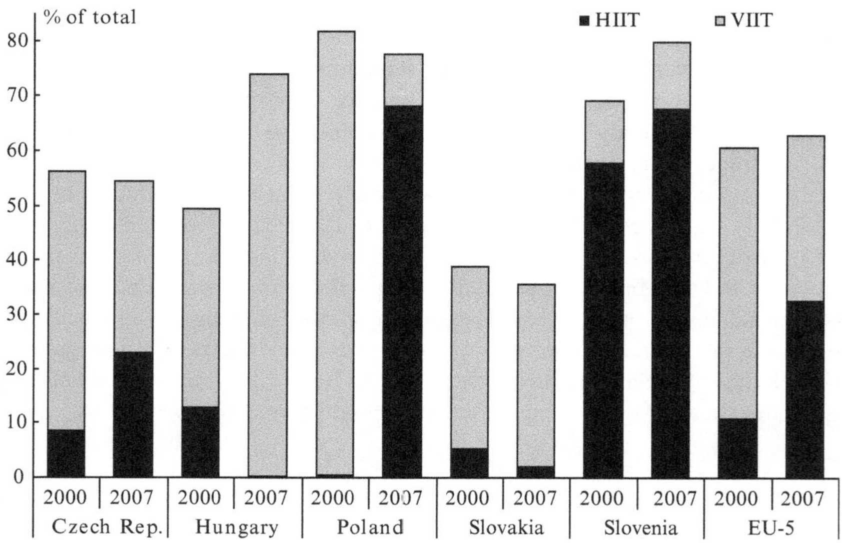

Fig. 2.2 Horizontal and vertical intra-industry trade in the automotive industry in some new Member States in 2000 and 2007
Source: Data of Table 2.6

Table 2.7 Inward FDI stock in transport equipment in 2001–2006

Mio. of EUR	2001	2002	2003	2004	2005	2006	2007	2006/2001 change (in %)
Czech Republic	2192.0	2272.4	3407.6	3345.4	4740.1	5700.3	n.a.	260
Estonia	36.8	25.7	77.3	59.3	60.5	60.7	63.7	164
Latvia	2.0	3.0	1.2	7.9	12.7	15.1	19.5	735
Lithuania	42.9	43.2	70.3	75.5	84.7	93.6	97.9	218
Hungary	2833.1	3247.5	3761.7	4387.4	4855.6	5683.1	n.a.	201
Poland	2421.7	2280.3	2760.5	4465.1	4975.4	5692.1	n.a.	235
Slovenia	127.6	54.4	124.9	197.3	256.1	271.2	n.a.	212
Slovakia	141.3	149.1	156.2	314.7	563.5	879.0	n.a.	623
Bulgaria	n.a.	n.a.	n.a.	n.a.	n.a.	n.a.	n.a.	n.a.
Romania	n.a.	n.a.	527.0	860.0	1112.0	1406.0	n.a.	n.a.

Notes: Transport equipment: Motor vehicles and other transport equipment (DM NACE, NACE 34 and 35)
Source: WIIW Database

Table 2.8 FDI stock in transport equipment

% of total FDI stock	2001	2002	2003	2004	2005	2006	2007
Czech Republic	7.1	6.2	9.5	8.0	9.2	9.4	n.a.
Estonia	1.0	0.6	1.4	0.8	0.6	0.6	0.6
Latvia	0.1	0.1	0.0	0.2	0.3	0.3	0.3
Lithuania	1.4	1.1	1.8	1.6	1.2	1.1	1.0
Hungary	9.1	9.4	9.8	9.6	9.3	9.2	n.a.
Poland	5.2	4.9	6.0	7.0	6.5	6.0	n.a.
Slovenia	4.3	1.4	2.5	3.5	4.2	4.0	n.a.
Slovakia	2.2	1.7	1.2	2.0	2.8	3.0	n.a.
Bulgaria	n.a.	n.a.	n.a.	n.a.	n.a.	n.a.	n.a.
Romania	n.a.	n.a.	5.5	5.7	5.1	4.1	n.a.

Notes: Transport equipment: Motor vehicles and other transport equipment (DM NACE, NACE 34 and 35)
Source: WIIW Database

and other parts while such products were also imported to be assembled in the country and re-exported (Tables 2.7 and 2.8).

The low and even decreasing share of intra-industry trade in Slovakia (Fig. 2.2) can be explained to a great extent by this country's specialization in importing automotive parts and components and the subsequent export of assembled cars. Such flows did not translate into higher VIIT (or total IIT) explained by the detailed SITC classification applied in this study.

Bearing in mind the limitations of the approach followed based on IIT indices which are useful for comparisons over time or across products but have deficiencies when comparing absolute levels, there are nevertheless sufficient indications pointing at a positive relationship between FDI and intra-industry trade in the automotive sector. Countries with relatively high foreign investment in the automotive sector (Hungary, the Czech Republic and Poland) record usually higher IIT in this sector than in total trade (recently, the Czech Republic was an exception). Intra-industry trade in the automotive sector is not, as suggested by some previous studies (see overview of the literature above), mainly of vertical character. In some countries, an increase of horizontal intra-industry trade in the automotive sector has been recorded mirroring a fast catching up process and the involvement of transnational corporations.

2.8 Conclusion

Intra-industry trade, which is of greater benefit to the economy than inter-industry trade, has driven trade developments of the new Member States in recent years. Its share in total trade of the EU-10 countries increased from 42% in 2000 to 51% in 2007. The increasing role of IIT has been observed in all countries, but one (Malta). The EU-10 countries have made great strides in changing their production structures which became more similar to those of the old EU Members.

The fast development of IIT smoothened the adjustments of the EU-12 countries to the EU internal market, as resources had not to be re-allocated between industries. This is a noteworthy achievement against the background of increased competition in an uncertain and globalised environment in which new emerging markets are fighting for their place.

A new element is the relatively quickly changing pattern of specialization of a majority of the new Member States towards more horizontal intra-industry trade, usually typical for more developed countries. An increasing share of high quality vertical intra-industry trade was also identified. Moreover, this study confirms the important role of FDI for growth in intra-industry trade.

Acknowledgments The author wishes to thank Prof. Elżbieta Czarny for helpful comments. Data has been compiled by Łukasz Ambroziak and Maciej Sewerski, who produced the tables and figures.

References

Abd-el-Rahman, K. (1991). Firms' competitive and national comparative advantages as joint determinants of trade composition. *Weltwirtschaftliches Archiv, 127*(1), 87–97.

Aturupane, C., Djankov, S., & Hoekman, B. (1999). Horizontal and vertical intra-industry trade between eastern Europe and the European Union. *Weltwirtschaftliches Archiv, 135*(1), 62–81.

Balassa, B. (1966). Tariff reductions and trade in manufactures among industrial countries. *American Economic Review, 56*(3), 466–473.

Černoša, S. (2007). Horizontal and vertical intra-industry trade between the former CEFTA countries and the European Union. *Managing Global Transitions, 5*(2), 157–178.

Cieślik, A. (2008). *Multinational firms and international fragmentation of production in Poland.* Working Papers of International Business, Sopot: University of Gdańsk.

Czarny, E., & Śledziewska, K. (2008). Poland's intra-industry trade with the European Union at the beginning of the 21th century. In M. A. Weresa (Ed.), *Poland. Competitiveness report.*

Focus on services. Warszawa: World Economy Research Institute, Warsaw School of Economics.
Di Simone, G. (2007, May). *Trade in parts and components and central eastern European countries' industrial geography*. Department of Economics, University of Milan.
Falvey, R. (1981). Commercial policy and intra-industry trade. *Journal of International Economics, 11*(4), 495–511.
Falvey, R., & Kierzkowski, H. (1987). Product quality, intra-industry trade and (im)perfect competition. In H. Kierzkowski (Ed.), *Protection and competition in international trade*. Oxford: Blackwell.
Ferto, I., & Soos, K. A. (2006, February). *The development of intra-industry trade between the European Union and European former communist countries before the 2004 enlargement*. INDEUNIS Papers, Hungarian Academy of Sciences, Institute of Economics.
Fidrmuc, J., Grozea-Helmenstein, D., & Wörgötter, A. (1997, December). *Intra-industry trade dynamics in the east-west relations. Comparison of Austrian, Dutch, German, Italian and Swedish trade with the CEEC*. East European Series, No. 52, Vienna: Institute for Advanced Studies.
Finger, J. M. (1975). Trade overlap and intra-industry trade. *Economic Inquiry, 13*, 581–589.
Flam, H., & Helpman, E. (1987). Vertical product differentiation and north-south trade. *American Economic Review, 76*(5), 810–822.
Gacs, J. (1994). The economic interpenetration between the EC and eastern Europe: Hungary. *European Economy, 6*, 191–224.
Greenaway, D., Hine, R. C., & Milner, C. (1994). Country-specific factors and pattern of horizontal and vertical intra-industry trade in the UK. *Weltwirtschaftliches Archiv, 130*, 77–100.
Grubel, H. G., & Lloyd, P. J. (1975). *Intra-industry trade: The theory and measurement of intra-industry trade in differentiated products*. London: Macmillan.
Helpman, E. (1981). International trade in the presence of product differentiation, economies of scale and monopolistic competition: A Chamberlin-Heckscher-Ohlin approach. *Journal of International Economics, 11*(3), 305–340.
Helpman, E., & Krugman, P. (1985). *Market structure and foreign trade*. Brighton: Harvester Wheatsheaf.
Hine, R. C., Greenaway, D., & Milner, Ch. (1998). Vertical and horizontal intra-industry trade: An analysis of country- and industry-specific determinants. In M. Brülhart & R. C. Hine (Eds.), *Intra-industry trade and adjustment*. London: Macmillan.
Kaminski, B. (2001, April). *How accession to the European Union has affected external trade and foreign direct investment in central European countries*. Policy Research Working Paper, No. 2578.
Krugman, P. R. (1979). Increasing returns, monopolistic competition and international trade. *Journal of International Economics, 9*, 469–479.
Krugman, P. R. (1980). Scale economies, product differentiation, and the pattern of trade. *American Economic Review, 70*(5), 950–959.
Lancaster, K. (1980). Intra-industry trade under perfect monopolistic competition. *Journal of International Economics, 10*(2), 151–175.
Loertscher, R., & Wolter, F. (1980). Determinants of intra-industry trade: Among countries and across industries. *Weltwirtschaftliches Archiv, 116*, 280–293.
Przystupa, J. (Ed.). (2006). *Economy and foreign trade of Poland in 2006*. Warsaw: Institute for Market, Consumption and Business Cycles Research.
Ruffin, R. J. (1999). The nature and significance of intra-industry trade. *Economic and Financial Review*, Federal Reserve Bank of Dallas, Fourth Quarter.
Tirpak, M. (2006, November). The automobile industry in central Europe. Washington DC: IMF.
Verdoorn, P. J. (1960). The intra-block trade of Benelux. In E. A. G. Robinson (Ed.), *Economic consequences of the size of nations*. London: Macmillan.

Chapter 3
FDI Spillovers in the Czech Republic: Takeovers Versus Greenfields

Juraj Stančík

Abstract This contribution analyzes the effects of foreign direct investment on the sales growth rate of domestic companies in the Czech Republic. Using firm-level panel data from 1995 to 2005, it studies both horizontal and vertical spillovers with respect to two kinds of foreign investment – takeovers and greenfields. This is the first paper applying this framework on firm level. The study allows also for the lagged nature of these spillovers. The results suggest that the sales growth rates of domestic companies mostly decrease in the presence of foreign companies, especially in upstream sectors. The impact through horizontal spillovers is mixed – positive from foreign takeovers, negative from greenfields. Positive forward spillovers are present mainly in recent years. Time sensitivity is revealed for horizontal as well as vertical spillovers.

3.1 Introduction

Foreign direct investment (FDI) is a driving force of growth for every developing economy. It brings new capital, technology and know-how. This investment comes either in the form of a greenfield project, where a new plant is built and therefore a new company formed, or in the form of foreign capital inflow to an existing domestic company. In both cases, this company is typically characterized by higher productivity and competitiveness (Arnold and Javorcik 2005).

Besides these direct effects from FDI, there are also varieties of indirect effects. The entry of any high productivity company should naturally encourage other companies within the same sector to improve their performance and competitiveness. The increase in efficiency of the production process can happen by copying

J. Stančík
Center for Economic Research and Graduate Education, Charles University, Prague, Czech Republic
e-mail: juraj.stancik@cerge-ei.cz

F. Keereman and I. Szekely (eds.), *Five Years of an Enlarged EU*,
DOI 10.1007/978-3-642-12516-4_3, © Springer-Verlag Berlin Heidelberg 2010

new technologies or by hiring trained workers and managers from foreign-owned companies (Javorcik 2004). On the other hand, those domestic companies that are not able to catch up with the higher performance of other companies within the sector may be crowded out of the market. In general, these effects are referred to as horizontal spillovers.

However, companies from sectors other than that of the foreign enterprise might be affected by its presence as well if they are in direct business contact with it. This includes companies that supply or provide services for foreign firms, as well as companies that are supplied by foreign firms. It is likely that foreign companies require higher standards from their suppliers. On the other hand, it is also likely that higher standards are provided by foreign companies to domestic companies as well, which might improve the domestic companies' efficiency and performance. In general, these effects are referred to as vertical spillovers.

An extent of these spillovers depends also on the type of foreign investment. Based on the industry where they operate, foreign investors have several options. If they are in non-tradable business, they can pick the best local company, take over and price others out of the local market. Or they can pick the industry with weak local companies and put in a greenfield. In both of these cases we can expect negative horizontal spillovers. On the other hand, if they operate in exporting industry, they do not have to care about local companies within a sector. They can find good suppliers and concentrate on export. This may result in positive horizontal and backward spillovers. Another important factor is a characteristic of the investment itself. Takeovers usually start by improving acquired companies' organization and management; new technologies may arrive much later. Moreover, they are likely to use an existing network of suppliers and customers. Whereas greenfields often bring state-of-the-art technologies immediately and may not use local markets at all.

Governments in transition and developing countries often compete to attract foreign investors by offering them various advantages. The Czech Republic is no exception. In 1998 its government approved a system of subsidies for foreign investors that was supposed to increase the competitiveness of Czech industry. One of the supporting arguments was that foreign investors would help other domestic companies to improve. However, contrary to these arguments and expectations, the recent study by Stančík (2007) shows that the impact on domestic companies is actually negative. This brings up new interesting questions. Does this negative impact differ with different type of investment? Is there a type of investment that we should support more?

The goal of this paper is therefore to answer these questions by analyzing the effects of FDI on the performance of domestic companies in the Czech Republic with respect to different types of foreign investment – acquisitions and greenfields. We study these effects within the same sector as well as through vertical linkages. We employ up-to-date data that cover the period 1995–2005. We also focus on the time structure of these effects.

To our best knowledge, this is the first paper analyzing FDI spillovers on firm-level data by dividing them into takeovers and greenfields. Therefore, one of the goals of this paper is to suggest a framework that might be used and further developed in future empirical studies.

This paper finds that there are differences between the two types of foreign investment; in sign of their impact on domestic companies as well as in magnitude. Particularly, supplying domestic companies are affected by the presence of foreign investors downstream through negative backward spillover effects. Since foreign investors prefer to import their supplies from abroad, Czech supplying companies oriented mainly on domestic markets consequently lose on sales. The impact is double in case of greenfields. Regarding horizontal spillover effects, they are much smaller in magnitude. However, the main difference is that they differ in sign. The impact of greenfields remains negative, while the impact of takeovers on domestic companies within the same sector is now positive. No forward spillover effects are present. Furthermore, the results suggest a dynamic pattern in FDI spillovers. Initial positive/negative horizontal spillovers from takeovers/greenfields are later translated into positive/negative forward spillovers.

This contribution is structured as follows. The Sect. 3.2 deals with the previous studies relevant for this research. Our research strategy is explained in the Sect. 3.3. The Sect. 3.4 contains the data description. The empirical results are presented in the Sect. 3.5. The Sect. 3.6 concludes.

3.2 Literature Review

One of the first studies investigating the benefits for domestic companies from FDI using company-level panel data is Aitken and Harrison (1999) who employ data from Venezuela during the years 1976–1989. They find a positive effect of FDI on smaller domestic companies and a small negative effect of FDI on all domestic companies. They further claim that the positive effect of the presence of foreign enterprises is gained by joint ventures with foreign capital. According to the authors, the overall effect is thus only slightly positive. Javorcik (2004) goes a little bit further and besides horizontal spillovers, she stresses also the role of vertical spillover effects. Her research is based on a sample of Lithuanian companies in the period 1996–2000. She does not find any significant spillover effect or effects within a region. However, she finds a positive significant vertical spillover effect of FDI on domestic companies. She also claims there is no difference in magnitude between the effects from partially or fully foreign-owned companies.

There are also several company-level studies of the Czech Republic. Djankov and Hoekman (2000) study the impact of FDI on total factor productivity growth of recipient firms and find that this impact is positive and significant. On the other hand, the effect of joint ventures is less positive and not statistically significant. As regards the spillover effects, they find a negative horizontal spillover effect of FDI and joint ventures, taken together, on domestic companies. Kinoshita (2000) finds no significant technology spillover effect of joint ventures or FDI on productivity growth neither within the firm nor within the industry. The author further examines the two roles of the firm's R&D – innovation and absorptive capacity. She claims that the latter is far more important. According to her results, the effects of FDI are significant for firms that perform their own R&D – the horizontal spillover is positive and the direct effect is negative, whereas the effect of just R&D remains insignificant. Jarolím (2001) concentrates mainly on the performance of foreign-owned companies, but he examines also the horizontal spillover effects of FDI on domestic companies within the same sector. In line with the previous literature, he shows that foreign-owned companies are characterized by higher total factor productivity. However, he does not find any significant horizontal spillover effects. Moreover, he compares the performance of greenfield ventures with foreign acquisitions and concludes that the former perform significantly better.

Damijan et al. (2003a) examine the direct effect of FDI, intra-industry knowledge spillovers from FDI and the impact of firms' own R&D accumulation on productivity growth using a sample of eight transition countries.[1] Regarding the Czech Republic, they find a positive direct effect of FDI on domestic recipient companies. Intra-industry knowledge spillovers are found to be insignificant, but, similarly to Kinoshita (2000), their significance increases when controlling for a firm's own R&D. Surprisingly, the productivity growth of Czech companies that perform their own R&D decreases with foreign presence in the industry. In a closely related study, Damijan et al. (2003b) use the same sample and add Lithuania and Latvia. Their analysis now incorporates not only horizontal but also vertical spillovers. They conclude that vertical spillover effects are more important than horizontal effects. Particularly, both of these effects are positive in the Czech Republic.

These previous studies about the Czech Republic have some similar characteristics. Most of them suffer from small samples and from focusing on the early transition period. Early transition (i.e., 1991–1996) is characterized by mass privatization and unclear ownership structures, whereas the main boom of foreign investment came in and after 1998 (Fig. 3.1), which is the last sample year in almost all of these studies. Therefore, there is no surprise that they often did not succeed in finding any significant spillover effects. Furthermore, most of this previous literature is limited to manufacturing sectors only. However, it is likely that especially domestic companies from service sectors would be affected by the presence of foreign investors. Unlike manufacturing companies, these companies are not able to export their services abroad and they are limited to domestic market only. Finally, they incorporate mostly only horizontal spillovers.

Stančík (2007) attempts to improve over this literature by analyzing the effects of FDI on sales growth rate using a panel of 4,067 Czech companies from all sectors during the period of 1995–2003. He studies both horizontal and vertical spillovers. Moreover, he pays attention also to the potential endogeneity of FDI with respect to future industry growth. The results suggest that domestic companies are mostly suffering in the presence of foreign companies, especially in upstream sectors.

A slightly different concept is studied in Kosová (2006) where she concentrates on the crowding-out effect from the presence of foreign companies. She uses a

[1]Bulgaria, Czech Republic, Estonia, Hungary, Poland, Romania, Slovakia, and Slovenia.

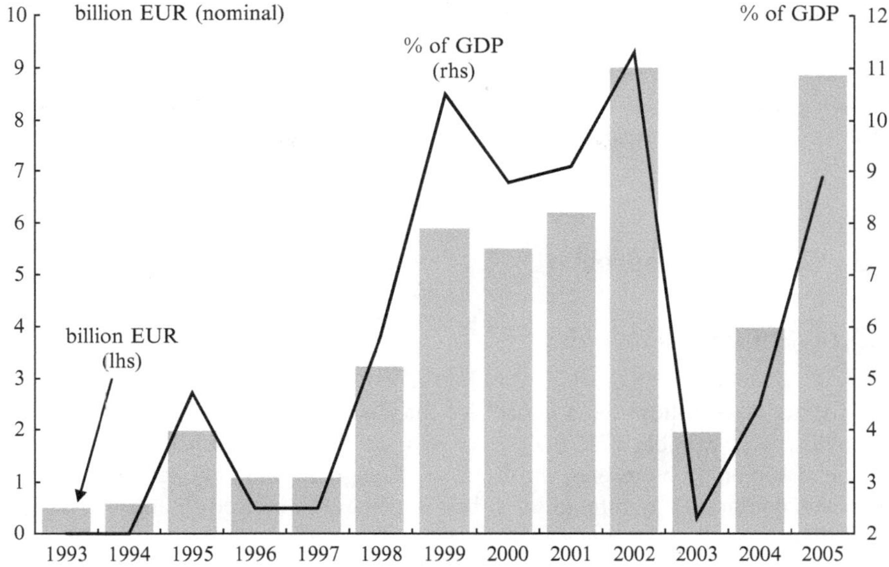

Fig. 3.1 FDI inflow into the Czech Republic
Source: Czech National Bank

sample of 9,986 Czech companies from all sectors covering the period 1994–2001. She finds a positive effect of foreign capital presence on domestic firms' growth and survival. She claims that exit rates are lower for companies in industries with foreign presence. On the other hand, Kosová and Ayyagari (2006) deal with the impact of FDI on domestic entrepreneurship. They find that foreign presence contributes positively to the entry rates of domestic companies through both horizontal and vertical spillovers. Although both of these effects are statistically significant, they claim the dominance of vertical spillovers over horizontal spillovers, especially through forward linkages. For this research they use a sample of 9,979 Czech companies covering the period 1994–2000.

There is another string of literature which focuses more closely on different types of foreign investment, not necessarily in the Czech Republic. However, instead of studying spillover effects, one part of this literature concentrates on direct impact of FDI on its recipients (Evenett and Voicu 2003; Hanousek et al. 2007; Arnold and Javorcik 2005). The common finding from these studies is that acquired companies are positively affected by the presence of foreign investors. The other part of literature then studies distinct modes of entry of foreign investors. It usually deals with strategies of foreign investors or factors contributing to their decision process (Zejan 1990; Hennart and Park 1993; Harzing 2002; Aminian et al. 2005).

Regarding the literature that would clearly connect these two concepts – FDI spillovers and the type of foreign investment, there is almost nothing. One of the attempts is Wang and Wong (2007). They separate FDI into greenfields and cross-border mergers & acquisitions and study the impact on economic growth. However, this is a country level study and greenfield FDI is only estimated from total FDI inflow values. The main reason for shortage of studies about this issue is probably a lack of information in data that would allow to distinguish between acquisitions and greenfields.

3.3 Research Approach

3.3.1 Spillover Variables

In this study we follow the approach of Stančík (2007) and create six spillover variables. The variable $THORIZ_{jt}$ measures the foreign presence[2] in takeovers within a sector. It represents the share of foreign capital invested in acquired domestic companies by foreign ones, i.e., in takeovers, in sector j at time t and is defined as

$$THORIZ_{jt} = \frac{\sum_{i:i \in j, FA_{ijt} \geq 0.1} FS_{ijt} FA_{ijt}}{\sum_{i:i \in j} FA_{ijt}} \tag{3.1}$$

where FS_{ijt} denotes the share of foreign capital in firm i at time t in sector j, given that firm i is a takeover, and FA_{ijt} denotes the fixed assets of firm i at time t in sector j.

The variable $TBACK_{jt}$ represents the weighted share of foreign capital in takeovers in all sectors that are supplied by sector j at time t and, conversely, the variable $TFORW_{jt}$ represents the weighted share of foreign capital in takeovers in all sectors that supply sector j at time t. $TBACK_{jt}$ measures the presence of foreign takeovers downstream and $TFORW_{jt}$ measures the presence of foreign takeovers upstream. They are defined as

$$TBACK_{jt} = \sum_{k:k \neq j} \beta_{jkt} THORIZ_{kt} \tag{3.2}$$

$$TFORW_{jt} = \sum_{k:k \neq j} \beta_{kjt} THORIZ_{kt}, \tag{3.3}$$

where β_{xyt} stands for the fraction of output from sector x supplied to sector y at time t.

---

[2]We interpret a company as foreign if it has at least 10% of its equity owned by a foreign investor. The same threshold is also used in the Czech National Bank official definition of FDI and in Damijan et al. (2003b), Javorcik (2004), and Stančík (2007).

In a similar fashion we define three remaining variables $GHORIZ_{jt}$, $GBACK_{jt}$, $GFORW_{jt}$. The only difference is that instead of foreign capital in takeovers these variables are now related to foreign capital invested in greenfields that are built by foreign investors.

3.3.2 Theoretical Model

The goal of this paper is to examine whether sales growth is affected by the share of foreign capital within and across sectors and whether these effects differ with respect to the type of foreign investment (takeovers vs. greenfields). For this purpose, we follow the methodology of Haddad and Harrison (1993). They assume a production function with value-added Y that is a function of two inputs, capital K and labor L:

$$Y_{ijt} = A_{jt}f(K_{ijt}, L_{ijt}).$$

The level of productivity is given by A_{jt}. It is assumed to vary across sectors j and time t. By using total differential, taking logs, and using the fact that the value of the marginal product for each factor equals its cost, we now have

$$\Delta \ln Y_{ijt} = \frac{\Delta A_{jt}}{A_{jt}} + \alpha_1 \Delta \ln K_{ijt} + \alpha_2 \Delta \ln L_{ijt}, \tag{3.4}$$

where $\frac{\Delta A}{A}$ is productivity growth.

The coefficients on the growth of labor and capital are simply their share in value-added. We test the hypothesis that productivity growth is affected by the share of foreign capital both within and across sectors and that there are differences between takeovers and greenfields in these effects. Thus, we proceed by assuming that productivity growth can be decomposed into the following components:

$$\begin{aligned}\frac{\Delta A_{jt}}{A_{jt}} &= \alpha_0 + \alpha_3 THORIZ_{jt} + \alpha_4 TBACK_{jt} + \alpha_5 TFORW_{jt} + \alpha_6 GHORIZ_{jt} \\ &\quad + \alpha_7 GBACK_{jt} + \alpha_8 GFORW_{jt} + \alpha_t + \varepsilon_{ijt}\end{aligned} \tag{3.5}$$

where *THORIZ, TBACK, TFORW:* measuring effects from foreign takeovers *GHORIZ, GBACK, GFORW:* measuring effects from foreign greenfields α_t: set of dummy variables to control for year-specific effects ε_{ijt}: disturbance term to account for possible changes in productivity growth due to stochastic shocks at the firm or sector level over time.

Combining (3.4) and (3.5) yields the equation we estimate:

$$\Delta \ln Y_{ijt} = \alpha_0 + \alpha_1 \Delta \ln K_{ijt} + \alpha_2 \Delta \ln L_{ijt} + \alpha_3 THORIZ_{jt} + \alpha_4 TBACK_{jt} + \alpha_5 TFORW_{jt} + \alpha_6 GHORIZ_{jt} + \alpha_7 GBACK_{jt} + \alpha_8 GFORW_{jt} + \alpha_t + \varepsilon_{ijt} \quad (3.6)$$

3.4 Data

The company-level annual data used here come from the ASPEKT database, which is a Czech source for the Amadeus database[3] and is widely used in empirical research (Earnhart and Lízal 2002; Hanousek et al. 2007; Bena and Hanousek 2006). Financial data cover the period 1993–2006, include almost 30,000 Czech firms in total and form an unbalanced panel, where the number of usable companies varies from almost 2,000 in 1993 to more than 19,000 in 2004. The *ASPEKT* database also provides information about companies' ownership structure. However, due to the limited availability of this information, the total number of companies is significantly reduced. Ownership information allows us to distinguish foreign companies from domestic ones. Unfortunately, this ownership information does not allow to distinguish foreign takeovers from greenfields. For this purpose, we use internet and search web pages for the history of all foreign companies in our sample. In contrast to most previous studies about FDI spillovers, we do not limit the analysis only to the manufacturing sectors. With few exceptions, we employ data from all sectors; only sectors with a strong regulatory role of the government are excluded (see Annex for details).

Table 3.1 shows the summary statistics of all the variables used in this research. As regards the ownership structure, the average share of a foreign investor in a Czech company is almost 20%.

For studying vertical spillover effects, we employ inter-industry data (input–output matrices) that come from the Czech Statistical Office and are available for every year during 1995–2005. There is an often used assumption in previous studies (Damijan et al. 2003b; Javorcik 2004 or Kosová and Ayyagari 2006) that these matrices do not change much over time. However, a descriptive analysis in Stančík (2007) reveals that for almost 30% of relations[4] the standard deviation over time is bigger than the mean value. Therefore, in order to remove possible measurement errors, we follow the approach in Stančík (2007) and use fitted values of time trends based on these matrices instead of the original values. In other words, we still have

[3]Amadeus is a pan-European financial database.

[4]A relation is a time series of the flow of goods and services from sector X to sector Y for the whole period 1995–2005. There are almost 7,000 such relations – for every combination of sectors X and Y, as well as for the supply and demand relationship. These relations are used to generate a mean value and standard deviation for every time series.

Table 3.1 Summary statistics of the variables used

	Observations	Mean	Std. deviation	Min	Max
Sales (1,000 CZK)	23,680	663,282	3,453,186	1	177,800,000
Fixed assets (1,000 CZK)	23,680	410,876	2,792,964	1	130,500,000
Staff costs (1,000 CZK)	23,680	71,009	279,695	1	8,499,800
Δln sales	23,680	0.019	0.997	−10.979	14.458
Δln fixed assets	23,680	0.030	0.745	−9.543	11.785
Δln staff costs	23,680	0.062	0.617	−9.641	9.968
Foreign (%)	23,680	19.900	37.328	0	100.275
Domestic (%)	23,680	37.854	40.290	0	109.678
$THORIZ_{jt}$	23,680	0.095	0.128	0	0.929
$TBACK_{jt}$	23,680	0.073	0.065	0	0.648
$TFORW_{jt}$	23,680	0.073	0.051	0.004	0.323
$GHORIZ_{jt}$	23,680	0.143	0.158	0	1.000
$GBACK_{jt}$	23,680	0.086	0.058	0.001	0.411
$GFORW_{jt}$	23,680	0.076	0.049	0.007	0.322

Notes: Foreign: share of foreign capital in a company. Domestic: denotes the share of domestic capital in a company
Source: ASPEKT Database

Table 3.2 Number of companies by year

	All	Domestic	Foreign	Takeover	Greenfield
1995	1,336	1,066	127	176	94
1996	2,007	1,558	273	256	193
1997	2,370	1,816	400	309	245
1998	2,570	1,924	507	330	316
1999	2,682	1,936	636	357	389
2000	2,788	1,937	777	401	450
2001	2,644	1,763	838	413	468
2002	2,599	1,674	910	410	515
2003	2,361	1,528	833	370	463
2004	1,199	722	473	201	276
2005	1,124	665	459	178	281
Total	23,680	16,589	6,233	3,401	3,690

Notes: Domestic denotes only always-domestic companies
Source: ASPEKT Database

a different input–output matrix for each year but these matrices now capture trends in supplying and demanding rather than just oscillating official values.

After merging all variables and performing several data cleaning procedures,[5] the resulting sample covers the period 1995–2005 and contains information about 4,253 companies from 44 sectors,[6] 23,680 observations in total. An overview of the time, sector and ownership structure of the final sample is provided in Tables 3.2 and 3.3. The number of companies varies from 1,124 in 2005 to 2,788 in 2000. Foreign companies represent 26% of all observations. As regards sectors, most of the

[5] All of these procedures are described in the Annex.

[6] At 2-digit NACE classification (Classification of Economic Activities in the European Community).

Table 3.3 Number of companies by NACE classification

NACE	All	Domestic	Takeover	Greenfield
10 Mining of coal and lignite; extraction of peat	10	9	1	0
14 Other mining and quarrying	33	25	5	3
15 Manufacture of food products and beverages	280	228	35	17
16 Manufacture of tobacco products	3	0	0	3
17 Manufacture of textiles	78	61	10	7
18 Manufacture of wearing apparel; dressing and dyeing of fur	14	13	1	0
19 Manufacture of leather and leather products	12	10	2	0
20 Manufacture of wood and wood products	75	59	13	3
21 Manufacture of pulp, paper and paper products	33	19	8	6
22 Publishing, printing and reproduction of recorded media	50	33	9	8
23 Manufacture of coke, refined petroleum products and nuclear fuel	4	3	1	0
24 Manufacture of chemicals and chemical products	91	55	21	15
25 Manufacture of rubber and plastic products	53	25	14	14
26 Manufacture of other non-metallic mineral products	152	97	40	15
27 Manufacture of basic metals	75	59	13	3
28 Manufacture of fabricated metal products	151	110	23	18
29 Manufacture of machinery and equipment n.e.c.	222	165	34	23
30 Manufacture of office machinery and computers	4	1	0	3
31 Manufacture of electrical machinery and apparatus n.e.c.	95	55	21	19
32 Manufacture of radio, TV and communication equipment	37	23	4	10
33 Manufacture of medical, precision and optical instruments	38	29	4	5
34 Manufacture of motor vehicles, trailers and semi-trailers	62	28	18	16
35 Manufacture of other transport equipment	30	21	8	1
36 Manufacture of furniture; manufacturing n.e.c.	32	20	8	4
37 Recycling	15	15	0	0
45 Construction	225	190	26	9
50 Sale, maintenance and repair of motor vehicles and motorcycles	106	81	3	22
51 Wholesale trade, except of motor vehicles and motorcycles	647	341	52	254
52 Retail trade; repair of personal and household goods	182	113	12	57
55 Hotels and restaurants	70	55	5	10
60 Land transport; transport via pipelines	107	96	7	4
63 Supporting and auxiliary transport activities; travel agencies	50	24	8	18
64 Post and telecommunications	43	17	8	18
65 Financial intermediation, except insurance and pension funding	207	150	19	38
66 Insurance and pension funding, except compulsory social security	1	1	0	0
67 Activities auxiliary to financial intermediation	19	15	1	3
70 Real estate services	260	206	24	30
71 Renting of machinery and equipment without operator	14	8	1	5

(*continued*)

Table 3.3 (continued)

NACE	All	Domestic	Takeover	Greenfield
72 Computer and related services	84	45	7	32
73 Research and development	28	24	2	2
74 Other business services	460	332	42	86
90 Sewage and refuse disposal, sanitation and similar activities	63	56	4	3
92 Recreational, cultural and sporting activities	32	27	1	4
93 Other service activities	6	6	0	0
Total	4,253	2,950	515	788

Source: ASPEKT Database

companies are from service sectors (56%) and manufacturing sectors (38%). Table 3.3 in the annex also includes information about the structure of our sample regarding takeovers and greenfields. From the total 4,253 companies, 12% are acquisitions and almost 19% are greenfields.

3.5 Estimation Results

3.5.1 Baseline Specification

In order to study the horizontal and vertical spillover effects from FDI, the following modification of model (3.6) is estimated:

$$\begin{aligned}\Delta \ln SALES_{ijt} = {} & \gamma_i + \alpha_1 \Delta \ln FA_{ijt} + \alpha_2 \Delta \ln SC_{ijt} + \alpha_3 THORIZ_{jt} \\ & + \alpha_4 TBACK_{jt} + \alpha_5 TFORW_{jt} + \alpha_6 GHORIZ_{jt} + \alpha_7 GBACK_{jt} \\ & + \alpha_8 GFORW_{jt} + \alpha_t + \varepsilon_{ijt} \qquad (3.7)\end{aligned}$$

where $SALES_{ijt}$, FA_{ijt}, and SC_{ijt}: sales, fixed assets, and staff costs, respectively, for firm i at time t in sector α_t: year dummy variables because sales, fixed assets, and staff costs are originally collected in nominal values γ_i: capturing unobserved firm characteristics (e.g., better management or technologies) assumed constant over time (thus a model with firms' fixed effects is estimated).

A positive value of the variable $THORIZ_{jt}$ would imply that the presence of foreign takeovers in the sector has a positive impact on the productivity of domestic companies within a sector. A positive value of the variable $TBACK_{jt}$ would imply that the presence of foreign takeovers has a positive impact on the productivity of those domestic companies that supply the foreign companies' sectors. Similarly, a positive value of the variable $TFORW_{jt}$ would imply that the presence of foreign takeovers has a positive impact on the productivity of those domestic companies that are supplied by the foreign companies' sectors. Furthermore, variables measuring spillover effects from greenfields are defined accordingly. A positive value of the variable $GHORIZ_{jt}$ would imply that the presence of foreign greenfields in the sector has a positive impact on the productivity of domestic companies within a sector. A positive value of the variable $GBACK_{jt}$ would imply that the presence of foreign greenfields has a positive impact on the productivity of those domestic companies that supply the foreign companies' sectors. Similarly, a positive value of the variable $GFORW_{jt}$ would imply that the presence of foreign greenfields has a positive impact on the productivity of those domestic companies that are supplied by the foreign companies' sectors.

Since the goal of this paper is to study the effects on domestic companies, model (3.7), as well as all further models, are estimated on a sample of "always-domestic" companies only. This sample excludes companies that are foreign at any time during the sample frame. It allows one to study the pure spillover effects of FDI that are not affected by the better performance of either foreign greenfield companies, local companies that have been taken over by a foreign entity or local companies that are about to become foreign in the near future. However, for comparison, we estimate model (3.7) using the whole company population as well, including foreign companies.

Furthermore, in this kind of study, one has to be aware of the potential endogeneity of ownership at the firm level. In that case, foreign investors would acquire better domestic companies, while the worse ones would remain domestic. As a result, estimated coefficients would be biased towards negative values. In order to check whether this is the case, we also run regression (3.7) on a sample of companies that are always domestic plus the companies that will be acquired by foreign investors in the future during the period 1995–2005 but are still domestic now.

The estimates from these regressions are summarized in Table 3.4. The first column includes the estimated coefficients using a sample of always-domestic companies. The coefficients of capital and labor inputs are positive and significant, which is in line with expectations. The coefficient of the horizontal spillover variable from takeovers is positive and weakly significant. On the other hand, the coefficient of the same variable but from greenfields is negative and more significant. This implies that domestic companies are gaining in the presence of foreign takeovers within the same industry but losing from the presence of foreign greenfields within the same sector. However, it is necessary to emphasize that economically, these effects are very small: a 1% point increase in foreign capital's share in takeovers/greenfields within a sector causes an increase/decrease in the growth rate of the sales of domestic companies in the same sector by only 0.14/0.26% points. Since there are no previous studies dealing with an FDI impact of takeovers and greenfields separately, it is possible to compare these results only in global aspects. In this sense, these results are in line with previous studies, which mostly find only weak or non-significant horizontal spillover effect. One of the reasons can be exactly the fact that the impact of takeovers differs from the impact of greenfields and put together, these impacts negate each other.

Regarding backward spillovers, the situation is different when both coefficients are negative and strongly significant. These results correspond to previous finding by Stančík (2007) who finds negative backward spillover effects from FDI, though

Table 3.4 FDI spillover effects: the baseline specification

	Always-domestic	To-now-domestic	Whole population
Constant	0.267***	0.270***	0.269***
	(0.037)	(0.036)	(0.035)
$\Delta lnFA$	0.065***	0.063***	0.049***
	(0.021)	(0.020)	(0.018)
$\Delta lnSC$	0.601***	0.609***	0.632***
	(0.043)	(0.043)	(0.038)
$THORIZ_{jt}$	0.144*	0.164**	0.165**
	(0.081)	(0.080)	(0.072)
$TBACK_{jt}$	−0.714***	−0.732***	−0.787***
	(0.265)	(0.263)	(0.224)
$TFORW_{jt}$	0.463	0.501	0.132
	(0.398)	(0.412)	(0.366)
$GHORIZ_{jt}$	−0.255**	−0.247**	−0.153
	(0.115)	(0.113)	(0.098)
$GBACK_{jt}$	−1.468***	−1.391***	−1.235***
	(0.411)	(0.403)	(0.411)
$GFORW_{jt}$	−0.278	−0.302	0.526
	(0.568)	(0.561)	(0.498)
Year dummies	Yes	Yes	Yes
Number of observations	16,589	17,447	23,680
F statistic	40.64	42.11	60.82

Notes: The dependent variable is Δln *SALES*. Spillovers are examined on the sample of always-domestic companies, of to-now-domestic companies, of all companies, including foreign owned. Regressions with firms' fixed effects. Robust standard errors are in parentheses, corrected for clustering for each company. Significance at the 1%, 5%, and 10% levels is denoted by ***, ** and *, respectively

neither his study recognizes takeovers from greenfields. The current estimates suggest that domestic companies supplying both foreign takeovers and greenfields are negatively affected by their presence: a 1% point increase in foreign capital's share in takeovers/greenfields in a downstream sector causes a decrease in the growth rate of the sales of supplying domestic companies by 0.7/1.5% points. These impacts are about 5–6 times bigger than horizontal ones. The interesting fact is that the impact of greenfields is double in magnitude compared to takeovers and this holds for horizontal as well as for backward spillover effects. Finally, the coefficients of the forward spillover variables are in both cases insignificant so there are no spillover effects on consuming domestic companies.

Table 3.4 also presents the results from the estimation using a population of "to-now-domestic" companies in order to verify the potential endogeneity of foreign ownership. The results are consistent with little cherry picking by foreign investors because the estimated coefficients have basically the same magnitudes as when the sample of "always-domestic" companies was employed.

Summarizing the results, domestic companies are mainly negatively affected by the presence of foreign investors, either takeovers or greenfields, in downstream sectors. The explanation for this finding can be found in Tables 3.5 and 3.6. Table 3.5 shows the results from a regression of industry imports, the amount of

Table 3.5 The relationship between FDI and import

Constant	19,366.840***
	(2,164.019)
$THORIZ_{jt}$	98,220.337***
	(13,581.524)
$GHORIZ_{jt}$	12,035.839*
	(7,109.411)
Number of observations	441
R^2	0.135

Notes: Dependent variable *is* $IMPORT_{jt}$. () and ***, **, *, see Table 3.4

Table 3.6 FDI spillover effects by non-exporting and exporting sectors

Sectors	Non-exporting	Exporting
Constant	0.331***	0.112**
	(0.045)	(0.045)
$\Delta lnFA$	0.068***	0.030
	(0.022)	(0.057)
$\Delta lnSC$	0.583***	0.704***
	(0.048)	(0.084)
$THORIZ_{jt}$	0.262**	0.019
	(0.106)	(0.120)
$TBACK_{jt}$	−1.156***	0.037
	(0.353)	(0.329)
$TFORW_{jt}$	1.126**	−0.053
	(0.504)	(0.657)
$GHORIZ_{jt}$	−0.381**	−0.138
	(0.150)	(0.150)
$GBACK_{jt}$	−2.109***	−0.446
	(0.517)	(0.694)
$GFORW_{jt}$	−0.005	−2.944***
	(0.660)	(1.064)
Year dummies	Yes	Yes
Number of observations	13,383	3,206
F statistic	33.90	15.92

Notes: The dependent variable is Δln *SALES*
Sample: always-domestic companies variable. () and ***, **, *, see Table 3.4

goods and services imported to sector *j* at time *t* from abroad ($IMPORT_{jt}$), on the share of foreign capital. The positive coefficients of $THORIZ_{jt}$ and $GHORIZ_{jt}$ suggest that both types of foreign investors tend to import their supplies from abroad rather than use domestic suppliers. In addition, according to the Table 3.6, domestic companies oriented at foreign markets are able to deal with this fact. The regression in Table 3.6 is run on the firm level, although companies are divided into export- and non-export-oriented groups based on data on the sector level. A sector is considered to be export-oriented if it exports on average over the period 1995–2005 at least 50% of its production abroad. The coefficients of both backward spillover variables are statistically insignificant. However, domestic companies oriented mostly on the domestic market have nobody else to supply. In this case, there are significant and negative backward spillover effects, from takeovers as well as from greenfields. Since the number of these domestically-oriented companies is bigger than the export-oriented, these negative effects dominate when the sample of all "always-domestic" companies is employed.

3.5.2 FDI Spillovers on Various Subsamples

The previous results indicate that there are strong backward spillover effects from FDI on domestic companies, either from takeovers or from greenfields. Horizontal spillover effects are present as well but they are much less statistically or economically significant. Additionally, there are no forward spillovers present. However, these effects may be prevalent or stronger only in some period of time or in some specific group of companies. Fortunately, our sufficiently big sample allows us to create several smaller subsamples. Thus, regression (3.7) is run stepwise on two subsamples from the periods 1995–2000 and 2001–2005. Moreover, it is run on a subsample from the period 1998–2005 to see the impact of FDI on domestic companies after the boom in 1998. Then, it is run also on a subsample of "smaller" companies. In this case, a company is defined as "smaller at time *t*" if its amount of fixed assets in year *t* is lower than the average amount of fixed assets of all companies within a sector in year *t*. This case is interesting because there are potentially two opposite effects. Due to their smaller size, these companies may be flexible and capable to quickly adjust to a new situation in a market. On the other hand, precisely because of their smaller size, they have only limited sources for improving their technologies or hiring new managers. Finally, regression (3.7) is run on subsamples of only-manufacturing companies as well as only-service companies to see the impact of FDI on these specific industries.

The results of the estimated coefficients from the six regressions on subsamples of always-domestic companies are summarized in Table 3.7. The coefficients of inputs are almost the same as with the original sample. The only difference is that the coefficient of fixed assets is not significant for later periods. The results for the period 1998–2005, i.e., the period of FDI boom in the Czech Republic, are almost the same as for the whole sample. However additionally, there are positive and significant, though only weakly, forward spillover effects from takeovers as well as from greenfields. These results are even more obvious during the years 2001–2005 when positive and strongly significant forward spillover effects are the only found effects. Thus, it might suggest an ability of domestic companies to improve themselves once they are offered better or improved products and services from foreign companies from upstream sectors and their enhanced ability to learn and adjust in this later period. It is also interesting that while at the beginning domestic companies used to only suffer from the presence of foreign investors, especially greenfields, the situation turned around recently and domestic companies mostly gain from the presence of these foreign investors.

Table 3.7 FDI spillover effects in different subsamples according to time span on sector

Specification	1995–2000	2001–2005	1998–2005	*FA*<mean	Manufacture	Service
Const	0.337***	−0.700***	0.047	0.244***	0.034	0.483***
	(0.053)	(0.262)	(0.155)	(0.045)	(0.040)	(0.066)
$\Delta lnFA$	0.066**	0.026	0.036	0.056***	0.081**	0.053**
	(0.026)	(0.043)	(0.025)	(0.021)	(0.038)	(0.025)
$\Delta lnSC$	0.617***	0.528***	0.565***	0.604***	0.639***	0.567***
	(0.051)	(0.083)	(0.051)	(0.043)	(0.083)	(0.052)
$THORIZ_{jt}$	0.080	−0.155	0.157*	0.206**	0.027	0.211
	(0.183)	(0.197)	(0.093)	(0.096)	(0.101)	(0.160)
$TBACK_{jt}$	1.033	0.671	−0.947***	−0.741**	0.438	−1.720***
	(0.673)	(1.202)	(0.344)	(0.314)	(0.293)	(0.496)
$TFORW_{jt}$	−1.360	3.106***	0.909*	0.344	0.482	2.833***
	(1.058)	(1.048)	(0.480)	(0.468)	(0.577)	(0.668)
$GHORIZ_{jt}$	−0.055	−0.067	−0.270**	−0.245*	0.100	−0.475***
	(0.202)	(0.223)	(0.131)	(0.138)	(0.164)	(0.173)
$GBACK_{jt}$	−2.366***	−0.919	−1.602***	−1.194**	−0.640	−3.191***
	(0.734)	(0.930)	(0.507)	(0.468)	(0.519)	(1.005)
$GFORW_{jt}$	−2.521**	4.422***	1.328*	0.035	0.044	0.448
	(1.133)	(1.523)	(0.767)	(0.665)	(0.670)	(1.221)
Year dummies	Yes	Yes	Yes	Yes	Yes	Yes
Number of observations	10,237	6,352	12,149	13,007	6,891	8,380
F statistic	39.25	8.83	23.75	34.86	24.38	25.06

Notes: The dependent variable is $\Delta \ln SALES$. Regressions with firms' fixed effects. () and ***, **, *, see Table 3.4

The situation for "smaller" companies just copies the overall results with mixed results for horizontal spillovers and negative backward spillovers. Thus, as regards the potential opposite effects mentioned above, none of them dominates the other one. While the results for manufacturing companies do not reveal any significant spillovers, the last column shows that especially the service sector is the one that loses in the presence of foreign investors. Both backward spillovers from takeovers and greenfields are negative, significant and more than double in magnitude compared to the overall results. Regarding horizontal spillovers, the overall positive spillover effect from takeovers now diminishes and the negative impact from greenfields is even bigger. These are natural results because service companies are almost completely domestically oriented and usually they are not forced by the domestic market to improve their products. Therefore, it is even harder for them to adjust to the presence of foreign companies. However, a forward spillover effect from takeovers is found to be positive, which is partially in line with the results from the previous paragraph.

3.5.3 *Time Aspects of FDI Spillovers*

The sections above assume that horizontal and vertical spillover effects from takeovers as well as greenfields are constant over time. But it is reasonable to assume that since foreign investors are usually one step ahead of domestic companies, these domestic companies need some time to improve their technology or efficiency. Moreover, the inflow of FDI has increased substantially since 1998, but this increase takes some time to have an effect. It is often the case, particularly for big greenfield investments, that although they are assigned to one specific year, it takes 1–2 years till these new companies start to produce and consequently to have an impact on a market. The similar reasoning holds also for acquisitions by foreign investors; an impact on these companies' production is often not immediate.

Therefore, in order to allow for the lagged effects of horizontal and vertical spillovers, two separate modifications of model (3.7), already with the lagged spillover variables, are estimated. The estimation results are reported in Table 3.8. For comparison, the first column comprises the results from the baseline model (3.7). Although there are positive/negative significant horizontal spillovers from takeover/greenfields in time *t*, they are now insignificant for both lags. Hence, initially domestic companies are slightly affected by the presence of foreign companies within their sector. But already after 1 year both of these positive and negative effects disappear. Regarding backward spillovers, they show some persistence for takeovers but only for 1 period. Otherwise, the situation is similar to horizontal spillovers. Domestic companies tend to adjust within a year, so after an initial negative shock they are able to regain their positions within 1–2 years. Thus, horizontal and backward spillover effects are sensitive to time and they occur mostly within the same year as a foreign investment. However, forward spillover effects on consuming domestic companies are significant only after 1 or 2 years after a foreign investment. In case of takeovers, this effect is positive, while for greenfields this effect is negative. This is an interesting result, especially in connection with the results from time *t*. It suggests a dynamic pattern in FDI spillovers. At first, domestic companies are positively affected by the presence of foreign takeovers within their sector. Then, this positive impact is translated through forward spillovers on their consumers in the next period. At the same time, foreign greenfields cause an opposite effect – negative initial impact on domestic companies, later translated through negative forward spillovers.

3.6 Conclusion

In this paper we analyze the horizontal and vertical spillover effects of FDI on the sales growth of Czech domestic companies over the period 1995–2005. In contrast to the previous literature, we study these spillovers with respect to two kinds of foreign investment – acquisitions and greenfields.

The results suggest that especially supplying domestic companies are affected by the presence of foreign investors downstream through negative backward spillover effects. The impact is bigger in case of greenfields: a 1% point increase in foreign capital in takeovers/greenfields in a downstream sector causes a decrease in the growth rate of the sales of supplying domestic companies by 0.7/1.5% points.

Table 3.8 FDI spillover effects with lags

	t	*t–1*	*t–2*
Constant	0.267***	0.274**	0.064
	(0.037)	(0.115)	(0.133)
$\Delta lnFA$	0.065***	0.061***	0.054**
	(0.021)	(0.022)	(0.022)
$\Delta lnSC$	0.601***	0.588***	0.599***
	(0.043)	(0.042)	(0.047)
$THORIZ_{jt}$	0.144*		
	(0.081)		
$THORIZ_{jt-1}$		0.028	
		(0.100)	
$THORIZ_{jt-2}$			−0.038
			(0.127)
$TBACK_{jt}$	−0.714***		
	(0.265)		
$TBACK_{jt-1}$		−0.742**	
		(0.289)	
$TBACK_{jt-2}$			0.175
			(0.311)
$TFORW_{jt}$	0.463		
	(0.398)		
$TFORW_{jt-1}$		1.847***	
		(0.486)	
$TFORW_{jt-2}$			2.119***
			(0.637)
$GHORIZ_{jt}$	−0.255**		
	(0.115)		
$GHORIZ_{jt-1}$		−0.125	
		(0.111)	
$GHORIZ_{jt-2}$			0.026
			(0.142)
$GBACK_{jt}$	−1.468***		
	(0.411)		
$GBACK_{jt-1}$		0.221	
		(0.451)	
$GBACK_{jt-2}$			0.544
			(0.526)
$GFORW_{jt}$	−0.278		
	(0.568)		
$GFORW_{jt-1}$		−2.427***	
		(0.647)	
$GFORW_{jt}$			−1.968**
			(0.798)
Year dummies	Yes	Yes	Yes
Number of observations	16,589	15,523	13,965
F statistic	40.64	33.79	29.93

Notes: The dependent variable is Δln SALES. Regressions with firms' fixed effects. Sample: always-domestic companies only. () and ***, **, *, see Table 3.4

This evidence can be explained by the fact that both types of foreign investors tend to import their supplies from abroad instead of using domestic suppliers. As a consequence, those domestic companies that are oriented mainly on the domestic market lose their sales. Regarding horizontal spillover effects, they are statistically weaker and much smaller in magnitude. However, the main difference is that foreign takeovers have a positive impact on domestic companies within their sector. The impact of greenfields remains negative. These contradictory results are probably the reason why the most of previous studies find only weak or insignificant horizontal spillovers. No forward spillover effects are present. Negative spillovers, horizontal or backward, are present especially in service sectors, which is again the consequence of their mainly domestic orientation. However, once they are offered "better" products from upstream sectors with foreign takeovers presence, their sales growth increases.

Furthermore, we consider also the time aspect of these spillovers. In this case, the results suggest a dynamic pattern in FDI spillovers. At first, domestic companies are positively affected by the presence of foreign takeovers within their sector. Then, this positive impact is translated through forward spillovers on their consumers in the next period. At the same time, foreign greenfields cause an opposite effect – negative initial impact on domestic companies, later translated into negative forward spillovers. Thus, we can conclude that all of these spillover effects are sensitive to time. Horizontal and backward spillovers occur mostly within the same year as a foreign investment, whereas forward spillovers need at least 1 year.

To conclude, we find that Czech domestic companies are not profiting from the presence of foreign investors. The overall impact on their sales growth rate is mostly negative, although the impact from takeovers is mixed and differs for supplying and consuming domestic companies. On the other hand, the results from the recent period are quite promising. Especially consuming domestic companies start to gain and their sales growth rates increase. Nevertheless, we are still not able to answer the question laid at the beginning – whom should we support more? Takeovers partially promote sales growth rate of other domestic companies, while the impact from greenfields is rather negative. But in fact, it is greenfields who create new jobs or start production in previously sleeping sectors.

Acknowledgments I would like to thank Štěpán Jurajda and Peter Katuščák for valuable consultations on this research, and Jan Hanousek and Evžen Kočenda for providing data and useful comments. Financial support from GAČR grant No. 402/06/1293 is gratefully acknowledged.

Annex: Data Cleaning Procedure

Starting with the original data set we perform the following procedures:

(a) Sales, fixed assets, staff costs

- Observations other than from December 31 are dropped.
- If there are more observations (from various accounting systems) for the same company and year, we use only the one from the most frequent accounting system.
- Missing values are replaced by interpolated values.

(b) Ownership structure

- The sum of weighted averages, according to the number of reported days out of 365, of all owners within a year is used for creating a company's ownership structure. This structure after wards includes the share of foreign as well as domestic capital for each company in each particular year.
- When in two consecutive years (t and $t+1$) the share of domestic capital does not change and the value of the share of foreign capital in time t is missing, then this missing value is replaced with the value of foreign share from time $t + 1$.
- We also assume the foreign share to be non-decreasing which al lows considering a company as foreign also in the next year even in absence of ownership structure information once it is found to be foreign in any previous year with a known ownership structure.
- Observations from the years 1993 and 1994 are dropped due to missing ownership information.
- Observations from the year 2006 are dropped as well because they are recorded only till June 30, 2006.

(c) Cleaning of variables

- Companies with only 1 year-observation are dropped since it is not possible to compute a growth rate for them.
- Negative values of ownership shares are dropped.
- If the sum of percentage ownerships of foreign and domestic owners is greater than 110%, the observation is dropped.
- Sectors with a strong regulatory role of the government are dropped:
  - NACE-01 Agriculture, hunting and related service activities
  - NACE-02 Forestry, logging and related service activities
  - NACE-05 Fishing, fish farming and related service activities
  - NACE-40 Electricity, gas, steam and hot water supply
  - NACE-41 Collection, purification and distribution of water
  - NACE-75 Public administration & defence; compulsory social security
  - NACE-80 Education
  - NACE-85 Health and social work

See Tables 3.2 and 3.3

References

Aitken, B. J., & Harrison, A. E. (1999). Do domestic firms benefit from direct foreign investment? Evidence from Venezuela. *American Economic Review, 89*(3), 605–618.

Aminian, N., Campart, S., & Pfister, E. (2005). *Macroeconomic determinants of cross-border mergers and acquisitions: European and Asian evidence*. Paper for conference.

Arnold, J., & Javorcik, B. S. (2005). *Gifted kids or pushy parents? Foreign acquisitions and plant performance in Indonesia*. Policy Research Working Paper Series, 3597. *The World Bank*.

Bena, J., & Hanousek, J. (2006). *Rent extraction by large shareholders: Evidence using dividend policy in the Czech Republic*. CERGE-EI Working Paper, 291.

Damijan, J. P., Knell, M., Majcen, B., & Rojec, M. (2003a). The role of FDI, R&D accumulation and trade in transferring technology to transition countries: Evidence from firm panel data for eight transition countries. *Economic Systems, 27*(2), 189–204.

Damijan, J. P., Knell, M., Majcen, B., & Rojec, M. (2003b). *Technology transfer through FDI in top-10 transition countries: How important are direct effects, horizontal and vertical spillovers*? WDI Working Paper, No. 549.

Djankov, S., & Hoekman, B. (2000). Foreign investment and productivity growth in Czech enterprises. *The World Bank Economic Review, 14*(1), 49–64.

Earnhart, D., & Lízal, L. (2002). *Effects of ownership and financial status on corporate environmental performance*. CEPR Discussion Paper, 3557.

Evenett, S., & Voicu, A. (2003). *Picking winners or creating them? Revising the benefits of FDI in the Czech Republic*. Oxford University Working Paper.

Haddad, M., & Harrison, A. (1993). Are there positive spillovers from direct foreign investment? Evidence from panel data for Morocco. *Journal of Development Economics, 42*, 51–74.

Hanousek, J., Kočenda, E., & Švejnar, J. (2007). Origin and concentration: Corporate ownership, control and performance. *Economics of Transition, 15*(1), 1–31.

Harzing, A.-W. (2002). Acquisitions vs. greenfield investments: International strategy and management of entry modes. *Strategic Management Journal, 23*, 211–227.

Hennart, J.-F., & Park, Y.-R. (1993). Greenfield vs. acquisition: The strategy of Japanese investors in the United States. *Management Science, 39*(9), 1054–1070.

Jarolím, M. (2001). Foreign direct investment and productivity of Czech manufacturing firms. *CERGE-EI Dissertation*.

Javorcik, B. S. (2004). Does foreign direct investment increase the productivity of domestic firms? In search of spillovers through backward linkages. *American Economic Review, 94* (3), 605–627.

Kinoshita, Y. (2000). *R&D and technology spillovers via FDI: Innovation and absorptive capacity*. WDI Working Paper, 349.

Kosová, R. (2006). *Do foreign firms crowd out domestic firms? Evidence from the Czech Republic*. Working Paper, 6, School of Business and Public Management, George Washington University.

Kosová, R., & Ayyagari, M. (2006). *Does FDI facilitate domestic entrepreneurship? Evidence from the Czech Republic*. School of Business, GWU Working Paper, 8.

Stančík, J. (2007). *Horizontal and vertical FDI spillovers: Recent evidence from the Czech Republic*. CERGE-EI Working Paper, 340.

Wang, M., & Wong., M. C. S. (2007). *What drives economic growth? The case of cross-border M&A and greenfield FDI activities*. Working Paper.

Zejan, M. C. (1990). New ventures or acquisitions. The choice of Swedish multinational enterprises. *The Journal of Industrial Economics, 38*(3), 349–355.

Chapter 4
Comments on Chapter 2 and 3

Sándor Richter

Abstract Both Ms. Kawecka-Wyrzykowska's and Mr. Stančík's paper were important, interesting and useful contributions to the workshop. In the first paper the central issue is distinction between horizontal and vertical type of the IIT. The separation of the two types of trade is based on the comparison of unit values in exports and imports. Where the spread is relatively small, the products involved in trade are considered horizontally differentiated, where it is relatively large, the products are vertically differentiated. With a good portion of simplification the former is the 'good' while the latter is the 'bad' ITT, as relative prices are thought to reflect quality differences. That may be true in general, but in particular cases differences in unit value may be misleading. Especially in the case of the new-Member States a poor image inherited from the communist era may lead to misinterpretations in this field. In the second paper the author is concerned about domestic firms' "suffering" caused by emerging foreign competitors following inward FDI projects. Actually what we see described and analysed in the paper is, in a broader context, an adjustment process to increased competition. New players appear with better equipment, management, marketing, etc. and, with a minimal time lag, growth rates of sales of market incumbents go down. I think that is part of the game in an open and highly integrated economy. Moreover, as it was shown, the impact is provisional and in hardly more than one year is absorbed.

4.1 Introductory Remarks

Part I on "Trade and foreign direct investment in an enlarged EU: opportunities and challenges" contains a first paper by Elzbieta Kawecka-Wyrzykowska on 'Evolving Patterns of Intra-industry Trade Specialization of the New Member States of the

S. Richter
The Vienna Institute for International Economic Studies, Vienna, Austria
e-mail: richter@wiiw.ac.at

F. Keereman and I. Szekely (eds.), *Five Years of an Enlarged EU*,
DOI 10.1007/978-3-642-12516-4_4, © Springer-Verlag Berlin Heidelberg 2010

EU: the Case of the Automotive Industry' where she analyses trade developments in the recently acceded countries. The second contribution by Juraj Stančík on 'FDI Spillovers in the Czech Republic: Takeovers vs. Greenfields' is more specific and focuses on foreign direct investment in a particular country.

This workshop is devoted to discuss various respects of the first 5 years of the enlarged EU as experienced by new and old EU members. The topic of this session, namely trade and foreign direct investment is a specific one in as much as in these two areas of economic integration no dramatic changes were induced by the accession itself. Movement of capital had long been liberalized (except for real estate in the accession countries), just as trade barriers had been removed (except for certain agricultural and food products). For this reason it is no wonder that new member states accomplished a "smooth landing" in both trade and foreign direct investment upon their EU accession.

The most remarkable, and to some extent indeed surprising development took place in trade. In new member states' mutual trade there began a sudden upturn right after their accession to the EU. In 2007 the value of aggregate intra-CEEC trade was two and a half times more than in 2003. The rate of growth in new members trade with the 'old' EU member states was only half as much as that. Moreover, new members' mutual trade had substantially higher growth rates in the post accession years than in the years before their accession. This development is clearly shown in the paper of Elzbieta Kawecka-Wyrzykowska even if this is not the immediate topic of the paper.

4.2 Comments on Chap. 2

Ms. Kawecka-Wyrzykowska focused her attention to the automotive industry in the new Member States. At this juncture I have to recall a comment made by the famous late Polish reform economist Wladzimir Brus at a conference in 1991 who expressed his doubts whether it was a wise decision by the then Hungarian government to invite Suzuki to produce cars in Hungary. Why should a country like Hungary produce cars? – was his question, most probably referring to his preference for specialization patterns fitting better the long term traditions of Hungary (e.g. food industry). Nevertheless the decision that seemed so strange in the early 1990s was followed by many similar decisions in Central Europe which have transformed this region into a host for a remarkable automotive cluster of the global economy. For this reason it was a good decision to choose this sector for a intra-industry trade (IIT) analysis.

In the introductory section of her paper Ms. Kawecka-Wyrzykowska finds that IIT indicators can be regarded as a tool for comparing economic levels of development of the countries concerned. IIT may be seen as an indicator supplementing the traditional measurement of GDP levels at purchasing power parity when evaluating the success of NMS' convergence to old EU members. Indeed, IIT indicators reflect, in most cases, how developed the economies involved in bilateral trade really are. Nevertheless that statement needs a comment. In the case of countries being rich in one or another natural resources (e.g. Canada and Finland in wood, Norway in natural gas, etc.) relatively high shares of inter-industry trade in their total trade do not necessarily mean lower level of development of the trading countries. Anyhow, none of the new Member States possess of a natural endowment which would jeopardize the interpretation of IIT indicators as measuring rod for convergence with the EU-15.

Distinction between horizontal and vertical type of the IIT is a central issue of the paper. The separation of the two types of trade is based on the comparison of unit values in exports and imports. Where the spread is relatively small, the products involved in trade are considered horizontally differentiated, where it is relatively large, the products are vertically differentiated. With a good portion of simplification the former is the 'good' while the latter is the 'bad' ITT, as relative prices are thought to reflect quality differences. That may be true in general, but in particular cases differences in unit value may be misleading. Especially in the case of the new Member States a poor image inherited from the communist era may lead to misinterpretations in this field. To remain in the automotive industry, the first Skoda cars produced after the Volkswagen had taken over the Czech factory were of excellent quality but relatively cheap, because otherwise nobody would have been ready to buy it. Customers had still the poor quality of the 'old' Skoda in mind and years were needed to change this disposition. In most cases, however, the image problem does not appear as the cars produced in the new Member States are sold under the mother company's trademark and costumers typically are not aware of the location of their car's producer. E.g. in Hungary produced Suzuki cars are seen as a Japanese car by Hungarians even if they are advertised in the country as 'our car'.

Another problem with the unit values is related to the fact that a huge though unknown share of new Member States exports and imports are intra-firm transactions of multinational corporations. According to an expert estimation this share may range between 50 and 80% in CEEC exports[1]. Multinational corporations may have various considerations for setting the export/import prices of their own products in intra-firm trade. To what extent such accounting prices may divert from market prices is an open question, but this distortion must be big enough to reckon with.

The author's suggestion to take IIT as a supplementary indicator for measuring convergence receives an interesting justification by data in Table 2.1. Here IIT shares in NMS trade with the world are displayed, specified by clearly defined categories as low quality vertical IIT, high quality vertical IIT and horizontal IIT. Taken the IIT shares in trade by individual IIT categories the figures do not seem to convey a clear message. However, if we add the shares of high quality vertical IIT and horizontal IIT, the two categories that can be seen as the 'good' IIT (contrary to low quality IIT and the ab ovo 'bad' inter-industry trade) we receive figures which surprisingly fit the ranking of NMS by level of economic development if measured

[1]Estimation by Gábor Hunya, wiiw.

by per capita GDP. In the year 2007 the share of 'good' IIT in total trade was 39% for Slovenia, 38% for the Czech Republic, 35% for Poland, 34% for Estonia, 32% for Hungary, 29% for Slovakia, 28% for Lithuania, 22% for Latvia, 24% for Romania and finally 19% for Bulgaria.

Table 2.6 displays the development of IIT shares in the automotive industry's trade between 2000 and 2007 for the central European NMS. We have surprising data for two countries, Hungary and Poland. In Hungary's automotive trade horizontal IIT's share dropped from 12.9 to 0.3% in 7 years. Parallel to this a large increase took place (from 36.5 to 73.9%) in the share of vertical IIT. It would be interesting to know what explains this change, new type of division of labour or price changes which pushed part of the trade from horizontal to vertical IIT. In Hungary a special type of horizontal trade may have appeared. In the early 2000s Audi started with the production of very expensive sports car models in the Hungarian town Györ. Practically the total production is exported. Audi's exports from its Györ factory deliver a considerable part of the Hungarian automotive (and total) exports. In this case a sort of 'inverse' horizontal IIT may have emerged, where the less developed trading partner is exporting high quality (with high unit value) products to its more developed trading partner, but simultaneously imports products of much lower quality (unit value) in order to cover domestic demand (consumption/industry-intern input for production).

A final remark to Ms. Kawecka-Wyrzykowska's paper: there are interesting data in Table 2.3 on the IIT indices of the EU-15, with partly surprising results. Some EU-15 members have fairly low IIT indicators. The results are understandable to a large extent, as Finland exports a lot of paper and wood based on its natural endowments, Greece and Portugal are relatively underdeveloped countries and Luxembourg is too small to have a diversified export structure. But how did Ireland get to this group? Ireland, the shooting star of convergence in the 1990s and first part of 2000s attracted a huge number of foreign companies, most of them export oriented. What may explain the relatively low share of IIT in Ireland's trade?

4.3 Comments on Chap. 3

FDI is one of those economic issues in Central Europe (and for sure in many other countries and regions of the world economy) which is strongly loaded emotionally. The emotions of the broader public concerned are rarely positive. I do not remember to have seen any political demonstration for more FDI anywhere. Just the opposite is true. Populist political movements both on the left and right often rely on hostile sentiments in wide segments of the population against multinational firms. They argue against 'selling out' the national fortune in privatisation deals, or blame foreign owned enterprises – predatory capitalists – for all kind of problems in the country concerned. With all this in mind I had a pretty bad feeling when I read in the abstract of Mr. Stančík's paper the following sentence about the situation in the Czech Republic: "Domestic companies are mostly suffering in the presence of foreign companies" Will this paper follow an emotional line of arguments?

Then reading the paper my fears were certainly dissolved, it is a well established, deeply researched and correctly documented piece of work. Nevertheless, I am still not convinced that the expression: "domestic companies *suffer* in the presence of foreign companies" is the best possible way how we can describe the issue in question.

Actually what we see described and analysed in the paper is, in a broader context, nothing else than an adjustment process to increased competition. New players appear with better equipment, management, marketing, etc. and, with a minimal time lag, *growth rates of sales* of market incumbents go down. I think that is part of the game in an open and highly integrated economy. Moreover, as it was shown, the impact is provisional and in hardly more than 1 year is absorbed.

The author writes 'The current estimates suggest that domestic companies supplying both foreign takeovers and greenfields are negatively affected by their presence: a 1% point increase in foreign capital's share in takeovers/greenfields in a downstream sector causes a decrease in the growth rate of the sales of supplying domestic companies by 0.7/1.5% points'. We must put these figures in context: if the *ex-ante sales growth rate* was 25%, and that decreases by 0.7/1.5% points, the effect is negligible. In the case the ex-ante sales growth rate was 2.5% or 0.5% the impact is considerable, nevertheless it is still a question whether the expression 'suffering' is appropriate here. It is also an important question how abruptly does the share of foreign capital increase, as rapid penetration would cause certainly greater losses in sales growth rates in a given year.

In the conclusion of the paper the above argumentation is repeated, as one of the main findings of the paper. Nevertheless the reader may raise the question, whether the whole story is valid for foreign enterprises only? Why should a new player come in only from another country? Is the domestic market so 'sleepy' that any new player should come from abroad? And if there were new *domestic* competitors, would they behave differently than penetrating foreign companies? The real question is therefore, in my view, if the number of actors in a certain product market increases, what happens to the sales growth rates of established actors.

That the central problem investigated here is not that of foreign penetration but lack of competition of any kind is underlined by the following citation in Stancik: '...especially the service sector is the one that loses in the presence of foreign investors. Both backward spillovers from takeovers and greenfields are negative, significant and more than double in magnitude compared to the overall results. Regarding horizontal spillovers, the overall positive spillover effect from takeovers now diminishes and the negative impact from greenfields is even bigger. These are natural results because service companies are almost completely domestically oriented and usually they are not forced by the domestic market to improve their products'.

In the conclusion part of the paper, however, the author takes up a more amicable position towards foreign companies: "to conclude, we find that Czech companies are not profiting from the presence of foreign investor...in fact, it is greenfields who create new jobs or start production in previously sleeping sectors". I appreciate that the author acknowledges the positive impact of FDI on job creation and appreciates the impact fostering increased competition. I think it is very important to analyse the FDI impact in the possible broadest context. Perhaps we also can agree that more competition, even if it is unpleasant for individual companies, is good for the Czech (and any other) economy, and in the longer run for individual companies as well, if fitness is regarded an important feature of a company.

The author raises an important question in the conclusion of the paper: whom should the government support, takeovers or greenfield investments? The author concludes that based on the results of his analysis this question cannot be answered. He is right, the impact of foreign firms' arrival on sales growth of domestic players can only be a part, and not even the most relevant part, of the picture. The consequences for job creation, perspectives of underdeveloped regions, the development of knowledge intensive technologies may be more important than possible deterioration in sales growth rates.

The paper analyses the foreign companies along the division between takeover and greenfield FDI, although the author mentions that the really big difference appears between export vs. domestic oriented foreign companies. It would be interesting to learn more about this division: what are the proportions between them in the Czech Republic, is that proportion similar or different in other new Member States?

Enlargement was not in the focus of the research. Nevertheless Fig. 3.1 shows data of FDI inflow in 1993–2005. It is remarkable that 2003, the last year before the EU accession and 2004, the year of accession were exceptionally bad years for Czech FDI inflow unlike in other new Member States. It would be interesting to know what was the reason for that weak performance?

A final remark on Table 3.2 (number of companies by year). In this table the number of companies investigated suddenly drops to its half from 2003 to 2005. This refers to both domestic and foreign owned companies. The reasons for this change are not mentioned. It is not clear whether the results are not influenced by the substantially smaller number of observations in those 2 years.

Concluding my comment I think that both Ms. Kawecka-Wyrzykowska' and Mr. Stančík's paper were important, interesting and useful contributions to the workshop on the fifth anniversary of the 2004 EU enlargement.

Part II
Migration in an enlarged EU: solution or problem for labour market woes and cash-strapped social security systems?

Chapter 5
Migration in an Enlarged EU: A Challenging Solution?

Martin Kahanec and Klaus F. Zimmermann

Abstract The 2004 and 2007 enlargements of the European Union were unprecedented in a number of economic and policy aspects. This essay provides a broad and in-depth account of the effects of the post-enlargement migration flows on the receiving as well as sending countries in three broader areas: labour markets, welfare systems, and growth and competitiveness. Our analysis of the available literature and empirical evidence shows that (1) EU enlargement had a significant impact on migration flows from new to old Member States, (2) restrictions applied in some of the countries did not stop migrants from coming but changed the composition of the immigrants, (3) any negative effects in the labour market on wages or employment are hard to detect, (4) post-enlargement migration contributes to growth prospects of the EU, (5) these immigrants are strongly attached to the labour market, and (6) they are quite unlikely to be among welfare recipients. These findings point out the difficulties that restrictions on the free movement of workers bring about.

5.1 Introduction

Europe as a crossroads of cultures and migration of people has been rather the rule than the exception. Since the 1960s immigration has been on rise especially in Western Europe (Fig. 5.1). In 2006 foreigners, whether non-citizens or foreign-born, constituted a substantial share of the population in most of the old Member States of the European Union and also in some of the new Member States

M. Kahanec (✉)
Institute for the Study of Labor, Bonn, Germany
Central European University, Budapest, Hungary
kahanec@iza.org

K.F. Zimmermann
Institute for the Study of Labor, Bonn, Germany
Bonn University, Bonn, Germany
DIW Berlin, Berlin, Germany

F. Keereman and I. Szekely (eds.), *Five Years of an Enlarged EU*,
DOI 10.1007/978-3-642-12516-4_5, © Springer-Verlag Berlin Heidelberg 2010

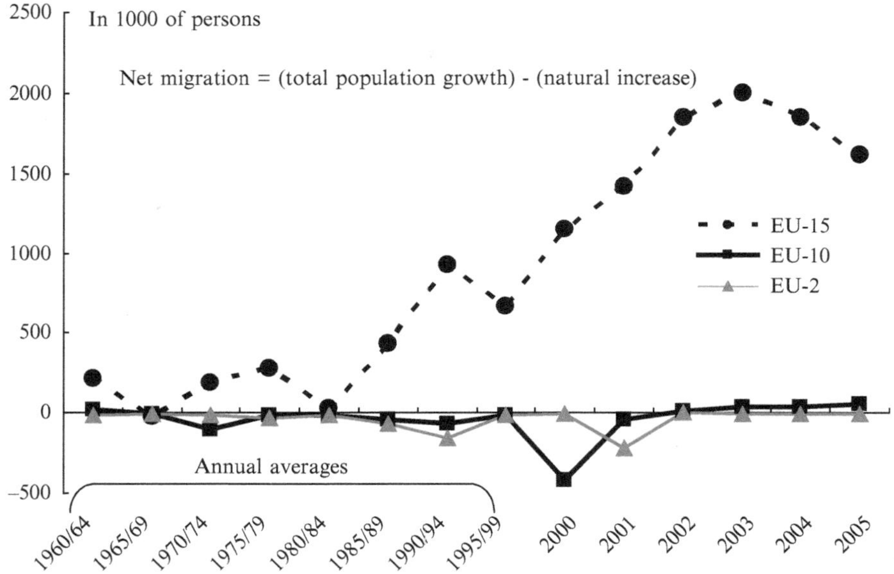

Fig. 5.1 Net migration in Europe in EU-15, EU-10 and EU-2
Notes: Cyprus (government-controlled area only) from 1975; 2000–2001: corrections due to census
Source: Eurostat

(Table 5.1). Yet the enlargement of the European Union in May 2004 involving eight Central and Eastern European countries[1] (EU-8) along with Malta and Cyprus, and the accession of Bulgaria and Romania (EU-2) in January 2007 were unprecedented in how they changed the European migration landscape. The differences in income and employment opportunities between the old EU Member States[2] and most new EU Member States were large; there was essentially no history of free migration between the Eastern and Western parts of Europe during the decades of separation by the "Iron Curtain"; and the new members from Central and Eastern Europe had undergone a transition from a centrally-planned economy to a market-based one. These specific circumstances partly explain the sensitivity of the migration issue among policy makers and the general public across Europe, which traditionally stems from the apprehension of the potential economic, social, cultural and political consequences of migration. Concerns about labour markets and welfare systems have received particular attention.

---

[1]Including the Czech Republic, Estonia, Latvia, Lithuania, Hungary, Poland, Slovakia and Slovenia. EU-10 includes also Cyprus and Malta.

[2]The old member states (EU-15) in the context of these enlargements include Austria, Belgium, Denmark, Finland, France, Germany, Greece, Ireland, Italy, Luxembourg, the Netherlands, Portugal, Spain, Sweden and the United Kingdom.

Table 5.1 Proportion of foreign-born and foreign citizens in European Union countries by region of origin in 2006

In percent of total population	Foreign citizens		Foreign-born	
	Other EU	Non-EU	Other EU	Non-EU
EU-15:				
Austria	4.1	5.0	6.7	8.7
Belgium	6.4	2.6	6.8	6.7
Denmark	2.9[a]	2.4	2.0	4.6
Finland	0.7	1.0	1.4	1.8
France	2.3	3.3	3.4	7.8
Germany	3.1	2.8	n.a.	n.a.
Greece	1.3	4.8	1.7	5.9
Ireland	5.4[b]	2.6[b]	8.8[b]	3.4[b]
Italy[a]	1.3	3.8	2.2	5.3
Luxembourg	41.2	5.6	37.9	8.6
Netherlands	1.7	1.9	2.8	9.1
Portugal	0.6	2.8	1.8	5.7
Spain	3.9	8.3	4.5	10.0
Sweden	2.5	2.7	5.5	10.0
UK	2.6	4.3	3.5	8.8
EU-12:				
Bulgaria	(0.1)[c]	(0.1)	n.a.	n.a.
Cyprus	8.1	6.5	8.1	11.0
Czech Republic	0.4	0.4	1.3	0.6
Estonia	0.7	16.8	0.6[c]	13.6
Hungary	0.5	0.2	1.3	0.4
Latvia	n.a.	0.7[d]	1.1[c]	9.6
Lithuania	n.a.	(0.6)	(0.3)[c]	3.8
Malta	1.2	1.8	1.7[e]	3.0
Poland	(0.1)	0.1	0.2	0.3
Romania	0.1[a]	0.1	n.a.	(0.1)[b]
Slovakia	(0.2)	(0.1)[b]	0.6[c]	(0.1)
Slovenia	(0.2)[c]	(0.2)	(0.7)[e]	4.6

Notes: Share of active working age residents is reported. Data in parentheses lack reliability due to small sample size
[a]Data are from 2004
[b]Data are from 2005
[c]Residents of EU-10 and EU-2 only
[d]The number for non-EU citizens is suspiciously low, and similarly low numbers are reported in the 2005 Labour Force Survey. This may arise because non-citizens were grouped together with nationals as in Eurostat (2006, p. 65)
[e]Residents of EU-15 only
Source: Bonin et al. (2008)

The free movement of workers constitutes a fundamental principle of the European Union, as stated in Article 39 of the Treaty establishing the European Community.[3] Nevertheless, transitional periods of up to 7 years were implemented, which restricted access of citizens from the new Member States to the labour markets in the

[3]Article 39 entitles nationals of one EU member state to work in another EU member state under the same conditions as that member state's own citizens.

old Member States. Only a few old Member States opened their labour markets with no or mild transitional measures. Given this institutional variation and other important factors, such as geographic, linguistic or cultural distances, the recent EU enlargements have had heterogeneous effects on migration flows across Europe.

The European Union faces a number of fundamental policy challenges, including an aging population, global competitiveness and growth, and the sustainability of social security systems. The diverse post-enlargement migration flows of a predominantly young labour force constitute an important policy issue that interacts with these challenges in both receiving and sending countries. Since a significant proportion of these migrants are women, their successful integration in the labour market is another important prerequisite for tackling these challenges adequately. Understanding the causes and effects of migration in an enlarged EU is a precondition for designing effective migration policies in Europe and thus a precondition for reaching the Lisbon targets as well as the key objectives of the European Employment Strategy and the Social Agenda.

A focal objective of this essay is to advance and broaden our understanding of the effects of the post-enlargement migration flows and thus provide a well-founded insight into the functioning of an enlarged EU[4] The essay will simultaneously address the opportunities and challenges brought about by the recent EU enlargements.

Methodologically we adopt a multilevel comparative analytical framework based on existing evidence, descriptive empirical analysis, as well as a number of in-depth case studies. Specifically we evaluate the existing evidence of the effects of migration flows in an enlarged EU on both source and destination countries. Three broader domains of the economic effects of migration are studied: labour markets; social security systems; and economic growth. We highlight the role of the determinants and temporal character of migration on its effects and study the benefits and costs of migration.

5.2 The Contexts of the Recent EU Enlargements

During its post-World War II history, Western Europe witnessed substantial movements of people. Following the periods of post-war adjustment and decolonisation, growth-driven labour migration in the late 1950s and 1960s, post oil-shock policy change and the resulting migration slowdown in the 1970s and 1980s, refugee and asylum seeker flows in the early 1990s, and the ensuing "Fortress Europe" policy reaction, EU enlargement opened gateways for new migration trajectories. Given the complexity of the issues related to migration, transitional arrangements were specified by the Accession Treaties of the 2004 and 2007 EU enlargements. These

[4]We cover the whole EU wherever possible and relevant, including Romania and Bulgaria as the most recent member states. While the 5 year period between 2004 and 2009 is the focus of the analysis, a broader time frame is called upon whenever necessary. The confounding effects of the ongoing financial and economic crisis, which began in 2007 in the US and spread to the global economy in 2008, are beyond the scope of this essay.

are based on the 2-3-2 formula: for the first 2 years following accession, access to the labour markets of the incumbent Member States is governed by their national laws and policies. National measures may be extended for a further period of 3 years. However, should an EU member state find after that period that its labour market has been severely disrupted, it is possible to have these national measures extended for a further 2 years.

Following the 2004 EU enlargement, Ireland, the UK and Sweden opened access to their labour markets immediately.[5] As for social benefits, access to the welfare systems in Ireland and the UK depends on the duration of residence and employment. This is in contrast to Sweden, which decided to apply European Community rules. In the second phase of these arrangements (European Commission 2006a), ten more Member States opened their labour markets (Greece, Spain, Portugal, Finland, Italy, the Netherlands, Luxembourg, France, Belgium and Denmark). Germany and Austria have announced they will continue to impose restrictions on labour mobility until 2011, although they have simplified and liberalised the access rules in some sectors and professions. For instance Germany passed legislation in late 2008 facilitating access for high-skilled migrants. As for the 2007 enlargement, ten EU-25 Member States (the Czech Republic, Estonia, Cyprus, Latvia, Lithuania, Poland, Slovenia, Slovakia, Finland and Sweden) liberalised the access of Bulgarian and Romanian workers to their labour markets during the first phase.[6] In the second phase as of August 2009 Greece, Hungary, Portugal, Spain and Denmark have also opened their labour markets to EU-2 nationals. Most of the remaining EU-25 Member States have simplified their procedures or have reduced restrictions in some sectors or professions.

5.3 The Scale of Post Enlargement Migration

One of the main reasons for adopting the transitional arrangements was a fear of mass migration from the new Member States. There is a relatively large body of literature that attempts to estimate potential migration after enlargement [for example: Bauer and Zimmermann (1999), Boeri and Brücker (2000), Alvarez-Plata et al. (2003) and Zaiceva (2006); see Zaiceva and Zimmermann (2008) for an extensive review]. These studies generally predict that between 2 and 4% of the new Member States' population will move to the EU-15 countries in the long run, which constitutes about 1% of the EU-15 population. Some studies, however, estimate the upper bound of potential migration to be 7–8% of the new Member

[5]In the UK immigrants from the EU-8 have to register with the Home Office administered Worker Registration Scheme if they are employed in the UK for a month or more. This requirement allows the authorities to monitor immigration and its impact on the British labour market. In Ireland individual identification, Personal Public Service Numbers, is required in order to gain employment or access to state benefits and public services.

[6]In Finland, Cyprus and Slovenia employment must subsequently be registered for monitoring purposes.

States' population (Sinn et al. 2000). All these studies are based on strong assumptions, project counterfactual scenarios for out-of-sample countries, and do not take into account differences in transitional arrangements.

A number of recent studies scrutinise migration intentions after the EU enlargement (Fouarge and Ester 2007a, b; Bonin et al. 2008; Zaiceva and Zimmermann 2008; Blanchflower and Lawton 2009). Remarkably the proportion of individuals intending to emigrate after the 2004 enlargement was found to be larger in the new Member States than in the old EU-15, while it was smaller before the enlargement (Fouarge and Ester 2007a; Zaiceva and Zimmermann 2008; and Drinkwater 2003). This finding suggests that with open borders an increasing number of individuals in the EU-8 considered the option of working abroad, since after EU accession the option to return or migrate again became permanently available.

A comprehensive account of the actual post-enlargement migration flows is currently very difficult to provide, mainly due to the general scarcity of migration data. Early evidence reported by the European Commission (2006a, b) suggests that migration flows between the EU-8 and EU-15 Member States have been quite modest on average. However as a result of coordination failures and migration diversion (Boeri and Brücker 2005) these immigrants are unequally distributed across different Member States, with some countries experiencing a relatively large increase in the number of immigrants. According to these reports, the UK, Austria and Ireland have most probably experienced an increase in immigration as a consequence of EU enlargement. Nevertheless in the first quarter of 2005 the proportion of the working age population from the ten new member states in the EU-15 "was rather small, ranging from 0.1% in France and in the Netherlands to 1.4% in Austria and 2% in Ireland" (European Commission 2006a, p. 9). The European Commission reports also suggest that there is no conclusive evidence of a direct link between the magnitude of migration flows and the transitional arrangements in place. The data also show that a significant fraction of permits is granted to short-term or seasonal workers, that employment rates among immigrants from the new Member States are comparable to those of the EU-15 nationals, and that they are generally higher than for non-EU nationals.

There are several country studies that document actual migration in destination countries after enlargement. Zaiceva and Zimmermann (2008) evaluate the scale, diversity and determinants of labour migration in Europe, suggesting that there was an increase in immigration from the new Member States into most EU-15 countries, albeit this increase varied quite substantially. While in most of EU-15 countries Poland was the main sending country, Estonians are dominant in Finland, and Romanians in Spain.

Gilpin et al. (2006) report a substantial increase in the number of nationals from new Member States in the UK following enlargement. According to the UK Home Office (2007) there was however a decline in the number of applicants to the Worker Registration Scheme in the first quarter of 2007 compared to the last quarter of 2006. The most recent Accession Monitoring Report (Home Office 2008) states that the number of applicants to the Worker Registration Scheme, the majority of whom were from Poland, followed by Slovaks and Lithuanians, rose from 134,550 in May–December 2004 to 234,725 in 2006 and fell slightly to 217,740 in 2007. According to Blanchflower and Lawton (2009) 850,000 workers from the new Member States registered to work in the UK between May 2004 and June 2008 with the WRS, and there have been an additional 19,525 and 31,080 worker registrations from Bulgaria and Romania between April and June 2008, respectively.

These authors warn however that the Worker Registration Scheme numbers overstate actual immigration flows since the registered people are temporary workers, while the size of net migration from the eight new Member States is much lower (71,000 in 2006). Drinkwater et al. (2009) analyse the performance of Polish immigrants in the UK labour market. Overall no evidence of "welfare tourism" was found. In most cases the majority of migrants were male, young, tended to come from Poland and the Baltic states, had relatively high or medium skill levels and were concentrated in relatively low-skilled sectors (or self-employed), pointing to such issues as downgrading and transferability of human capital (Blanchflower et al. 2007). Ruhs (2007) reports that almost half of the workers who registered under the Worker Registration Scheme since May 2004 have taken temporary jobs.

According to a study by Doyle et al. (2006), which documents the situation in Ireland and Sweden, the number of immigrants from the new Member States in Sweden increased between 2003 and 2005. The authors also argue that the number of post-enlargement EU-10 immigrants is still small and suggest several reasons for this observation, such as few job vacancies, linguistic distance and the lack of established migration networks. They report however a different situation in Ireland. Although there are no data available for Ireland before 2005 which distinguish between accession country nationals and foreigners from the rest of the world, there is a remarkable increase in the number of foreigners between 2003 and 2005, and the majority in 2005 were nationals from the new Member States. Indeed Hughes (2007) reports that there were about 54,000 EU-10 immigrants in May–December 2004, 112,000 in 2005, and 139,000 in 2006 measured by the Personal Public Service Number registration scheme. Barrett et al. (2008) documents that nationals from the new Member States constituted 3% of Ireland's population in 2006. Remarkably Brenke and Zimmermann (2007) document an increase in net immigration flows from the new Member States into Germany, despite the "closed door" policy, acting through a rise in self-employment, especially among Poles.

As for the sending countries, Iglicka (2005) argues that the majority of emigration from Poland to the EU (mainly Germany and the UK) is of a temporary nature, and emigration to the West is being replaced by immigration from the East (Ukraine) and by return migration. Kaczmarczyk and Okólski (2008) report that the accession of Poland and the Baltic states significantly increased emigration from these countries, mainly to Ireland and the UK.

The World Bank (2006) documents that Lithuania is the country with the largest emigration rate among the new Member States, with 3.3% of its population having emigrated between May 2004 and December 2005, followed by Latvia (2.4%), Slovakia and Poland (1%). An interesting observation is that while prior to enlargement most Lithuanians migrants went to Germany, Estonia, Russia, Ireland and the US, after the enlargement they headed towards the UK and Germany. These migrants were predominantly young with medium or high skills. Kadziauskas (2007) reports that the number of migrants from Lithuania has increased after the enlargement, warning that these outflows may be severely understated by official statistics. The World Bank (2006) documents a similar upward trend in emigration using the Polish Labour Force Survey data, with 20% more Poles staying abroad in 2004 than in 2003.

Based on the same data, Kaczmarczyk and Okólski (2008) report that the number of Polish residents who stayed abroad for at least 2 months tripled from early 2004 to early 2007 from around 180,000 to around 540,000. Germany remains the most important destination country for immigrants from Poland (especially regarding seasonal migration), although its share is decreasing; whereas the importance of the UK and Ireland is increasing (World Bank 2006; Frelak and Kazmierkiewicz 2007; Kaczmarczyk and Okólski 2008). Kaczmarczyk and Okólski (2008) confirm the findings from the receiving countries: these migrants tend to be males, work-oriented, young, relatively well-educated and temporary. The proportion of individuals with tertiary education among migrants has increased after enlargement, leading to an emergence of two distinct emigrants groups – low-skilled individuals from the periphery and highly-skilled ones from the cores (Kaczmarczyk and Okólski 2008).

What is the outlook concerning the migration flows from the new to the old Member States? On the one hand emigration intentions are larger in the new EU-10 than in the old EU-15. On the other hand growth in the EU-10 and wage convergence, as well as new vacancies and skills shortages at home combined with the remaining cultural barriers, could negatively influence these migration flows in the future. Figure 5.2 shows that a significant proportion of people in the new Member

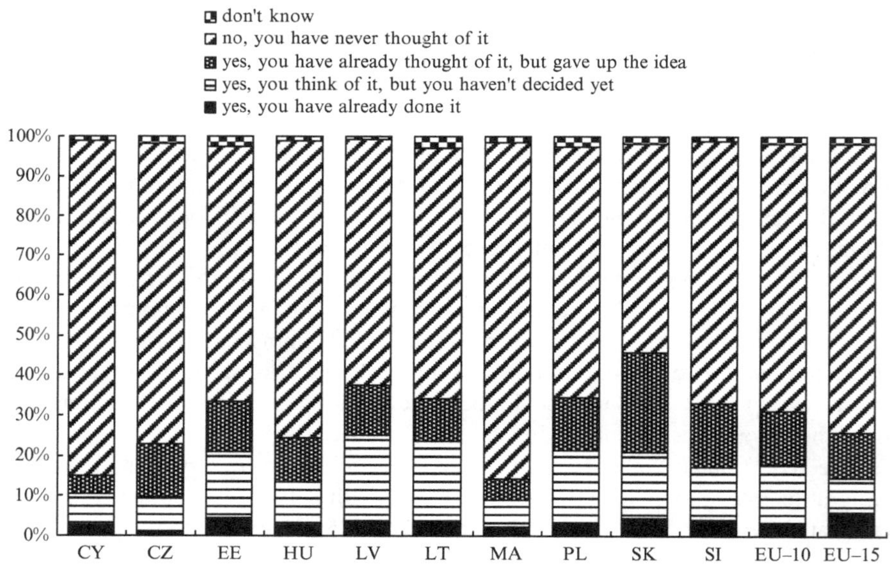

Fig. 5.2 Migration intentions, February–March 2006
Notes: Response to "Have you yourself ever considered living in another Member State in order to work?", in percent
Source: Eurobarometer EB 65.1

States (15%) is still thinking about "living in another Member State in order to work, but haven't decided yet". However a large proportion of respondents have already thought about it but gave up the idea.

5.4 The Effects of Post-Enlargement Migration

5.4.1 The Determinants of Migration

Understanding the determinants of migration flows is crucial for the understanding of their composition and characteristics and thus for evaluation of their effects on the source and destination countries. It is especially important to distinguish the nature of the economic or other migration motives and their interaction with individual characteristics to draw conclusions not only about the skill level and age structure but also duration of migration, which all condition the effects of migration on the source and destination countries.

Early theories of the migration decision stress the significance of (expected) regional disparities in prosperity (Harris and Todaro 1970). These theories imply the significance of earnings and income levels, costs of living, unemployment rates, quality of public goods, and the generosity of the welfare systems. Theories based on the human capital model (Becker 1964) identify the importance of age, as older potential migrants have a shorter expected lifetime gain from moving than younger ones. More educated individuals may be in a better position to gain valuable information about the destination country, thereby reducing their costs of adjustment and thus be more inclined to migrate. Inter-regional cultural, linguistic and geographical distances should also affect the adjustment costs and thus affect the migration flows. Needless to say the decision to move is affected by the costs of moving, which also include, besides the well-understood pecuniary costs, significant psychological and social costs of forgone contacts with friends and family as well as social contacts. Indeed family issues, such as having a child or spouse, and broader social relationships, such as ethnic networks, play a significant role (Mincer 1978; Massey 1990). While having children may increase the costs of moving, ethnic networks may facilitate important information about the destination labour market.

The character of the earnings distribution in the source country affects the migration incentives of high and low-skilled workers differently. In a country that has a relatively flat earnings distribution, the opportunity costs of migration are higher for the low-skilled workers, who enjoy wealth redistribution in their favour. On the other hand in a country with a relatively steep income distribution, it is the high-skilled workers who enjoy high returns to skills and have high opportunity costs of migration (Borjas 1985, also Roy 1951). Overall migrants may be positively or negatively self-selected with respect to their observable and unobservable characteristics, both upon entry and exit (Borjas 1987b; Chiswick 1999).

One of the most interesting questions in the European context is whether generous welfare systems attract immigrants and whether they affect the type of immigrant inflows. Borjas (1999a) studies this issue in a model that assumes variation in terms of the generosity of welfare provisions and returns to human capital across US states. The model predicts that, relative to the native population, low-skilled immigrants should be more prone to cluster in welfare-generous states and the effect of a change in the level of welfare benefits should have stronger effects on immigrant welfare participation, that is, the benefits elasticity of immigrants should be higher than that of the native population. Borjas empirically corroborates the prediction of immigrants' excess propensity to cluster in welfare generous states, even when controlling for demographic and socioeconomic factors as well as for possible network effects.

What are the main determinants of East–West migration flows in an enlarged EU? While family and other social relationships as well as housing and local environment conditions are important, Fouarge and Ester (2007a) and Bonin et al. (2008) show that employment-related factors such as higher income, better working conditions, and opportunities of finding a suitable job are key migration motivators in Europe, and in the new Member States in particular. Bonin et al. (2008) show that language and cultural barriers also play an important role. The authors do not find evidence that migration is primarily attracted by access to welfare payments or better public services. This is in line with De Giorgi and Pellizzari (2009), who find, using data from the European Community Household Panel, that welfare benefits are a factor which influences an immigrant's choice of destination; however it is a small effect relative to the impact of wages.

Blanchflower et al. (2007) show that the propensity to migrate is correlated with income per capita, unemployment rates and life satisfaction in the new Member States. In line with this study, unhappiness with their lives, dissatisfaction with their salaries and working conditions, concerns about the availability of good jobs and insecurity about their jobs were shown by Blanchflower and Lawton (2009) to be some of the key reasons for moving abroad for Eastern Europeans. Kadziauskas (2007) reports that 90% of the respondents in Lithuania, a country with high levels of emigration, name low salaries as the main motive of seeking employment abroad. Zaiceva and Zimmermann (2008) show that linguistic and geographical distances, migrant networks, as well as scale seem to have played a role in the allocation of migrants across destination countries. So in general we can conjecture that most of the post-enlargement East–West migration flows have been economic in nature, pushed by the dissatisfaction with economic opportunities in the new Member States and attracted by better labour market opportunities in the old Member States. Welfare does not seem to be a key factor in determining the nature of these migration flows.

5.4.2 The Impact of Migration on Wages and Their Distribution

The effects of migration on labour markets are complex and multifaceted. Migration involves relocation of workers and thus affects the supply of labour and human capital in source and destination labour markets. Depending on the character of the implied changes in labour supply, migration may affect wages, employment and other labour market outcomes of not only the natives and stayers but also of other migrants. As a corollary, migration potentially has significant effects on economic inequality.[7]

The impact of immigration on the destination labour market has been modelled by a number of studies, including Chiswick et al. (1992), and Chiswick (1980, 1998). In these models the effects of migration on income inequality in receiving countries largely depend on the socioeconomic and demographic characteristics of the immigrant and native populations as manifested by the substitutability or complementarity of their labour. Concerning the empirical evidence for the US, Grossman (1982) finds that foreign-born workers are substitutes for native workers, and Borjas (1983) reveals complementarity between Black and Hispanic labour, and Hispanic and White male workers. Borjas (1987a) provides some evidence that White, Black, Hispanic and Asian immigrant male workers are substitutes for Whites born in the US. All these studies report effects of small magnitudes.

More recent studies however provide evidence of diverse and non-negligible labour market effects of immigration. Using data from the 1990 US census, Card (2001) distinguishes the effects of immigration for various occupational groups and finds significant negative employment effects in most cases. In a similar study, Orrenius and Zavodny (2007) find negative wage effects of immigration on unskilled natives but do not find significant effects in skilled occupations. Borjas et al. (1997) report that immigration explains a significant proportion of the increase in the wage gap between high and low-skilled labour in the US in the 1980s and early 1990s. Negative wage effects of immigrants on their co-ethnics in the same linguistic group are reported by Chiswick and Miller (2002). Borjas (1999b, 2003, 2006) and Filer (1992) provide further evidence on the negative effects of immigration in the US. In the natural experiment setting of the Mariel boatlift, which brought an influx 45,000 Cubans into Miami in 1980, Card (1990) finds that any effects of unexpected immigration were cancelled out by a mobility response of natives and former immigrants.

Considering the international evidence, Roy (1987) reports detrimental effects of immigration on native employment prospects in Canada. However no negative employment effects of immigration are found by Akbari and DeVoretz (1992) for Canadian natives and Addison and Worswick (2002) for Australian natives. Roy (1997) reports no clear patterns of substitutability or complementarity between foreign and Canadian-born labour. Friedberg (2001) finds no negative effects of Russian immigration on Israeli wages or employment. On the positive side, Chapman and Cobb-Clark (1999), and Parasnis et al. (2005) find positive effects of immigration on the employment prospects of Australian natives.

---

[7]Kahanec and Zimmermann (2008, 2009) extensively summarise this literature and argue that migration potentially has important consequences for economic inequality, which are driven by the skill-composition of migrant flows.

As concerns Europe, Winkelmann and Zimmermann (1993) find only small negative effects of immigration on German employment. Hunt (1992) studies the impact of the Algerian repatriates on the French labour market after Algerian independence and finds detrimental yet weak wage and employment effects for the natives. Similarly, Carrington and de Lima (1996) find some evidence of negative effects on native wages in Portugal of refugees from the former colonies. Angrist and Kugler (2003) report negative effects of immigration from the former Yugoslavia on employment in Europe, especially in countries with more restrictive market institutions. However no negative effects of immigration on employment are reported by Pischke and Velling (1997) for Germany, and Dustmann et al. (2005) in the case of the UK. Zorlu and Hartog (2005) report few effects of immigration on native wages for the Netherlands, the UK and Norway. De New and Zimmermann (1994) support the complementarity hypothesis by finding negative effects of (largely unskilled) immigration on the wages of the German unskilled but positive wage effects on the wages of native high-skilled.

The book "*European Migration: what do we know?*", edited by Zimmermann (2005), contains 15 chapters on European countries and the US, Canada and New Zealand and summarises migration experiences since the Second World War. The conclusion reached is that immigration is largely beneficial for the receiving countries. There can be phases of adjustment, but there is no overall evidence that natives' wages are strongly depressed or that unemployment substantially increases as a consequence of immigration.

To evaluate the post-enlargement migration flows we need to analyse empirical evidence on the quality of post-enlargement migrants, their position in the destination labour markets, and also whether they leave employment, unemployment or inactivity (Kaczmarczyk and Okólski 2008). While aggregate statistical data do not identify any causal links, they do provide a broad picture of economic development in receiving countries in the pre- and post-enlargement periods. Aberrant patterns in aggregate statistics following enlargement could hint at some effects of post-enlargement developments, while their normality would be consistent with the hypothesis that enlargement had no extraordinary effects on the receiving labour markets.

Figure 5.3 shows that there is no evidence of employment growth slow down after the 2004 enlargement in the EU-15, Germany and Sweden. Ireland exhibited increasing employment growth up until the third quarter of 2005 but deceleration thereafter. In the UK employment growth was fairly steady throughout the period. There was an increasing or steady unemployment rate in the EU-15, Germany and Sweden up until 2005 and a decline thereafter. The opposite pattern occurs in the UK and Ireland. Together with steady vacancy rates, the overall picture is that there was strong demand for labour in these countries, even in manufacturing, a sector with a high concentration of accession country citizens. In the same vein, average wages did not exhibit any observable slow down during the studied period (Fig. 5.4). We can thus summarise that aggregate data do not provide discernible signs of negative economic effects of post-enlargement migration, perhaps with the exception of Ireland and the UK, where employment growth and unemployment

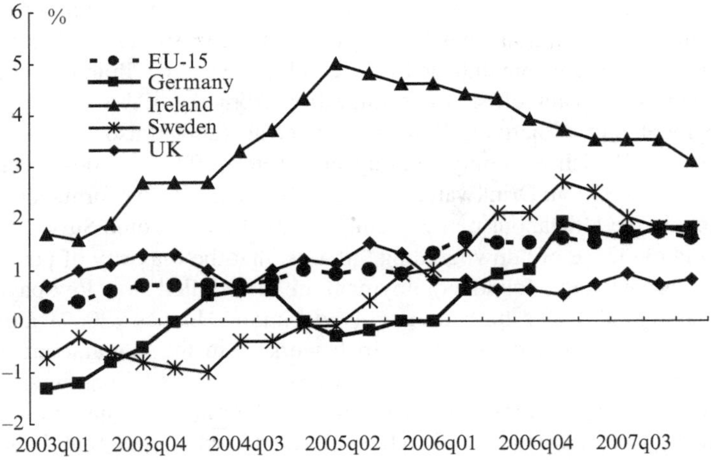

Fig. 5.3 Employment growth rates in selected old Member States, 2003Q1–2008Q1
Source: Eurostat

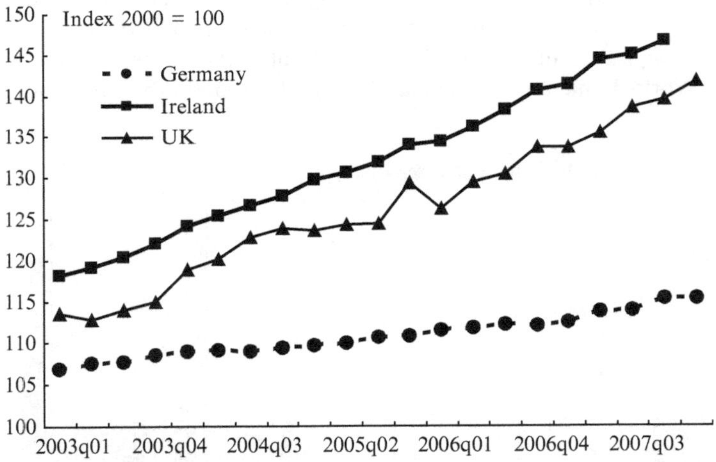

Fig. 5.4 Labour cost index in selected old Member States, 2003Q1–2008Q2
Notes: Wages and salaries in industries and services excluding public administration; seasonally adjusted and adjusted by working days, nominal value
Source: Eurostat

rates have exhibited some negative trends since 2005. It remains an open question however whether these can be ascribed to post-enlargement migration flows.

Evidence on the direct effects of post-enlargement migration is still relatively scarce but rising. The UK Home Office (2007) provides evidence that immigrant workers from the EU-10 go to sectors where the demand for their labour is the greatest (hospitality and catering, agriculture, manufacturing, food processing, and business and administration) thus helping to fill the gaps in the UK labour market while placing only few demands on the UK welfare system. Gilpin et al. (2006) do not find any significant effect of immigration from the EU-8 on the claimant unemployment rate of natives. Blanchflower et al. (2007) also find no negative impact on the British economy, hinting at curbing effects of post-enlargement immigrants on inflation. Drinkwater et al. (2009) analyse the performance of Polish immigrants in the UK labour market using the UK Labour Force Survey data. The authors find evidence of "downgrading," that is, that the majority of post-enlargement immigrants have found employment in low-skilled and low-paying jobs despite having relatively high levels of education. Hughes (2007) argues that foreign workers continued to replace Irish workers in the manufacturing sector, but that earnings growth has recently increased. Moreover he continues to argue that the recent vacancies data show that the demand for labour remained strong after enlargement. This is in line with Doyle et al. (2006), who argue that displacement does not appear to affect the Irish labour market negatively since the aggregate unemployment rate remain stable, and even if some displacement takes place, native workers probably move to better-paid jobs.

Concerning the sending countries, aggregate data document decreasing unemployment (Fig. 5.5) as well as an increasing number of vacancies, employment growth and increasing wages in the post-enlargement period.[8] However emigration of skilled specialists may exacerbate structural weaknesses in national labour markets (World Bank 2006). Kadziauskas (2007) reports that in Lithuania there

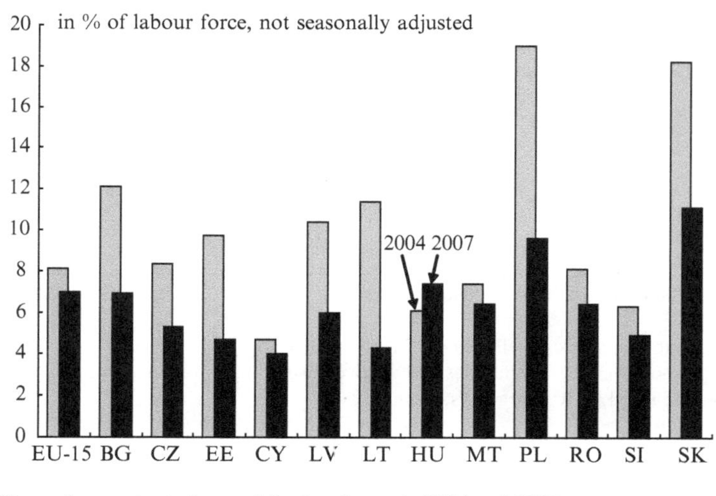

Fig. 5.5 Unemployment rate in new Member States in 2004 and 2007
Source: Eurostat

[8]The World Bank (2006) warns that increasing wages may generate inflation pressures.

were around 12,000 unfilled vacancies at the end of 2005, especially in manufacturing and trade sectors. Kaczmarczyk and Okólski (2008) document similar shortages in Poland, especially in manufacturing, trade and construction, arguing that around 80% of the registered job seekers do not match regional labour market requirements. A consequence of such a mismatch is increased demand for immigrant labour, as documented for Poland, where the number of immigrants in 2004 was the highest since 1960, mainly coming from Ukraine, Belarus and Russia (Frelak and Kazmierkiewicz 2007; Iglicka 2005). Iglicka (2005) argues that post-enlargement emigration from Poland has contributed to the decrease in the aggregate unemployment rate in Poland after 2004, and that there are already shortages of low and medium-skilled workers, lending evidence of a mismatch between jobs and workers. One needs to be careful when interpreting these results as causal however: overall restructuring and business cycle, rather than emigration, may be the key driving factors (Rutkowski 2007; Kaczmarczyk and Okólski 2008).

Kahanec and Zimmermann (2008, 2009) provide and empirically test a theoretical model that predicts a positive (negative) effect of skilled (unskilled) immigration on earnings inequality in developed destination countries with relatively high shares of skilled workers. The effects in source countries similarly depend on the skill level of those who leave and the skill composition of the labour force. In the context of EU enlargement, the labour force in the EU is relatively skilled. This would imply that in sending (receiving) countries skilled migration increases (decreases) inequality and unskilled migration decreases (increases) it. According to this argument, brain circulation between sending and receiving countries can be expected to generate a win–win situation in terms of reduction in inequality in both sending and receiving countries.

5.4.3 *The Consequences of Migration for Welfare Systems*

The question of whether immigrants use welfare more or less intensively than natives has generated the most papers in the general area of immigrants and welfare (for an extensive review of the literature see Barrett and McCarthy 2008). Brücker et al. (2002) discuss a number of reasons why such native-immigrant differences could arise. First, immigrants may have unobserved characteristics that make them more prone to migrating to countries with more generous welfare systems (self-selection). For example economic migrants are typically less likely to claim welfare benefits, but their dependants or non-economic migrants are more likely to become welfare claimants. Second, employers' discrimination may disadvantage immigrants in the labour market by reducing their chances of finding employment. Third, language problems or psychological trauma may lead immigrants to be more dependent on welfare benefits. Fourth, legislation in the host country may exclude immigrants from participating in welfare systems. Fifth, ethnic enclaves may facilitate immigrant employment, for instance by providing relevant information about the labour market, but may also lead to separation from the host society.

Thus ethnic enclaves and networks may decrease or increase immigrants' welfare use, depending on which of the two effects prevails. Finally, any factor that leads immigrants to be in low-pay or low-quality employment, such as exclusion from public employment, also tends to reduce their capacity to provide for themselves and thus increases their probability of welfare use.

Considering the US evidence, Jensen (1988) compares unadjusted rates of welfare receipt and finds only a marginally greater probability that an immigrant is on welfare compared to a native. Once he controls for relevant characteristics, it even turns out that immigrant households are less likely to be among the recipients of welfare benefits. However Borjas and Hilton (1996) show that if non-cash benefits are accounted for, immigrants appear to be more likely to be in welfare receipt than natives. Borjas and Trejo (1991) report a cohort effect concerning immigrant welfare use: as opposed to earlier immigrant cohorts, more recent immigrants are more likely to be among recipients of welfare benefits. Furthermore their welfare use is increasing with the length of stay in the US: the longer their stay, the more likely they are to be in receipt of welfare benefits, which implies assimilation into welfare rather than out of it.

For a European perspective of this area, Brücker et al. (2002) carry out an EU-wide analysis. Using the European Community Household Panel (1994–1996) they study the relative rates of welfare use for non-EU immigrants in eleven of the EU-15 countries, assessing whether there is an "immigrant" effect on welfare receipt when controlling for individual characteristics such as education or family situation. Their results suggest that two groups of countries can be defined. One group contains Germany, the UK, Greece and Spain, where the rates of welfare receipt for non-EU immigrants and EU citizens are similar. In some instances it is even lower for immigrants. The other group of countries, comprising Denmark, the Netherlands, Belgium, France, Austria and Finland, and includes those where there is a significantly higher rate of welfare use among non-EU immigrants than the natives. When controlling for observable characteristics, non-EU immigrants have an immigrant impact on unemployment benefits in Denmark, the Netherlands, France, Austria and Finland; but no such effects in Germany, the UK, Greece or Spain. The evidence of welfare dependency of post-enlargement migrants is scarce. One exception is Doyle et al. (2006), who find no evidence of "welfare tourism" in Ireland and argue that the immigration to Ireland is primarily demand-driven and does not affect native employment significantly.

From a different perspective, Åslund and Fredriksson (2005) look at the impact of immigrant networks on immigrant welfare receipt in Sweden.[9] Their quasi-experimental approach alleviates the issue of the endogeneity of locational choice and thus enables conclusions to be drawn about neighbourhood effects on individuals. They make use of a government housing programme which took place in the late 1980s, whereby communities were selected for refugees. Their findings suggest

[9]See Borjas and Hilton (1996) and Hao and Kawano (2001) for evidence on the US. See also Wadensjö (2007) on immigrant inflows to Sweden.

that it is rather the rate of welfare receipt among their co-ethnics rather than the size of their population that affects individual likelihood of being in receipt of welfare. They estimate a near 7% increase in the rate of welfare receipt when there is a 10% increase in the number of welfare dependents among the co-ethnics.

As for the sending countries, the significant outflows of young and skilled individuals may have negative impacts on the demographic situation and public budgets. For example Kadziauskas (2007) estimates that the elderly dependency ratio will more than double in Lithuania by 2050, and unless significant policy change occurs (for example adjusting the age of eligibility), the social security system may fail entirely. A significant decline in population and labour force over the next 50 years was also forecasted for Poland, posing a serious threat to its labour market and public budgets (Kaczmarczyk and Okólski 2008). In a similar vein, Kupiszewski and Bijak (2007) warn about the demographic consequences of post-enlargement out-migration and their effects on the labour market as well as social security system in Poland. However if the current migration flows lead to efficient brain circulation, empowering people to leave inactivity, increase their human capital abroad, and then utilise it at home, current outflows of migrants from the new Member States may in fact lead to more stable welfare systems in the medium or long-run.

5.4.4 The Growth Effects of Migration

Economic migration typically contributes to a more efficient allocation of production factors, most notably human capital, thereby improving the prospects for economic growth. Indeed some of the main arguments for increased geographic mobility are economic. Perhaps even more important than these direct effects are the indirect effects on productivity and growth through technology transfer. Indeed, skilled migrants often act as agents of knowledge transfer. On the other hand the loss of the best and brightest participants in the work force to developed countries, commonly known as "brain drain," may have adverse effects on source economies. In view of circular migration the resultant transfer of human capital and knowledge represents a "brain circulation" between the host country and the country of emigration. This phenomenon is giving way to a more complex process of sharing information between the immigrants' countries of origin and destination, which is being fuelled by a continual fall in the costs of international travel and communications. Additional second-order effects arise through the supply of labour and skills, which is a function of migrant flows, that affects investors' decisions on the allocation of their investments and thus technologies in the global context.[10]

---

[10]The implied industrial structure has further repercussions for the adjustment capacity in the case of economic shocks.

With these factors in mind it is necessary to stress that although migration may change the economic growth rate simply by changing the size of the labour force, it does not necessarily affect per capita income. A social planner who was concerned not only with maximising national income but also about its distribution would therefore aim at per capita growth. Complementarities in the labour market and improved skill matching are a prerequisite for positive per capita economic growth effects as well as externalities through educational choices, human capital formation, and those of a fiscal nature.

Much of the literature on brain circulation focuses on the economic and growth aspects of geographic mobility, especially when discussing the brain circulation and youth mobility aspects of migration (for an extensive review of the literature see Bonin et al. 2008) A number of studies have calculated quite large additional income growth from extending the free circulation of human capital (Bloom and Grant 2001; European Foundation for the Improvement of Living and Working Conditions 2006; Kaba 2004). The overall conclusion is also in agreement with studies attempting to forecast potential migration and any welfare gain or loss resulting from EU enlargement (Alvarez-Plata et al. 2003).

A potential negative externality of the brain gain and circulation aspects of geographic mobility may be a loss of economic potential in the sending countries that experience a brain and labour force loss. On the other hand, migrants are often not required, economically speaking, in their region of origin at the time of the migration decision, and can be found moving from unemployment in the region of origin into employment in the destination region. A recent IMF-study (IMF 2005, see also Kaba 2004) concludes that human capital flight, especially in the case of doctors and teachers, generates a permanent reduction of per capita income growth rate in the country of emigration. When considering the drain of young, well-educated people, another potential negative externality of geographic mobility is governed by the fact that this part of the labour force is the most inventive in relative terms: it has the most recent edition of human capital and would bear, if the members of the labour force were to stay in the country of origin, the highest fiscal burden over the course of their lives. However different studies do point to the positive innovation, productivity and export potentials of geographic mobility when considering brain gain and circulation (Branstetter 2001; Peri 2005).

Migration of highly skilled workers has repercussions for technological and scientific progress measured as innovation, which are likely to affect the future growth rates of per capita income. Indeed such repercussions include discoveries and technological improvements that are transferred on total factor productivity. Several empirical studies which analyse innovation as measured by the number of patents capture such positive effects of highly educated and talented workers on the rate of scientific and technological innovation of a country. A study by Wasmer et al. (2007) arrives at the conclusion that in the long run the most important effects of immigration might be those on the innovation potential of the economy, as highly skilled experts repeatedly migrating between source and destination countries often function as major catalysts for expanding knowledge, businesses and venture initiatives. A consequence of their actions is a general enhancement of cross-border knowledge transaction and exports (Teferra 2004; Kaba 2004; Saxenian 2002).

These potential positive externalities may however be outweighed by the risk that out-migration of highly productive and well-educated members of the labour force reduces the average productivity of the sending country. In such a context, as highlighted by Straubhaar et al. (2000), limited mobility could allow industries to make more efficient use of firm or country-specific knowledge in production. However such potential negative externality of migration is rather hard to document empirically.

The evidence of these effects in the context of post-enlargement migration flows in Europe is unfortunately limited. Brücker (2007) argues that migration from the new Member States yields substantial gains for the GDP of an enlarged EU in the long-run, and that migrants themselves are the main winners of free movement. He contends further that the effects on the natives in sending and receiving countries are ambiguous and in general rather small. Wasmer et al. (2007) suggest that the economic and social dynamism in the 2004 and 2007 accession states will, sooner or later, draw skilled immigrants homeward. Those who choose not to return home will still contribute to the economic efficiency of both sending and receiving countries by acting as intermediaries: they will connect businesses which are based in Western Europe to their home regions.

In summary the consequences of brain gain and circulation resulting from geographic mobility may be economically favourable for both the sending and receiving country. If the effect is one mainly of a brain drain scenario, the sending country may experience a multitude of negative externalities. Whether or not the total outcome is positive is hindered by the difficulty in estimating the exact size of the different effects arising from the positive and negative externalities.

5.4.5 The Temporal Dimension of Migration

One of the key factors behind the dynamism and circularity of migration are the temporal choices of migrants. Whether the observed migration flows and thus their effects are temporary or persistent determines which of the aspects of circular migration shapes the costs and benefits for sending and receiving countries. Although source countries may worry about the emigration of their most able workers and losing them to the brain drain, they may simultaneously gain know-how and human capital through return migration in the form of brain gain. Migrants may move from unemployment in the sending country to employment in the receiving country, and then return to the sending country as easily employable workers with additional skills. While research in this area is scarce, it seems that much of the migration is of a temporary nature, and that the aforementioned measures on gross inflows are likely to overstate the long-term permanent immigration. According to Home Office (2008) figures, 60% of the applicants in the United Kingdom in March 2008 intended to stay for fewer than 3 months. Epstein and Radu (2007) also report evidence in line with this finding in the case of Romania.

The issue, as discussed by Constant and Zimmermann (2008), of whether migrants adjust over time to become like natives or whether they stay distinct in terms of their economic characteristics and outcomes are yet to be explored in the post-enlargement context. It appears that temporary migrants typically do not invest in the destination country's specific human capital; and even long-term immigrants often do not fully adjust to the economic conditions in the destination country. The degree and time path of immigrant adjustment is thus an important factor driving the effects of migration.

5.4.6 Remittances

Migrants, especially temporary ones, typically have relatives in their country of origin. Such social relationships often channel financial resources to the source countries, as people working abroad transfer a part of the money earned to support the family back home. These flows are further increased by migrants planning to return to their country of origin and invest there accordingly. Migrant remittances are often substantial and affect the source and destination economies directly: not only through wealth transfers, which may be distributed unequally, but also indirectly, especially through the labour market choices of remittance recipients. When economies become dependent on the remittances, the adverse incentives that such dependency may create can slow down economic development.

The literature on the effects of emigration on various measures of inequality in sending rural areas of poor countries dates back to Lipton (1977), who argues that such emigration increases interpersonal and inter-household inequality within and between rural villages (Kahanec and Zimmermann 2009). A number of studies addressing this issue in national and international settings deliver conflicting findings: the direction of effects depends on applied methodologies, type of migration, and stages of the studied migration histories.[11] Stark et al. (1986) find that remittances from emigrants reduce income inequality in a Mexican village with an extensive experience of emigration to the US. In a later study Stark et al. (1988) use an extended Gini index of inequality to examine the sensitivity of the estimated positive effect of remittances from the US on a Mexican village. They find that this effect decreases as incomes of people at the bottom of the distribution are assigned higher weights. In contrast Adams (1989) finds that remittances increase inequality in three Egyptian villages comparing the actual migration history to the no migration counterfactual. Replicating the study for four Pakistani villages (Adams 1992), he finds neutral effects however. Barham and Boucher (1998) find that migration reduces inequality,

[11]Stark et al. (1986, 1988), Taylor (1992), Adams (1989, 1992), Lipton (1980), Stahl (1982), Barham and Boucher (1998), and McKenzie and Rapoport (2007).

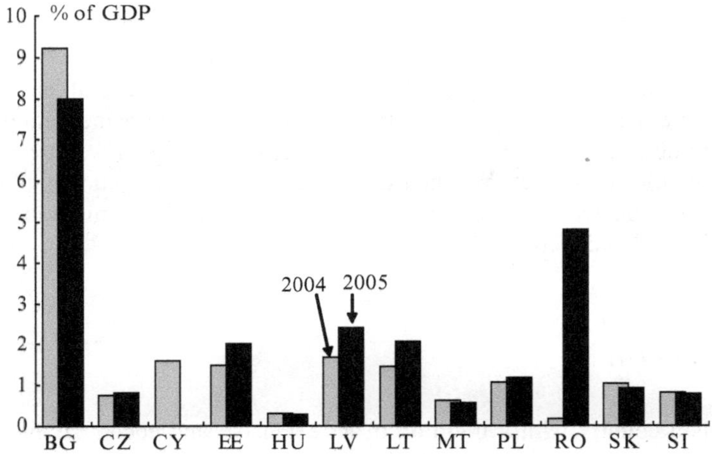

Fig. 5.6 Remittances to the new Member States in 2004 and 2005
Source: World Bank World Development Indicators

assuming exogeneity of remittances; however they find the opposite effects when endogeneity of remittances is accounted for. In fact a recent World Bank report (World Bank 2006) concludes that migration helps alleviate poverty in the sending country, regardless if the migrant is educated or not. The report goes on to state that remittances mean less child labour, more hours worked in self employment, and a higher education rate of people starting capital intensive enterprises – all together with positive impacts on economic growth. And the greater the proportion of the remittances directed into human capital or physical investment, rather than consumption, the greater the positive impact on the country which receives them. However even if remittances are just consumed by the recipient and no investment externalities arise, welfare increases (World Bank 2007).

As an exception to the general scarcity of literature on remittances in post-enlargement Europe, Epstein and Radu (2007) highlight the role of remittances for the Romanian economy. In general remittances constitute a significant share of the country's GDP in Bulgaria and Romania, but also in the Baltic states (Fig. 5.6). Countries can be divided into two groups: one in which remittances have increased from 2004 till 2005 (Poland, Lithuania, and also Bulgaria and Romania); and another one in which workers' remittances have decreased after enlargement (Latvia, Estonia, Hungary, Slovenia). Kaczmarczyk and Okólski (2008) report that remittances equalled 2.6% of GDP in Estonia, 2.5% in Latvia, 2.1% in Lithuania and 1.3% in Poland; and that their volume also increased substantially in Estonia and Lithuania after enlargement. In the case of Poland most of the money earned abroad is spent in Poland, mostly on consumption, but more recently also on investment (World Bank 2006; Kaczmarczyk and Okólski 2008). The remittances are mostly of a seasonal nature in Poland and the Baltic states, pointing to a temporary seasonal pattern of migration from these countries (Kaczmarczyk and Okólski 2008).

5.5 Case Studies

To better understand the topics discussed we examine several case studies providing a more detailed account of the effects of post-enlargement migration in source and destination countries. We first look at differences in welfare receipt in four destination countries.[12] We then study the effects of emigration on the Polish economy and conclude with a discussion of the structure of the migration patterns between Poland and Germany.

5.5.1 Sweden

Sweden is a country with a tradition of an extensive and encompassing welfare system, which is relatively open to immigration. Hansen and Lofstrom (2003) analyse longitudinal administrative data compiled over the years between 1990 and 1996 to assess whether immigrants exhibit a more intensive use of welfare compared to natives. They find that although immigrants account for just a tenth of the population in Sweden, the social assistance expenditure on them is equivalent to the amount spent on natives. The result that immigrants are more likely to receive welfare than natives is robust when controlling for individual characteristics. However welfare receipt decreases with length of stay: immigrants tend to assimilate out of welfare. Yet the authors conclude that this rate of convergence is not sufficiently high to erode differences between the propensity of welfare receipt of natives and immigrants in the long-run. Expanding this framework Hansen and Lofstrom (2009) study the native-immigrant differences in transition rates between employment, unemployment and social assistance receipt. They report that the degree of structural state dependence is significantly greater among refugees than among natives. However non-refugee immigrants are similar to natives in this respect. This has important consequences for welfare policy design, as it needs to reflect the different underlying mechanisms that govern welfare use among refugee and non-refugee immigrants.

Hansen and Lofstrom (2006) focus on transitions in and out of welfare. They examine longitudinal administrative data over a longer time period (1991–2001). Their findings show that differences between the rates of welfare receipt exhibited by immigrants and natives result from a higher rate of entry into welfare and not a lower rate of exit out of it. Their results also suggest that the key driver of the difference in welfare receipt between natives and immigrants is the time invariant differences in unobserved characteristics rather than the differences in observable characteristics between the two groups.

So in general it appears that immigrants are overrepresented among welfare recipients in Sweden. Does this hold for those arriving from the new Member States?

[12] We draw on Barrett and McCarthy (2008).

A study by Andrén (2007) tackles the question of welfare use in a dynamic framework and examines the extent of structural state dependency for immigrants and Swedes. His findings indicate that although state dependence is witnessed in both groups, the effect is three times larger for immigrants. However he does not find any significant effect of being of an Eastern European origin on welfare use in the 1990s.

The study of Wadensjö (2007) shows that this result holds even after the 2004 EU enlargement. Studying the people born in one of the new Member States and comparing them to those born in Sweden at the end of 2005, Wadensjö documents that these immigrants are overrepresented in some sectors of the Swedish economy; earn somewhat lower wages other things equal; and remarkably are not overrepresented in various income transfer programmes.

5.5.2 *Germany*

We now turn to the case of Germany, a country with an extensive welfare system and a more restrictive immigration policy, fully applying transitional arrangements vis-à-vis the nationals of the new Member States. Following a study by Frick et al. (1999), which showed that an immigrant living in Germany was 3.7 times more likely to receive benefits compared to a native, Castronova et al. (2001) attempt to explain the difference. They examine whether it is higher rates of eligibility or higher rates of taking up welfare, conditional on eligibility, which account for the discrepancy. They conclude that there is no difference in the rate of taking up welfare payments between immigrants and natives, but immigrants are more likely to be eligible to claim welfare due to their income or social situation.

Riphahn (2004) examines the role of differences in group characteristics in explaining the differences in welfare use between natives and immigrants. She finds that the immigrant characteristics explain their higher propensity to be in welfare receipt and that dropping out of the labour force is a considerably stronger predictor of welfare use for an immigrant than for a native. However she finds neither an "immigrant effect" nor an "assimilation effect." Her results show quite the opposite: the longer an immigrant stays in Germany, the greater the likelihood of receiving benefits.

The evidence of welfare use of post-enlargement migrants from Eastern Europe is scarce. The aforementioned studies however hint at a conjecture that, other things equal, immigrants in Germany are not more likely to be recipients of welfare benefits and that this might hold for the post-enlargement migrants from the new Member States as well.

5.5.3 *Ireland*

Ireland is an interesting case study when comparing the receipt of welfare between immigrants and natives: Barrett and McCarthy (2007) find that immigrants in

Ireland are less intensive users of the welfare system. The raw figures imply that an immigrant's probability of being among welfare recipients is just one half of the corresponding probability for a native. This finding could be explained by the high levels of immigrant educational attainment in Ireland. Barrett and McCarthy (2007) investigate this issue and find that lower rates of welfare use among immigrants persist even when controlling for standard socioeconomic factors, including education. When unemployed immigrants and natives are compared, they conclude that immigrants are significantly less likely to be in receipt of welfare. However this could be a result of eligibility requirements rather than lower residual take-up rates. Barrett and McCarthy (2008) use the 2005 wave of the EU Survey of Income and Living Conditions and largely confirm the results found in their 2007 paper that used the 2004 wave of the same dataset. While the data do not enable immigrants from the new Member States to be distinguished, they constitute a large proportion of the group labelled "non-English speaking" origin. These immigrants are found to be 8% less likely to be among welfare recipients, ceteris paribus. This finding may be due to the 2-year residency requirement for welfare receipt in Ireland. The authors also find that immigrants of a non-English speaking origin are less likely to be among welfare recipients if unemployed, and receive significantly lower welfare payments. Barrett and McCarthy (2008) conclude that immigrants do not seem to pose any significant burden on the Irish welfare system.

5.5.4 Poland

Literature on remittances in post-enlargement Europe is scarce, but a pioneering study by Kaczmarczyk and Okólski (2008) summarises the evidence on Poland and provides several findings. Although Poland has a longstanding tradition of emigration, its EU accession triggered substantial additional outflows of people, who mainly headed to Ireland and the UK but were visible in all pre-2004 EU and EEA countries. Polish migrants became the largest immigrant group by inflows in a number of countries, most notably Ireland and the UK.[13] According to Kaczmarczyk and Okólski the post-enlargement migrant flows are structurally different from those prior to enlargement. Not only do the flows appear to be more individualistic and regular, but legally speaking they are more solidly based and more diversified with respect to both immigrant characteristics and destination countries. In the area of age and education Polish workers fare well: the post-enlargement migrants from Poland are younger and better educated. Two trends seem to be at work here: the emigration of "redundant" labour from peripheries contributing to better labour and human capital allocation; and the emigration of high-skilled workers from economic cores. This could be a first sign of brain circulation. EU enlargement has thus had a significant effect on the Polish labour market. While

[13]There is also evidence of substantial inflows of Polish migrants in Germany. See the section on Polish–German migration flows below.

more time is needed for all the effects to unfold, it is already clear now that Poland, and more generally new Member States with significant out-migration, will need to adapt to the outflows of their skilled workers and perhaps attract replacements from third countries.

5.5.5 Polish–German Migration

We now evaluate the effects (and determinants) of migration flows for Poland and Germany. There are two reasons why Poland was selected as a source country and Germany as a destination country. First, the effects of post-enlargement migration are relatively well understood in the case of more open destination countries, such as the UK, Ireland or Sweden. Germany by contrast is a country that fully applied transitional measures and yet has received significant numbers of immigrants from the new Member States. Thus Germany is a good example to enable us to shed light on the lesser known facts about post-enlargement migration. Second, most immigrants from the new Member States in Germany come from Poland (as is also the case for many other old Member States).

According to Brenke and Zimmermann (2007) there were about 530,000 foreigners in Germany in 2006 who had citizenship of one of the EU-10 new Member States. They came mainly from Poland, Slovakia, Hungary and the Czech Republic, and were mostly first generation. They constitute about 8% of the foreigner population in Germany and about 20% of them have a German spouse (80% of these are women). Although these foreigners have lower participation rates than natives and foreigners originating from the EU-15, they outperform all other immigrant groups. This pattern is mirrored in the unemployment rates. Furthermore these immigrants exhibit rates of self-employment higher than the natives; however they are lower than those of immigrants from Asia or the EU-15. The immigrants from the new Member States are also distinguished in having good educational and occupational attainment, albeit lower than Germans without an immigrant background; however somewhat higher than Germans with such a background.

Brenke and Zimmermann (2007) continue their study to examine the effect of the 2004 enlargement. They observe for the most part a significant positive effect on immigration from EU-8, mainly from Poland. Most of these migrants are of prime age, mainly in the 25–35 age group, and exhibit higher participation rates and lower unemployment rates than other immigrants arriving in the same period. A relatively high proportion of these migrants have middle levels of education and not too many are in the high-education group. This finding is consistent with the hypothesis that the closed-door policy led to a diversion of high-skilled migrants to more open countries like the UK and Ireland, and those who migrated to Germany concentrated on semi-skilled occupations operating as self-employed. Furthermore a large share of these migrants are self-employed. This suggests that a closed-door policy motivates immigrants to find inventive ways of how to penetrate the labour market, in our case using self-employment as means of avoiding restrictions imposed on immigrants in wage employment. The fact that Polish immigrants in Germany are somewhat older and their educational distribution has a thin upper tail may indicate the role of linguistic and geographical factors. Namely it is the young and highly skilled that are the most mobile and thus willing to migrate to more distant labour markets. Furthermore the tradition of speaking German is stronger among the older generations in Poland; whereas English is the dominant second language among the young.

5.6 Summary and Policy Conclusions

The objectives of the EU, as outlined in the Lisbon Agenda and the European Employment Strategy and Social Agenda, are the development and application of first-rate migration practices and policies. The achievement of these aims is not possible outside the framework of a better understanding of the determinants and effects of migration.

Our analysis is a contemporary perspective focusing on the 5 years after the 2004 enlargement. The importance and relevance of this essay is based on several insights that consistently came out from the comparative study of various aspects of migration, its determinants and effects, and a number of case studies. First, we comprehensively and comparatively describe the landscape of post-enlargement migration trajectories and their relationships to labour markets, social security systems and growth, identifying the policy considerations and stylised facts of migration in an enlarged EU. We find that EU enlargement has had a significant impact on migration flows from new to old Member States. While we do observe various forms of migrant diversion to those old Member States that adopted the open-door policy, countries like Germany or Austria, which have not opened their labour markets, have also experienced significant inflows of migrants from the new Member States. We also observe some signs that if diversion occurred, it mostly worked through migrant characteristics, whereby more open economies attracted more educated and younger migrants.

Second, we provide an in-depth analysis of the effects of migration in the three important areas: labour markets, welfare systems, and growth. Not only does this advance our understanding of these effects in the source and destination countries, but it also allows us to evaluate the relationships between the effects in these domains as well as between determinants and effects of migration from the selection perspective. Our findings by and large confirm the international evidence on this issue: any negative effects in the labour market on wages or employment are hard to detect. In fact there is evidence that post-enlargement migration contributes to growth prospects of the EU by ensuring a better allocation of human capital, that these migrants are strongly attached to the labour market, and that they are quite unlikely to be among welfare recipients.

Third, these results are strengthened by a study of a matrix of country case studies, in which we highlight the different labour market and welfare effects in the source and destination countries, as well as across countries with different transitional arrangements. The case study on migration flows between a sending and a receiving country – Poland and Germany – further deepens our understanding of the effects of migration and their interaction with the determinants and institutional framework of migration flows, quite in line with our general results.

Fourth, throughout the study we look into the specific migration issues in the market for high-skilled labour as one of the main determinants of the growth potential of the EU, highlighting the role of brain circulation.

In summary we offer a number of insights relevant for the development of migration policies and good practice in dealing with migration issues. While our ambition was not to provide an exhaustive account of such practices, we point out the difficulties that restrictions on the free movement of workers bring about, including the forgone increase in the efficiency of human capital allocation at the transnational level, and the diversion of migration flows at the country level. We also highlight the important positive role of brain circulation for the sending as well as receiving countries. We thus believe that the free movement of workers constitutes not only a fundamental principle of the European Union, but also a key precondition to reap the benefits from the opportunities offered in the labour market, to ensure the sustainability of the welfare systems of the Member States, and to strengthen the EU's global competitiveness.

Acknowledgment We thank Anzelika Zaiceva for providing us with invaluable data.

References

Adams, R. H. (1989). Worker remittances and inequality in rural Egypt. *Economic Development and Cultural Change, 38*(1), 45–71.

Adams, R. H. (1992). The effects of migration and remittances on inequality in rural Pakistan. *Pakistan Development Review, 31*(4), 1189–1206.

Addison, T., & Worswick, C. (2002). The impact of immigration on the earnings of natives: Evidence from Australian micro data. *Economic Record, 78*, 68–78.

Akbari, A., & DeVoretz, D. (1992). The substitutability of foreign-born labour in Canadian production: Circa 1980. *Canadian Journal of Economics, 25*(3), 604–614.

Alvarez-Plata, P., Brücker, H., & Siliverstovs, B. (2003). *Potential migration from central and eastern Europe into the EU-15 – an update.* Report for the European Commission, DG Employment and Social Affairs, Berlin: German Institute for Economic Research (DIW Berlin).

Andrén, T. (2007). *The persistence of welfare participation.* IZA Discussion Paper, No. 3100.

Angrist, J. D., & Kugler, A. D. (2003). Protective or counter-productive? Labour market institutions and the effect of immigration on EU natives. *The Economic Journal, 113*(488), F302–F331.

Åslund, O., & Fredriksson, P. (2005). Peer effects in welfare dependence: Quasi-experimental Evidence. *Journal of Human Resources, 44*(3), 799–825.

Barham, B., & Boucher, S. (1998). Migration, remittances and inequality: Estimating the net effects of migration on income distribution. *Journal of Development Economics, 55*(3), 307–331.

Barrett, A., & McCarthy, Y. (2007). Immigrants in a booming economy: Analysing their earnings and welfare dependence. *Labour, 21*(4–5), 789–808.

Barrett, A., & McCarthy, Y. (2008). Immigrants and welfare programmes: Exploring the interactions between immigrant characteristics, immigrant welfare dependence, and welfare policy. *Oxford Review of Economic Policy, 24*(3), 542–559.

Barrett, A., McGuinness, S., & O'Brien, M. (2008). *The immigrant earnings disadvantage across the warnings and skills distributions: The case of immigrants from the EU's new Member States in Ireland.* IZA Discussion Paper No. 3479.

Bauer, T., & Zimmermann, K. F. (1999). *Assessment of possible migration pressure and its labour market impact following EU enlargement to central and eastern Europe.* IZA Research Report No. 3.

Becker, G. S. (1964). *Human capital.* New York: National Bureau of Economic Research.

Blanchflower, D. J., & Lawton, H. (2009). The impact of the recent expansion of the EU on the UK labor market. In M. Kahanec & K. F. Zimmermann (Eds.), *EU labor markets after post-enlargement migration* (pp. 181–215). Berlin: Springer.

Blanchflower, D. G., Saleheen, J., & Shadforth, C. (2007). *The impact of the recent migration from eastern Europe on the UK economy.* IZA Discussion Paper, No. 2615.

Bloom, M., & Grant, M. (2001). *Brain gain – the economic benefits of recognizing learning and learning credentials in Canada.* The Conference Board of Canada.

Boeri, T., & Brücker, H. (2000). *The impact of eastern enlargement on employment and labour markets in the EU Member States.* Brussels: European Commission.

Boeri, T., & Brücker, H. (2005). Why are Europeans so tough on migrants? *Economic Policy, 20* (44), 629–703.

Bonin, H., Eichhorst, W., Florman, C., Hansen, M. O., Skiöld, L., Stuhler, J., et al. (2008). Geographic mobility in the European Union: Optimising its economic and social benefits. *IZA Research Report,* No. 19.

Borjas, G. J. (1983). The substitutability of black, hispanic, and white labor. *Economic Inquiry, 21*(1), 93–106.

Borjas, G. J. (1985). Assimilation, changes in cohort quality, and the earnings of immigrants. *Journal of Labor Economics, 3*(4), 463–489.

Borjas, G. J. (1987a). Immigrants, minorities, and labor market competition. *Industrial and Labor Relations Review, 40*(3), 382–392.

Borjas, G. J. (1987b). Self-selection and the earnings of immigrants. *American Economic Review, 77*(4), 531–553.

Borjas, G. J. (1999a). Immigration and welfare magnets. *Journal of Labor Economics, 17*(4), 607–637.

Borjas, G. J. (1999b). *Heaven's door: Immigration policy and the American economy.* Princeton, New Jersey: Princeton University Press.

Borjas, G. J. (2003). The labor demand curve is downward sloping: Reexamining the impact of immigration on the labor market. *The Quarterly Journal of Economics, 118*(4), 1335–1374.

Borjas, G. J. (2006). *Immigration in high-skill labor markets: The impact of foreign students on the earnings of doctorates.* National Bureau of Economic Research, Working Paper, No. 12085.

Borjas, G. J., Freeman, R. B., & Katz, L. F. (1997). How much do immigration and trade affect labor market outcomes? *Brookings Paper of Economic Activity, 1,* 1–90.

Borjas, G. J., & Hilton, L. (1996). Immigration and the welfare state: Immigrant participation in means-tested entitlement programs. *The Quarterly Journal of Economics, 111*(2), 575–604.

Borjas, G. J., & Trejo, S. J. (1991). Immigrant participation in the welfare system. *Industrial and Labor Relations Review, 44*(2), 195–211.

Branstetter, L. G. (2001). Are knowledge spillovers international or intranational in scope? Microeconometric evidence from the U.S. and Japan. *Journal of International Economics, 53*(1), 53–79.

Brenke, K., & Zimmermann, K. F. (2007). Zuwanderung aus Mittel- und Osteuropa trotz Arbeitsmarktbarrieren deutlich gestiegen. *DIW Wochenbericht, 74*(44), 645–653.

Brücker, H. (2007). *Migration after the EU's eastern enlargement: Who wins, who loses?* Paper presented at Second IZA Migration Workshop: EU enlargement and the labor markets, Bonn 7–8 September 2007.

Brücker, H., Epstein, G. S., McCormick, B., Saint-Paul, G., Venturini, A., & Zimmermann, K. F. (2002). Managing migration in the European welfare state. In T. Boeri, G. H. Hanson, & B. McCormick (Eds.), *Immigration policy and the welfare system* (pp. 1–159). Oxford: Oxford University Press.

Card, D. (1990). The impact of the Mariel boatlift on the Miami labor market. *Industrial and Labor Relations Review, 43*(2), 245–257.

Card, D. (2001). Immigrant inflows, native outflows, and the local labor market impacts of higher immigration. *Journal of Labor Economics, 19*(1), 22–64.

Carrington, W. J., & de Lima, P. J. F. (1996). The impact of 1970s repatriates from Africa on the Portuguese labor market. *Industrial and Labor Relations Review, 49*(2), 330–347.

Castronova, E. J., Kayser, H., Frick, J. R., & Wagner, G. G. (2001). Immigrants, natives and social assistance: Comparable take-up under comparable circumstances. *International Migration Review, 35*(3), 726–748.

Chapman, B., & Cobb-Clark, D. (1999). A comparative static model of the relationship between immigration and the short-run job prospects of unemployed residents. *Economic Record, 75*(231), 358–368.

Chiswick, B. R. (1980). *An analysis of the economic progress and impact of immigrants.* Employment and Training Administration, U.S. Department of Labor, National Technical Information Service, PB80-200454.

Chiswick, B. R. (1998). The Economic consequences of immigration: application to the United States and Japan. In M. Weiner & T. Hanami (Eds.), *Temporary workers or future citizens? Japanese and U.S. migration policies* (pp. 177–208). New York: New York University Press.

Chiswick, B. R. (1999). Are immigrants favorably self-selected? *American Economic Review, 89*(2), 181–185.

Chiswick, C. U., Chiswick, B. R., & Karras, G. (1992). The impact of immigrants on the macroeconomy. *Carnegie-Rochester Conference Series on Public Policy, 37*(1), 279–316.

Chiswick, B. R., & Miller, P. W. (2002). Immigrant earnings: Language skills, linguistic concentrations and the business cycle. *Journal of Population Economics, 15*(1), 31–57.

Constant, A., & Zimmermann, K. F. (2008). Measuring ethnic identity and its impact on economic behavior. *Journal of the European Economic Association, 6*(2–3), 424–433.

De Giorgi, G., & Pellizzari, M. (2009). Welfare migration in Europe. *Labour Economics, 16*(4), 353–363.

De New, J. P., & Zimmermann, K. F. (1994). Native wage impacts of foreign labor: A random effects panel analysis. *Journal of Population Economics, 7*(2), 177–192.

Doyle, N., Hughes, G., & Wadensjö, E. (2006). Freedom of movement for workers from central and eastern Europe. experiences in Ireland and Sweden. *Swedish Institute for European Policy Studies Report* No. 5.

Drinkwater, S. (2003). *Go west? Assessing the willingness to move from central and eastern European countries.* University of Surrey Discussion Paper No. 05/03.

Drinkwater, S., Eade, J., & Garapich, M. (2009). Poles apart? EU enlargement and the labour market outcomes of immigrants in the UK. *International Migration, 47*(1), 161–190.

Dustmann, C., Fabbri, F., & Preston, I. (2005). The impact of immigration on the British labour market. *The Economic Journal, 115*(507), F324–F341.

Epstein, G., & Radu, D. (2007). *Returns to return migration and determinants of subsequent moves.* Paper presented at Second IZA Migration Workshop: EU Enlargement and the Labour Markets. Bonn 7–8 September 2007.

European Commission. (2006a). *Report on the functioning of transitional arrangements set out in the 2003 accession treaty (period 1 May 2004–30 April 2006).* Communication from the Commission to the Council, the European Parliament, the European Economic and Social Committee and the Committee of the Regions. Brussels: European Commission.

European Commission. (2006b). *Enlargement, two years after: An economic evaluation.* European Economy, Directorate-General for Economic and Financial Affairs. Occasional Papers, No. 24, Brussels: European Commission.

European Foundation for the Improvement of Living and Working Conditions. (2006). *Long-distance mobility in Europe: Getting the balance right*. Dublin: Eurofound.

Eurostat. (2006). *Population statistics*. Luxembourg: Office for Official Publications of the European Communities.

Filer, R. K. (1992). The effect of immigrant arrivals on migratory patterns of native workers. In G. J. Borjas & R. B. Freeman (Eds.), *Immigration and the work force: Economic consequences for the United States and source areas* (pp. 245–269). Chicago: University of Chicago Press.

Fouarge, D., & Ester, P. (2007a). *Determinants of migration intentions in Europe. Exodus or bounded mobility?* Institute for Labour Studies, Tilburg University, mimeo.

Fouarge, D., & Ester, P. (2007b). *Factors determining international and regional migration in Europe. European foundation for the improvement of living and working conditions*. Dublin: Eurofound.

Frelak, J., & Kazmierkiewicz, P. (2007). Labor mobility: The case of Poland. In J. Smith-Bozek (Ed.), *Labor mobility in the European Union: New members, new challenges* (pp. 60–79). Washington DC: Center for European Policy Analysis.

Frick, J. R., Smeeding, T. M., & Wagner, G. G. (1999). Immigrants in two modern nations: Characteristics of the foreign and native born populations in Germany and the United States. *Vierteljahrshefte zur Wirtschaftsforschung, 68*(2), 287–307.

Friedberg, R. M. (2001). The Impact of mass migration on the Israeli labor market. *The Quarterly Journal of Economics, 116*(4), 1373–1408.

Gilpin, N., Henty, M., Lemos, S., Portes, J., & Bullen, C. (2006). *The impact of free movement of workers from central and eastern Europe on the UK labour market*. Department of Work and Pensions, Working Paper, No. 29.

Grossman, J. B. (1982). The substitutability of natives and immigrants in production. *Review of Economics and Statistics, 64*(4), 596–603.

Hansen, J., & Lofstrom, M. (2003). Immigrant assimilation and welfare participation: Do immigrants assimilate into or out of welfare? *Journal of Human Resources, 38*(1), 74–98.

Hansen, J., & Lofstrom, M. (2006). *Immigrant-native differences in welfare participation: The role of entry and exit rates*. IZA Discussion Paper, No. 2261.

Hansen, J., & Lofstrom, M. (2009). The dynamics of immigrant welfare and labor market behavior. *Journal of Population Economics, 22*(4), 941–970.

Hao, L., & Kawano, Y. (2001). Immigrants' welfare use and opportunity for contact with co-ethnics. *Demography, 38*(3), 375–389.

Harris, J. R., & Todaro, M. P. (1970). Migration, unemployment and development: A two-sector analysis. *American Economic Review, 60*(1), 126–142.

Hughes, G. (2007). *EU enlargement and labour market effects of migration to Ireland from southern, central and eastern Europe*. Paper presented at Second IZA Migration Workshop: EU Enlargement and the Labour Markets, Bonn 7–8 September 2007.

Hunt, J. (1992). The impact of the 1962 repatriates from Algeria on the French labor market. *Industrial and Labor Relations Review, 45*(3), 556–572.

Iglicka, K. (2005). *The impact of the EU enlargement on migratory movements in Poland*. Center for International Relations, Report No. 12/05. Warsaw: CSM.

IMF (2005). World Economic Outlook (Chapter 2: Two current issues facing developing countries). *IMF International Migration and Development Research Program*.

Jensen, L. (1988). Patterns of immigration and public assistance utilization, 1970–1980. *International Migration Review, 22*(1), 51–83.

Kaba, A. J. (2004). Africa's migration brain drain. *Chimera – improving the environment for intercontinental exchanges, 2*(3), 19–30.

Kaczmarczyk, P., & Okólski, M. (2008). *Economic impacts of migration on Poland and the Baltic states*. Fafo-Paper 2008:01

Kadziauskas, G. (2007). Lithuanian migration: Causes, impacts and policy guidelines. In J. Smith-Bozek (Ed.), *Labor mobility in the European Union: New members, new challenges* (pp. 80–100). Washington DC: Center for European Policy Analysis.

Kahanec, M., & Zimmermann, K. F. (2008). *Migration, the quality of the labour force and economic inequality*. IZA Discussion Paper, No. 3560.
Kahanec, M., & Zimmermann, K. F. (2009). International migration, ethnicity and economic inequality. In W. Salverda, B. Nolan, & T. M. Smeeding (Eds.), *The Oxford handbook of economic inequality* (pp. 455–490). Oxford: Oxford University Press.
Kupiszewski, M., & Bijak, J. (2007). *The impact of the EU enlargement on the Polish labor Market*. Paper presented at Second IZA Migration Workshop: EU Enlargement and the Labour Markets, Bonn 7–8 September 2007.
Lipton, M. (1977). *Why poor people stay poor: Urban bias in world development*. London: Temple Smith.
Lipton, M. (1980). Migration from rural areas of poor countries: The impact on rural productivity and income distribution. *World Development, 8*(1), 1–24.
Massey, D. S. (1990). Social structure, household strategies, and the cumulative causation of migration. *Population Index, 56*(1), 3–26.
Mckenzie, D., & Rapoport, H. (2007). Network effects and the dynamics of migration and inequality: Theory and evidence from Mexico. *Journal of Development Economics, 84*(1), 1–24.
Mincer, J. (1978). Family migration decisions. *Journal of Political Economy, 86*(5), 749–773.
Office, H. (2007). *Accession monitoring report May 2004–September 2007*. London: Crown.
Office, H. (2008). *Accession monitoring report May 2004–June 2008*. London: Crown.
Orrenius, P. M., & Zavodny, M. (2007). Does immigration affect wages? A look at occupational-level evidence. *Labour Economics, 14*(5), 757–773.
Parasnis, J., Fausten, D., & Smyth, R. (2005). *The impact of immigration on native workers in Australia*. Monash University, mimeo.
Peri, G. (2005). Determinants of knowledge flows and their effect on innovation. *Review of Economics and Statistics, 87*(2), 308–322.
Pischke, J.-S., & Velling, J. (1997). Employment effects of immigration to Germany: An analysis based on local labor markets. *Review of Economics and Statistics, 79*(4), 594–604.
Riphahn, R. T. (2004). Immigrant participation in social assistance programs: Evidence from German guestworkers. *Applied Economics Quarterly, 50*(4), 329–362.
Roy, A. D. (1951). Some thoughts on the distribution of earnings. *Oxford Economic Papers, 3*(2), 135–146.
Roy, A. S. (1987). An analysis of substitutability and complementarity of immigrants and canadian-born workforce. *Labour Market Bulletin, 4*(9), 5–11.
Roy, A. S. (1997). Job displacement effects of canadian immigrants by country of origin and occupation. *International Migration Review, 31*(1), 150–161.
Ruhs, M. (2007). Greasing the wheels of the flexible labour market: East European labour immigration in the UK. In J. Smith-Bozek (Ed.), *Labor mobility in the European Union: New members, new challenge* (pp. 4–34). Washington DC: Center for European Policy Analysis.
Rutkowski, J. (2007). Labor markets in EU8+2: From the shortage of jobs to the shortage of skilled workers. *World Bank EU8+2 Regular Economic Report Special Topic*, Washington, DC: The World Bank.
Saxenian, A.-L. (2002). *Local and global networks of immigrant professionals in Silicon Valley*. San Francisco, California: Public Policy Institute of California.
Sinn, H.-W., Flaig, G., Werding, M., Munz, S., Düll, N., Hofmann, H., et al. (2000). *EU-Erweiterung und Arbeitskräftemigration: Wege zu einer schrittweisen Annäherung der Arbeitsmärkte*. München: Ifo Institut.
Stahl, C. W. (1982). Labor emigration and economic development. *International Migration Review, 16*(4), 869–899.
Stark, O., Taylor, J. E., & Yitzhaki, S. (1986). Remittances and inequality. *Economic Journal, 96*(383), 722–740.
Stark, O., Taylor, J. E., & Yitzhaki, S. (1988). Migration, remittances and inequality: A sensitivity analysis using the extended Gini index. *Journal of Development Economics, 28*(3), 309–322.

Straubhaar, T., Fischer, P. A., Holm, E., & Malmberg, G. (2000). *Why do people stay? Insider advantages and immobility*. Hamburg Institute of International Economics, HWWA Discussion Paper 112.

Taylor, J. E. (1992). Remittances and inequality reconsidered: Direct, indirect, and intertemporal effects. *Journal of Policy Modeling, 14*(2), 187–208.

Teferra, D. (2004). *Brain circulation: Unparalleled opportunities, underlying challenges and outmoded presumptions*. Paper prepared for the Symposium on International Labour and Academic Mobility: Emerging Trends and Implications for Public Policy. World Education Services, Toronto; Center for International Higher Education, Boston College.

Wadensjö, E. (2007). *Migration to Sweden from the new EU Member States*. IZA Discussion Paper, No. 3190.

Wasmer, E., Fredriksson, P., Lamo, A., Messina, J., & Peri, G. (2007). The macroeconomics of education. In G. Brunello, P. Garibaldi, & E. Wasmer (Eds.), *Education and training in Europe* (pp. 1–35). Oxford: Oxford University Press.

Winkelmann, R., & Zimmermann, K. F. (1993). Ageing, migration and labour mobility. In P. Johnson & K. F. Zimmermann (Eds.), *Labour markets in an ageing Europe* (pp. 255–282). Cambridge: Cambridge University Press.

World Bank. (2006). *International migration, remittances and the brain drain*. Washington, DC: World Bank.

World Bank. (2007). *Migration and remittances: Eastern Europe and the former Soviet Union*. Washington, DC: World Bank.

Zaiceva, A. (2006). *Reconciling the estimates of potential migration into the enlarged European Union*. IZA Discussion Paper No. 2519.

Zaiceva, A., & Zimmermann, K. F. (2008). Scale, diversity, and determinants of labour migration in Europe. *Oxford Review of Economic Policy, 24*(3), 428–452.

Zimmermann, K. F. (2005). *European migration: What do we know?* Oxford/New York: Oxford University Press.

Zorlu, A., & Hartog, J. (2005). The effect of immigration on wages in three European countries. *Journal of Population Economics, 18*(1), 113–151.

Chapter 6
The Consistency of EU Foreign Policies Towards New Member States

Jean-Claude Berthélemy and Mathilde Maurel

Abstract While European countries have been very generous by opening their frontiers to trade, investing in transition countries, and accepting as EU new members some of the latter, their migration policies were less liberal. The policy coherence debate is an old theme in the international economics literature, which is revisited here by looking at the relationships between aid and migration policies towards new Member States. Are they substitutes or complements? What happens if eastern European labour markets conditions improve? In theory, potential migrants will stay home, and the concern of being invaded by skilled or unskilled workers searching for better conditions and higher wages in the old Member States can be alleviated. But in practice, at low levels of income in the origin countries, economic progress can result in lowering the budget constraint of moving, leading to more migration pressures. We therefore compute the critical level of GDP, above which an increase in transfers and improvement in the economic situation will not lead to an increase in migration. It amounts to USD 2,837 for migration within Europe. We argue that this critical level is not the same for a skilled and unskilled individual. The critical income level, under which a skilled individual with better opportunities abroad decides to migrate, will be higher than for an unskilled worker, who may be better off by staying and looking for a job at home: USD 15,085 for the former, and USD 4,384 for the latter. This has important implications, namely that in some cases, more financial transfers will result in increasing the gap between skilled and unskilled departures from countries already suffering from a brain drain.

J.-C. Berthélemy
Pantheon Sorbonne University Paris 1, Centre d'Economie de la Sorbonne, Paris, France
e-mail: berthele@univ-paris1.fr

M. Maurel
Centre National de la Recherche Scientifique, Centre d'Economie de la Sorbonne, Paris, France

F. Keereman and I. Szekely (eds.), *Five Years of an Enlarged EU*,
DOI 10.1007/978-3-642-12516-4_6,

6.1 Introduction

Considerable progress in the re-unification process between Western and Eastern Europe has been achieved over the last fifteen years. This progress is the result of different factors, including trade and financial opening, particularly with the EU, reforms, privatisation and macro-economic stabilisation. For the countries, which eventually entered the EU, the implementation of the European set of values like democracy, the rule of law, respect for minorities and the Acquis Communautaire, has played a key role in attracting investors and implementing a strong and reliable business environment. Last but not least, important amounts of financial aid have been provided to countries, including EU neighbours. The last chapter of the European reconstruction which followed the fall of the Berlin wall has been the complete opening of borders for individuals.

Can we think of a sort of rationale behind this apparent inconsistency of European policies towards Eastern countries, being very liberal in the extent of trade and financial opening and generous in terms of the financial or technical assistance, but at the same closing the borders to immigration? Relying upon the seminal work of Schiff (2006), this study will try to answer the question. We present in the first section the objectives of the analysis followed by the stylised facts in the second and data, methodology and results in the third. In section four we extend the analysis of the migration/aid relationship by taking into account the skilled versus unskilled nature of the migrants coming to Western Europe. Conclusions summarize.

6.2 Objectives of This Study

The policy coherence debate is an old theme in the international economics literature since the seminal work of Mundell (1957). In principle trade and migration are substitutes, implying that opening trade dampens migration pressures. However, they can also be complementary (Markusen 1983; see Schiff 2006 for an overview).

What about aid and migration policies? Being substitutes means that improving local labour market conditions reduce the incentives for emigrating. Hence, concerns of being invaded by skilled/unskilled workers searching for better conditions and higher wages can be alleviated. If aid and migration are complements, then economic progress can lead to more migration pressures. This can occur at low levels of income when potential migrants cannot afford the cost of moving because of a liquidity constraint which is alleviated by the supplied aid. We therefore ask the question whether improving living standards in Eastern and Central Europe result in an increase or decrease of migration flows to the industrialized countries.

To our knowledge very few empirical papers have dealt with these questions. Recently Beuran et al. (2009) analysed the aid/migration relationships by focusing on a broader range of countries. The question is particularly relevant from a policy perspective in Europe. "Structural Fund" policies have played a key role in the catching-up process in Ireland, Greece, Portugal and Spain, and a similar policy is now implemented in favour of the new Member States. Our objective is to compute the critical level of GDP, above which an increase in European transfers and improvement in the economic situation will not lead to an increase in migration pressures. In other words, we want to compute the level of GDP above which aid and migration are consistent.

Another key issue is the skill content of migration. Recall that if trade and migration were substitutes, trade would be specialized and migration should provide EU-15 countries with unskilled workers. This does not necessarily occur for two reasons. First, migration and trade are not always substitute, and the composition of migration does not necessarily follow the logic of specialisation. Second, migration policies tend to favour skilled migration. As a result, all categories of workers have incentives for moving to Western Europe.

Our prior is that the threshold, below which the migration payoff is positive, may not be the same for a skilled and unskilled individual. In other words, the critical income, under which a skilled individual with better opportunities abroad decides to migrate, will be higher than for an unskilled worker, who may be better off by staying and looking for a job at home. This has an important implications, namely that in some cases, increasing financial transfers will result in increasing the gap between skilled and unskilled departures from countries suffering already from brain drain.

6.3 The Stylised Facts: European Trade, Finance and Aid

6.3.1 Trade and Finance

The restructuring of trade and output has been extremely fast in the Central and Eastern European countries[1] as well as the accession (Duchêne et al. 2004). In order to become eligible for accession to the EU, the Central and Eastern European countries had to remove, albeit gradually, their barriers to trade with the EU, introduce trade-facilitating measures, and reform their customs administration, as well as make reforms to converge to the Acquis Communautaire.

Taken together, these measures have contributed to the emergence of well-functioning service blocs and a business-friendly environment, both necessary conditions for participation in a fragmentation-induced division of labour. As reflected by the evolution of trade, European transition countries rapidly changed

[1]The Central and Eastern European countries referred at in this contribution are Estonia, Latvia, Lithuania, Poland, Czech Republic, Slovakia, Slovenia, Hungary, Croatia, Romania and Bulgaria. The Central European countries are Poland, Czech Republic, Slovakia, Slovenia and Hungary, while the Eastern European countries refer to the six remaining.

their specialisation from traditional low value-added sectors, like textiles, clothing, and agriculture, to sectors requiring more knowledge, managerial skills, and technological competencies, i.e., high value-added sectors (Freudenberg and Lemoine 1999). Moreover, their trading volume, especially with EU-15 countries, increased dramatically, suggesting an increasing integration of the Central and Eastern European countries into EU-15 production networks. This evolution was driven mainly by FDI (Lefilleur and Maurel 2010), mostly from the EU-15.

6.3.2 European Aid Policies

The candidate countries of Eastern Europe were asked to achieve the conditions for being capable of participating in the Single Market and for transforming themselves into liberal economies and political democracies (the so-called Copenhagen criteria). Such ambitious conditions called for the implementation of a no less ambitious programme of assistance. The 'Europe Agreements' were intended to establish bilateral free trade in industrial products between the EU and each of the Central and Eastern European countries, and to develop industrial, technical and scientific cooperation.

In addition to the trade and financial agreements, a programme of financial aid was implemented (Table 6.1). The Phare programme (Poland and Hungary Assistance for the Restructuring of the Economy) was extended in 1990 to all the countries of Central and Eastern Europe. It aimed to support candidate countries in the process of adopting and implementing the Acquis Communautaire and in preparing them for the management of the Structural Funds. During the period 2000–2006, the Phare programme was supplemented by the Instrument for Structural Policies for Pre-Accession (ISPA) for the environment and transport and the Special Accession Programme for Agriculture and Rural Development (SAPARD).

For the period 2007–2013, the European Union has established new external aid instruments. Phare and the other pre-accession instruments (ISPA and SAPARD) have been replaced by IPA (Instrument for Pre-Accession Assistance) as well as CARDS (Community Assistance for Reconstruction, Development and Stabilisation), a neighbourhood programme, which aimed to provide Community assistance to the countries of South-Eastern Europe to foster stabilisation and prepare accession. As EU candidate countries, Turkey, Croatia and the former Yugoslav Republic of Macedonia, along with the potential candidate countries (Western Balkans), benefit from IPA. The Technical Assistance to the Commonwealth of Independent States (Tacis) was intended for the former USSR and was a neighbourhood instrument, not a pre-accession instrument, like phare. Moreover, the European Bank for Reconstruction and Development (EBRD) was established on 15 April 1991 to grant loans for productive investment in transition countries.

As can be seen from the comparison of Tables 6.1 and 6.2, European aid goes far beyond official development aid, in terms of volumes, areas covered and objectives pursued.

Table 6.1 Overview of aid provided by the EU to candidate countries, potential candidates and neighbours

Programmes	Period covered	Sector	Countries	Disbursements	Commitments
Phare	1990–2006	Restructuring of the economy	BG, CZ, EE, LV, LT, HU, PL, RO, SI, SK	EUR 5.6 bn. (up to1998) EUR 5.7 bn. (1999–2006)	EUR 8.9 bn. (up to 1998)
ISPA	2000–2006	Environment and transport		EUR 0.6 bn. (2000–2005)	EUR 2.4 bn. (2000–2004)
SAPARD	2000–2006	Agriculture	Ten candidate Central and Eastern European countries	EUR 1.0 bn.	2.4 bn. EUR (2000–2004)
CARDS	2000–2006	Reconstruction, aid to refugees, stabilisation, implementation of democracy, rule of law	South Eastern Europe: AL, BA, HR, MK, RS, ME	EUR 4.65 bn.	
IPA	2007–2013		Candidates: HR, MK, TR Potential candidates: AL, BA, ME, RS, KS		EUR 11.5 bn. (2006 prices)

Source: Europa, http://europa.eu/scadplus/scad_fr.htm

Table 6.2 Total development aid, net disbursements

Million EUR (2006 prices)	1997	1998	1999	2000	2001	2002	2003	2004	2005	2006	Total
EU donors	42	31	62	126	97	137	202	211	121	246	1,277
All donors	172	272	517	355	196	276	388	402	329	406	3,313

Notes: Original data in USD
Source: OECD (DAC)

6.3.3 Consistency of European Policies

Aid can be understood as having many components such as trade promotion, financial assistance and migration, but these policies are not always consistent. The Centre for Global Development with its "Commitment to Development Index" (Roodman 2005) makes the point. For instance, France and Japan, which are among the biggest donors of foreign assistance, are also among the countries that implement the hardest immigration policies. Nordic countries are ranked very high by the Centre for Global Development for their aid policies, but do not perform particularly well with respect to immigration. By attracting skilled migrants from developing countries, donors destroy the capacities that they have contributed to build.

Similarly in the EU, the liberal trade policy, the generous financial and the fast accession procedure did not appear consistent with the restrictive attitude towards migration from Central and Eastern European countries. Governments in the old Member States feared that migration could lead to unemployment, exert downward pressure on wages or undermine the welfare system. The inflows of workers have indeed been quite limited. In 2004, the year of accession, about 1 million individuals from the Central and Eastern European countries lived in the old Member States, accounting for only 0.3% of the EU-15 population. This migration, however, was unevenly spread with a relative concentration on Germany (450,000) and Austria (70,000).

There are also concerns on the side of new Member States. The demographic conditions (Table 6.3) are worrying with fertility rates below the reproduction level of 2.1 level. The dependency ratios are slightly better than in Western Europe, but they are expected to deteriorate. The main fear is now the exodus of young and skilled nationals. It has to be noted, though, that in some countries net emigration is positive.

Most countries in the EU-15 decided to implement some transitory restrictions on access to their labour markets. Austria, Belgium, Finland, France, Germany, Greece, Italy, Luxembourg, Portugal and Spain opted to set labour limitations to citizens of the new Member States. Contrarily, Ireland, Sweden and the United Kingdom did not implement restrictions. Migration was not allowed during an initial period of two years. Restrictions could then be extended for three additional years. After these first five years, another assessment of the situation had to be undertaken, and only in cases when a serious labour-market disturbance or threat is proven, further limitations of two years will potentially be accepted.

Table 6.3 Demographic indicators in the new Member States for 2005

	Birth rate, crude (per 1,000 people)	Fertility rate, total (births per woman)	Net migration (1,000)	Population aged 15–64 (% of total)$^{(1)}$	Population aged 65 and above (% of total)$^{(2)}$	Dependency ratio$^{(2)/(1)}$
Bulgaria	9.0	1.3	–43.1	69.4	16.8	0.4
Czech Republic	10.0	1.3	67.0	71.2	14.2	0.4
Estonia	10.7	1.5	0.9	68.3	16.5	0.5
Hungary	9.6	1.3	65.0	69.1	15.2	0.5
Latvia	9.3	1.3	–19.6	68.4	16.9	0.5
Lithuania	8.9	1.3	–29.8	67.8	15.5	0.5
Poland	9.4	1.2	–200.0	70.7	12.9	0.4
Romania	10.2	1.3	–270.0	69.8	14.8	0.4
Slovakia	10.0	1.3	3.0	71.5	11.8	0.4
Slovenia	8.8	1.2	21.5	70.5	15.6	0.4
EU	10.3	1.5	5035.7	66.8	17.7	0.5

Source: World Bank Development Indicators

This implies that, at the latest, restrictions will have to be eliminated in 2011, and that, from relatively conservative in the past, migration policies will be very liberal in a near future. As a consequence, migration policy towards the new Member States is likely to be more consistent with the other components of assistance to the region. This is not the case with regard to the EU's neighbours where the general framework of tight migration policies remains in place.

6.4 Data, Methodology, Results

6.4.1 Data

Our main data source is a panel of flows of migrants from 187 sending countries, which are developing, emerging and transition economies, to 22 OECD member countries, over the period 1995–2005. We will consider whether these migration flows are influenced by economic, geographic, demographic and cultural factors. We pay particular attention to the interaction that may exist between foreign assistance policy and migration.

For disaggregated migration at educational level (primary, secondary and tertiary), we take advantage of the World Bank's recent release (Development Research Centre on Migration, Globalisation and Poverty) of an update of its global database. This database consists of a 226x226 matrix of origin-destination stocks by country (see Parsons et al. 2007 for more information). It provides, however, only a one point observation in time, for the year 2000, which restricts the quantitative research. The complete description of the sources used and the list of countries in the sample can be found in Berthélemy and Maurel (2009).

6.4.2 *Methodology: An Equation for Migration*

6.4.2.1 Migration and Aid: The Hump-Shaped Pattern

According to purely economic determinants, migration should decrease linearly with GDP per capita of the origin country. Observed migrations fit relatively well this intuition (Massey et al. 1998), except for low levels of GDP per capita. The hump-shaped pattern hypothesis, which is recurrent in the empirical literature (Faini and Venturini 1993; Hatton and Williamson 2002; Adams and Page 2003), refers to a positive correlation between GDP per capita and migration for relatively low levels of GDP per capita, and to a negative correlation only for relatively higher levels of GDP per capita. We observe this pattern in our dataset (Fig. 6.1).

The hump-shaped pattern can be related to the existence of migration costs, which reduce the possibility of emigration from the poorest countries. Such costs can be reduced by geographical proximity (bordering countries are generally more open to bi-directional migration), common language as well as historical ties implying overall knowledge of the destination country.

Migration has been also explained in the literature by other factors. First, a demographic factor (Hatton and Williamson 1994): poorer countries have a younger population and young adults are more likely to migrate. Second, an industrialization factor: a rural population is reputed to be more reluctant to international migration (according to Hatton and Williamson 2002 this effect is weak).

Faini and Venturini (1993) analyse the evolution of migration observed in Europe from the 1960s to the 1980s in this hump-shaped framework. They find a positive relationship between migration and development for Greece, Portugal and Turkey, but not for more advanced Spain or Italy. Clark et al. (2002), studying

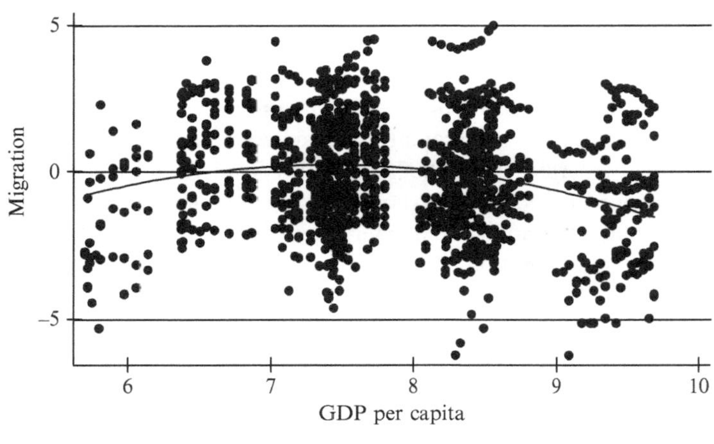

Fig. 6.1 The hump-shaped pattern of migration.
Notes: data set restricted to East–West European migration.
Source: OECD, Word Bank

immigration to the United States between 1971 and 1998, find a negative relationship between income and migration from middle-income and high-income countries that reverses for low-income countries. Hatton and Williamson (2002) contrast emigration from a typical Western European, East Asian, South American and African country: for the latter does an increase in income per capita increase migration to the US.

Aid can influence migration indirectly through its impact on income, as suggested by Faini and Venturini (1993). However, this impact is not robust (Doucouliagos and Paldam 2008). We assume instead that by augmenting the available income of the recipient country, an increase in total aid might result in a lower budget constraint and a greater propensity to migrate. For the poorest transition countries,[2] any increase in income is likely to rise rather than decreases migration.

6.4.2.2 The Gravity Model of International Migration

According to Sjaastad (1962) and Borjas (1989, 1994), migration can be viewed as an investment in human capital. Migrants chose the destination, where their expected payoff is higher than that of any other alternative, including the home wage. Several predictions can be done from the investment in human capital approach: emigration is higher (lower) the greater the mean income in the host (source) country; migration is lower the larger migration costs; migration is higher the greater the payoff in the host country relative to the host country.

Based upon the human capital approach, the gravity model of international migration is commonly used for quantifying the potential of migration (Karemera et al. 2000; Rotte and Vogler 2000). Hönekopp (1999) in a literature survey on East-West migration based on the gravity model finds that estimates of the migration potential vary between 41,000 and 680,000 annually. Those figures are not far away from reality.

Combining supply factors in the sending country and demand factors in the receiving country (both represented by GDP per capita[3]) with trade intensity and variable representing factors restraining or facilitating migration such as transport costs, language or presence of historical ties, like being a former colony, yields the following basic migration equation:

$$Migration_{ij} = a_0(GDPpc_i - GDPpc_j)^{a_1} GDPpc_j^{a_2} GDPpc_j^{2a_3} X_{ij}^{a_4} / R_{ij}^{a_5} \tag{6.1}$$

[2]For an interesting application of this assumption to Russia and Russian inter-regional mobility, see Andrienko and Guriev (2004).

[3]Due to lack of information, particularly for developing countries, variables for wages, unemployment (even if both reflect imperfectly employment opportunities), tax and social security systems have not been included.

Taking logarithms from both sides:

$$m_{ij} = \alpha_0 + \alpha_1 diff_{ij} + \alpha_2 gdppc_j + \alpha_3 gdppc_j^2 + \alpha_4 x_{ij} + \alpha_5 r_{ij} + u_{ij} \quad (6.2)$$

Where u_{ij} stands for the error term; m_{ij} is the log of the migration flows between countries i and j, respectively receiving and sending country;

$diff_{ij}$ is the difference between GDP per capita of the receiving and sending country. In principle it has a positive parameter, implying that higher this difference, the stronger the incentive of moving. GDP per capita of the sending country and its square are introduced to fit the hump-shaped pattern.

x_{ij} is the logarithm of trade intensity, measured by bilateral exports from country of emigration to country of immigration, as a ratio of GDP of the country of emigration. A positive parameter would imply that labour flows and external trade are complements, while a negative parameter would imply that there are substitutes.

r_{ij} consists of variables representing the costs of migration and historical ties. Bilateral distance between sending and receiving country (ldist) is the proxy used for the costs related to migration (transport, income losses during the migration, psychological costs due to separation from relatives, general difference between countries). Dummy variables represent historical ties where past colonial relations are assumed to facilitate migration (colcountry equal to one). Similarly, a common language might favour cross border movement of people (comlang equal to one). Finally, there is a dummy variable that takes account that "western offshoots" (offshoot) have more immigrants than Europe reflecting the strong link between the United States and Latin America and the cultural specificity of Japan, which has very restrictive attitudes vis-à-vis immigration.

There is a standard technical estimation problem with the migration equation, related to the censored nature of the dependent variable, which cannot be negative. Estimating such equations with all observations would result in potentially large biases. This problem is frequently treated by restricting the sample to strictly positive variables. This permits also to specify equations in logarithmic form, which facilitates interpretation of parameters as elasticities, what has been done in this research. This method may result, however, in another bias, known as the selection bias, which results from the fact that the selection of a country as a destination of migration may depend on variables that also influence the number of migrants. There is no perfect solution to this problem in the absence of variables that would explain the selection of a country, but not the number of migrants, that it receives. The most frequent approach is to assume that the selection bias is of second order.

6.4.3 Results: Migration and Aid, Complement or Substitute?

In Table 6.4 we present the results for the migration equation. The coefficients have the expected signs: positive for the difference in GDP per capita, suggesting that richer countries attract more migrants and that migration is determined by the

Table 6.4 Migration equation over 1995–2005

	Coefficient	Standard error
Constant	−17.706***	1.342
$diff_{ij}$	1.450***	0.078
$gdppc_j$	2.946***	0.271
$gdppc_j^2$	−0.086***	0.016
x_{ij}	1.129**	0.587
ldist	−0.576***	0.053
colbritish	1.138***	0.303
colfrance	1.853***	0.499
colportugal	2.231***	0.826
colspain	1.978***	0.445
comlang	0.768***	0.151
offshoot	2.295***	0.194

Number of observations: 7,453. Number of pair countries: 1,116. R^2: 0.3282.

Notes: ***, **, * significant at 1%, 5%, 10%, respectively

income differential, positive for the sending country GDP per capita and negative for its squared. We interpret those latter results as confirming the hump-shaped pattern of migration. For low levels of income, an increase in GDP per capita results in more migration instead of less.

As expected, migration is a decreasing function of the physical distance. Sharing a common language or a common colonial past with the host country has a positive influence on migration flows. Trade intensity as measured by the ratio of export of the origin country on its GDP is significant and positive, suggesting that migration and trade are more complement than substitute. However, its level of significance is not very high. Time dummies (not reported in the table, but available in Berthélemy and Maurel 2009) were introduced for taking account of a possible trend in migration flows. Parameters attached to these time dummies are significant, at least partially, but do not exhibit any clear dynamic pattern.

The presence of squared GDP per capita of the sending country allows taking into account that citizens in the poorest countries do not migrate to the industrialized world as a simple theory of supply and demand determinants would imply. Using the coefficients in Table 6.4 above, we find that migration increases with incomes up to a critical income value of USD 6,084.[4] This is higher that the threshold reported in Adams and Page 2003 (USD 1,630 in 1995 prices) or USD 7,400 in PPS prices reported in Berthélemy and Maurel (2009).

At the policymaking level, a case-by-case discussion will be necessary. Emigration from relatively poor countries such as Albania, Armenia, Azerbaijan, Georgia, or Moldova may be positively influenced by taking initial steps toward development of their economies. Such migrations are, however, dampened by the distance of these countries from Western Europe. Conversely, emigration from relatively rich countries may be slowed by further development of their economies. This is

[4]The threshold can be derived using the following formula: log(critical threshold)=(2.946−1.450)/(2×0.086).

Table 6.5 GDP per capita, European countries

Constant 2,000 USD prices		1995	2001	2007
May 2004	Hungary	3,549	3,677	5,045
	Poland	3,411	4,537	5,935
	Slovak Republic	3,174	3,910	5,734
	Slovenia	7,975	10,145	13,016
	Czech Republic	5,100	5,684	7,408
	Lithuania	2,561	3,498	5,772
	Estonia	2,986	4,438	7,424
	Latvia	2,364	3,588	6,315
	Malta	8,260	9,745	–
	Cyprus	11,870	13,811	15,071
January 2007	Bulgaria	1,564	1,658	2,407
	Romania	1,742	1,770	2,594
Candidate countries	Turkey	3,549	3,677	5,045
	Macedonia, FYR	1,578	1,699	2,064
	Croatia	3,337	4,333	5,798
Potentialcandidate countries	Albania	897	1,279	1,677
	Bosnia and Herzegovina	480	1,502	2,037
	Montenegro	–	1,479	2,152
	Serbia	–	1,252	1,764
	Low and middle income	1,034	1,207	1,628
	Low income	310	339	415
	Lower middle income	701	901	1,359
	Russian Federation	1,618	1,870	2,868
	Moldova	331	334	516
	Ukraine	672	701	1,125

Source: World Bank (World Development indicators)

particularly the case for all twelve new members of the European Union, whose GDP per capita is close to USD 6,084. According to Table 6.5, only one country, Slovenia, which is the richest amongst the European transition countries, would face a decrease in migration outflows when income raises (for whatever reason, be it aid or not). For all other transition countries considered here, economic progress leading to higher income would induce more emigration. This result may however depend on the specification of our equations. Further results below suggest a smaller threshold.

Migration within Europe differs from migration between developing and developed countries for several historical reasons. Until the first world war, Europe had a geopolitical structure very different from what it became in the 20th century. The Austro-Hungarian Empire has been dismantled and Central and Eastern Europe had been separated from the West during the cold war. The end of the cold war sparked a wave of migration from East to West, which had been suppressed before. Migration within Europe further accelerated in the past 15 years as the European Union expanded its membership. The civil war in former Yugoslavia and its dismantlement has spurred emigration from South-eastern Europe.

Three models of within European migration are usually distinguished. The Nordic model was introduced as early as 1954 and granted free mobility of labour within Scandinavia. The EFTA[5] model promoted the liberalization of trade flows, but not factor flows. Some EFTA countries, in particular Switzerland and Austria, allowed a large inflow of labour from abroad, but limited social integration of the foreign work force by not allowing equal access to the labour market, to social assistance, housing and political participation. Finally, the European Community followed yet another model of integration. While free trade was on the agenda from the very beginning, free mobility of labour between the six founding countries[6] was allowed only when the common market was launched in 1992.

In Europe traditional linkages and history matter, e.g. the colonial past in the case of Netherlands, France, Belgium, the United Kingdom and Portugal. Countries like Germany, Finland, and Greece give preferential treatment to returning migrants, who are descendants of former emigrants (Aussiedler in Germany, Ingrians in Finland, Pontean Greeks in Greece). For instance during the 1980s, 300,000 Poles were given authorization to emigrate, and amongst them, 60% went to Germany, with the status of Aussiedler (in recognition of their ethnic German origin). Similarly, 300,000 Bulgarian of Turkish origin left their country for joining Turkey. It is worth noticing that Switzerland has a long standing tradition of taking refugees and asylum seekers, i.e., migration on humanitarian grounds. Germany and Austria adopted the Swiss guestworker model of migration after the second world war, intended to satisfy labour needs, perceived to be only of a short-term nature. These historical links explain partially why Germany and Austria became the main destination countries of immigration from East Europe.

In addition, the labour mobility within Europe is shaped by the EU's ambitious policy of integration of its former Eastern neighbours. Hence migration takes place in an institutional set-up in which the ultimate goal is to facilitate the free movement of goods, capital and persons, including of labour, with new Member countries, while the policy vis-à-vis non-member countries is more restrictive.

Despite this favourable context, the freedom of labour has been neglected during the European enlargement process. If the freedom of labour became unavoidable once the Central and Eastern European countries entered the EU, during the pre accession period the movements of workers were regulated mostly by bilateral agreements, such as the agreement between Poland and Germany or between Austria and both Hungary and the Slovak Republic. Such bilateral agreements have provided an important framework for the temporary movement of workers from the Central and Eastern European countries, and they have brought advantages to both employers in the EU and to the workers themselves. They have had a positive effect in channelling irregular migration into legal seasonal work.[7] But they reflected also the willingness of the EU countries not to open too dramatically

[5]EFTA: European Free Trade Association. At a certain moment following countries were member: Austria, Denmark, Norway, Portugal, Sweden, Switzerland, the United Kingdom, Finland, Iceland, Liechtenstein.

[6]France, Germany, Italy, Belgium, the Netherlands and Luxembourg.

[7]The large majority of workers who benefit from bilateral employment agreements with Member States of the European Union are seasonal workers, mainly Polish, employed in Germany.

Table 6.6 The migration equation with European specificities

	Coefficient	Standard error
Constant	−17.355***	1.375
$diff_{ij}$	1.546***	0.082
diff_eu	−0.710***	0.179
$gdppc_j$	2.767***	0.276
$gdppc_j$_eu	0.999***	0.367
$gdppc_j^2$	−0.068***	0.017
$gdppc_j^2$ _eu	−0.116***	0.031
x_{ij}	0.709	0.600
x_{ij} _eu	9.628***	2.710
ldist	−0.616***	0.068
ldist_eu	0.383***	0.112
colbritish	1.232***	0.301
colfrance	1.955***	0.496
colportugal	2.386***	0.818
colspain	2.167***	0.442
comlang	0.723***	0.154
comlang_eu	−1.686**	0.829
offshoot	2.281***	0.192
Number of observations: 7,453		
Number of country pairs: 1,116		
R^2: 0.3282		

Notes: ***, **, * significant at 1%, 5%, 10%, respectively

their labour markets when increasing unemployment in North Western Europe would have rendered this liberal policy unpopular. These bilateral agreements were worded in loose terms and often a source of abuse by employers in some countries seeking to avoid the costs of employment.

Against these historical and institutional specificities in Europe, we are now testing whether European migrants behave the same as non-Europeans, notably with respect to the income levels and differences. Specific behaviour was examined by introducing a dummy variable equal to 1 when the country of origin is in Central and Eastern Europe, Cyprus or Malta and the country of destination is a EU member. A Wald test performed shows that the interaction of this vector of parameters with the European dummy variable is significantly different from zero at the 10% level.

Further scrutiny of results obtained for each variable which we interacted with the European dummy variable suggests that all of them are significant: the difference in GDP per capita, GDP per capita of the East-European sending country and its square, the distance, language, trade intensity (Table 6.6).

Migrants from Eastern Europe are less reactive to the income differential. Also the hump-shape effect is different: its weight is higher and the threshold at which the own income effect starts declining is lower.[8] The end result of these two shifts, according to our computations, is that the income level under which migration and

[8]This threshold is easy to compute as the half of the ratio of the parameter of GDP per capita to the parameter of the squared GDP per capita.

income are complements falls to 2,837 $US. According to Table 6.5, this implies that for most East-European countries, which entered the EU already, migration and income have not been or are no more complement: Hungary, Poland and the Slovak republic did not create migration pressures induced by their economic progress. Hence, there was a win–win situation for old Member States and these new Member States as income progression went hand in hand with reduced emigration pressure. By contrast, Bulgaria and Romania, which entered the EU only in 2007, all countries classified as potential candidate countries (Albania, Bosnia and Herzegovina, Montenegro and Serbia), and, amongst candidate countries, Macedonia, would experience higher emigration outflows when their GDP per capita increase. Hence, for this second group of countries, we may understand why their accession has been delayed. They are on the left hand side of the hump shape and opening EU borders to such countries would lead to more migration at least for a while. This could create policy reversals and inconsistencies between EU transfers and labour market liberalization policies.

Distance is less of an impediment for Eastern European migrants than for other migrants. Speaking the same language does not significantly influence European migration, simply because there are few instances of common languages. However, our result may be blurred by the fact that within Europe some similarities exist between different languages (e.g. Romanian is close to Italian). There are also minorities in Eastern Europe who speak the language of the destination country (e.g. German). Moreover, significant cultural and historical proximities within Europe may offset differences in languages.

The trade intensity coefficient is much higher, with a positive parameter, implying that labour flows and external trade are more complements than in North-South relations. Referring to Markusen (1983), such complementarity is associated with technological progress and increasing returns to scale, which are more prevalent in European East-West trade than in North-South trade. Trade within Europe is of the intra-industry type (see Chap. 2), while North-South trade is more related to standard comparative advantages.

6.5 Skilled/Unskilled Migration Stocks and Aid: Complement or Substitute?

We continue our analysis by addressing the question of the impact of aid on migration with respect to the level of education. Our gravity equation based on the model by Borjas (1989, 1994) assumes that the decision to migrate depends on education and dispersion of earnings in both the source and destination countries. As a consequence, (1) educated persons migrate to the country where the return to education is the highest and (2) less educated migrants can earn less in both home and source countries (negative selection) if the host country taxes high income workers relatively more than the source country in order to provide better insurance for low income workers against poor labour market outcomes.

Table 6.7 The migration equation with different education levels

	Primary level		Secondary level		Tertiary level	
	Coefficient	Standard error	Coefficient	Standard error	Coefficient	Standard error
Constant	0.626	1.470	−2.619**	1.339	−0.604	1.314
$diff_{ij}$	0.786***	0.082	1.225***	0.074	1.037***	0.072
$gdppc_j$	2.070***	0.314	2.274***	0.287	1.831***	0.282
$gdppc_j^2$	−0.077***	0.020	−0.060***	0.018	−0.041**	0.018
x_{ij}	2.376***	0.523	1.771***	0.479	1.907***	0.473
ldist	−1.075***	0.063	−1.086***	0.058	−1.006***	0.058
colonizer	0.002	0.007	0.010*	0.006	0.016***	0.006
colbritish	3.801***	0.325	3.567***	0.298	3.676***	0.296
colfrance	4.653***	0.476	2.877***	0.436	3.905***	0.432
colportugal	5.425***	0.992	4.443***	0.909	4.280***	0.987
colspain	3.505***	0.578	4.312***	0.529	3.406***	0.525
comlang	0.336***	0.115	0.129	0.105	0.187**	0.104
offshoot	2.649***	0.137	2.799***	0.124	3.627***	0.120
repl. rate	−0.020***	0.003	−0.018***	0.002	−0.024***	0.002
No. of obs.	2,634		2,661		2,705	
R^2	0.2868		0.3360		0.3868	

Notes: The dependant variable is the migrant stock of different education levels. ***, **, * significant at 1%, 5%, 10%, respectively

In compressing the earning distribution, redistribution can be expected to produce a migration pattern consisting of negatively selected individuals with below average skill levels. Conversely, individuals with above average skill levels will prefer destinations where earnings are higher (and wealth is not redistributed).

This idea is tested with replacement rates (over 60 months of unemployment). The replacement rates are a proxy for redistribution policies: the higher they are, the more compressed the earnings distribution is likely to be. We expect that unskilled migrants will prefer destinations with high replacement rates.[9]

Table 6.7 report the result for primary, secondary and tertiary education migrants. These results are based on stocks of migrants, available for one year only, but they are consistent with our previous results based on migration flows.

Distance has the same impact on the migration of all types of workers, while language is more of an impediment to the migrating decision of unskilled people compared to the skilled. Interestingly, coming from a former colony is in general not significant for unskilled migrants, while coming from former British, French, Spanish and Portuguese colonies is. Moreover, skilled migrants seem to be more attracted to western offshoots. We do not find any evidence that migrants are particularly attracted by access to welfare payments or better public services, nor do we find any evidence of a negative (positive) self-selection of unskilled (skilled) migrants more attracted towards high (low) redistributive countries. Our findings corroborate the empirical literature on this specific issue (see Chap. 5).

[9]Hatton and Williamson (2002) use the Gini coefficient as a proxy for the return to skills. A low Gini index suggests a more evenly income or wealth distribution.

Following the approach of the previous section, we can compute the threshold for each level of education under which migration and income are complementary, and above which they become substitute. We find a hump-shaped curve whatever migration variable considered: stocks of skilled or unskilled migrants, or flows of migrants.

This similarity of results obtained with either flows or stocks deserve a particular comment. According to Lucas (2004), the hump-shaped pattern is suspected to be a statistical artefact, due to the use of OECD data, which are stocks. Indeed OECD data are likely to overestimate migrations to industrialized countries because they fail to take into account migration flows occurring across poor (African notably) countries. By contrast, Lucas finds that migration flows do not reveal any inverted U pattern, because they are not biased.

Having at our disposal both types of data, we can check whether they are consistent. Indeed, they do deliver not only the same inverted U pattern between migration and income, but also more or less, on average, the same income threshold. Table 6.7 indicate that migration and income are complementary up to USD 4,384 for primary education, USD 6,367 for secondary education, and USD 15085 for tertiary education, which on average are not far from the figures we obtained in the previous section using flow data.

Furthermore, it is important to notice that there is an income range, over which skilled migrants may continue to enjoy better opportunities abroad, while unskilled individuals are better off at home, given their expected salary on the local labour market. For any income in this range, an increase in GDP per capita will accentuate the brain drain by favouring the departures of skilled workers. This will happen for all East European countries and the potential or candidate countries, in as much as their GDP per capita exceeds in most cases US$ 4,384, but is lower than US$ 15,085.[10]

6.6 Conclusion

We have shown that foreign assistance and migration are substitute above a threshold of about USD 6,084 for the entire sample; for within European migration the threshold falls to USD 2,837. This contrasting result echoes the specificities of the European integration process, which has emerged after the fall of the Berlin Wall. This EU model embraces many dimensions: a trade and financial dimension (enforced by the Europe Agreements), a strong institutional and aid dimension (the

[10]Those results corroborate the finding of Gudrun Biffl (2001, p. 159) that EU citizens working in another EU country are increasingly highly skilled. The mobility of people with "high and specialized skills, in particular in the information-communication technology field, has increased. This does not mean, however, that unskilled labour migration has come to a halt in Western Europe. It is still the major group of migrants in Western Europe. The source countries of un- and semi-skilled migrants changed, however, as the supply of these skills dried up in less developed regions of the EU as a result of human resource and economic development."

implementation of the Acquis Communautaire, accession to the EU at an unprecedented speed) and finally an aid dimension (large financial transfers embodied in the successive Phare programmes and subsequently, the Structural funds).

As a result the level under which migration and economic progress are substitutes turns out to be much lower within Europe. Any improvement in the economic situation translates therefore into less migration pressures. This is a welcome result for governments that fear (justified or not) of being invaded by workers from abroad. According to our findings, most East-European countries, which entered the EU already, did not create migration pressures induced by their economic progress and this is a win–win situation for all involved. By contrast, Bulgaria and Romania, which entered the EU only in 2007, all countries classified as potential candidate countries (Albania, Bosnia and Herzegovina, Montenegro and Serbia), and, amongst candidate countries, Macedonia, would face higher emigration outflows when their GDP per capita increases. Hence, for this second group of countries, the opening the EU borders would lead to more migration pressures at least for a while and could create policy reversals and inconsistencies between EU transfers and labour market liberalization policies.

Our last investigation analyses the tradeoffs faced by skilled and unskilled individuals when they consider migrating. A well-known stylised fact is that skilled individuals are more mobile than unskilled ones. First we provide a rationale for this higher mobility, which is that skilled individuals face lower migration costs including a lower liquidity constraint and less linguistic and psychological barriers, and they anticipate higher benefits. Second we turn to the migration hump framework and we compute three different income thresholds below which migration and income are complements: USD 4,384 for primary education, USD 6,367 for secondary education and USD 15,085 for tertiary education. We emphasise that for any income higher than USD 4,384 but lower than USD 15,085, an increase in GDP per capita accelerates brain drain by favouring the departures of skilled workers. This negative outcome is expected to happen for most East European countries and potential or candidate countries.

Acknowledgments We are grateful to Alba Lorena Arbelaez Toro for her excellent research assistance.

References

Adams, R., & Page, Jr. J. (2003). *International migration, remittances and poverty in developing Countries*. World Bank Policy Research Working Paper 3179, Washington, D.C.

Andrienko, Y., & Guriev, S. (2004). Determinants of Interregional Mobility in Russia. *Economics of Transition, 12*, 1–27.

Berthélemy, J. C., & Maurel, M. (2009). *The consistency of EU foreign policies towards new Member States*. European Economy Economic papers, No. 365, March.

Beuran, M., Berthélemy, J. C., & Maurel, M. (2009). Aid and migration: Substitutes or complements? *World Development, 37*, 1589–1599.

Biffl, G. (2001). Migration Policies in Western Europe and the EU-Enlargement In OECD (Ed.), Migration Policies and EU Enlargement: The Case of Central and Eastern Europe, Paris.

Borjas, G. J. (1989). Economic theory and international migration. *International Migration Review, 23*(3), 457–485.

Borjas, G. J. (1994). The economics of immigration. *Journal of Economic Literature, 32*, 1667–1717.

Clark, X., Hatton, T., & Williamson, J. (2002). Explaining US immigration 1971–1998. *Review of Economics and Statistics, 89*(2), 335–342.

Doucouliagos, H., & Paldam, M. (2008). Aid effectiveness on growth: a meta study. *European Journal of Political Economy, 24*(1), 1–24.

Duchêne, G., Maurel, M., & Najman, B. (2004). Elargissement de l'UE: présentation générale. *Economie et Prévision, 163*, 1–16.

Faini, R., & Venturini, A. (1993). Trade, aid and migrations: some basic policy issues. *European Economic Review, 37*, 435–442.

Freudenberg, M., & Lemoine, F. (1999). *Central and eastern European countries in the international division of labour in Europe*. CEPII, Working Paper 1999–2005.

Hatton, T., & Williamson, J. G. (1994). *Migration and the international labor market, 1850–1939*. London, UK: Routledge.

Hatton, T., & Williamson, J. (2002). *What fundamentals drive world migration*? Paper presented at the Conference on Poverty, International Migration and Asylum. Helsinki, September 27–28.

Hönekopp, E. (1999). *Auswirkungen der EU – Osterweiterung auf die Arbeitsmärkte der Mitgliedsländer der Europäischen Union*. (Schwerpunkt Arbeitsfreizügigkeit). Nürnberg: Manuscript, IAB.

Karemera, D., Iwuagwu Oguledo, V., & Davis, B. (2000). A gravity model analysis of international migration to North America. *Applied Economics, 32*, 1745–1755.

Lefilleur, J., & Maurel, M. (2010). The logics of Eastern European firms integration: location close to input suppliers and export markets, Economic Systems (in press).

Lucas, R. E. B. (2004). *International migration to the high income countries: Some consequences for economic development in the sending countries*. Paper prepared for the Annual World Bank Conference on Development Economics, Europe, Brussels.

Markusen, J. R. (1983). Factor movements and commodity trade as complements. *Journal of International Economics, 14*(3–4), 341–356.

Massey, D. S., Arango, J., Hugo, G., Kouaouci, A., Pelligrino, A., & Taylor, J. E. (1998). *Worlds in motion: Understanding international migration at the end of the millennium*. Oxford: Clarendon Press.

Mundell, R. A. (1957). International trade and factor mobility. *American Economic Review, 47*(3), 321–335.

Parsons, C. R., Skeldon, R., Walmsley, T. L., & Winters, L. A. (2007). *Quantifying international migration: A database of bilateral migrant stocks*. World Bank, Working Paper No 4165.

Roodman, D. (2005). *An index of donor performance – Revised August 2005*. Center for Global Development, Working Paper No 67.

Rotte, R., & Vogler, M. (2000). The effects of development on migration: Theoretical issues and new empirical evidence. *Journal of Population Economics, 13*(3), 485–508.

Schiff, M. (2006). *Migration, investment and trade: Substitute or complements*? Paper presented at the AfD/EUDN Conference on "Migration and Development: Mutual Benefits?, Paris. http://www.eudnet.net/download/Schiff.pdf

Sjaastad, L. A. (1962). The costs and returns of human migration. *Journal of Political Economy, 70*(5), 80–93.

Vogler, M., & Rotte, R. (2000). The effects of development on migration: theoretical issue and new empirical evidence. *Journal of Population Economics, 13*, 485–508.

Chapter 7
Comments on Chapters 5 and 6

Filip Keereman and Karl Pichelmann

Abstract In their comments to the first paper in this chapter the discussants express broad agreement with its main message that the post-enlargement labour flows have been positive with little negative impact. In the second paper, an interesting perspective is offered on the relation between economic development and migration, which leads, though, to some question marks.

7.1 Introductory Remarks

This chapter on "Migration in an enlarged EU: solution or problem for labour market woes and cash-strapped social security systems?" contains two papers which are very different in approach. The contribution by Martin Kahanec and Klaus F. Zimmermann reviews the literature on EU migration after enlargement. The study by Jean-Claude Berthélemy and Mathilde Maurel focuses on one aspect and analyses the relation between migration and development aid to the sending countries.

7.2 Comments on Chap. 5

"Migration in an enlarged EU: A challenging solution?" by Kahanec and Zimmermann is an interesting review paper about post-enlargement mobility flows. Yet, to begin with, its title requires a clarification. A challenging solution for what? The

F. Keereman
European Commission, Directorate General Economic and Financial Affairs, Brussels, Belgium
K. Pichelmann (✉)
European Commission, Directorate General Economic and Financial Affairs, Université Libre de Bruxelles, Brussels, Belgium
e-mail: karl.pichelmann@ec.europa.eu

F. Keereman and I. Szekely (eds.), *Five Years of an Enlarged EU*,
DOI 10.1007/978-3-642-12516-4_7,

explanation can be found in that the paper was produced for a session in the workshop which asked whether migration in an enlarged EU poses a solution or a problem for labour market woes and cash-strapped social security systems. The paper addresses this question adopting a multilevel analytical framework based on existing evidence, descriptive empirical analysis, as well as a number of case-studies. Reviewing the effects of the post-enlargement migration flows on the receiving as well as sending countries in three broader areas, namely labour markets, welfare systems, and growth and competitiveness, the authors conclude that post-enlargement mobility flows contribute to growth prospects of the EU and that any negative effects on wages, employment or welfare dependency are hard to detect. These findings are very much in line with the assessment in other studies and the recent Communication from the European Commission on the impact of the free movement of workers in the context of EU enlargement. There appears to be a broad consensus now that post-enlargement intra-EU mobility flows have not led – and are unlikely to lead – to serious labour market disturbances, and that the migration-induced re-allocation of labour resources across countries has already brought sizeable economic benefits for the enlarged EU.

But it has not always been like that. Indeed, a major uncertainty surrounding the May 2004 EU enlargement process was the effect it would have on East–West migration flows, both in terms of the actual numbers moving across borders as well as the economic impact of those flows on the sending and receiving EU Member States. The sizeable income differentials which existed in the pre-enlargement period sparked concerns that there could be a massive surge of workers from poorer central and eastern European countries flooding into the labour markets of the old EU-15 Member States and impacting negatively on the wages and employment prospects of local workers. These fears led to many old Member States imposing temporary restrictions on the flow of new Member States' workers into their countries, with just three Member States (i.e. the UK, Ireland and Sweden) fully opening their labour markets in May 2004. In the new Member States, however, initially the predominant perception was that the availability of "surplus" labour should ensure that they gain from declines in unemployment and from an influx of emigrants' remittances, with the migrants themselves benefiting strongly either as a result of moving out of unemployment or from finding a better remunerated job; only more recently, with tightening labour markets, emerging skill shortages and associated inflationary pressures, concerns were growing that the outflow of workers could have accentuated labour market imbalances and be hampering growth prospects.

The exact size of post-enlargement mobility flows is of course difficult to determine due both to several shortcomings in the existing data and to the largely open borders which exist between Member States. However, the available population statistics, as well as data from the EU's Labour Force Survey, suggest that since 2004 the stock of EU-10 citizens resident in the EU-15 has essentially doubled over the period to 2007 from roughly 1 to 2 million. While these numbers are significant in absolute terms, they represent – with the notable exception of Ireland – a relatively small share of the working-age population of the host countries. In fact, in almost all of the EU-15 Member States the number of recent arrivals from countries outside the

EU-25 substantially exceeds the numbers arriving from the EU-10 Member States. Moreover, in most of the EU-15 countries, the inflow of other EU-15 nationals has also been larger than the number of recent arrivals from the EU-10.

Overall, these mobility flows have clearly contributed to growth. Results presented in D'Auria et al. (2008) suggest that the GDP effect on the EU25 as a whole of recent intra-EU mobility has been substantial and positive at about 0.3% of GDP. This is equivalent to an income gain of around €30 billion for the enlarged EU. Thus, a migration shock of this magnitude is in fact much more potent, in economic terms, than a one percentage point increase in the EU-25's investment to GDP ratio. This positive effect from cross-border mobility within the EU-25 is in keeping with the view that migration increases the productive use of human resources within the enlarged area and hence adds to GDP as well as boosting productivity and GDP per capita.

However, whilst positive for the EU-25 as a whole, the analysis cited above also shows that migration has potentially less clear-cut effects for the receiving (EU-15) and sending (EU-10) groups of countries. For example, whilst the receiving countries are expected to gain in GDP terms, the effects on GDP per capita, real wages and the employment rate are more ambiguous, with gains dependent on the time horizon chosen for the simulations and the assumptions regarding both the skill characteristics of migrant and native labour as well as for the overall speed of adjustment of economies. For the sending countries, the simulation results point to the possibility of some negative effects on total GDP which must be balanced against capital deepening induced gains for real wages, productivity and GDP per capita. Moreover, it suggests that whilst labour mobility from the new Member States has helped to reduce inflationary pressures in most receiving countries, it has also contributed to emerging labour shortages and a (temporary) increase in inflation in some of the main sending countries.

Despite these caveats, it is certainly fair to conclude from the available evidence that the overall impact of post-enlargement mobility flows has been positive, with any negative effects for individual countries or for specific skill groups generally being both small in magnitude and time limited. And while the findings confirm that migration and mobility are certainly no panacea for labour market woes and ageing-related pressures on social security systems, they show that migration has a key role to play in realising the full benefits of an integrated economic area in the EU as a whole. In this respect, it is necessary to stress that a commitment to the free movement of workers remains perhaps the most symbolic and important of the four fundamental freedoms of the EU's internal market programme.

7.3 Comments on Chap. 6

In contrast to the broad-brushed review of the previous paper, in "The consistency of EU foreign policies towards new Member States", Barthélemy and Maurel zoom in on a specific topic in the migration debate and examine the relation between cross border movement of people and development aid. They start from the observation that there may be an inconsistency in the EU policy framework towards the new Member States. The EU liberalized trade and capital flows and the old Member States are generous in providing financial support to the recently acceded countries, while at the same they are quite restrictive towards migration from the Central and Eastern European countries. This appears a contradiction as financial transfers and general economic progress in less developed regions should reduce the incentives to migrate as income differentials narrow. If this is correct, there is no need for rich countries fearing an invasion of poor migrants to impose tights controls.

In an effort to rationalize the apparent incoherent policy mix between generous aid supply and quite severe restrictions on the free movement of people, the authors make a link to the literature where the issue is traditionally discussed by asking the question if aid and migration policies are complements or substitutes. The reasoning is as follows. At low levels of income, potential migrants cannot afford moving because they cannot bear the costs of leaving the country. If financial support is received which increases the income level, the liquidity constraint may be overcome and people start moving. Hence, up to a certain income threshold aid and migration are complements implying a justification for limiting the cross border movement of people, while beyond this critical level aid and migration are substitutes when maintaining restrictions does not make sense.

With other words there does not exist a negative linear relation between income levels and migration, but a hump-shaped one. Up to a certain threshold migration increases with income, while beyond this threshold it declines. The authors use a gravity model to determine the critical level when the relation between migration and income changes in sign. The migration equation contains the traditional demand and supply factors in receiving and sending countries as well as the income differential between the two groups of countries, all represented by GDP per capita. To test for a hump-shaped relation between migration and income, GDP per capita in the sending country and in addition its square are introduced in the equation. Further explanatory variables are bilateral trade and a series of indicators for the affinity between sending and receiving countries including distance and historical and language links.

Based on more than 7,000 observations and more than 1,000 country pairs spanning the whole world, the results from the panel estimations confirm the expectations of the authors. In particular, they find evidence for the hump-shaped relationship between income in the sending country and migration. However, compared to the world as a whole, the threshold until which migration and income growth are positively related, is lower in the new Member States (USD 2837 versus USD 6084). Language differences and distance are less an impediment to migrate inside the EU, while trade intensity is a complement rather than a substitute for the cross border movement of people. The authors explain these differences with the world as a whole by referring to some European specificities including the historical context, enlargement and the *Acquis Communautaire*, which is the set of rules that governs the integration process. The complementarity of trade and migration is associated with the large share of intra-industry within Europe, while North–South trade is based on comparative advantages consistent with trade and migration being substitutes.

Looking at the numbers, the authors find that most of the inconsistencies in the policies towards the new Member States are alleviated as their income level is above the critical threshold. Only in Romania and Bulgaria, will an increase in GDP per capita lead to more emigration. However, for most of the EU's neighbours, aid and economic progress will stimulate the movement of people rather than hold them in the country.

The skilled are more mobile than the unskilled. Against this well-established stylised fact, the analysis is further refined and the critical income levels according to educational attainment are calculated. It is as high as USD 15085 for migrants with tertiary education, while only USD 4384 for primary education. From this, the authors draw the conclusion that financial support to economic development within that income range will accelerate brain drain and worsen the skill composition of the sending country.

Overall, the authors have offered an interesting perspective on the migration debate by framing it into the general policy framework applied to the new Member States. Apparent inconsistencies were rationalised by pointing at non-linearities in the relation between economic development and migration. Several comments apply, though. First, the hump-shaped curve, as the authors themselves admit, is not generally accepted. This can already be deducted from the scatter plot in their paper where the inverted U-curve does not appear the only possibility. The reliability of the regression can also be questioned as many variables have been omitted. In particular, growth and unemployment in destination countries should be controlled for in the estimations. Second, to the extent that the hump shape does not correspond to reality, but that the migration regression slope is firmly negative with respect to income, the policy conclusions drawn in the paper are not warranted. In such a case imposing restrictions to labour movements are never justified. Third, even if at low income levels economic progress in the sending countries stimulates migration, one can wonder if this justifies impediments to labour movement in Europe. In the United Kingdom, Sweden and Ireland, where migrants from the new Member States could enter freely, the inflows were not of that magnitude to disturb the functioning of the labour markets. Migration appeared good for both the receiving and sending country. Fourth, more at the technical level, the paper addressing European issues and would have come easier across, at least to the European reader, if the critical income threshold were expressed in euro rather than US dollars.

Reference

D'Auria, F., McMorrow, K., Pichelmann, K. (2008). Economic impact of migration flows following the 2004 EU enlargement process: a model based analysis. *European Economy Economic Papers, 349*.

Part III
Financial integration and stability in an enlarged EU

Chapter 8
Real Convergence, Financial Markets, and the Current Account: Emerging Europe Versus Emerging Asia

Sabine Herrmann and Adalbert Winkler

Abstract Global financial integration has been associated with divergent patterns of real convergence and the current account in emerging markets. While countries in emerging Asia have been running sizeable current account surpluses, countries in emerging Europe have been facing large current account deficits. In this paper we test for the relevance of financial market characteristics in explaining this divergence in the catching-up process in Europe and Asia. We assume that the two regions constitute distinct convergence clubs, with the euro area and the United States respectively at their cores. In line with the theoretical literature, we find that better developed and more integrated financial markets increase emerging markets´ ability to borrow abroad. Moreover, the degree of financial integration within the convergence clubs – as opposed to the state of financial integration in the global economy – and the extent of reserve accumulation are significant factors in explaining the divergent patterns of real convergence and the current account in the regions under review.

8.1 Introduction

Over the past decade, the process of financial globalisation has been associated with strongly divergent current account patterns in emerging market economies engaged in a rapid catching-up process. While countries in emerging Europe and emerging Asia have been receiving substantial gross financial inflows, the two regions have differed significantly with regard to direction and size of net capital flows. Most countries in emerging Europe, in keeping with standard economic theory, have

S. Herrmann (✉)
Deutsche Bundesbank, Frankfurt, Germany
e-mail: sabine.herrmann@bundesbank.de

A. Winkler
European Central Bank, Frankfurt, Germany

F. Keereman and I. Szekely (eds.), *Five Years of an Enlarged EU*,
DOI 10.1007/978-3-642-12516-4_8, © Springer-Verlag Berlin Heidelberg 2010

been reporting substantial current account deficits over the past 10 years (Bussière et al. 2004). Growth has been driven by domestic demand, in particular by investment, partly financed by foreign savings. By contrast, in emerging Asia – as described by the so-called *Lucas paradox*[1] – the convergence process has been associated with current account surpluses,[2] while periods of expansionary domestic demand and deteriorating net exports proved to be indicators of an ensuing crisis (Asian Development Bank 2005).

There is a large body of literature on the determinants of current account balances, globally, in both advanced and emerging market economies. From this literature, a broad consensus has emerged that the state of financial development and international financial integration plays a key role in explaining why emerging economies' current account patterns contradict standard theory (Prasad et al. 2007) or conform with predictions based on consumption-smoothing behaviour (Abiad et al. 2007). Against this background, this paper analyses the relationship between real convergence and current account developments in emerging market economies in Europe[3] and Asia.[4] It aims at shedding light on the extent to which financial market characteristics have been at the heart of the strikingly different current account patterns observed in two emerging market regions experiencing a rapid catching-up process. In doing so, we test for the significance of different types and dimensions of financial integration, namely an overall as well as an intra-regional form of financial integration. To this end, we employ the concept of *convergence clubs*, with two peripheries (the two regions) and two cores. The United States is identified as emerging Asia's core, while the euro area/EU-15 is the core of the convergence club in Europe. Finally, we go beyond identifying statistically significant determinants and reveal the extent to which these variables actually contribute to the level of the current account balances.

Our analysis suggests that financial markets and financial integration are important factors in determining current account balances and their dispersion in the two regions. At the same time, the overall state of financial development and integration does little to explain the divergent patterns of real convergence and the current account in emerging Europe and emerging Asia. Rather, the differences reflect the different ways financial integration with the respective core has been proceeding.

---

[1]According to Lucas (1990) capital seems to flow *uphill* from poor to rich countries contradicting the prediction of standard neoclassical growth models.

[2]In recent years, other emerging market economies have seen improving current account balances as well, mainly reflecting the rise in oil and other raw material prices, which has supported trade and current account balances in many resource-rich countries.

[3]The emerging European countries are the new EU Member States Bulgaria, Czech Republic, Estonia, Hungary, Latvia, Lithuania, Poland, Romania, Slovakia and Slovenia as well as the candidate (Croatia, FYR Macedonia and Turkey) and potential candidate countries (Albania, Bosnia & Herzegovina, Montenegro and Serbia) for EU accession.

[4]The emerging Asia group refers to developing Asian countries such as China, Indonesia, Malaysia, Philippines and Thailand, as well as the newly industrialized Asian economies, i.e. Hong Kong, Korea, Singapore and Taiwan. India and Vietnam are also part of the sample.

Moreover, different financial integration methods may reflect strong differences in the two convergence clubs' overall approaches to integration between core and periphery.[5]

The paper is structured as follows: Sect. 8.2 introduces the convergence club concept, while Sect. 8.3 provides an overview of real convergence and current account developments in emerging Europe and emerging Asia. This provides a context for analysing major breakdowns of the current account positions, their financial account counterparts and saving-investment balances. Sects. 8.4 and 8.5 discuss the role of the financial markets with respect to the current account by confronting theoretical approaches with the status quo of financial development and integration in the two regions. In Sect. 8.6, an econometric analysis identifies the major determinants of the current account positions in the European and Asian emerging market economies. Sect. 8.7 includes a summary and conclusion.

8.2 The Convergence Club Concept

Standard economic theory predicts that, driven by differences in the marginal returns to capital, countries with a relatively low per capita income will catch up with richer ones. Globally, however, empirical evidence suggests increasing divergence of income levels over time. This contradiction between theory and evidence has triggered the convergence club concept (Abramovitz 1986), among others. It takes a historical perspective by noting two features of modern growth processes: (a) certain countries have led in terms of growth and development; (b) only a small group of countries have managed to converge with the leader over time. Leaders and followers form specific convergence clubs with a core (leader) and a periphery (converging countries). Convergence is driven by spillovers from the core to the periphery as converging economies engage in similar lines of production and develop extensive trade and financial linkages with the core.

We apply the concept to emerging Europe and emerging Asia, as – following Eichengreen (2004) – the process of globalisation can be very much analysed in a core – periphery framework, with the industrial countries acting as the core and emerging markets acting as the periphery. However, several indicators suggest that the two emerging regions converge to two different cores.

In Europe emerging economies' convergence process has been largely shaped by European integration, i.e. the process of accession to the European Union. This is most obvious with regard to institutional integration, but applies to economic integration as well. Trade and financial integration have mainly taken the form of integration with the euro area/EU-15, and euro area/EU-15 residents have been the

[5] It should be stressed that these results are not to be seen as a contribution to the debate on the causes and roots of global imbalances. By focusing on two sub-regions of the emerging market world, our analysis neglects developments in countries not covered by our analysis.

most important foreign investors in the region. Moreover, when taking a monetary perspective, the countries in emerging Europe predominantly use the euro as the main anchor currency (ECB 2007). Against this background we identify a European convergence club with the euro area as the core and emerging Europe as the periphery.

In institutional terms, the convergence process in emerging Asia has been very different, as there is no framework comparable to that of European integration in linking the periphery to the core. However, from an economic perspective, there are several indicators pointing to the United States as the core country to which emerging Asian economies' convergence is aimed. For example, the US dollar serves as the main anchor upon which they base exchange rate policy or to which they keep a fixed or quasi-fixed peg. Furthermore, all Asian countries – except for Indonesia – show strong trade integration with the United States. Exports to the United States in 2006 represented the largest share for any single country, significantly exceeding that of Japan or the euro area.[6] The same applies to the degree of financial integration, as the stock of consolidated foreign bank claims by US banks predominate in most of the Asian countries under review.[7] Thus, we identify a second convergence club with the United States as the core and emerging Asia as the periphery.

The convergence club concept and the identification of two different convergence clubs with emerging European and emerging Asian countries constituting the respective peripheries broadens the analysis of financial development and financial integration in both regions by adding an additional, regional dimension. Current account patterns in both peripheries may be influenced not only by progress in domestic financial development and integration in global financial markets, but also by the depth and form of financial integration between core and periphery within the respective convergence club.

8.3 Real Convergence and Current Account Developments in Central, Eastern and South-Eastern Europe and in Emerging Asia: An Overview

Reviewing the process of real convergence in both peripheries suggests that between 1994 and 2006, emerging Europe and emerging Asia witnessed similar dynamics of catching up.[8] On average, Asian countries experienced a slightly higher (non-weighted) growth rate (5.6%) than the emerging European countries

[6] See Direction of Trade Statistics, IMF.

[7] In China, Hong Kong, Indonesia and Thailand Japanese banks hold the largest claims on the respective countries. See Consolidated Banking Statistics, BIS.

[8] For Bosnia and Herzegovina, the average applies to the period 1999–2006 to avoid a bias from the immediate post-war recovery, when annual growth rates were exceptionally strong. Data for Serbia are available only from 1999. Montenegro is not included in the analysis.

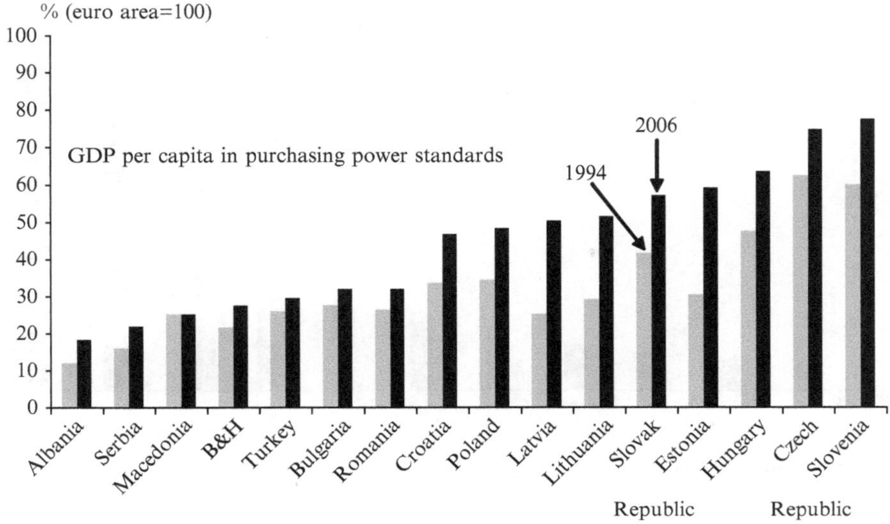

Fig. 8.1 GDP per capita in emerging Europe, 1994/2006
Source: IMF

(4.1%), with China (9.7%) and Estonia (6.6%) being the fastest growing countries within the respective convergence clubs. In emerging Europe, GDP per capita rose by more than 12% points compared with the euro area average in the period under review (Figs. 8.1 and 8.2). By contrast, Asian countries improved their relative per capita income position[9] vis-à-vis the United States by only 6% points on average, mainly reflecting strong population growth and the fact that Asia's core country grew faster than Europe's.[10] The convergence process was strongly influenced by the 1997–1998 financial crisis. Thailand, Indonesia, the Philippines and Malaysia, i.e. four of the five countries that were hit hardest, rank last in terms of catching-up with US per capita income between 1994 and 2006.[11]

In 2006, the dispersion of per capita incomes varied from approximately 19% (Albania) to almost 77% (Slovenia) of the euro area average in emerging Europe, and from 8% (Vietnam) to about 88% (Hong Kong) of the US average in emerging Asia. Broadly speaking, the newly industrialised Asian countries may be compared to the central and eastern European countries, while the per capita income level in

[9]The GDP per capita is reported in purchasing-power-parity (PPP) adjusted terms.

[10]While all Asian countries increased their population between 1994 and 2006, 10 out of 16 CEE/SEE countries report a decline in population. Furthermore, it should be noted that in 1994 euro area GDP per capita was about USD 20,000 compared with around USD 26,000 in the US. Over the review period, euro area GDP per capita rose by 57%, while growth of US GDP per capita reached 65%.

[11]However, the relative income position of Korea, although strongly affected by the crisis, increased by almost 30% in the review period.

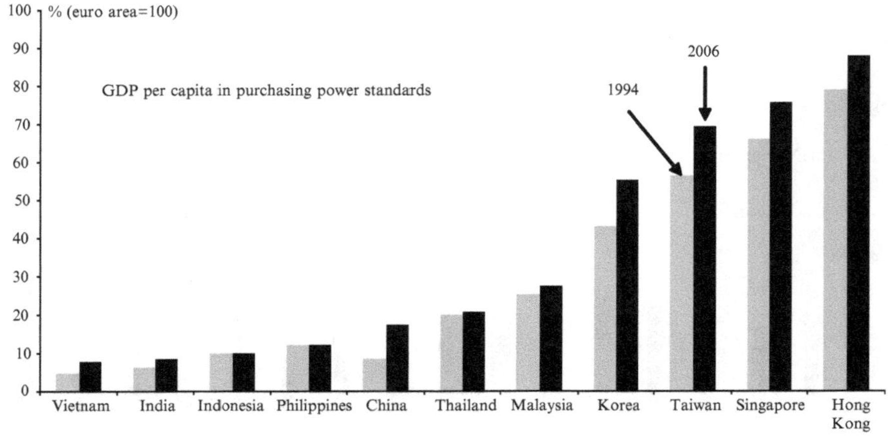

Fig. 8.2 GDP per capita in emerging Asia, 1994/2006
Source: IMF

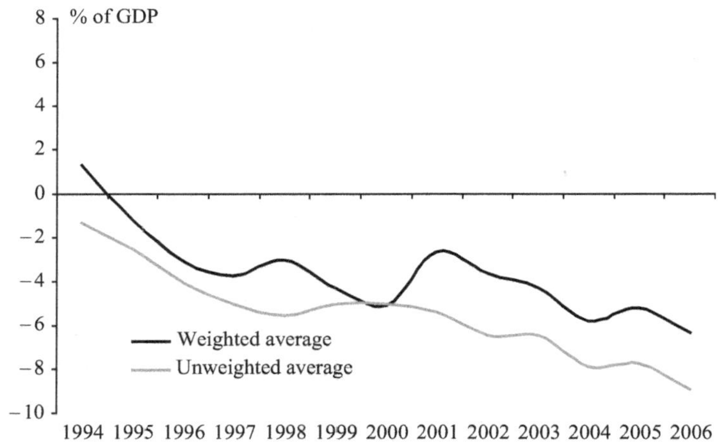

Fig. 8.3 Current account balances in emerging Europe, 1994–2006
Source: IMF

developing Asian countries is somewhat lower than in the poorest south-eastern European countries.

In Europe the convergence process has been accompanied by substantial current account deficits (Fig. 8.3).[12] Between 1994 and 2006, only seven countries recorded

[12]In general, smaller countries recorded higher current account imbalances, explaining the wedge between the weighted and non-weighted average of current account balances in Figures 3.1.5 and 3.1.6.

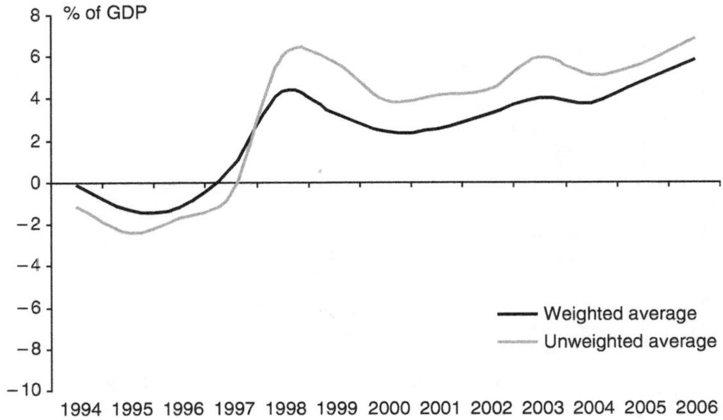

Fig. 8.4 Current account balances in emerging Asia, 1994–2006
Source: IMF

1 or 2 years with current account surpluses, either in the mid-1990s or as part of an adjustment process after a period of financial turbulence.

By contrast, Asian countries show, on average, a positive current account position in most of the years under consideration (Fig. 8.4). The 1997 financial crisis marks a clear turning point, as five countries, Indonesia, Malaysia, Thailand, Hong Kong and Korea, saw a shift from deficits to sustained surpluses. China, Singapore and Taiwan recorded current account surpluses over the whole review period, while developments in the remaining countries have been more heterogeneous.

In both samples (Figs. 8.5 and 8.6), a higher per capita income[13] – relative to the core – has been associated with an improving current account position (correlation coefficient Europe: 0.3, Asia: 0.6), which is in line with the predictions of standard theory. However, there is a strong level effect which distinguishes the European from the Asian sample. In emerging Asia, even countries with a comparatively low per capita income have not borrowed abroad to raise present consumption based on the expectation that income will rise in future.

In both samples, a negative correlation (correlation coefficient Europe: −0.6, Asia: −0.2) between growth and the current account balance can be observed (Figs. 8.7 and 8.8). Thus, within the peripheries patterns are in line with the predictions of standard theory, suggesting a positive correlation between net capital inflows and growth (Prasad et al. 2007). However, there is again a significant level effect between the two regions, as in emerging Asia even the fastest growing countries have not been characterized by significant current account deficits, but mainly by smaller surpluses.[14]

[13]If not explicitly mentioned differently, GDP per capita figures are in PPP terms.

[14]On a global scale, Gourinchas and Jeanne (2007) found that capital flows have been more pronounced to emerging market countries with – on average – lower rates of growth. Like the

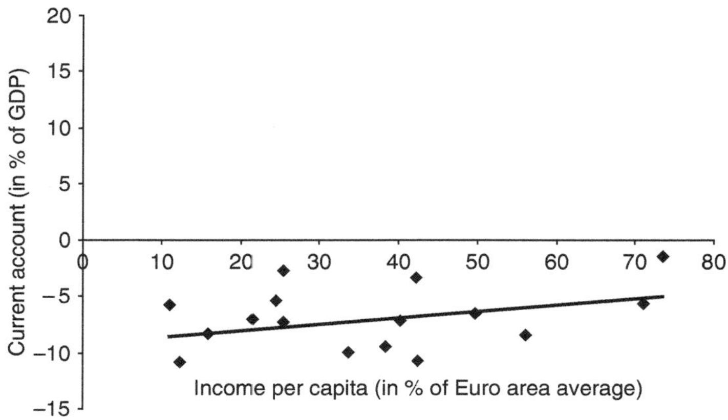

Fig. 8.5 Current account balances and relative income per capita in emerging Europe, averages 1994–2006
Source: IMF

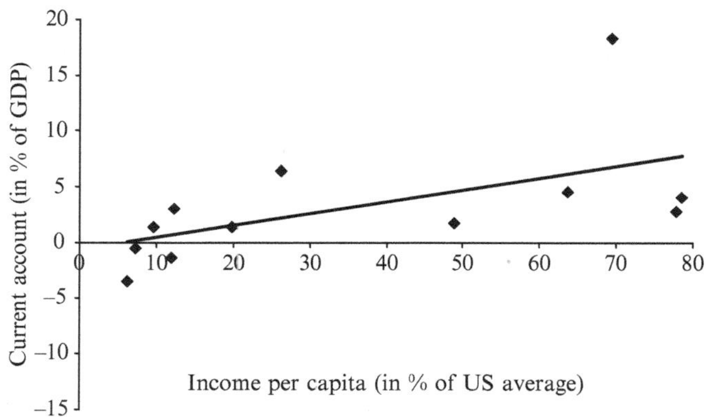

Fig. 8.6 Current account balances and relative income per capita in emerging Asia, averages 1994–2006
Source: IMF

A closer look at the sub-balances of the current account reveals that in emerging Europe trade balances have been negative in all countries under consideration. Moreover, large transfers in the form of remittances (Albania, Bosnia and Herzegovina and FYR Macedonia) or a strong service balance, also reflecting substantial tourism revenues (Croatia, Turkey), reduced current account compared with trade

Lucas paradox, this contradicts the predictions of standard economic theory, which is why they refer to the empirical evidence as the *allocation puzzle*.

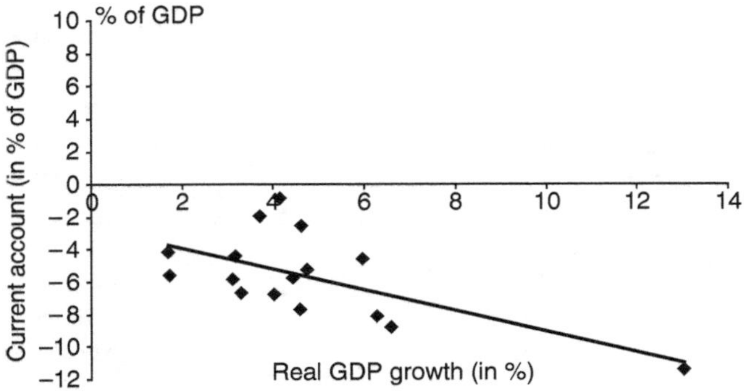

Fig. 8.7 Current account balances and real GDP growth in emerging Europe, averages 1994–2006
Source: IMF

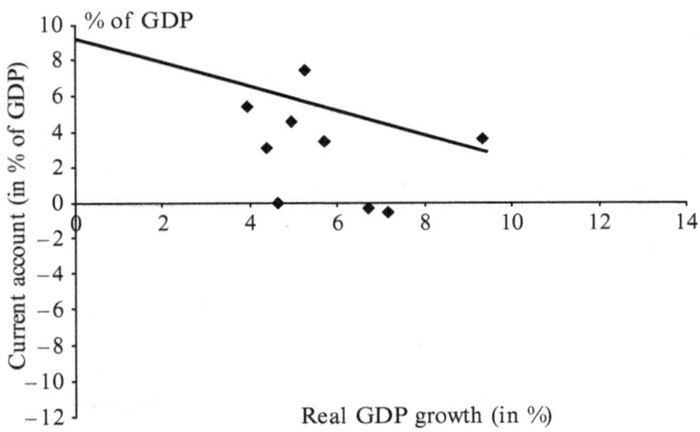

Fig. 8.8 Current account balances and real GDP growth in emerging Europe, averages 1999–2006
Source: IMF

deficits.[15] In emerging Asia, a more heterogeneous picture emerges. While six countries have been recording – on average – trade balance surpluses, trade balances in Hong Kong, India, Philippines and Vietnam have been – on average – negative. In all trade surplus countries except Singapore, pronounced deficits in the service or income balances – mainly due to retained earnings of foreign-owned

[15] In Hungary and the Czech Republic a negative income balance has contributed significantly to the current account deficit. Furthermore, in most European countries the income balance has been worsening over time, indicating that non-distributed earnings of foreign-owned firms might have played an increasing role in these countries.

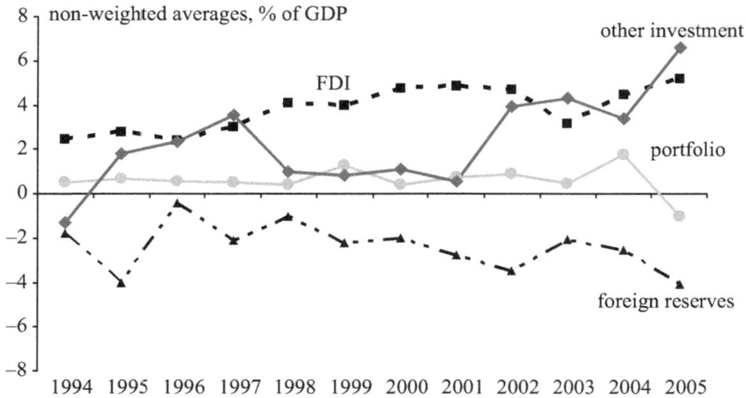

Fig. 8.9 Main counterparts of the current account in emerging Europe, 1994– 2005
Source: IMF

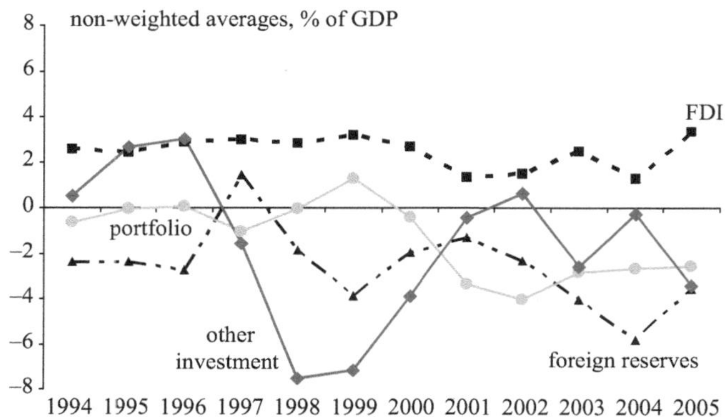

Fig. 8.10 Main counterparts of the current account in emerging Asia, 1994–2005
Source: IMF

firms – can be observed. By contrast, in all countries with a trade deficit, the current account deficit was considerably smaller.[16]

Current account developments are reflected in the financial account balance (Figs. 8.9 and 8.10). In emerging Europe, net non-weighted average FDI inflows increased almost continuously from 2.5% of GDP in 1994 to 5.2% of GDP in 2005. There has been a steep increase in other investment, mainly in the form of loans, since the early 2000s, amounting to 6.6% of GDP at the end of 2005. Portfolio

[16]Hong Kong even recorded a trade deficit and a current account surplus due to a strong service balance. In the other deficit countries, transfers in the form of remittances have played a major role, in particular in the case of the Philippines, the only country in emerging Asia showing a pronounced trade deficit (on average it corresponds to approximately 9% of GDP).

inflows have been small and rather stable. In total, net private capital inflows surpassed the level of current account deficits, which is reflected in substantial reserve accumulation by the monetary authorities.

In emerging Asia, non-weighted average net FDI inflows, expressed as a percentage of non-weighted average GDP, have been relatively stable, fluctuating around the 2% mark. By contrast, other investment flows have been highly volatile. While net inflows had accelerated before the Asian crisis, there were substantial outflows in the post-crisis period. Net portfolio flows, which had been marginal in the mid to late 1990s, have recorded outflows of more than 2% of GDP since 2000. Following a substantial loss of reserves in 1997, rapid reserve accumulation has been a feature in all countries exposed to the crisis. More recently, however, the pronounced foreign reserve build-up has been largely due to China.

In emerging Europe, current account deficits have mainly been a reflection of rising investment (Fig. 8.11), while in emerging Asia (Fig. 8.12), the current account surpluses that emerged after the financial crisis were almost entirely due to a decline in investment (*investment drought*). The strong rise in the weighted savings rate in Asia is almost exclusively due to developments in China, where public sector saving in particular has been continuously increasing over time (*public savings glut*).

In the following, we evaluate whether the characteristics of the financial markets might have an important bearing on the development of the current account and to what extent they can explain divergent external balances in emerging Europe and Asia. This is done, first, by reviewing the literature, second, by pointing out the main characteristics of financial sector developments in both regions and third, by running the empirical estimations.

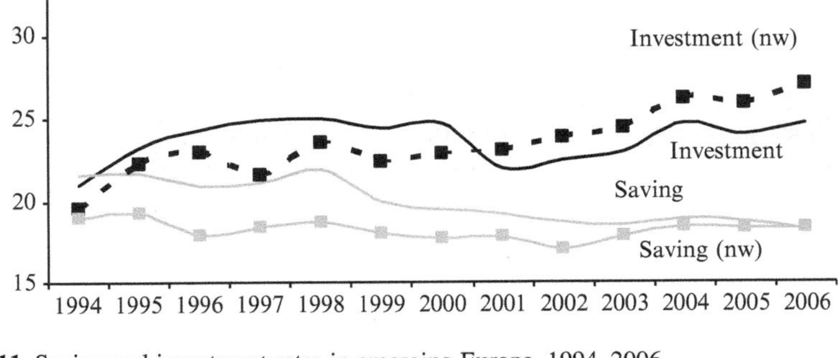

Fig. 8.11 Saving and investment rates in emerging Europe, 1994–2006
Source: IMF

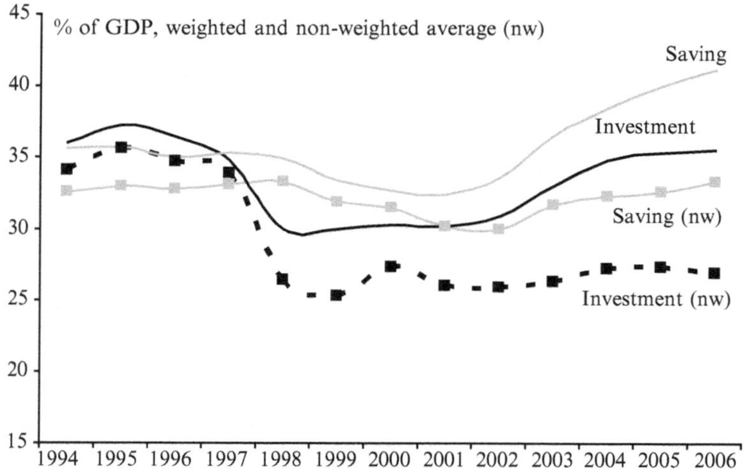

Fig. 8.12 Saving and investment rates in emerging Asia, 1994–2006
Source: IMF

8.4 Current Account Developments and the Financial Sector: A Review of the Literature

In recent years, a broad consensus has emerged in the literature that underdeveloped and weak financial markets represent one factor explaining why many emerging markets have not recorded substantial current account deficits as predicted by standard theory.[17] Underdeveloped and weak domestic financial markets hamper emerging markets' ability to transform domestic savings into domestic investment and to engage in substantial foreign borrowing. Thus, emerging markets with underdeveloped financial markets will – in principle – invest less than predicted by standard theory and hence will show a tendency towards current account surpluses.

Financial development is difficult to quantify. In the literature a low degree of financial development has been associated with

- A low level of financial intermediation and financial sector quality
- A strong accumulation of foreign exchange reserves, serving as a signalling and shock-absorbing device substituting for highly developed financial markets
- A limited ability to engage in international financial integration

[17]By contrast, most of the traditional literature neglected financial sector development as a potential determinant of the current account balance (Gosh and Ostry 1992).

Concretely, three approaches linking underdeveloped financial markets with current account developments in emerging markets can be distinguished.

1. *Financial intermediation and financial sector quality*. Underdeveloped financial sectors are seen as an impediment to emerging economies converting domestic savings and capital inflows into high-quality assets and thus investment, creating a shortage of assets (Caballero 2006). As a result, financial capital flows *uphill*, i.e. from emerging to mature markets where funds can be invested in a stronger institutional setting offering higher returns.[18] This might lead to current account surpluses in emerging economies despite their low capital–labour-ratios. As financial development would induce a rise in domestic investment, a higher degree of financial intermediation and financial sector quality should be associated with a deterioration in the current account (Clarida 2005).
2. *Built-up of foreign exchange reserves*. The *precautionary savings view* (Aizenman 2007) identifies foreign exchange reserve accumulation by emerging market economies as a substitute for developed financial markets in absorbing terms of trade shocks. Episodes of financial crisis reveal financial sector weaknesses in emerging economies and reinforce the need to build up foreign reserves. The *new mercantilist view* (Dooley et al. 2007) claims that financial markets in emerging economies are unable to integrate with the global financial system because they lack credibility. To gain credibility, emerging markets have to accumulate foreign assets, mainly foreign exchange reserves. These assets, placed at the core of the convergence club, serve as collateral for private capital inflows from mature markets, mainly in the form of FDI.
3. *Financial integration*. Underdeveloped financial sectors are regarded as a major obstacle to the financial sector's international integration, which hampers borrowing abroad and thus weakens the link between income convergence and the current account. Vice versa, a high degree of financial integration, like that achieved in Europe for example (Abiad et al. 2007), allows catching-up economies to run sizeable current account deficits.[19]

The literature suggests that a lack of financial development is a key obstacle to emerging markets engaging in consumption-smoothing activities, thereby affecting the current account. Before empirically testing the various propositions associated with the different dimensions of financial sector development for the two peripheries under review, we point out the main characteristics of financial sector developments in both regions.

---

[18]This idea is similar to the approach of Ju and Wei (2007), assuming that underdeveloped financial sectors are by-passed by economic agents through integrating with mature market economies.

[19]However, financial integration may also support behaviour in line with the Lucas paradox, if it is a precondition for emerging market economies to invest in mature financial markets (Greenspan 2003).

8.5 Financial Development: Emerging Europe Versus Emerging Asia

Standard indicators of financial sector quality, i.e. the intermediation (credit to the private sector relative to GDP, Fig. 8.13) and monetisation ratios (M2 to GDP, Fig. 8.14), suggest that financial sectors in emerging Asia are more advanced than in emerging Europe. On average, private sector credit – as a percentage of GDP – and the M2 to GDP ratio are approximately twice as high in emerging Asia as in the European sample. Over the review period, the monetisation ratio increased in both regions, more strongly in emerging Asia after the financial crisis. By contrast, the intermediation ratio dropped by about 10% points in Asia after the financial crisis and then showed a high degree of stability, while private sector credit has been increasing rapidly in emerging Europe after 2002.[20]

While capturing financial sector quality by quantitative indicators is inherently difficult, the available evidence on non-performing loans and lending-deposit spreads, loan quality and banking sector efficiency suggests an improvement in both indicators over time in both regions (Figs. 8.15 and 8.16).[21]

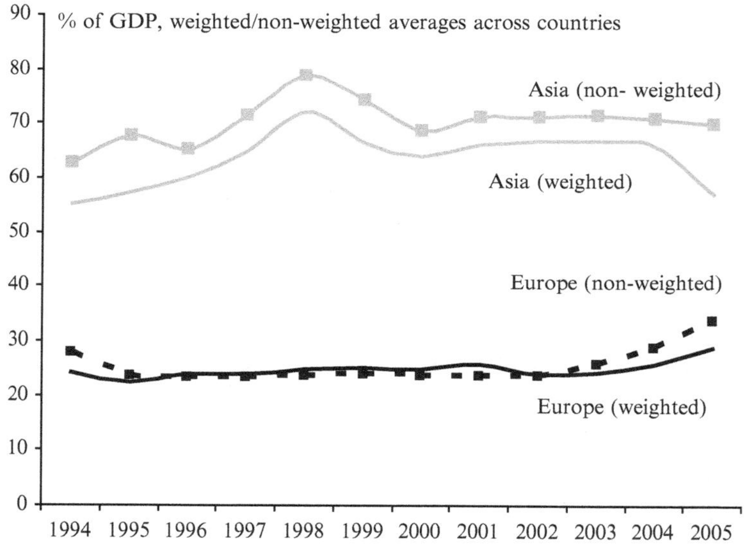

Fig. 8.13 Private credit in emerging Europe/Asia, 1994–2005
Source: IMF

[20]Standard indicators of financial development might fail to capture the borrowing constraints businesses and households effectively face (IMF 2006).

[21]It should be noted that in emerging Europe, due to a high level of asset substitution on the banks' asset as well as liability side (ECB 2007), the spread of local currency interest rates may be less important than the spread on foreign currency loans and deposits.

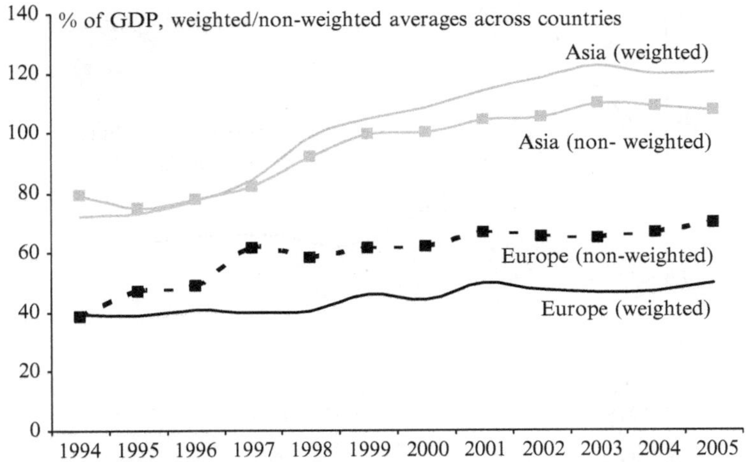

Fig. 8.14 M2 in emerging Europe/Asia, 1994–2005
Source: IMF

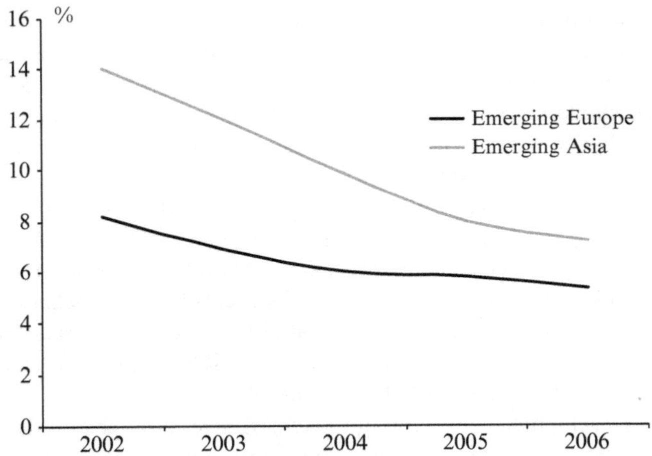

Fig. 8.15 Non-performing loans to total loans in emerging Europe and Asia
Source: IMF

A low level of financial sector quality and poor governance of financial institutions are most clearly displayed in times of financial sector crisis (Caprio and Klingebiel 1996). Countries in both peripheries have been facing financial crises, in particular in the first part of the review period, with the Asian financial crisis being the most pronounced.

According to the new mercantilist/precautionary savings view, emerging market economies accumulate foreign exchange reserves to compensate for underdeveloped financial markets. Thus, the size of foreign exchange reserves may serve as an

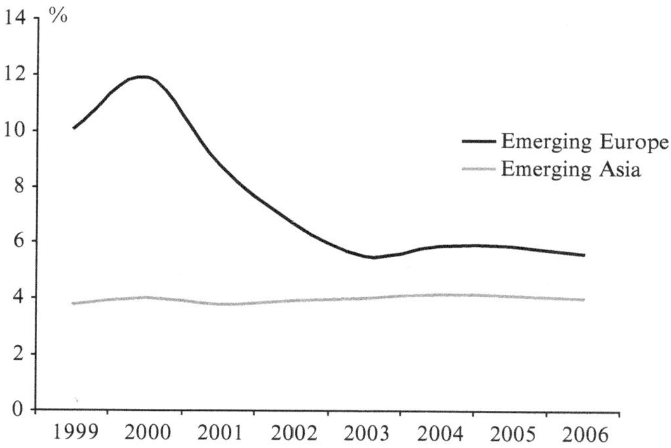

Fig. 8.16 Spread lending/deposit rate in emerging Europe and Asia
Notes: Excluding Bosnia and Herzegovina (2001), Vietnam (2004), Lithuania (2005/2006), FYR of Macedonia, and Poland (2006)
Source: IMF

indicator of domestic financial development. Emerging Asia has been experiencing a substantial rise in foreign exchange reserves since the 1997 financial crisis, most notably in China. A similar tendency, albeit on a significantly smaller scale in absolute US dollar terms, can also be observed in most emerging European countries.

Foreign exchange interventions and the associated build-up of foreign exchange reserves may also reflect countries' preferences for stable real effective exchange rates, either in the framework of an explicit export-led growth strategy or as a means of compensating for underdeveloped financial markets. Figures 8.17 and 8.18 depict developments of real effective exchange rates in the peripheries of both convergence clubs. In emerging Europe, developments have been characterised – in principle – by a trend appreciation of the real effective exchange rate. In emerging Asia the impact of the financial crisis is clearly visible, with significant appreciations after 1997 being limited to Indonesia and Korea.

Financial development and foreign exchange reserve accumulation in the regions under review have been taking place in different environments with respect to the openness of their financial sectors (Fig. 8.19).[22] For the period 1998–2005 the Chinn/Ito index,[23] in which higher values indicate a greater degree of financial openness, depicts a continuous liberalisation in emerging Europe, including an acceleration since 2000. This reflects the process of capital account liberalisation, a key criterion for accession to the European Union.[24] By contrast, the index values

[22]See Kose et al. (2006) and IMF (2007) for a review of financial globalisation and liberalisation.

[23]See Chinn and Ito (2007).

[24]Capital account liberalisation is part of the *acquis communautaire*, the body of legislation of the European Union, which candidate countries must accept before they can join the EU.

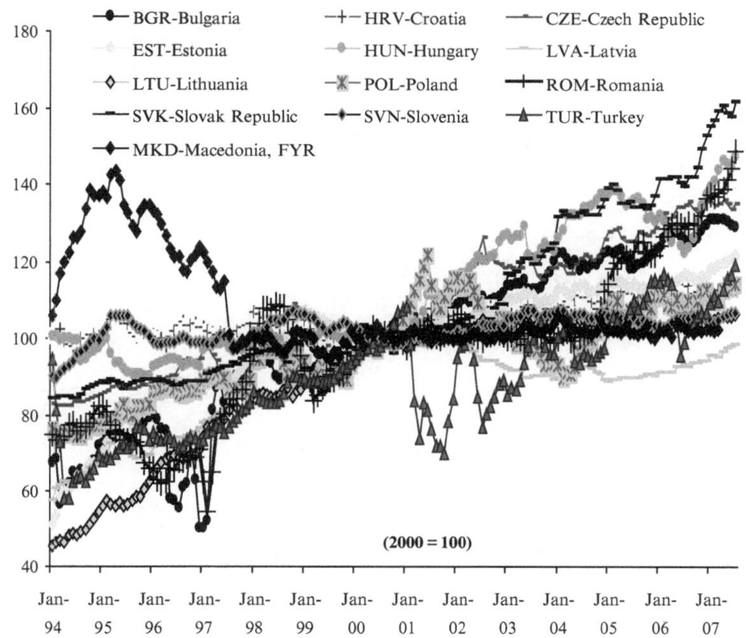

Fig. 8.17 Real effective exchange rates in emerging Europe
Source: IMF

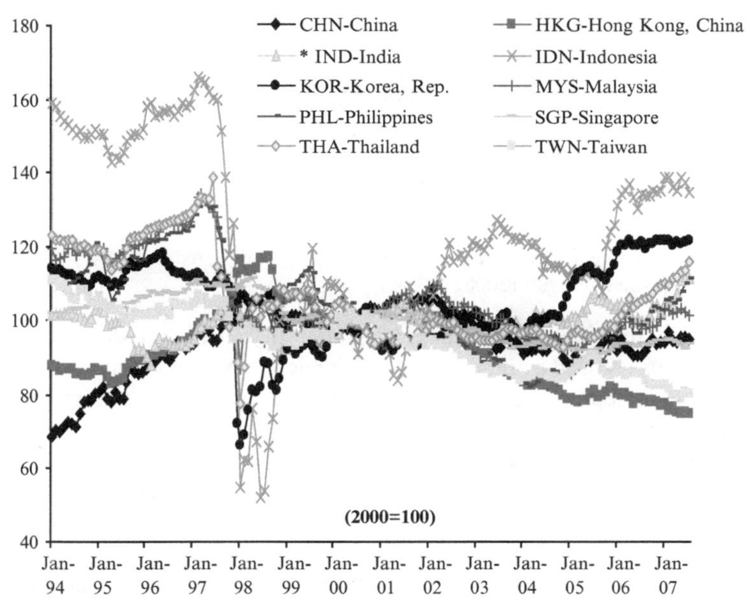

Fig. 8.18 Real effective exchange rates in emerging Asia
Source: IMF

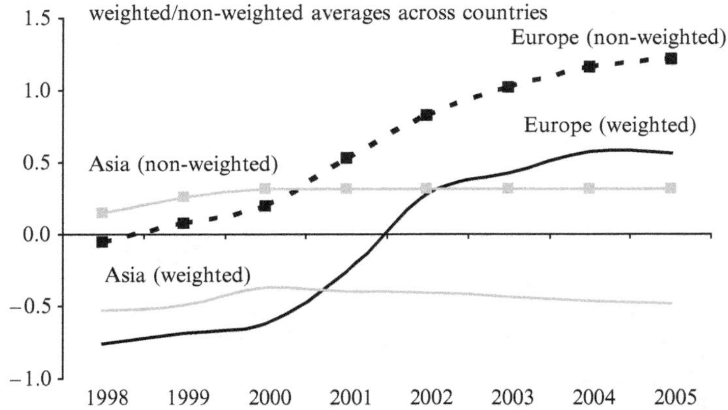

Fig. 8.19 Chinn-Ito-index in emerging Europe/Asia, 1998–2005
Source: Chinn and Ito (2007)

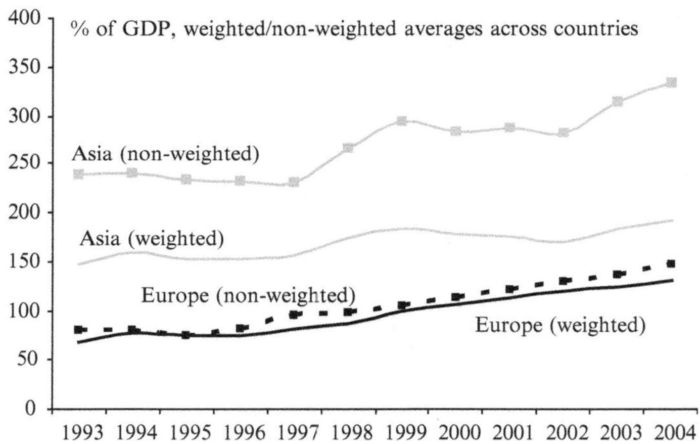

Fig. 8.20 Sum of foreign assets and liabilities in emerging Europe/Asia, 1993–2004
Source: Lane and Milesi-Ferretti (2006)

for emerging Asia show a high degree of stability. Thus, at the end of 2005, emerging Europe showed a higher degree of financial openness than emerging Asia.

Turning to the degree of actual financial integration, as measured by the sum of outstanding foreign assets and liabilities divided by GDP, emerging Europe has been engaged in a steady process of financial integration (Fig. 8.20).[25] Thus, actual financial integration has followed greater openness with respect to regulatory

[25]We focus on quantity-based measures of financial integration, as price-based indicators are more vulnerable to bias from common factors or and/or similarities in fundamentals (Baltzer et al. 2007).

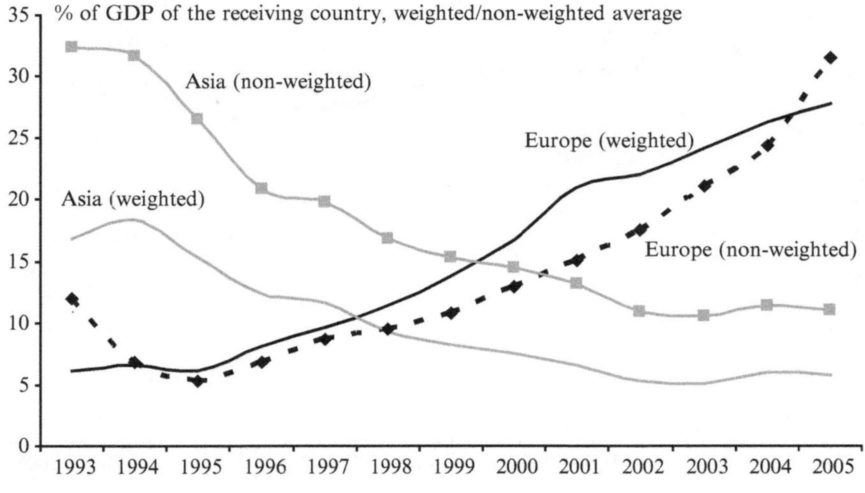

Fig. 8.21 Consolidated euro area/US bank claims in emerging Europe/Asia, 1993–2005
Source: BIS, IMF

restrictions. In terms of levels, however, on average, the sum of foreign assets and liabilities held by emerging European countries – expressed as a percentage of GDP – is still lower than in emerging Asia.[26]

Within the convergence clubs, financial integration has been much higher in Europe than in Asia according to the benchmark of consolidated foreign claims of BIS reporting banks in the euro area and United States on the respective periphery regions. These claims, expressed as a percentage of the respective region's (weighted/unweighted) GDP, have been increasing continuously over the review period in emerging Europe, but have trended downward in emerging Asia (Fig. 8.21).

In 2005, the weighted average of BIS reporting euro area banks' consolidated claims on emerging Europe accounted for approximately 28% of the region's GDP, while the respective figure for BIS reporting US banks' consolidated claims on emerging Asia added up to only 6% of the region's GDP. Moreover, there is evidence suggesting that intra-club financial integration has been much more prominent as a means of achieving overall financial integration in the case of emerging Europe. Euro area banks account for the bulk of total consolidated claims on emerging Europe, while US banks' share of total claims on emerging Asia has been declining for most of the observation period (Fig. 8.22).

[26] Thus, the evidence provided by Abiad et al. (2007) suggesting an extraordinary degree of financial integration in Europe is largely driven by cross-border asset accumulation in the core. According to this approach, Europe is financially much more integrated than Asia, as the sum of European economies' foreign assets and liabilities, expressed as a percentage of GDP (weighted average), is almost twice as high at the end of the current observation period as in emerging Asia.

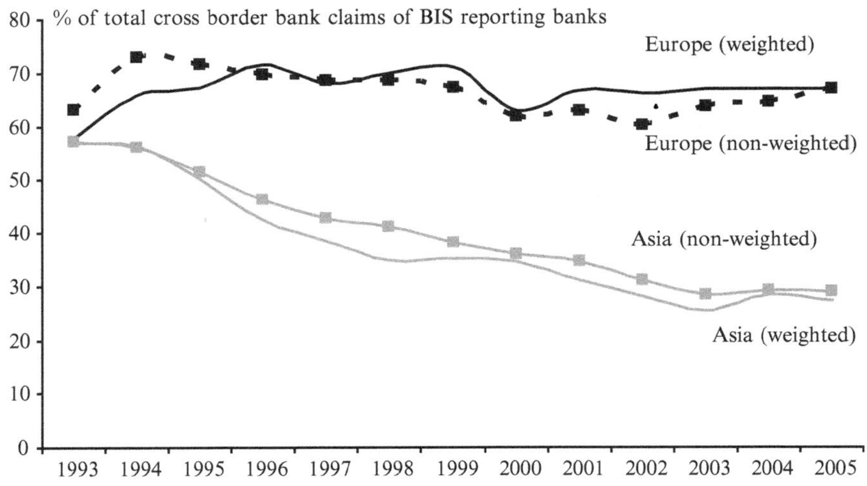

Fig. 8.22 Consolidated euro area/US bank claims in emerging Europe/Asia, 1993–2005
Source: BIS, IMF

Intra-club financial integration in Europe has also advanced in the form of foreign-owned banks', i.e. euro area banks' massive entry into emerging European banking sectors.[27]

The share of banking sector assets held by foreign-owned banks increased steadily in emerging Europe (Fig. 8.23) from 1995 to 2006, as foreign banks became the driving force of financial development in emerging Europe. They accounted for roughly 75% of total banking assets at the end of 2006 (non-weighted terms). By contrast, financial development in emerging Asia continues to be largely based on domestic institutions.

In the following section, we test empirically whether the various indicators of financial development and financial integration are significant in explaining the strikingly different current account developments in emerging Europe and Asia.

8.6 Current Account Balances and the Financial Sector: An Empirical Investigation

The database covers 27 emerging markets in Europe and Asia, namely the 16 countries in central, eastern and south-eastern Europe and 11 developing and newly industrialised Asian economies from 1994 to 2006. The estimation results

[27] See also ECB (2007).

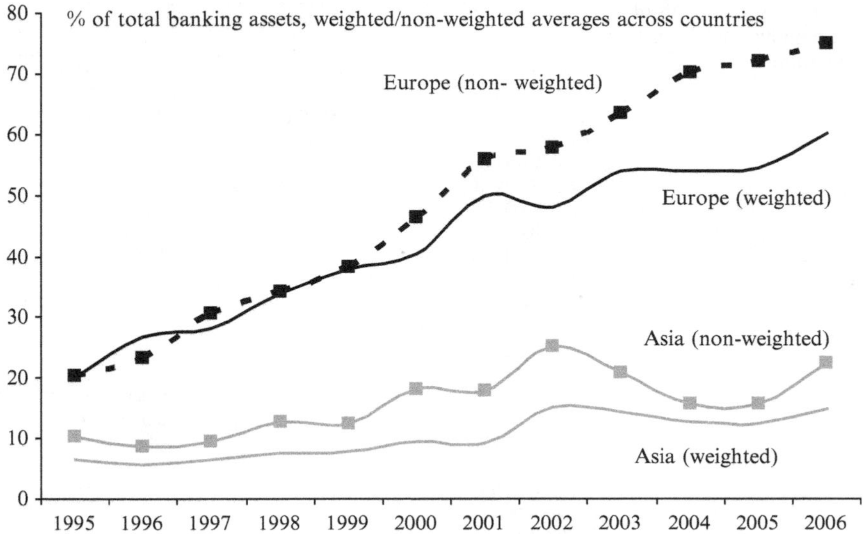

Fig. 8.23 Foreign bank assets in emerging Europe/Asia, 1995–2006
Source: World Bank, EBRD

are presented in Table 8.1. (For a detailed description of the models and the estimation techniques see Herrmann and Winkler 2009).[28]

The results stress the importance of the domestic macroeconomic variables and confirm the expected coefficients. Countries in emerging Europe and emerging Asia experiencing more pronounced income growth (relative to the core country) are found to record higher current account deficits or lower surpluses. Moreover, as in Masson et al. (1998) and Chinn and Prasad (2003), countries with a higher dependency ratio show a higher current account deficit. Furthermore, larger gross inflows of capital as well as stronger FDI inflows, both expressed as a percentage of GDP of the recipient country, increase the current account deficit significantly. Our hypothesis is that foreign capital acts as a major source of investment funding. In doing so, the impact of FDI on the current account seems to be remarkably stronger than the influence of capital inflows in general.

[28]The following variables are part of the empirical investigation: INCOME: country´s relative GDP per capita (PPP); DEPENDENCY: dependency ratio; CAPITAL: gross capital flows (as % of GDP); FDIGDP: FDI (as % of GDP); RESERVES: stock of foreign exchange reserves (as % of GDP); EXCHANGE: real effective exchange rate (log.); CREDIT: private credit (as % of GDP); CRISIS: banking crisis index; CHINN_ITO: capital account openness index; OVERALL INTEGRATION: foreign assets plus liabilities (as % of GDP); INTRA INTEGRATION: consolidated cross border banking claims of euro area/US banks on an emerging country (as % of GDP of the recipient country); FOREIGN BANKING: foreign-owned banking assets (as % of total banking sector assets in the periphery country).

Table 8.1 Determinants of the current account – results of the estimations

	Basic model	Financial development model
D(INCOME)	−0.506 (−2.74)***	−1.163 (−9.03)***
DEPENDENCY	−20.220 (−2.25)**	−33.483 (−2.00)**
CAPITAL (−1)	−0.080 (−3.55)***	−0.048 (−3.39)***
FDIGDP (−1)	−0.151 (−2.97)***	−0.199 (−4.27)***
RESERVES		0.253 (7.73)***
EXCHANGE		−0.311 (−0.23)
D(CREDIT)		−9.226 (−3.70)***
M2GDP		−0.031 (−1.76)*
CRISIS (−1)		1.880 (4.25)***
D(CHINN_ITO)		−0.337 (−1.26)
OVERALL INTEGRATION		−0.017 (−2.54)***
INTRA INTEGRATION		−0.154 (−3.60)***
FOREIGN BANKING		−0.086 (−3.13)***
Interaction term: Overall Integration *Income		0.0003 (3.66)***
Interaction term: Intra Integration *Income		0.001 (1.61)*
Interaction term: Foreign Banking *Income		0.001 (1.88)*

Notes: ***, **, * denote significance at the 1%, 5%, 10% level, respectively; t-values in parentheses

In addition, the estimation confirms – in accordance with Chinn and Ito (2007) – that financial markets do matter for saving and investment decisions. This is indicated by significant negative coefficients of real credit growth and the M2 ratio on the current account balance.[29] We assume this relationship to hold because more developed financial markets allow emerging economies to invest more due to a more sophisticated financial intermediation. Furthermore, the experience of a banking crisis seems to be an incentive for countries to run current account surpluses. This result supports the empirical findings of Gruber and Kamin (2005), implying that recent patterns of current account surpluses in emerging Asia can be linked to the financial crisis of 1997. In addition, a higher stock of foreign exchange reserves is significantly linked with an improvement in the current account balance in both model specifications. By contrast, we find that an appreciation of the real effective exchange rate, while being associated with a higher current account deficit (lower current account surplus), is not significant.

[29]As the private credit to GDP ratio has been differentiated, the variable represents the change in the private credit to GDP ratio.

The model confirms that all indicators of financial integration are negatively correlated with the external balance, with only the Chinn/Ito index failing to be significant. Thus, the model lends support to the hypothesis that the degree of overall financial integration, the extent of financial integration within the convergence clubs and the penetration of foreign banks into domestic banking sectors matter for developments in the current account balance. This result is in line with the findings of Chinn and Ito (2007) that a greater degree of financial openness is typically associated with a smaller current account balance in developing countries. It is also consistent with the results of Abiad et al. (2007), suggesting that financial integration in Europe is a major reason for capital flowing downhill from rich to poor.

Finally, all variables representing the de facto degree of financial integration interact positively and significantly with the relative income level. Two major results arise:

- First, the relationship between financial integration and the current account depends on the level of income. As a result, the parameter of overall financial integration (−0.0169 + 0.0003* per capita income), intra-regional financial integration (−0.1543 + 0.001* per capita income) and foreign banking asset share (−0.0864 + 0.001* per capita income) is negative for low-income countries and positive for high-income countries. Thus, in line with the findings of Abiad et al. (2007), a higher level of financial integration leads to an increased dispersion of current account balances, as – given a certain income level – deficits and surpluses will be larger compared with a situation in which there is a low level of financial integration.
- Second, the degree of financial integration has a positive impact on the link between the relative income position and the current account, as a higher level of financial integration contributes to a higher income coefficient (0.0003* overall financial integration +0.001* intra-regional financial integration + 0.001* foreign banking asset share). Thus, depending on the underlying relationship between per capita income and the current account, a higher degree of financial integration will either strengthen consumption-smoothing behaviour or be associated with a shift in the underlying relationship between relative per capita income and the current account from the Lucas paradox to consumption-smoothing.

Overall, our analysis indicates that more developed financial systems in emerging economies and deeper financial integration are associated with a deteriorating current account balance. Thus, at the current income level of the countries under review, financial development and integration seem to enhance countries' ability to perform consumption-smoothing activities. This might imply that more developed financial sectors and deeper financial integration allowed these countries to increase consumption relative to the baseline scenario with a less developed financial system and a lower degree of financial integration. The concomitant decrease in the saving ratio may result in a negative saving ratio, i.e. consumption is financed by capital flows from abroad based on expectations of higher income in future.

As a further step, we perform a contribution analysis that provides information on the economic significance of the estimated variables. In particular, we estimate the contributions of the individual variables to the current account balances as a percentage of GDP for the average of the European and Asian samples between 1994 and 2006.[30] As a result, the analysis reveals the extent to which financial development and integration give rise to different current account developments in emerging Europe and Asia.

Except for 1998/1999, the post-financial crisis years, and 2001, the change in relative per capita income (INCOME) contributes negatively to the current account in both peripheries. In emerging Europe the income effect gains strength in the second half of the observation period due to a more rapid convergence process. In 2006, around 2% points of the current account deficits in emerging Europe can be traced to the rapid catching-up of per capita income levels compared with the euro area. These results indicate that – based on their lower relative income compared with the core – both regions smooth their consumption via the inflow of capital flowing downhill from rich to poor and "financing" the catching-up process in the countries under review. However, in Asia, this negative effect of the relative income position on the current account is compensated by the impact of other variables, leading in total to net capital outflows.

In both samples, the demographic situation (DEPENDENCY) has a strongly negative impact on current account developments. The impact, the size of which is almost equal in both peripheries, declines slightly over time, as the ratio of the non-working population to the working population has been decreasing in both regions under review. However, at the current end of the sample, the ratio still accounts for more than 15% points of the current account deficit in both samples.

In both regions, a negative current account balance emerges due to size and composition of capital inflows. While the contribution of CAPITAL and FDIGDP was of almost equal size and direction in the years preceding the 1997 Asian financial crisis, since the turn of the century both variables have been contributing to larger current account deficits in emerging Europe relative to emerging Asia. Moreover, compared with other variables, the overall contribution of both variables is rather small.

Due to the strong accumulation of foreign exchange reserves (RESERVES) in emerging Asia, the positive impact of this variable on the current account is substantially more pronounced in Asia. In 2006, reserves account for a current account surplus in emerging Asia of more than 10% of GDP, compared with 5% in emerging Europe in 2006, with the wedge increasing over time. In particular, the much more rapid pace of reserve accumulation in emerging Asia, in particular after 2001, has a sizeable impact on the (lack of) improvement of current account balances in emerging Asia (emerging Europe).

[30]The data result from multiplying the estimated parameters by the annual figures of each factor using the average in the two regions. Thus, the analysis informs about the relative contributions of the various variables to the predicted current account/GDP ratio for both peripheries.

As there has been broad stability of real effective exchange rates (EXCHANGE) since the financial crisis in emerging Asia, the negative contribution of this variable to the predicted current account balance in emerging Asia has been broadly stable as well. By contrast, as emerging Europe has experienced a constant revaluation of the real effective exchange rate over time, the variable slightly reduces the model's prediction of current account balances in emerging Europe.

Strong growth in private sector credit (CREDIT) leads the model to predict slightly larger current account deficits in emerging Europe in the second half of the review period, while a rising M2 to GDP ratio (M2GDP) adds 2% points on the negative side for predicted current account balances in emerging Asia. The impact of the 1997 crisis on current account balances in emerging Asia, which is also seen in other variables, is most visible in the contribution of the banking sector crisis variable (CRISIS), driving the current account into a surplus for several years after the financial crisis. While this is in line with Gruber and Kamin (2005), a comparison of the contribution of the crisis variable to predicted current account balances in both peripheries leads to the conclusion that it does little to help explain the increasing divergence of current account patterns in the two regions under review since the early 2000s.

The results of the contribution analysis also suggest that the divergence in current account patterns in both peripheries cannot be strongly linked to differences in the level of overall financial integration (OVERALL INTEGRATION). Indeed, as emerging Asia has a higher degree of overall financial integration, *ceteris paribus* this variable leads the model to predict higher current account deficits in emerging Asia than in emerging Europe. Moreover, since overall financial integration has increased in both regions over time, the variable does not contribute to the explanation of divergent current account patterns over time. Finally, when assessing the *net* impact of overall financial integration by controlling for the interaction terms, the contribution of overall integration to predicted current account balances is close to zero in both regions.

By contrast, the variables depicting financial integration between the core and the periphery play a key role in explaining the different pattern of current account balances in the two peripheries. This is because the decline in US banks' claims on emerging Asian countries halved the contribution of this variable to predicted current account balances over the review period. Thus, the net impact of the intra-regional financial integration (INTRA INTEGRATION) on current account balances in emerging Asia, again calculated by controlling for the interaction term, is only slightly negative at the end of the review period. By contrast, in emerging Europe the net impact is strongly negative, dropping only slightly from about −7.7 to −6.2% of GDP. The rise of intra-regional financial integration in Europe via the expanding presence of euro area banks (FOREIGN BANKING) in the region has an additional negative impact on current account balances in emerging Europe, which even after controlling for the interaction term, is increasing over time. By contrast, the net effect of the variable FOREIGN BANKING on predicted current account balances in emerging Asia is again close to zero.

8.7 Conclusions

In recent years, financial factors have been identified as key determinants of current account balances in emerging markets. Against this background, we analysed whether financial factors can explain divergent current account developments in the catching-up process of emerging Europe and emerging Asia. In doing this, we took the perspective that emerging Europe and the euro area/EU-15, and emerging Asia and the United States, can be perceived as two different convergence clubs. This allowed us to introduce indicators of financial integration within the convergence clubs as additional explanatory variables.

Our analysis confirms that financial market development and financial integration are important factors in determining current account balances. We find that better developed financial markets and a higher degree of financial integration are generally associated with higher current account deficits/lower current account surpluses. However, several indicators of financial development and financial integration fail to account for the divergent patterns of real convergence and the current account in emerging Europe and emerging Asia. Instead we find that the degree and institutional pattern of financial integration within the convergence clubs – together with the level of foreign exchange reserves – contribute significantly to the model's predictions of strikingly different current account patterns in both regions.

From this we draw the conclusion that the character of financial integration matters when explaining patterns of real convergence and current account balances in emerging markets. Emerging Europe has not been different because it has significantly better developed financial systems or because it is financially more integrated in the global economy than emerging Asia.[31] Rather, emerging Europe has been different because its financial integration with its core has been very different than in emerging Asia. This result can be interpreted as follows:

- European integration has created a very special environment for financial sector quality in emerging Europe,[32] which may not be captured by the standard variables. This may be the reason why their economic relevance in explaining divergent current account patterns in both regions has been rather marginal. The adoption of EU laws and directives has significantly improved financial sector quality in emerging Europe by holding the legal, regulatory and supervisory framework in emerging Europe to the same standard as in the core. Furthermore, the entry of foreign banks has also served as an instrument for improving the quality of domestic banking sectors in the region (Mehl et al. 2006).

[31] At least, this conclusion cannot be drawn when financial development and financial integration are measured by indicators commonly used to account for both factors.

[32] Comparing financial sector development in all transition countries, i.e. including emerging Europe as defined in this paper as well as the CIS, Berglöf and Bolton (2002) use the term "great divide" to stress the different character and environment of financial sector development in transition countries caused by the fact that some countries have an EU accession perspective.

- The European integration process as such may have erased – at least to a large extent – the inherent credibility gap between core and periphery identified by the new mercantilist view. This is because the very process of European integration implies that the periphery (the new EU Member States as well as candidate and potential candidate countries) joins the core by accepting key European institutions, laws and governance practices. This may have given emerging Europe more leeway to run substantial current account deficits and limit reserve accumulation compared with emerging Asia, and could also explain why foreign banks from the euro area/EU-15 have entered the domestic banking sectors in the region. Their presence has channelled funds to the periphery on a large scale and made it easier for emerging European countries to borrow abroad, either directly from their parent banks or indirectly by establishing contacts between companies and parent banks abroad.

To conclude, a peculiar environment conducive to financial integration between core and periphery appears to have allowed emerging Europe to enter a growth path that has been driven by domestic demand, in particular by investment, partly financed by foreign savings. As a result, emerging Europe has shown substantial current account deficits as predicted by standard theory. Of course, rapid financial deepening and the associated current account deficits have important macroeconomic and financial stability implications. (Eichengreen and Choudhry 2005). Thus, while the example of emerging Europe illustrates the impact of financial integration on current account developments in a process of real convergence, it does not imply that this process does not involve risks.

Acknowledgment Excellent research assistance by Silvia Magnoni, Livia Chitu and Michael Grill is gratefully acknowledged. The authors would also like to thank Neeltje van Hooren (World Bank) for data support. The paper has benefited from valuable comments by an anonymous referee, Gerard Korteweg, Heinz Herrmann, Peter Backé and participants in a seminar at the Deutsche Bundesbank, the ECB conference on central, eastern and south-eastern Europe and the ESCB Workshop on Emerging Markets in Helsinki.

Data Appendix

We provide below a listing of mnemonics, sources and descriptions for all the variables included in the empirical investigation. Additionally, we supply a listing of all countries belonging to the Asian and European sample. Unless otherwise noted, data were available from 1994 through 2006.

Mnemonic	Source*	Variable description
CAGDP	WEO	Current account to GDP ratio
CAPITAL	IFS	Gross capital flows (as % of GDP)
CHINN_ITO	CI	Capital account openness index
CREDIT	FSD	Private credit by deposit money banks to GDP ratio
CRISIS	CK	Systemic banking crisis index

(continued)

Mnemonic	Source*	Variable description
DEPENDENCY	IFS	Dependency ratio (dependents to working-age population)
EXCHANGE	BIS	Logarithm of the real effective exchange
EXTERNPOSITION	IFS	Foreign assets minus foreign liabilities to GDP ratio
FDIGDP	IFS	FDI as % of GDP
FOREIGN BANKING	WB	Foreign-owned banking assets (in % of the total banking sector assets in the periphery country)
GOVERNMENT BALANCE	WEO	General government balance to GDP ratio
INCOME	WEO	Country's GDP per capita (PPP terms) to euro area average/US GDP per capita (PPP terms)
INTEREST SPREAD	IFS	Lending rate minus deposit rate
INTRA INTEGRATION	BIS	Consolidated foreign claims of euro area/US banks on the respective emerging country as a percentage of GDP of the recipient country
M2	IFS	M2 to GDP ratio
NPL	GFSR	Non-performing loans to total loans
OVER ALL INTEGRATION	IFS	Foreign assets plus liabilities to GDP ratio
RESERVES	WEO	Stock of foreign exchange reserves at year-end to GDP ratio
RIR	WDI	Real interest rates in %
TOT	WEO	Terms of trade, goods and services
TRADE	WEO	Trade openness (world exports/imports in % of GDP)
STOCKMARKET	WEO	Stock market turnover (shares traded/GDP)
GDP GROWTH	WEO	Real GDP growth rate to euro area average/US

**BIS* Bank for International Settlements, *CI* Chinn/Ito (2007); *CK* Caprio/ Klingebiel (2003); *FSD* World Bank Financial Structure Dataset; *GFSR* IMF Global Financial Stability Report; *IFS* IMF International Financial Statistics; *WB* World Bank (Claessens, Stijn, Neeltje van Horen, Tugba Gurcanlar and Joaquin Mercado (2008); *WDI* World Bank World Development Indicator; *WEO* IMF World Economic Outlook.

Emerging Asian Countries: China (CHN), Hong Kong (HKG), India (IND), Indonesia (IDN), Korea (KOR), Malaysia (MYS), Philippines (PHL), Singapore (SGP), Taiwan (TWN), Thailand (THA), Vietnam (VNM).

Emerging European Countries: Albania (ALB), Bosnia and Herzegovina (BIH), Bulgaria (BGR), Croatia (HRV), Czech Republic (CZE), Estonia (EST), Hungary (HUN), Latvia (LVA), Lithuania (LTU), Macedonia (MKD), Poland (POL), Romania (ROM), Serbia (CS), Slovak Republic (SVK), Slovenia (SVN), Turkey (TUR).

References

Abiad, A., Leigh, D., & Mody, A. (2007). *International finance and income convergence: Europe is different*. IMF Working Paper No. 64, Washington, DC: International Monetary Fund.

Abramovitz, M. (1986). Catching up, forging ahead, and falling behind. *The Journal of Economic History, 46*(2), 385–406.

Aizenman, J. (2007). *Large hoarding of international reserves and the emerging global economic architecture*. NBER Working Paper No. 13277. Cambridge: National Bureau of Economic Research.

Asian Development Bank (2005). Export or domestic demand-led growth in developing Asia? In *Asian Development Outlook 2005*, Manila, Philippines.

Baltzer, M., Cappiello, L., De Santis, R., & Manganelli, S. (2007). *Measuring financial integration in the new EU Member States*. ECB Working Paper, mimeo.

Berglöf, E., & Bolton, P. (2002). The great divide and beyond. Financial architecture in transition. *Journal of Economic Perspective, 16*(1), 77–100.

Bussière, M., Fratzscher, M., & Mueller, G. J. (2004). *Current account dynamics in OECD and EU acceding countries – An intertemporal approach*. ECB Working Paper Series, No. 311, Frankfurt am Main: European Central Bank.

Caballero, R. J. (2006). *On the macroeconomics of asset shortages*. NBER Working Paper, No. 12753, Cambridge: National Bureau of Economic Research.

Caprio, G., & Klingebiel, D. (1996). *Bank insolvencies: Cross-country experience*. World Bank Policy Research Working Paper, No. 1620, Washington, DC: World Bank.

Caprio, G., & Klingebiel, D. (2003). Episodes of Systemic and Borderline Financial Crises, World Bank.

Chinn, M. D. & Ito, H. (2007). *East Asia and global imbalances: Saving, investment, and financial development*. NBER Working Paper, No. 13364. Cambridge: National Bureau of Economic Research.

Chinn, M. D., & Prasad, E. S. (2003). Medium-term determinants of current accounts in industrial and developing countries: An empirical exploration. *Journal of International Economics, 59*(1), 47–76.

Clarida, R. H. (2005). Japan, China, and the U.S. current account deficit. *The Cato Journal, 25*, 111–114.

Claessens, Stijn, Van Horen, Neeltje, Gurcanlar, Tugba and Mercado Sapiain, Joaquin (2008). Foreign Bank Presence in Developing Countries 1995–2006: Data and Trends (March 2008). http://ssrn.com/abstract=1107295

Dooley, M. P., Folkerts-Landau, D., & Garber, P. M. (2007). *The two crises of international economics*. NBER Working Paper, No. 13197, Cambridge: National Bureau of Economic Research.

Eichengreen, B. (2004). *Global imbalances and the lessons of Bretton Woods*. NBER Working Paper, No. 10497. Cambridge: National Bureau of Economic Research.

Eichengreen, B., & Choudhry, O. (2005). *Managing capital flows: Eastern Europe in an Asian mirror*. Berkeley: University of California. unpublished paper.

European Central Bank (2007). Review of the international role of the euro. Frankfurt am Main.

Gosh, A. R., & Ostry, J. D. (1992). *Macroeconomic uncertainty, precautionary savings and the current account*. Working Paper No. 72. Washington, DC: International Monetary Fund.

Gourinchas, P., & Jeanne, O. (2007). *Capital flows to developing countries: The allocation puzzle*. Peterson Institute for International Economics Working Paper 09–12. Washington DC.

Greenspan, A. (2003). Remarks at the 21st annual monetary conference. Cosponsored by the Cato Institute and *The Economist*, Washington, DC, November 20, 2003, http://www.federalreserve.gov/boarddocs/Speeches/2003/20031120/default.htm.

Gruber, J. W., & Kamin, S. B. (2005), *Explaining the global pattern of current account imbalances*. International Finance Discussion Papers No. 846. Washington, DC: Board of Governors of the Federal Reserve System.

Herrmann, S., & Winkler, A. (2009). *Real convergence, financial markets, and the current account – Emerging Europe versus emerging Asia. European Economy*. Economic Papers, No. 362. Brussels: European Commission.

IMF (2006). Private consumption in emerging Asia. *Asia and Pacific Regional Economic Outlook*, September 2006. Washington, DC: International Monetary Fund.

IMF (2007). *Reaping the benefits of financial integration.* IMF Staff Paper. June 2007. Washington, DC: International Monetary Fund.

Ju, J., & Wei, S.-J. (2007). *Domestic institutions and the bypass effect of international capital flows.* Working Paper No. 13148. Cambridge: NBER.

Kose, M. A., Prasad, E., Wei, S.-J., & Rogoff, K. (2006). *Financial globalisation: A reappraisal.* IMF Working Paper No. 06/189. Washington, DC: International Monetary Fund.

Lane, P. R., & Milesi-Ferretti, G. M. (2006). *The external wealth of nations Mark II: Revised and extended estimates of foreign assets and liabilities, 1970–2004.* IMF Working Paper No. 69. Washington, DC: International Monetary Fund.

Lucas, R. (1990). Why doesn't capital flow from rich to poor countries? *American Economic Review, 80*, 93–96.

Masson, P., Bayoumi, T., & Samiei, H. (1998). International evidence on the determinants of private saving. *The World Bank Economic Review, 12*(3), 483–501.

Mehl, A., Vespro, C., & Winkler, A. (2006). Financial sector development in South-Eastern Europe: Quality matters. In K. Liebscher, J. Christl, P. Mosslechner, & D. Ritzberger-Grünwald (Eds.), *Financial development, integration and stability – evidence from Central, Eastern and South-Eastern Europe* (pp. 186–203). UK: Cheltenham.

Prasad, E., Rajan, R., & Subramanian, A. (2007). The paradox of capital. *Finance and Development,* Vol. *44*, No. 1. Washington, DC: International Monetary Fund.

Chapter 9
Sustainable Real Exchange Rates in the New EU Member States: Is FDI a Mixed Blessing?

Jan Babecký, Aleš Bulíř, and Kateřina Šmídková

Abstract This essay focuses on the various macroeconomic opportunities and challenges created by the foreign direct investment (FDI) inflows in the new Member States. We question whether the macroeconomic performance of the new Member States is furthered through the overall positive impact of FDI on the trade balance or whether FDI can actually worsen the performance. Our findings suggest that in some new Member States the positive impact, foreseen by the financial markets, may be reflected in a sustainable appreciation of the real exchange rate. Such real appreciation is in most cases moderate enough to allow for smooth nominal convergence required for euro adoption. In some cases, however, this appreciation is very fast, especially in the new Member States with an initial low net external debt and massive inflows, making it challenging to fulfill the Maastricht criteria. The Maastricht criteria may be difficult to meet also in those new Member States where FDI has been channeled predominantly into services, housing construction, or non-tradable sectors in general, and where it might be required to depreciate currencies in real terms to sustain the external balance. In these countries we observe increasing net external debt without a corresponding improvement in the trade balance.

J. Babecký
Economic Research and Financial Stability Department, Czech National Bank, Prague, Czech Republic
e-mail: Jan.Babecky@cnb.cz

A. Bulíř
IMF Institute, International Monetary Fund, Washington, DC, USA

K. Šmídková
Economic Research and Financial Stability Department, Czech National Bank, Prague, Czech Republic

During our work we benefited from comments by Ignazio Angeloni, Martin Cincibuch, Zdeněk Čech, Carsten Detken, Balázs Égert, Vítor Gaspar, László Halpern, Katarina Juselius, Jan Kodera, Louis Kuijs, Kirsten Lommatzsch, Martin Mandel, Alessandro Rebucci, István P. Székely, Corina Weidinger Sosdean, and participants at seminars at the European Commission, European University Institute, International Monetary Fund, Prague University of Economics, Czech National Bank, and European Central Bank.

F. Keereman and I. Szekely (eds.), *Five Years of an Enlarged EU*,
DOI 10.1007/978-3-642-12516-4_9, © Springer-Verlag Berlin Heidelberg 2010

9.1 Introduction

Five years after the EU 2004 enlargement, the majority of the 12 new member states that joined the EU in May 2004 (the Czech Republic, Cyprus, Estonia, Hungary, Latvia, Lithuania, Malta, Poland, Slovakia, and Slovenia) and in January 2007 (Bulgaria, Romania) are still in the process of catching-up to the EU level of development. The catching-up process may have serious implications for macroeconomic policies of the new Member States. Specifically, it may affect both the sustainable real exchange rates (SRER) and the observed real exchange rates. Developments in the SRER are important variables for fulfilling the Maastricht criteria.

Our essay is motivated by a few selected stylized facts regarding the new Member States and their real exchange rates. First, the currencies of the new Member States currencies have appreciated substantially in real terms during the last decade. On average, the speed of real appreciation was very high at about 5% per year. Second, this appreciation either cannot be attributed to or it appears to contradict such frequently used justifications as excessive devaluation at the start of the transition process (Halpern and Wyplosz 1997); significantly rising total factor productivity in the tradable-good sector due to the Balassa–Samuelson effect (Cincibuch and Podpiera 2006); or the external wealth accumulation hypothesis according to which the new Member States' sizable external liabilities require trade surpluses supported by a depreciated real exchange rate (Lane and Milesi-Ferretti 2002). Third, new Member States have received massive inflows of FDI that may have affected investors' perceptions about the countries' long-term sustainable external balances.

We suggest that FDI is the main culprit in explaining the real exchange rate appreciation, which is otherwise at odds with the above-mentioned traditional explanations for real appreciation (initial disequilibrium, the Balassa–Samuelson effect, and the external wealth accumulation hypothesis). Assuming that export growth and productivity improvements are driven by FDI – as compared to being a simple function of price competitiveness and external demand – contemporaneous capital inflows may signal expected future net export gains consistent with an appreciation in real exchange rates that will be long-lasting and that will sustain external balance. These net export gains are in fact gains from financial integration, and we therefore use the term *integration gain* to refer to them further in the text. Clearly, the real appreciation is sustainable only if the net export gains are sufficient to prevent the increase of net external debt above some safe threshold. Of course, external debt may grow for a number of reasons, one of which is profit repatriation. The simple relationship between the increase in the stock of FDI and improvements in the trade balance in goods is suggestive – the new Member States with the biggest FDI accumulation export more than those with small FDI accumulation (Fig. 9.1).

Hence, on the one hand, the new Member States that are successful in attracting FDI should be able to appreciate their currencies in real terms without jeopardizing the long-term sustainable development of their economies. On the other hand, fast and strong financial integration with the EU can be a mixed blessing for those new

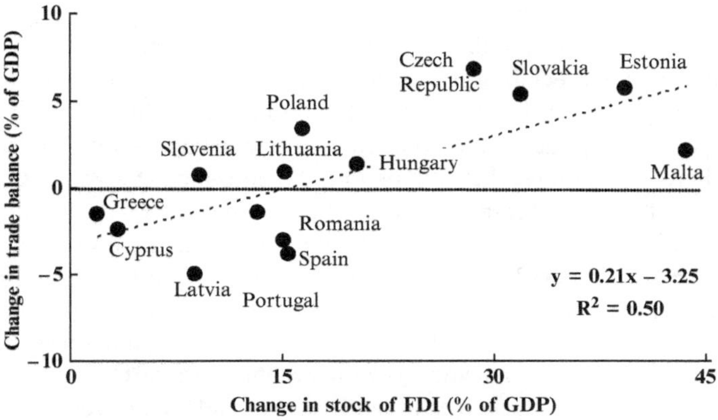

Fig. 9.1 Foreign direct investment is paying off
Notes: Changes are measured between 2001–2007 and 1998–1999. The simple linear regression implies that a 1% point increase in the stock of FDI corresponds to an improvement in the trade balance by 0.2% points. The linear trend is not sensitive to outliers.
Source: *World Economic Outlook*, authors' calculations

Member States that aim at adopting euro soon. For them fast and sustainable medium-term real appreciation may complicate the EMU preparations since it conflicts with the nominal convergence requirements. In contrast, moderate sustainable appreciation may be compatible with the EMU entry preparations in which case financial integration, represented by FDI inflows, is a pure blessing for the recipient new Member States. More difficult to appreciate is the impact on those countries that received FDI predominantly into the nontradable sectors as they may face a ballooning external debt, sizable income outflows on the current account, however, without any corresponding net export improvements. These countries may not view FDI as a blessing at all when approaching the euro adoption.

Monetary policy regimes differ across the sample countries and we therefore study the new Member States within three groups (inflation targeters (IT), hard pegs, euro area members) in order to see the potential impact of the monetary policy strategy on the interaction between the SRER and FDI. We work with the following three groups.

First, there are five IT (the Czech Republic, Hungary, Poland, Romania, and Slovakia) among the new Member States that announce explicit inflation targets and float their exchange rates. For these countries, real appreciation can go through two channels: nominal appreciation and/or higher inflation. However, the second channel is limited by the explicit inflation targets that are close to the definition of price stability used by the European Central Bank.

Second, there are four new Member States (Estonia, Lithuania, Bulgaria, and Latvia) that operate under either a currency board or a hard-peg regime that has not been readjusted for a considerable period of time. These countries have thus only one channel available to appreciate their currency in real terms vis-à-vis the euro, namely a higher inflation differential. As a result, they may have difficulties with the Maastricht criterion for inflation to which the policy response is a lot trickier than that to the volatile nominal exchange rates experienced by the IT. Note, however, that real appreciation is typically computed in effective terms and if the basket of trading partners is not completely dominated by the euro area countries, even hard-peggers can face some nominal effective exchange rate appreciation.

Third, there are three recent entrants into the euro area (Slovenia, Cyprus, and Malta) among the new Member States. (Slovakia has adopted the euro only on January 1, 2009 and is thus included in the inflation targeting groups instead.) We add also three forerunners (Greece, Spain, and Portugal) to this group in order to draw on their experience when discussing the interaction of FDI and the SRER in the new Member States. We select Greece, Portugal and Spain since they are the closest in their GDP levels to the new Member States. Other EU members that were significant receivers of FDI, such as Ireland, were already too developed in the time when our sample starts to form a comparable group (Barry 2000). The size of our sample is 13 countries when we compute the SRER (the full data set is not available for Cyprus and Malta).

There are various approaches to assess the interaction of the FDI and SRER. Empirical papers, especially those based on the time-series, single-equation approach, have been inconclusive with respect to the direction of currency misalignment. While currencies were found overvalued using one set of variables, they were often found balanced or undervalued in another. The puzzling ambiguity was explained by Driver and Westaway (2005), who found that alternative methods of computing equilibrium real exchange rates work with different time horizons and hence most of the differences can be explained away by the horizons of the individual studies. Long-term studies have found transition country currencies typically undervalued, whereas short-term studies have found them mostly without misalignments. We prefer to rely on structural medium-term model of SRER since this is the time horizon relevant for macroeconomic policies.

The starting point for our work is the SRER model. We estimate it for our restricted sample of 13 EU countries based on an updated set of economic fundamentals comparable to our previous research: net external debt, the stock of net FDI, terms of trade, international interest rates, and domestic and external demand variables. It is worth emphasizing that the set of economic fundamentals that determines SRER is broader than in the typical empirical studies of developed, fully-integrated EU economies, namely, the stock of FDI is added to capture the effect of integration gain. To obtain a wide range of plausible SRER estimates we produce them using both the previously estimated elasticities of export and import equations as well as newly produced estimates and calibrations.

We estimate both the current misalignment and future path for the SRER. First, we compute the indicator of misalignment that compares the SRER estimates with the observed values of the real effective exchange rates. This measure can be used to determine whether or not a certain group of the new Member States is more prone to overvaluation or undervaluation of their domestic currencies.

Second, we project the SRER trajectory (conditional on the projection of the fundamental economic variables and on the assumption of the sustainable net external debt) 5 years ahead to pinpoint those countries that may have difficulties with stabilizing both inflation and the nominal exchange rate in the medium-term. Countries with such difficulties are easy to recognize in our framework. One group of affected countries has a sharply downward sloping SRER trajectory implying either fast nominal appreciation, high inflation, or both. The other group has an upward sloping SRER trajectory due to a negative integration gain that would imply a need to either depreciate the domestic currency or deflate the domestic economy by limiting absorption.

Third, we subject our results to robustness tests related to estimated/calibrated parameters as well as exogenous variables projections. This analysis results into interval estimates of both the misalignment indicators and SRER trajectories, allowing us to encompass the various issues relevant for the new Member States. For example, it reflects the idea that once the new Member States are approaching the EMU entry, their risk premium ought to be reduced by financial markets to reflect their new prominent status of the euro area members. It also tackles the problem of normative nature of the SRER, namely the need to define the sustainable level of net external debt. Given the uncertainty of this level, we prefer to work with alternative trajectories, as opposed to a single targeted debt value. The robustness analysis also illustrates that the new Member States may face a less favorable international environment than in the last decade, and hence the real appreciation trends observed so far may not continue in the forthcoming years. Specifically, the analysis shows the potential impact of the current financial crises on the new Member States by estimating the impact of falling foreign demand on the SRER.

Somewhat paradoxically, unfavorable external demand developments are likely to limit the tensions between the preparatory process for the euro adoption and the integration gain in the most successful FDI recipients. Should the external trade environment become less advantageous for the new Member States, slowing demand for their exports, the scope for the sustainable real appreciation may be limited, offsetting the strong positive impact of FDI on trade balance.

We also suggest that the integration gain is likely to be longer-lasting than the medium-term negative effects of misalignment and the periods of sharp sustainable real appreciation. Our analysis focuses on the medium-term when the tradeoffs are likely to be the largest. If the impact of the initial, FDI-driven appreciation coincides with the preparatory process for the euro adoption, the integration-gain benefits may be limited in the medium term as the domestic currency may be pegged to the euro at an unfavorable rate or the costs of nominal convergence may be too high. After the period of medium-term adjustment, the integration gain may start playing a dominant role again. The first wave of the euro adopters and forerunners, such as Portugal or Greece, provide useful lessons for the new Member States in this respect.

9.2 Stylized Facts

Looking at our set of stylized facts, we see that they do not tell the same story for all the new Member States, even though certain trends appear to be common across the whole sample. Our data sample starts in 1995 and goes to 2007 and we use several

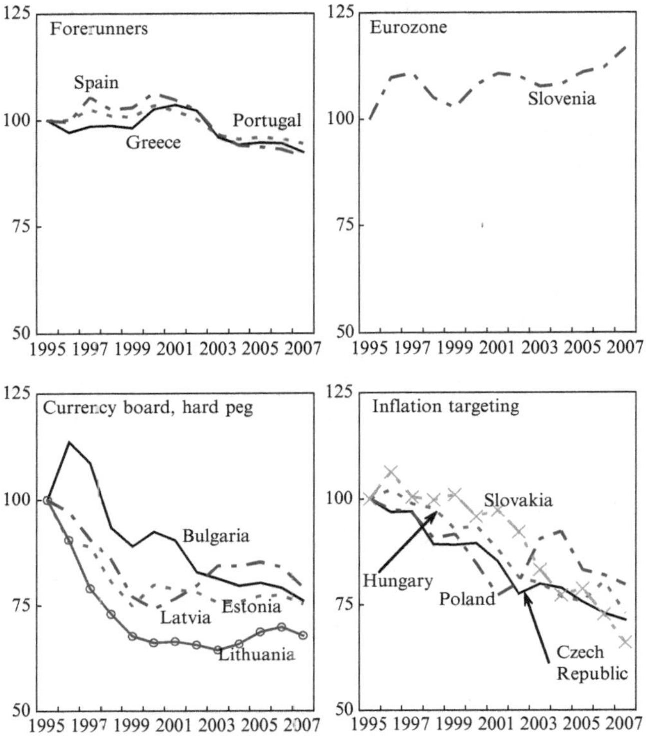

Fig. 9.2 Real effective exchange rates, NiGEM calculation, 1995–2007
Notes: 1995 = 100, decline = appreciation
Source: *NiGEM*

data sources, such as the IMF's International Financial Statistics and World Economic Outlook, EU's AMECO database, NiGEM[1] and Eurostat.[2]

The first common trend is the appreciation of the real effective exchange rate (Fig. 9.2). While all sample countries show some real appreciation during 1995–2007, the speed differs a lot across the sample and it does not seem to be correlated with the choice of a particular monetary policy strategy. Overall, sample-period real appreciation ranged between 10% in the forerunner countries and the early entrants into the eurozone, and 40–80% in the hard-peg and IT countries. As we noted earlier, the monetary policy strategy may limit the scope for alternative channels to effect the real exchange rate appreciation. Inflation performance in our

[1]NiGEM is the large-scale quarterly macroeconomic model of the world economy created and maintained by the London-based National Institute of Economic and Social Research (http://www.niesr.ac.uk). For a description, see National Institute Global Econometric Model (NiGEM 2008).

[2]Detailed description of the data and additional graphs, tables and results are available in the working paper version of this essay (see Babecký et al. 2009).

Table 9.1 Inflation and exchange rate developments (1998–2007)

Inflation					Average annual nominal effective exchange rate change (depreciation: -)
Romania	(1)	25.51	Romania	(1)	−18.65
Hungary	(1)	7.53	Slovenia	(3)	−3.27
Bulgaria	(2)	7.43	Latvia	(2)	−0.82
Slovakia	(1)	6.48	Hungary	(1)	−0.51
Slovenia	(3)	5.66	Greece	(3)	−0.48
Latvia	(2)	4.67	Bulgaria	(2)	−0.35
Poland	(1)	4.65	Poland	(1)	−0.02
Estonia	(2)	4.43	Portugal	(3)	0.12
Greece	(3)	3.34	Estonia	(2)	0.16
Czech Republic	(1)	3.33	Cyprus	(3)	0.19
Spain	(3)	2.98	Spain	(3)	0.37
Portugal	(3)	2.86	Malta	(3)	0.83
Cyprus	(3)	2.54	Czech Republic	(1)	2.94
Malta	(3)	2.46	Lithuania	(2)	2.99
Lithuania	(2)	2.22	Slovakia	(1)	3.02

Notes: In brackets monetary policy strategy: 1 = inflation targeters, 2 = hard-peggers, 3 = euro area members (both forerunners as well as recent entrants)

sample countries, when compared to their nominal effective appreciation rates, may suggests which channels were more important for respective groups (Table 9.1).

Without taking the concept of sustainable real appreciation into account, the differences in real appreciation could lead to a conclusion that the countries with massive real appreciation must have suffered from a loss in price competitiveness generating unsustainably large trade deficits and thus potentially endangering the macroeconomic stability.[3] However, the sample real GDP growth averaged 5% in 2001–2007, with only Portugal and Malta lagging significantly. Also, trade balances do not signal the problems with misalignment by large trade deficits in all fast appreciating countries. For many new Member States, real appreciation had no visible negative impact on their trade balances and these actually improved. Current account balances deteriorated in most sample countries. However, many countries stabilized current account deficits at around 5% of GDP or less. To conclude, there is no clear bi-variate link between the speed of real appreciation and the size of trade and current account balances (Fig. 9.3).

The previous results suggest that we should look at the factors behind the real appreciations more closely to see why in some countries fast real appreciation seems sustainable from the point of view of the external balance, while in others it leads to sizable external deficits. We will argue that FDI inflows may explain a substantial part of this puzzle.

All sample countries accumulated some stock of FDI. However, only seven countries managed to accumulate a stock of FDI in excess of 50% of GDP. These

[3]As argued earlier, the Balassa–Samuelson effect and its resulting impact on the productivity growth are not enough to explain the appreciation phenomenon.

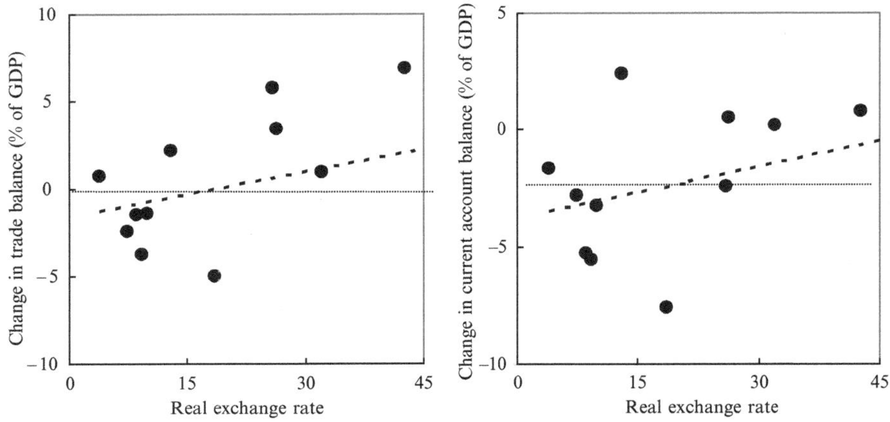

Fig. 9.3 Real appreciation has been consistent with trade and current account balance improvements
Notes: Change in a real exchange rate appreciation measured over 1998–2007. Change in average trade and current account balance measured between 2001–2007 and 1998–1999. The linear trends are not sensitive to outliers.
Source: *World Economic Outlook*, authors' calculations

countries belong to all three groups of countries – the eurozone, hard peg, and IT: Bulgaria, Cyprus, Czech Republic, Estonia, Hungary, Malta, and Slovakia. Six countries accumulated FDI equivalent to 25–50% of GDP, and two countries equivalent to 15–25% of GDP. A similar grouping arises when one looks at the increase in the FDI-to-GDP ratio. Seven countries (Bulgaria, Cyprus, Czech Republic, Estonia, Hungary, Malta, and Slovakia) attracted the new FDI of more than 30% of their GDP in the observed period (Table 9.2). From these data, it seems that the potential integration gain is related to neither a particular monetary policy strategy nor a particular exchange rate regime. If anything, there is some weak evidence that IT and countries outside the euro area were more successful in attracting the FDI. At the same time countries that attracted more FDI seem to exhibit faster real appreciation as well as smaller trade deficits as compared to the rest of the sample. This suggests that in their case, the faster real appreciation might have been sustainable.

FDI is a factor contributing to the recipient-country foreign indebtedness, providing the FDI inflows are not sterilized by the domestic central bank. A nonsterilized FDI inflow would have a corresponding foreign liability counter entry. If the sterilization strategy is employed, net foreign assets should not be affected much by the rapidly increasing stock of FDI. With the exception of Malta, all countries have had negative net foreign assets positions during the sample period. These negative net foreign assets ballooned the most in the forerunner countries and Latvia, while remaining constrained for the rest of the sample. This implies that countries with large FDI inflows were sterilizing these inflows by increasing their foreign exchange reserves, and that FDI inflows by themselves do not necessarily jeopardize the external debt position of a domestic country (Fig. 9.4). Because of

Table 9.2 Recipients of FDI

Country and monetary policy regimes (in brackets)		Increase in FDI in 1998–2007 (% of GDP)
Malta	(3)	78
Hungary	(1)	67
Slovakia	(1)	59
Bulgaria	(2)	55
Estonia	(2)	54
Cyprus	(3)	39
Czech Republic	(1)	38
Romania	(1)	30
Poland	(1)	27
Lithuania	(2)	26
Portugal	(3)	24
Spain	(3)	19
Latvia	(2)	17
Slovenia	(3)	15
Greece	(3)	7

Notes: In brackets monetary policy strategy: 1 = inflation targeters, 2 = hard-peggers, 3 = euro area members (both forerunners as well as recent entrants)
Source: *World Economic Outlook*, authors' calculations

this observation, we feel confident to model the sustainable trajectory for net external position independently from the FDI flows in the following part of the paper.

If it is not the FDI inflows that cause countries to accumulate negative net foreign asset positions, what other factors could be behind such developments? We suggest that there are two factors worth considering. First, private sector credit expanded fast, especially among the hard peggers, reflecting the consumption and investment booms financed by current account deficits.[4] Credit expansion among IT was more contained. It should be noted, however, that direct comparability of individual series is not perfect. Credit booms were typically accompanied by house price booms that have been more pronounced in the group of hard peggers, while comparatively contained in the group of IT. Second, government balances also contributed mildly to the external debt in some cases. On average, central government balances – with the exception of Hungary – showed gradual consolidation, mostly related to the cyclical position of economies in question. Some of the hard peggers ran sizable surpluses, while all IT ran gradually narrowing deficits.

All new member states are small open economies and are therefore affected by various international developments. The first such factor to consider is international price stability. The 1990s and the first half of the 2000s were a period of a low inflation, stable food and commodity prices, and declining nominal interest rates.[5]

[4]Note that the decision to borrow has been optimal under the existing circumstances: with much higher steady-state output and consumption, the firms and households attempt to smooth their investment and consumption profiles.

[5]This period has been known as the Great Moderation (Giannone et al. 2008).

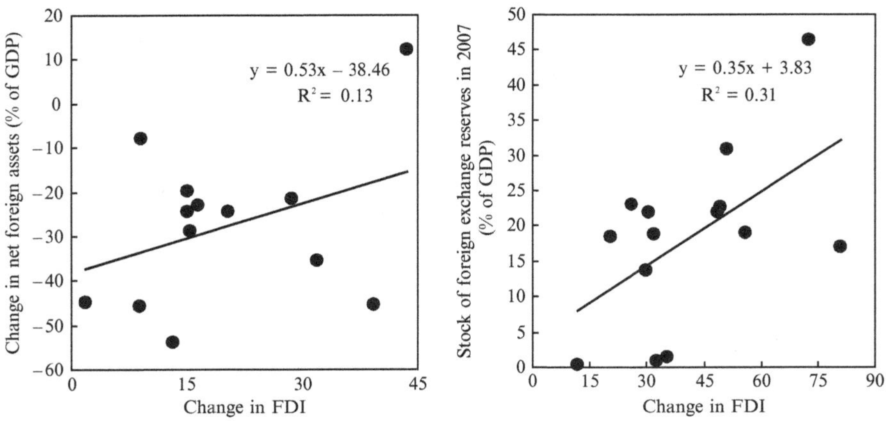

Fig. 9.4 FDI is unrelated to net external debt, because FDI recipients sterilized the inflows
Notes: Change in the stock of net FDI and in net foreign assets are measured between 2001–2007 and 1998–1999. In the first panel, the simple linear trend implies that a 1% point increase in the stock of FDI corresponds to an improvement in the net foreign asset position by 0.2%points. However, after removing Malta from the sample, the linear trend becomes horizontal. In the second panel the simple linear regression implies that a 1% point increase in the stock of FDI corresponds to an improvement in the stock of foreign exchange reserves by 0.3% points. The linear trend is not sensitive to outliers.
Source: *World Economic Outlook*, authors' calculations

The second factor affecting our sample countries was solid growth in both the US and euro area that favorably impacted the demand for sample country exports.

The current environment is of course much more volatile. The real exchange rates in the new Member States are affected by higher international inflation pressures in the second half of the 2000s, slowing foreign demand due to financial crisis, and also by changes in the terms of trade.

9.3 Analyzing Real Exchange Rates and FDI in New Member States

Stylized facts show clearly that new Member States must take the interactions between real exchange rates and FDI inflows into account. They cannot assume that real exchange rates will be stable in the process of financial integration with the EU that brings massive FDI inflows to most of the new Member States. Neither can they automatically assume that real exchange rate appreciation is sustainable in the medium-term no matter what the net external debt or international environment is. It is therefore important to analyze these interactions and decipher which real exchange rate changes are sustainable and which changes have policy implications for the new Member States preparing for the euro adoption.

Our approach, explained in more detail in our previous work (Babecký et al. 2009), defines the SRER as a real exchange rate that ensures a net external debt is sustainable in medium-term. This concept distinguish real exchange rate changes that are due to fundamental factors such as foreign demand for exports, initial external debt and FDI inflows from changes that are due to various short-term factors. The sustainability is a normative concept that depends on our definition of the steady-state level of net external debt. This steady-state level is taken from the empirical study that produced benchmarks for various types of economies. The more the current level of net external debt departs from its steady-state level, the more can real exchange rate deviate from the SRER.

The SRER concept is rooted in the pioneering studies that developed the empirical concept equilibrium (fundamental) real exchange rates (Williamson 1994). There are various approaches to estimating equilibrium real exchange rates that work with different sets of fundamental variables and different time horizons (Driver and Westaway 2005). Our approach belongs to the medium-term methodologies that work with both stock as well as flow variables. In comparison to previously applied methodologies, we put more emphasis on the role of FDI. Also, we implement the country-specific definition of sustainable external balance that reflects the fact that countries with favorable initial net external debts and recipients of massive FDI inflows can afford faster real appreciation in the medium-term while countries that are less lucky (with high initial debt levels or less FDI) face higher risks of overvaluation.

The advantage of the SRER approach is that is provides an aggregated framework for discussion about interaction of the real exchange rates and FDI. Alternative approaches provide an insight into several important issues that go beyond the scope of the SRER concept. First of all, there are alternative hypothesis explaining why the new Member States experienced sharp real appreciation of their exchange rates. We have already mentioned the excessive devaluation at the start of the transition process and the Balassa–Samuelson effect that is based on interaction between the tradable and non-tradable sectors. According to various empirical studies, the Balassa–Samuelson effect plays a very limited role in driving real exchange rate appreciation in new Member States (Cincibuch and Podpiera 2006 and Égert 2002). In addition, recent studies on globalization also claim that global prices are increasingly more important determinants of domestic price-setting behaviour for non-tradable goods (Borio and Filardo 2006).

An additional complication when the Balassa–Samuelson effect is employed is to explain the sharp real appreciation in the new Member States is the problematic empirical distinction between tradable and nontradable sectors. A firm may produce both types of products, or some notionally tradable goods are not really traded as they are directed primarily at the domestic market. Empirical studies available for the new Member States suggest that no clear distinction can be made between tradable and non-tradable goods, the "degree of non-tradability" varying between 10 and 85% (Čihák and Holub 2005). Also, Goldstein and Lardy (2005) use the example of car manufacturing in China that is predominantly serving the domestic market. Indeed, sectors producing tradable goods for the domestic market and for export tend to be fairly distinct in most newly industrialized and emerging or development countries.

The second important issue that goes beyond the scope of the SRER model is the non-homogeneity of the FDI. The impact of the FDI on the economy, trade balance and the real exchange rates depends on the capacity of domestic economy to absorb potential benefits and on recipient sectors. Hence, the impact is both country – as well as time-specific.

FDI has grown rapidly throughout the world in the last two decades, especially in developing countries, where it now accounts for almost half of total inflows (Kose et al. 2006). There is a strong presumption that FDI has a positive effect on economic growth and productivity through the transfer of technology and skills and by augmenting the recipient's domestic capital stock. The aggregate-data support the evidence regarding the positive growth effect of FDI. However, FDI inflows seem to contribute to growth only in countries with a high level of human capital beyond a certain threshold (Borensztein et al. 1998), when countries have well-developed financial markets (Alfaro et al. 2004), or in those with sufficient provision of infrastructure (Kinoshita and Lu 2006). FDI contributes to economic growth by augmenting capital accumulation (Mody and Murshid 2005) as evidenced by a strong "crowding-in" effect of FDI on domestic investment in developing countries between 1979 and 1999. Finally, the sectoral composition of FDI matters as positive externalities are realized through interactions between the sector receiving FDI and the rest of the economy. However, the evidence seems to suggest that if FDI is limited to the primary sector, the economy-wide externalities are smaller than if FDI concentrates in the manufacturing sector (Aykut and Sayek 2007).

Differential effects have been observed for the earlier FDI waves (see, for example, the historic overview in Baldwin and Martin (1999). Specifically, the first wave of FDI in the early 1990s – an example of which is the Volkswagen's bold purchase of the Czech carmaker Škoda – capitalized on the low wage level and a potential for productivity gains in the new Member States (Lansbury et al. (1996) and was directed primarily into sectors producing tradable goods and services. In the early 1990s, in part owing to sharply devalued exchange rates in the transition countries, it would not make much sense to invest into nontradable sectors: the purchasing power of domestic population was low and they distrusted domestically produced goods. In a sense, this FDI wave was a repetition of the much earlier wave observed during the pre-world war I period (Baldwin and Martin 1999). The second wave occurred in the late 1990s and early 2000s, with the process of real convergence well underway. With per capita incomes rising fast and the prospect of the EU accession looming, the flow of FDI was at least partly re-directed into the sectors producing non-tradable goods and services. Especially financial services were a big recipient of these inflows, fueling the credit boom (International Monetary Fund 2008).

Although it could be useful for the reasons mentioned above to distinguish the tradable and non-tradable FDI projects in the SRER model, it is extremely difficult to create a corresponding database. The data and measurement issues seem insurmountable. First, no such aggregate database exists, necessitating using primary sources, classification standards of which differ substantially across countries. Second, all difficulties with defining tradables and non-tradables mentioned in the context of the Balassa–Samuelson effect apply here as well.

The third issue related to the interaction of the real exchange rates and FDI is the measure of financial integration itself. The degree of financial integration can be measured either by quantitative indicators that compare volumes of capital inflows to the level of domestic product or by qualitative indicators that estimate price convergence or by (Baltzer et al. 2008). Our choice of the approximation of the integration process is given by the fact that the FDI brings capital, new technologies and management skills in the recipient economies (Sylwester 2005, and Hunya et al. 2007). The empirical effects of price convergence on exports and imports are not so well established. Similarly, the link between the total capital inflows and productivity of the real economy in the recipient country is supported by empirical studies less than the link between FDI and real economy. Moreover, the FDI stock is more homogenous variable than the total capital inflows.

9.4 Data Description, Empirical Estimates and Parameter Calibration

The SRER framework has been built around empirically estimated econometric trade equations relating exports and imports to fundamental variables such as the real exchange rate, the terms of trade, external debt, and domestic and foreign economic activity. The SRER model differs from its predecessors in several aspects. First, the FDI driven integration gain is incorporated directly into the model in a manner similar to Šmídková et al. (2003). Second, the current account balance is not restricted, as it is asset and liability stocks, not flows, that define the external equilibrium. The sustainable level of external debt is defined according to openness to trade. Third, all variables exogenous to the SRER are modeled within an underlying model framework (NiGEM), ensuring consistency and interdependency.

In this section we describe our data, empirical estimates of trade equations, and selected parameter calibrations. Data consistency is crucial for the SRER calculations, given the endogenous relationship between the various variables, such as domestic and foreign demand or the trade and financial flows. We rely on the global econometric model (NiGEM) maintained by the National Institute of Economic and Social Research, which allows us to project domestic and external variables consistently (Table 9.3). Our model simulations are based on an unconditional forecast – we implicitly assume that the NiGEM projection represents the optimal trajectory of macroeconomic developments.

We work with annual data, employing actual values for the period 1998–2007 and NiGEM and IMF projections for 2008–2013 data exogenous to the SRER model.

Table 9.3 Definition of variables

Variable	Notation	Data source
Effective foreign import demand (in millions of US dollars)	Y^*	NiGEM, September 2008
Effective world real interest rate (in %)	r	NiGEM, September 2008
Import prices (index)	P_m	NiGEM, September 2008
Export prices (index)	P_x	NiGEM, September 2008
US dollar exchange rate (in domestic currency terms)	E	NiGEM, September 2008
Real domestic output (in constant prices)	Y	NiGEM, September 2008
Real exports (volume)	X	NiGEM, September 2008
Real imports (volume)	M	NiGEM, September 2008
Domestic consumer price index (CPI)	P	NiGEM, September 2008
Initial level of external debt (in millions of US dollars)	D_0	IMF World Economic Outlook, October 2008
Stock of FDI (in % of GDP)	FDI	IMF World Economic Outlook, October 2008; and IMF IFS, September 2008
Net external debt target for time T	D^*	Own calculations based on International Monetary Fund (2002)

Notes: Calculations based on IMF World Economic Outlook projections of FDI flows for 2008–2013 and actual values of stock of FDI for 1998–2007

This projection horizon is sufficient to generate medium-term projections of the SRER. The FDI projections are taken from the IMF's World Economic Outlook, where the cutoff year is 2013. That predetermines our projection horizon. The net external debt trajectory – which defines the sustainable external position in the SRER model – is our own normative projection.

Throughout the paper we use the EViews (2007) package and the Gauss-Seidel simulation procedure with the solution period of 1998–2013. Exogenous variables are set equal to the observed values for the in-sample computations (1998–2007) and to the forecasted values for the out-of-sample computations (2008–2013).

To calibrate the SRER model we need to obtain estimates of export and import elasticities in equations. We estimate them in logs:

$$\ln(X_t) = A_0 + \alpha_1 \ln(RPX_t) + \alpha_2 \ln(Y_t^*) + \alpha_3 \ln(F_t) + \phi_t \tag{9.1}$$

$$\ln(M_t) = B_0 + \beta_1 \ln(RPM_t) + \beta_2 \ln(Y_t) + \beta_3 \ln(F_t) + v_t \tag{9.2}$$

where $A_0 = \exp(\alpha_0)$, $B_0 = \exp(\beta_0)$, $RPX = \left(\frac{EP_m}{P}\right).\left(\frac{P_x}{P_m}\right)$ is the relative price of exports, $RPM = \left(\frac{EP_m}{P}\right)$ is the relative price of imports, ϕ_t and v_t are white noise disturbances.

Since most of the variables in levels appear to be nonstationary, OLS estimates of the (9.1) and (9.2) would be biased. Our sample is too short for robust testing of the order of integration of the series and cointegration relationships. Therefore we specify the estimated equations directly in a dynamic error correction form, allowing for the long-run relationships between the variables in levels and at the same time capturing the short-run dynamics. In addition, we perform system estimates imposing common elasticities across countries, but allowing a separate constant term for each country to capture country-specific differences in the levels of the variables:

$$\Delta \ln(X_{i,t}) = A_{0,i} - \lambda[\ln(X_{i,t-1}) - \alpha_1 \ln(RPX_{i,t-1}) - \alpha_2 \ln(S_{i,t-1}) - \alpha_3 \ln(F_{i,t-1})] + \alpha_{4,i}\Delta \ln(RPX_{i,t}) + \alpha_{5,i}\Delta \ln(Y^*_{i,t}) + \varepsilon_{i,t} \quad (9.3)$$

$$\Delta \ln(M_{i,t}) = B_{0,i} - \delta[\ln(M_{i,t-1}) - \beta_1 \ln(RPM_{i,t-1}) - \beta_2 \ln(Y_{i,t-1}) - \beta_3 \ln(F_{i,t-1})] + \beta_{4,i}\Delta \ln(RPM_{i,t}) + \beta_{5,i}\Delta \ln(Y_{i,t}) + u_{i,t} \quad (9.4)$$

where λ and δ (expected to be positive) characterize the speed of adjustment towards long-run equilibrium, $\varepsilon_{i,t}$ and $\mu_{i,t}$ are white noise disturbances.

While generally preferring the country-specific estimates, we have to address the tradeoff between country-specific calibrations, based on estimated individual-country trade equations, and a generalized (average) calibration, based either on a full-size or selected-country panels. While the former would guarantee a better short-run fit for most countries, it would make the long-run, cross-country comparisons difficult if not downright doubtful. Specifically, basing the simulations on the estimated country elasticities would mix estimates from countries that are reasonably close to their steady states, with those that experience rapid convergence. While the former group would comprise the current eurozone members that serve as the control group in our paper (Greece, Spain, and Portugal), the latter group would comprise Bulgaria and Romania, with the somewhat richer Central European countries falling in between. As the convergence process runs its course, the initially poorer countries approach the economic level of the initially richer countries and trade patterns in the former countries start to resemble the patterns in the latter countries. However, mixing those two types of countries in a single panel would likely lead to misspecified equations.

We thus rely mostly on a generalized calibration tilted toward the more advanced EU countries. Naturally, there are risks associated with our approach. While we gain cross-country comparability, we have to make some ad hoc decisions on the selection of countries to be included in the initial estimation and the subsequent calibration. To ameliorate the potential criticism of data mining, we assess the robustness of our preferred econometric estimates vis-à-vis the full-sample panel with country dummies. In addition, we estimate country-specific elasticities for the FDI variable in order to capture the heterogeneity of the analyzed countries. This country-specific elasticity allow us to distinguish between countries in the pure-blessing, mixed-blessing or no blessing situations. In this setup, for example, the economies that received the FDI inflows into nontradable sectors

Table 9.4 Calibrated coefficients

		New estimates[a]	BBŠ (2008)[b]	Barrell et al. (2002)[c]
Real exchange rate elasticity of exports	α_1	4.03	1.95[e]	3.15
Terms of trade elasticity of exports	α_1	4.03	1.95[e]	3.15
Foreign demand elasticity of exports[d]	α_2	1.00	1.00	1.00
FDI (stock) elasticity of exports	α_3	0.56	0.18[e]	0.70[e]
Speed of adjustment to long-run equilibrium	λ	0.08	0.04[f]	0.13[e]
Real exchange rate elasticity of imports	β_1	−0.79[g]	−2.10[e]	−0.62[f]
Domestic demand elasticity of imports[d]	β_2	1.00	1.00	1.00
FDI (stock) elasticity of imports	β_3	0.20[e]	0.08[f]	0.24[e]
Speed of adjustment to long-run equilibrium	δ	0.55[e]	0.06[e]	0.13[e]

[a]Baseline scenario estimates in a panel comprising Greece, Portugal, Spain and Slovenia for the period 1998–2007
[b]Babecký et al. 2008 estimates in a panel comprising Greece, Portugal, Spain and Slovenia for the period 1995Q1–2007Q3
[c]Barrell et al. 2002 estimates in a panel comprising Czech Republic, Estonia, Hungary, Poland and Slovenia for the period 1994Q1–1999Q4
[d]The unitary values of demand elasticities are imposed
[e]Denote significance levels at 1%
[f]Denote significance levels at 5%
[g]Denote significance levels at 10%

(say, the residential housing construction or services) may face a negative integration gain (an "integration pain") while economies that received the FDI inflows into the tradable sectors (typically into car production or other manufacturing industries) may indeed benefit from a sizable and positive integration gain.

In order to calibrate the equations for all countries, we use the point elasticities (Table 9.4) of the exchange rate, terms of trade and demand variables obtained from the panel estimates of (9.3) and (9.4) for the euro-area country group (Greece, Portugal, Spain, and Slovenia). We will use the new estimates for our main simulation model (Table 9.4, left column), the previously obtained estimates are used for the sensitivity analysis purposes as the benchmark simulation model (Table 9.4, middle column). In addition to sample elasticities, we report the country-specific trade elasticities with respect to FDI in Table 9.5.

Regarding the panel parameters (Table 9.4), the FDI elasticities are in line with earlier research and the integration gain ($\alpha_3 > \beta_3$) is observable for the whole group. A 1% point increase in the stock of FDI increases long-run net exports by almost 0.4% (the difference between α_3 and β_3). Compared to the calibration Babecký et al. 2008, new estimates show somewhat higher export elasticities α_1 and α_3, a lower real exchange rate elasticity of imports β_1, and a higher FDI elasticity of imports β_3. Both calibrations produce broadly comparable estimates of elasticities to the previous studies Šmídková et al. 2002, Bulíř and Šmídková 2005, 2007, that relied on panel-data results from Barrell et al. 2002. Therefore, to assess the robustness of the model simulations, we employ two most recent of these sets of elasticities. The new estimates are used for the calibration of the main model. The elasticities from Babecký et al. 2008 are used for the calibration of the benchmark model.

Table 9.5 Country-specific FDI elasticities in export and import equations

	The main model: New estimates[a]		The benchmark model: BBŠ (2008)[b]	
	FDI elasticity of exports, α_3	FDI elasticity of imports, β_3	FDI elasticity of exports, α_3	FDI elasticity of imports, β_3
Bulgaria	−0.14	0.31[c]	−0.13	0.21[d]
Czech Republic	1.04[c]	0.38[c]	0.58[c]	0.03
Estonia	0.17	0.16[g]	0.07	0.05
Greece	−0.89[c]	0.12	−0.62[c]	0.00
Hungary	1.22[c]	0.25[c]	0.61[c]	−0.11
Lithuania	−0.60[e]	0.44[c]	−0.29[c]	0.33[c]
Latvia	−1.69[c]	0.57[c]	−1.07	0.85[c]
Poland	−0.03	0.30[c]	−0.02	0.35[c]
Portugal	0.44[c]	0.00	0.07	−0.22[e]
Romania	−0.58[e]	0.88[c]	−0.19[e]	0.92[d]
Slovenia	0.40[c]	0.23[d]	0.27[c]	0.13
Spain	0.24[d]	0.22[d]	0.05	0.03
Slovakia	0.52[c]	0.15[c]	0.27[c]	−0.01

[a]The main scenario estimates in the panel comprising Greece, Portugal, Spain and Slovenia for the period 1998–2007
[b]Babecký et al. (2008) estimates in a panel comprising Greece, Portugal, Spain and Slovenia for the period 1995Q1–2007Q3
[c]Denote significance levels at 1%
[d]Denote significance levels at 5%
[e]Denote significance levels at 10%

However, the impact of the FDI stock on the import and export volumes differs from country to country (Table 9.5). First, we observe a group of six countries with a significant integration gain: the Czech Republic, Hungary, Portugal, Slovenia, Spain, and Slovakia. Second, there are four countries with negative and significant FDI elasticities of exports (integration pain): Greece, Latvia, Lithuania, and Romania. For remaining three countries the evidence is mixed since the estimated elasticities are not statistically significant.

To our knowledge, there is no comprehensive empirical study that would look into the structure of FDI for all EU member states, in part owing to a lack of detailed data regarding the destination of FDI, and hence we rely on the following set of stylized facts (Table 9.6). For example, in Greece and Latvia we observe a relative expansion of the construction sector, while the industrial (manufacturing) sectors shrunk. In contrast, in countries like the Czech Republic or Estonia the manufacturing expanded, while the share of construction either stagnated or declined[6]. Given this evidence, we work with the hypothesis that the FDI flowed

[6]This finding is akin to the so-called "Rybczynski effect," according to which an increase in a country's endowment of a factor will cause an increase in output of the good which uses that factor intensively (Rybczynski 1955). In other words, if a country has specialized in tradable output, FDI is likely to continue to flow into these sectors.

Table 9.6 Developments in sectoral shares of output, 1995–97 and 2001–04

(In % of total value added)	Agriculture	Industry (without construction)	*Of which:* manufacturing	Construction	Services
Cyprus	−0.9	−2.0	−2.1	−0.8	3.2
Czech Republic	−1.3	−1.6	0.2	−1.6	4.5
Estonia	−2.9	−0.9	0.3	0.3	3.0
Greece	−2.6	−1.7	−1.3	1.9	0.9
Hungary	−2.7	−1.4	−0.7	0.6	3.4
Latvia	−2.9	−7.8	−6.3	1.2	9.1
Lithuania	−4.9	−0.3	0.3	−0.8	6.3
Poland	−2.7	−3.8	−3.0	−1.0	7.6
Portugal	−1.7	−2.3	−1.8	1.1	6.3
Slovakia	−1.4	−4.1	−3.2	−1.2	6.7
Slovenia	−1.3	−0.1	−0.2	0.0	1.3
Spain	−1.1	−2.6	−1.4	2.5	1.2

Notes: To capture the sectoral dynamics, we subtract the average share for 1995–1997 from the average share for 2001–2004. For example, the first cell shows that the relative share of the value added in agriculture in Cyprus declined by 0.9% points between those two periods.
Source: AMECO

predominantly in the construction and services sectors for the second group and thus FDI could not contribute to the improvement of net exports and worsened the net external debt position. For these countries, FDI was neither pure nor mixed blessing regarding the external balance.

The performance of the calibrated export and import equations and a comparison of the actual and predicted net exports for the main model can be found in Annex III in Babecký et al. (2009) The dynamics of both imports as well as exports is captured sufficiently well to proceed to the next step of preparing the SRER model.

In the next step, we reflect the various uncertainties related to both calibration as well as exogenous data projections. We use two sets of the estimated elasticities (denoted earlier as the "main model" and "benchmark model") and a total of 11 scenarios for exogenous variables, discussed below. For both models, we assume that the trade relationships are likely to settle at the euro group's levels, but allowing, first, for the country-specific FDI effects on exports and imports and, second, the country-specific constants. In total, we produce 22 SRER trajectories from which we construct the interval estimates of the SRER. The interval estimates are represented with means and with two standard deviation bands.

The first three scenarios relate to sustainable debt. Sustainable net external debt is a crucial normative concept in the SRER model. The earlier models assumed an all-purpose fixed net external debt target equal to 60% of GDP (Ades and Kaune 1997). Recent events have shown that the rule-of-thumb approach may not be flexible enough. Sustainable external debt ought to be related to countries' ability to service it (International Monetary Fund 2002), and the corresponding uncertainty

Table 9.7 Net external debt targets

Country	Exports-to-GDP ratio (in %)	External debt target
Bulgaria, the Czech Republic, Estonia, Latvia, Lithuania, Hungary, Slovakia, Slovenia	Higher than 40	65
Greece, Poland, Portugal, Romania, Spain	Higher than 30, but lower than 40	53

Source: Authors' calculations based on International Monetary Fund (2002)

related to the target can be large. We derive the steady-state debt levels from the countries' openness to trade (Table 9.7).

The three alternative paths for sustainable debt differ in the speed with which the steady-state debt target is reached. The first trajectory assumes that the sustainable net external debt position is close to the current one for the period 1998–2007 and that afterwards it converges slowly to the net debt target value (the steady-state value is not achieved until 2108). This trajectory gives the smallest scope for misalignment estimates due to the similarity between observed and sustainable debt. The second trajectory starts from the initial value equal to the observed debt value in 1998 and then it converges slowly toward the targeted steady-state value (again set to be achieved by 2108). This scenario would typically produce more visible misalignments for countries whose net external debts are significantly either below or above the debt target. The third trajectory starts from the same initial position in 1998 and it converges to the target rapidly, achieving the steady-state level of net external debt in 2017. This assumption implies that the level of sustainable debt can be much larger than the observed one for countries with small net external debt, and hence it will show a much larger scope for sustainable real appreciation. All three debt trajectories described above are plotted for each country in Annex IV in Babecký et al. 2009.

The remaining eight scenarios provide sensitivity analysis for four exogenous variables (positive and negative shocks to foreign demand for exports, domestic demand, FDI stock, and risk premium attached to interest rates paid on net external debt). More detailed description of all scenarios is provided in Tables 9.8 and 9.9. We include the risk premium scenarios since according to various authors euro adoption could be accompanied by a decrease in risk premium (Schadler et al. 2005).

It is worth noting that the conducted sensitivity analysis works with relatively large shocks (up to 10% of the exogenous variable values in 2007) and so the computed SRER intervals show quite robust estimates. In addition, the SRER intervals work implicitly with the uncertainty related to the euro adoption and implications of the current financial crises since the scenario of decreased risk premium and the scenarios of increased risk premium and reduced foreign demand for exports are included among our simulation scenarios.

To sum up, the SRER interval estimates and projections presented in the next section are obtained by computing the SRER values for the above-described 11 scenarios applied to both model calibrations (main model and benchmark model).

Table 9.8 Summary of 11 simulation scenarios

No.	Notation	Scenario description
1	D1	Debt trajectory: Polynomial extrapolation using actual data for 1998–2007 and debt target applied to 2108. The baseline sustainable debt trajectory
2	D2	Gradual net external debt convergence toward target: Logarithmic extrapolation using actual data for 1998 and debt targets applied to 2108
3	D3	Fast net external debt convergence toward target: Logarithmic extrapolation using actual data for 1998 and debt targets applied to 2017
4	R_low	Decrease in risk premium by 2 pp through 1998–2013
5	R_high	Increase in risk premium by 2 pp through 1998–2013
6	Y_low	Decrease in real domestic output by one standard deviation
7	Y_high	Increase in real domestic output by one standard deviation
8	Y*_low	Decrease in foreign import demand by one standard deviation
9	Y*_high	Increase in foreign import demand by one standard deviation
10	FDI_low	Decrease in stock of FDI by one standard deviation
11	FDI_high	Increase in stock of FDI by one standard deviation

Table 9.9 The calibration of the shocks

One standard deviation calculated over 2005–2007 as a ratio of the 2007 levels			
	Real domestic output, Y	Foreign import demand, Y*	Stock of FDI, F
Bulgaria	0.06	0.12	0.22
Czech Republic	0.06	0.12	0.06
Estonia	0.08	0.12	0.03
Greece	0.04	0.06	0.15
Hungary	0.03	0.12	0.28
Lithuania	0.07	0.12	0.09
Latvia	0.09	0.12	0.11
Poland	0.06	0.12	0.10
Portugal	0.02	0.06	0.11
Romania	0.06	0.12	0.17
Slovenia	0.06	0.06	0.06
Spain	0.04	0.06	0.09
Slovakia	0.08	0.12	0.16

Source: Authors' calculations

We suggest that this interval estimates should be robust to the most sensitive assumptions of our model.

9.5 Simulation Results

We report three types of simulation results. First, for period 1999–2007 we report our indicator for the currency misalignment. Second, we show the SRER projections 5 years ahead. Third, we report the outcome of one selected scenario simulation – falling foreign demand – that is relevant for the current policy discussion in the new Member States in order to show the potential impact of the financial crisis on the SRER trajectories.

9.5.1 Misalignment

The misalignment indicator is based on the simulation results from the above-described 22 scenarios, pointing toward real exchange rate overvaluation/undervaluation if the interval is above/below the zero horizontal line. In the case of overvaluation/undervaluation the estimated sustainable real exchange rate is weaker/stronger than the observed one, even after considering various uncertainties related to the model calibration, exogenous variable projections, and normative definition of the debt target.

While most currencies seem to be close to the sustainable level (Fig. 9.5), we identify at least one example of sizable misalignment in every group. Our simulations for the inflation targeting group identify at end-2007 only one country with a significantly overvalued currency (Romania), two countries with a marginally undervalued currencies (Hungary and Poland),[7] and two countries without visible currency misalignment (the Czech Republic and Slovakia). Among the hard-peggers, we find three countries with an overvalued currency (Bulgaria, Latvia, and Lithuania) and one country without currency misalignment (Estonia). In the control group of the euro area members, there are three countries without significant currency misalignment (Slovenia, Spain, and Portugal) and one country with an overvalued currency (Greece). Consistent with the often mentioned external trade developments in Spain and Portugal, our simulations indicate that both countries went through a prolonged period of overvaluation following the euro adoption.

From these results we conclude that the current misalignment of currencies may not be a serious problem for the IT group of countries, with the exception of Romania that is anyway a latecomer to inflation targeting. It is also not a problem for the euro area group, with the exception of Greece. The group of hard-peggers, with the exception of Estonia, is the group most likely to encounter problems in the year ahead stemming from the overvalued domestic currency.

9.5.2 The Sustainable Real Exchange Rate Projections

The SRER projections are computed for 5 years ahead in a similar fashion to the misalignment indicator, again relying on the interval indicator based on the 22 simulation scenarios. In our model, the countries with rapidly declining SRER trajectories, that is, sustainable appreciation, can withstand fast real exchange rate appreciation without endangering their development. On the one hand, appreciation is sustainable owing to a favorable set of fundamentals, such as the optimistic projection of FDI inflows, beneficial expected changes in terms of trade, or sustained increase in foreign demand for their exports. On the other hand, these countries may find themselves facing dilemma between the sustainable appreciation

[7]In both cases the upper band of the misalignment corridor is touching the zero horizontal line, thus suggesting that the domestic currency was not misaligned under some scenarios.

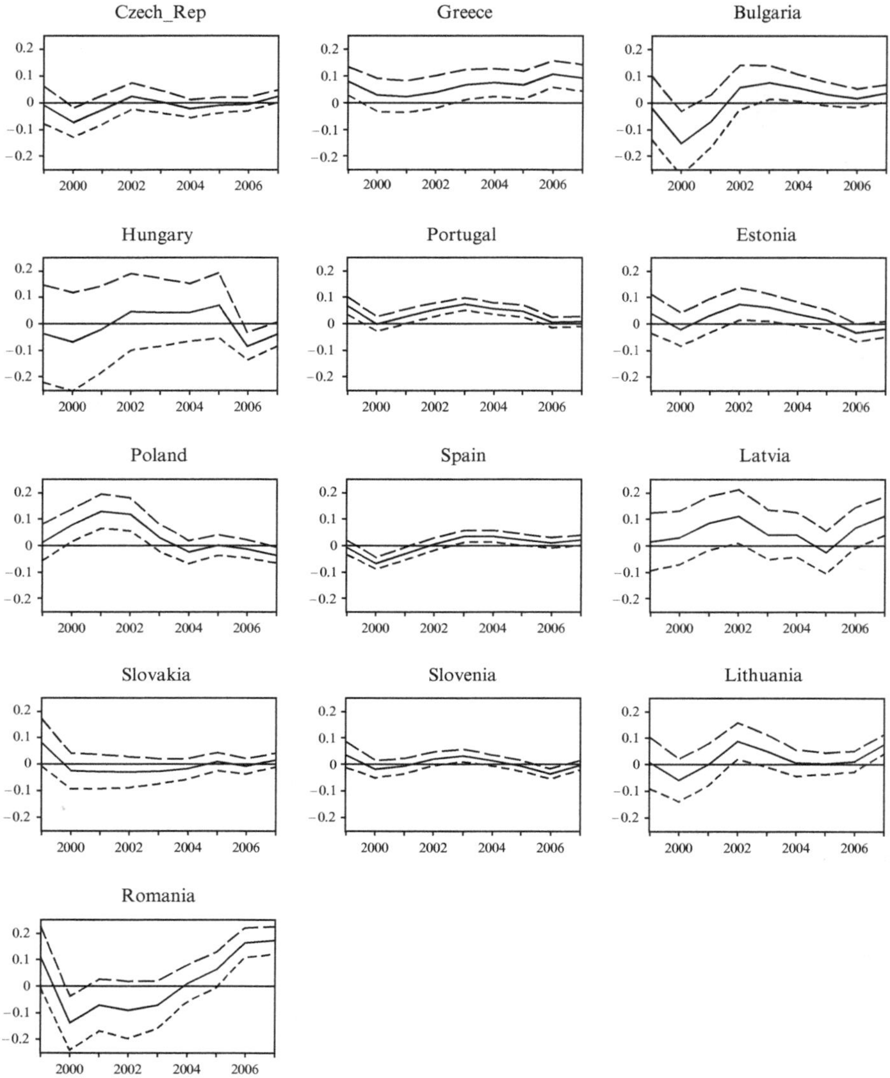

Fig. 9.5 Real exchange rate misalignments, 1999–2007, sustainable versus observed real effective values

Notes: The corridors are based on 22 scenarios

Source: Authors' calculations. Positive/negative values of misalignment indicator imply that the sustainable exchange rate is weaker/stronger than the observed one, and hence that there is a real overvaluation/undervaluation of a domestic currency. Bold line shows mean computed from 22 scenarios, dotted lines show +/−2 standard deviations benefits and obstacles to the euro adoption. This dilemma refers to the mixed-blessing case of the FDI integration gain defined in the introduction.

Some countries may face only slowly declining or stable SRER trajectories and would not face any policy dilemma because mild sustainable real appreciation would be compatible with the nominal convergence required for the euro area entry. This scenario would be analogous to the pure-blessing case described in the introduction. Alternatively, some countries may face upward sloping SRER trajectories in the model, and hence they will have to deal with policy implications similar to those of the negative integration gain. These countries cannot afford the existing real exchange rate appreciation, because it is not sustainable. Moreover, the nominal convergence required for the euro adoption may not be a feasible option for them in the medium-term.

The SRER projections indicate that for the 2008–2013 period there are three countries (Czech Republic, Bulgaria, Romania) that may face the mixed-blessing type dilemma, because the estimated sustainable real appreciation is more than 2% per year annually. The estimates of the average sustainable real appreciation for the 2008–2013 period for the remaining euro candidates are around 1% only. This result suggests that the above-mentioned tradeoffs will be faced only by some of the new Member States, specifically those who cumulated a large stocks of FDI and are at the same time faced with overall favorable conditions (such as a lower initial level of net external debt, growing external demand, and so on) or those who are in less advanced stages of convergence.

The projected sustainable real appreciation rates are significantly lower as compared to those estimated for the 1999–2007 period (Table 9.10).[8] First, we observe a visible deceleration in the sustainable real appreciation for six countries (Czech Republic, Hungary, Portugal, Slovakia, Slovenia, Spain). While four of them are either in the euro area already or will join soon, the remaining two have yet to enter the ERM2 regime. We interpret this result as an argument that the mixed-blessing problem is not a long-term phenomena. In other words, its relevance is likely to fade away gradually as the convergence process advances further. Second, we identify four countries where the sustainable real appreciation is likely to accelerate (Bulgaria, Estonia, Lithuania, and Poland). Finally, for three countries (Greece, Latvia, and Romania) we observe that the SRERs switch from sustainable depreciation to sustainable appreciation. Countries in the last two groups, with the exception of Greece, are comparatively less advanced in their convergence process and hence may face the above-mentioned tradeoffs in the future.

9.5.3 The Crisis Scenario

The SRER model simulations illustrate that massive FDI inflows are necessary but not sufficient causes of sustainable real exchange rate appreciation. The other

[8]See Babecký et al. 2009 for more details.

Table 9.10 Sustainable real exchange rate appreciation

(In %)	1999–2007	2008–2013
Countries with a decelerating speed of sustainable real appreciation		
Czech Republic (1)	−2.8	−1.7
Hungary (1)	−4.0	−0.8
Portugal (3)	−1.7	−0.8
Slovakia (1)	−2.9	−0.7
Slovenia (3)	−0.9	−0.6
Spain (3)	−0.7	−0.6
Countries with an accelerating speed of sustainable real appreciation		
Bulgaria (2)	−0.1	−2.9
Estonia (2)	−1.0	−1.7
Lithuania (2)	−0.3	−1.0
Poland (1)	−0.6	−0.7
Countries switching from SRER depreciation to SRER appreciation		
Romania (1)	1.5	−5.0
Greece (3)	0.1	−1.8
Latvia (2)	2.1	−1.2

Notes: In brackets monetary policy strategy: 1 = inflation targeters, 2 = hard-peggers, 3 = euro area members (both forerunners as well as recent entrants)

necessary conditions (low level of debt, demand for exports, and so on) must be present as well. The current financial crisis challenges the commonly applied assumption of smoothly increasing foreign demand for domestic exports. A scenario of a sustained medium-term slowdown in the euro area growth, global recession with a corresponding collapse of foreign trade is no longer a tail event. For example, a substantial fall in demand is projected presently by most of the professional forecasters surveyed by the Consensus Forecasts (2008).

The impact of a large decline in foreign demand, calibrated to be equal to two standard deviations of the series, is equivalent to sizable equilibrium depreciation and the SRER trajectories shift upwards. Although the SRER sensitivity to foreign demand differs case by case, the new Member States as a group should not count on a sustainable real appreciation trend. In some cases the estimated impact is sizable indeed – the most affected countries may need to target real depreciation to the tune of 10% annually to sustain the external balance.

9.6 Policy Implications

We asked whether FDI is a mixed blessing for the new Member States and we think that it indeed is in many of them. The new Member States try to reap the integration gain of massive FDI inflows and simultaneously prepare for the euro adoption. On the upside, the economic literature suggests that the macroeconomic performance may be boosted through the FDI's positive impact on the trade balance (we call this effect the integration gain) if FDI-financed projects expand the output of either exportable goods or substitutes for foreign imports. On the downside, this integration gain, foreseen by the financial markets, is likely to be reflected in the sharp appreciation of the real exchange rate that is sustainable in the medium-term, owing to the integration gain. The new Member States may have lessened their chances to fulfill the Maastricht criteria and to adopt the euro flawlessly and FDI can be indeed a mixed blessing for them.

Not everybody will have such dilemma, though. For some new Member States that have experienced only mild integration gains FDI can be a pure blessing as the resulting moderate real appreciation may be just compatible with the Maastricht criteria. Finally, for countries that have received FDI inflows predominantly into non-tradable goods and services sectors FDI can be no blessing at all. Such inflows may be associated with a deteriorating trade balance, and consequently, a sustainable path for economic development would require real depreciation. Of course, sustained equilibrium real depreciation is incompatible with the Maastricht criteria and may lessen the chances of the euro adoption even more than the sharp appreciation observed in the first group of countries.

Our results show that the new Member States do not form a homogenous group as far as the interaction of the real exchange rates and FDI is concerned. We identify only three new Member States that are not euro area members for which FDI has brought a significant integration gain: the Czech Republic, Hungary, and Slovakia. From these three countries, only the Czech Republic is likely to face the mixed blessing policy dilemma since the lack of other necessary factors for this dilemma, such as limited net external debt, seems to offset the integration gain for Hungary and Slovakia. Consequently, the projected sustainable real appreciation is mild for these two countries (Fig. 9.6). On the other side of the spectrum, we identify three countries (Latvia, Lithuania, and Romania) for which FDI can be no blessing at all since these inflows seem to have had a deteriorating impact on their trade balances. The two Baltic countries have strongly overvalued currencies because they have accumulated sizable net external debt without much integration gain.

Medium term appreciation of domestic currencies is not the only roadblock to the euro adoption and the new Member States have to assess the alignment of their currencies. Overvalued currencies are expected to contribute to external imbalances, including external debt accumulation. For example, we observe that a fast euro adoption process may not be advisable for Romania and Bulgaria as we project both fast, medium-term real appreciation of the national currencies and their current overvaluation.

On the one hand, a fast real exchange rate appreciation may be sustainable in the case of a strong integration gain and a favorable net external debt level. While such conditions would complicate the process of euro adoption, they would do so only in the medium term. On the other hand, a mild real exchange rate appreciation is not necessarily making the process of euro adoption more sustainable. Such appreciation may be associated with a strong overvaluation in the case of the integration loss and high net external debt. In the latter case, the process of euro adoption may be

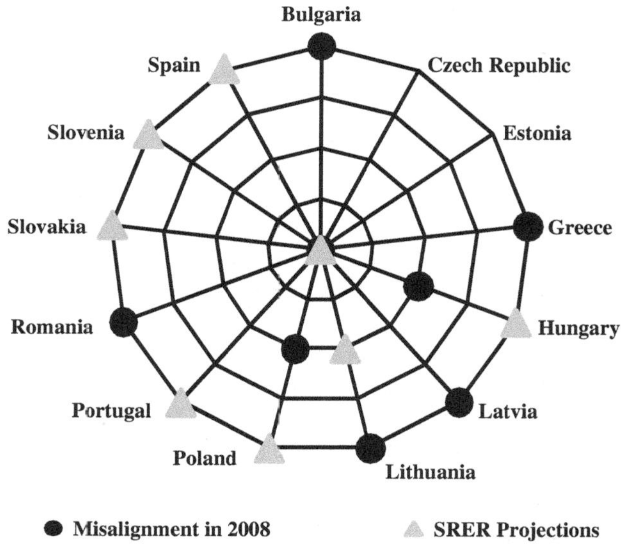

Fig. 9.6 FDI could be a mixed blessing: summary of the sustainable exchange rate indicators
Notes: The higher the country is on the axis, the less favorable the SRER indicators. Overvalued currencies (series Misalignment in 2008) and projected sustainable real depreciation (series SRER Projections) are the farthest from the center. If there is no triangle or circle for a country, then our simulation identified no misalignment, sustainable real depreciation, or both

more complicated and policymakers need to identify the starting position of their economies carefully and plan the process of the euro adoption adequately.

There are several policy implications of our findings. First, the real exchange rate developments in the new Member States need to be assessed carefully in light of the full set of fundamental variables. A special attention should be paid to the following two stock variables: the value of external indebtedness as measured by the net foreign assets variable and the stock of FDI. Our findings suggest that the FDI composition matters a lot. Although the necessary database is not available to conduct a more rigorous analysis, the estimates and stylized facts point out that the massive (non-productivity enhancing) FDI inflows into services, associated with credit booms and rapidly growing house prices, do not yield the integration gain observed in countries with export-sector directed FDI inflows.[9]

The second observation that follows from our work relates to the monetary policy strategy. We do not find particularly strong evidence that the choice of the monetary policy strategy may play an important role in the speed of real

[9]Nevertheless, in case of productivity enhancing FDI inflows into services there could be integration gain as well (Blanchard 2007). The mechanism is the following: an increase in productivity in services causes a decrease in prices, which in turn pushes down nominal wages in tradables, leading to an improvement in competitiveness in tradables and thus to higher activity and an improvement in the trade balance.

appreciation, and in the process of attracting FDI, or accumulating the stock of net external debt. The trend real appreciation and the real exchange rate developments observed in the past 10–15 years, seem to be determined mostly by real-economy factors, namely the speed of real convergence. However, it seems that IT and countries outside the euro area were more successful in attracting the FDI than the selected forerunners (Greece, Portugal, and Spain) and hard-peggers, in turn gaining a more favorable position with respect to the sustainable speed of real appreciation.

The third policy implication is important in the current financial turmoil: the SRER projections are very sensitive to projection of foreign demand. In the current international environment of volatile terms of trade, falling foreign demand, and nominal interest rates approaching the zero bound the policymakers need to be well aware of this sensitivity. Empirical results suggest that the positive impact of FDI on trade could be easily neutralized by the current international environment. As a result, policymakers could easily face a completely different dilemma. Instead thinking about the mixed blessing of FDI, they could be faced with a need to depreciate real exchange rates in order to sustain the external balance.

The fourth issue worth considering for policy makers is the dynamics in the interaction between real exchange rates and the FDI. We have found some support – in this paper and in the relevant literature – for the standard hypotheses regarding the short, medium and long term impact of FDI. First, large foreign capital inflows, irrespective of their nature, tend to appreciate the domestic currency in the short run and/or increase the stock of international foreign exchange rate reserves. Second, FDI inflows, to the extent they stimulate either tradable output or import substitution, have also an appreciating impact on the real sustainable exchange rate that is our approximation of the external equilibrium. This impact is of medium-term nature, and – according to our estimates – is likely to diminish in the long-term when even the advanced stages of convergence are completed. Third, leaving aside the impact on the real equilibrium rate, a more volatile nominal rate in the short run imposes welfare costs of its own. We have certainly observed that countries with sizable and irregular FDI inflows decided to sterilize at least a part of these inflows.

The last policy implication comes from the experience of forerunners, the EU members that adopted euro prior to the EU enlargement and that were relatively close to the new Member States and their convergence trajectory. Forerunners did not attract additional FDI after euro adoption. The new Member States should keep this in mind and work under assumption that FDI inflows are medium-term rather than long-term phenomena. As a result of diminishing integration gain and rapidly cumulating stock of net external debt, the forerunners went through a prolonged period of overvaluation after euro adoption. This period seems to be over for Portugal and Spain, but not for Greece where FDI inflows were associated with credit and house price booms. The forerunners' adjustment process to the overvalued currency might be worth analyzing specially for the hard-peggers among the new Member States. IT might be helped by nominal depreciation in the case they find themselves in a similar situation.

References

Ades, A., & Kaune, F. (1997). A new measure of current account sustainability for developing countries. New York: Goldman Sachs.

Alfaro, L., Chanda, A., Kalemli-Ozcan, S., & Sayek, S. (2004). FDI and economic growth: the role of local financial markets. *Journal of International Economics, 64*(1), 89–112.

Aykut, D., & Sayek, S. (2007). The role of the sectoral composition of FDI on growth. In L. Piscitello & G. D. Santangelo (Eds.), *Do multinationals feed local development and growth?* Amsterdam: Elsevier.

Babecký, J., Bulíř, A., Šmídková, K. (2009). Sustainable real exchange rates in the new EU Member States: is FDI a mixed blessing? *European Economy Economic Papers, 368,* 77 http://ec.europa.eu/economy_finance/publications/publication14297_en.pdf.

Babecký, J., Bulíř, A., & Šmídková, K. (2008). Sustainable real exchange rates when trade winds are plentiful. *National Institute Economic Review, 204*, 98–107.

Baldwin, RE., & Martin, P. (1999). *Two waves of globalisation: superficial similarities, fundamental differences.* NBER Working Paper, 6904. http://www.nber.org/papers/w6904.pdf.

Baltzer, M., Cappiello, L., De Santis, R.A., Manganelli, S. (2008) Measuring financial integration in new EU Member States. *ECB Occasional Paper Series, 81*, 1–34.

Barrell, R., Holland, D., Jakab, Z.M., Kovács, M.A., Šmídková, K., Sepp, U., Čufer, U. (2002). *An econometric macro-model of transition: policy choices in the pre-accession period. Proceedings of AMFET'2001 Conference – Modelling Economies in Transition.* Krag, Poland. Lodz: Absolwent.

Barry, F. (2000). Convergence in not automatic: lessons from Ireland for central and eastern Europe. *World Economy, 23*(10), 1379–1394.

Blanchard, O. (2007). Adjustment within the euro. The difficult case of Portugal. *Portuguese Economic Journal, 6*(1), 1–21.

Borensztein, E., De Gregorio, J., & Lee, J. W. (1998). How does foreign direct investment affect economic growth? *Journal of International Economics, 45*(1), 115–35.

Borio, C., & Filardo, A. (2006). Globalisation and inflation: new cross-country evidence on the global determinants of domestic inflation. Bank for International Settlements Working Paper, 227. Basel: Bank for International Settlements. http://www.bis.org/pub/work227.htm.

Bulíř, A., & Šmídková, K. (2007). Fast sailing toward the euro: dangers of the Lee shore. In N. Batini (Ed.), *Monetary policy in emerging markets and other developing countries* (pp. 67–92). New York: Nova Science Publishers.

Bulíř, A., & Šmídková, K. (2005). Sustainable real exchange rates in the new accession countries: what have we learned from the forerunners? *Economic Systems, 29*(2), 163–186.

Cincibuch, M., & Podpiera, J. (2006). Beyond Balassa–Samuelson: real appreciation in tradables in transition countries. *Economics of Transition, 13*(3), 547–73.

Čihák, M., & Holub, T. (2005). Price convergence in EU-accession countries: evidence from the international comparison. *Economie Internationale, 102*(2), 59–82.

Consensus Forecasts. (2008). Eastern Europe consensus forecasts and G-7 & Western Europe. *Consensus Economics* http://www.consensuseconomics.com/.

Driver, R., & Westaway, P.F. (2005). *Concepts of equilibrium exchange rates.* Bank of England Working Paper, 247. London: Bank of England. http://www.bankofengland.co.uk/workingpapers/wp247.pdf.

Égert, B. (2002). Estimating the impact of the Balassa–Samuelson effect on inflation and the real exchange rate during the transition. *Economic Systems, 26*, 1–16.

EViews. (2007). Version 6, A computer package for estimations and model simulations. Quantitative Micro Software: Irvine, CA. http://www.eviews.com/.

Giannone, D., Lenza, M., Reichlin, L. (2008). *Explaining the great moderation: It is not the shocks.* ECB Working Paper 865. Frankfurt: European Central Bank. http://www.ecb.int/pub/pdf/scpwps/ecbwp865.pdf.

Goldstein, M., & Lardy, N.R. (2005). *China's role in the revived Bretton woods system: a case of mistaken identity*. Washington, DC: Institute for International Economics Working Paper, WP 05–2 http://www.petersoninstitute.org/publications/wp/wp05-2.pdf.

Halpern, L., & Wyplosz, C. (1997). Equilibrium exchange rates in transition economies. *IMF Staff Papers, 44*, 430–461.

Hunya, G., Holzner, M., Wörz, J. (2007). *How to assess the impact of FDI on an economy*. OECD Concept Paper. http://www.oecd.org/dataoecd/9/0/38937107.pdf.

International Monetary Fund. (2002). *Assessing sustainability*. Washington, DC: International Monetary Fund. http://www.imf.org/external/np/pdr/sus/2002/eng/052802.htm.

International Monetary Fund. (2008). The European credit cycle: diverging patterns. In *Europe Regional Economic Outlook, Fall 2008*. Washington, DC: International Monetary Fund. http://www.imf.org/External/Pubs/FT/REO/2008/EUR/ENG/ereo1008.pdf.

Kinoshita, Y. & Lu, C.-H. (2006). *On the role of absorptive capacity: FDI matters to growth*. William Davidson Institute Working Paper, 845. http://www.wdi.umich.edu/files/Publications/WorkingPapers/wp845.pdf.

Kose, M.A., Prasad, E., Rogoff, K., Wei, S.-J. (2006). *Financial globalization: a reappraisal*. IMF Working Paper, WP/06/189. Washington, DC: International Monetary Fund. www.imf.org/external/pubs/ft/wp/2006/wp06189.pdf.

Lane, P. R., & Milesi-Ferretti, G. M. (2002). External wealth, the trade balance, and the real exchange rate. *European Economic Review, 46*, 1049–1071.

Lansbury, M., Pain, N., & Šmídková, K. (1996). Foreign direct investment in central Europe since 1990: an econometric study. *National Institute Economic Review, 156*, 104–114.

Mody, A., & Murshid, A. P. (2005). Growing up with capital flows. *Journal of International Economics, 65*(1), 249–66.

Rybczynski, T. M. (1955). Factor endowment and relative commodity prices. *Economica, 22*(87), 336–41.

Schadler, S., Drummond, P., Kuijs, L., Murgasova, Z., van Elkan, R. (2005). *Adopting the euro in central Europe – challenges of the next step in European integration*. IMF Occasional Paper, 234. Washington, DC: International Monetary Fund.

Sylwester, K. (2005). Foreign direct investment, growth and income inequality in less developed countries. *International Review of Applied Economics, 19*(3), 289–300.

Šmídková, K., Barrell, R., Holland, D. (2002). *Estimates of FRERs for the five EU accession countries*. CNB Working Paper, No. 3. Prague: Czech National Bank. http://www.cnb.cz/en/pdf/WP_3_2002.pdf.

Šmídková, K., Barrell, R., & Holland, D. (2003). Estimates of fundamental real exchange rates for the five EU pre-accession countries. *Prague Economic Papers, 4*, 291–318.

Williamson, J. (1994). *Estimating equilibrium exchange rates*. Washington, DC: Institute for International Economics.

Chapter 10
Comments on Chapters 8 and 9

Corina Weidinger Sosdean

Abstract This chapter provides comments on Chapter 8 and 9 included in the part on "Financial integration and stability in an enlarged EU". The comments on chapter 8 focus on the concept of "convergence clubs" as well as on the selection of variables and samples of countries included in the model used for explaining current account patterns in emerging Europe and emerging Asia. Regarding Chapter 9, comments touch upon the restrictive hypothesis on the impact of FDIs on the timing of the euro adoption in the new EU Member States, the concept of "integration gains" and some policy conclusions in the last section of the chapter.

10.1 Introductory Remarks

The chapter on "Financial integration and stability in an enlarged EU" contains two contributions, which address the topic from different points of view. The analysis by Sabine Herrmann and Adalbert Winkler focuses on the role of financial market characteristics in explaining the different current account patterns observed in emerging Europe and emerging Asia over the last decade. The contribution by Jan Babecký, Aleš Bulíř and Kateřina Šmídková assesses the impact of FDI inflows on the ability of the new EU member states to fulfil the Maastricht criteria and adopt the euro, given the effects these inflows have on the real exchange rate.

C. Weidinger Sosdean
European Commission, Directorate General Economic and Financial Affairs, Brussels, Belgium
e-mail: corina.weidinger-sosdean@ec.europa.eu

F. Keereman and I. Szekely (eds.), *Five Years of an Enlarged EU*,
DOI 10.1007/978-3-642-12516-4_10, © Springer-Verlag Berlin Heidelberg 2010

10.2 Comments on Chap. 8

The chapter on "Real Convergence, Financial Markets, and the Current Account – Emerging Europe versus Emerging Asia" by Herrmann and Winkler provides an interesting contribution to the strand of empirical studies on the determinants of current account patterns. Using both a standard model and a financial development model, as well as a time horizon of 12 years (1994–2006), the authors tested the significance of macroeconomic variables (i.e. per capita income, dependency ratio) and financial variables (i.e. private credit to GDP, the sum of foreign assets and liabilities to GDP) in explaining the different current account patterns in emerging Europe and emerging Asia. Moreover, a robustness check and a contribution analysis, which aims to provide information on the economic significance of the estimated variables, add value to the high quality of this analysis. Furthermore, the use of state-of-the-art modelling techniques coupled with an extensive literature survey indicates an in-depth knowledge of the subject at hand.

One of the main contributions of the analysis is to apply the concept of "convergence clubs" to describe the process of convergence in emerging Europe and emerging Asia. As meticulously explained by the authors, there are clear arguments for using EU-15 as "core" for emerging Europe, however, the rationale for using the US as the "core country" for emerging Asia appears less convincing. Undisputedly, the countries of emerging Asia have close trade and financial linkages with the US. However, at the same time, several countries of emerging Asia, and in particular the newly industrialized countries (i.e. Singapore, Taiwan) have also had very close trade and financial ties with Japan. Furthermore, the US and emerging Asia are not participating in a joint regional integration process. Consequently, the decision on the most appropriate "core country" in the case of emerging Asia appears to be a rather difficult call.

Concerning the catching-up process in emerging Asia, the authors rightly observe that, after the Asian crisis, convergence has been accompanied by sizeable current account surpluses, as current accounts have switched signs. Moreover, after the Asian crisis these countries not only switched from current account deficits to current account surpluses, but also their growth model changed. The countries of emerging Asia moved from a growth model with a more important contribution of domestic demand, large current account deficits and overvalued currencies to an export-led growth model characterized by an increased contribution of net exports and investment channeled more towards the production of tradable goods, undervalued currencies and widening current account surpluses (European Commission 2009).

The authors provided a good selection of variables in the financial development model used to quantify the contribution of financial market characteristics in explaining current account patterns in emerging Europe and emerging Asia. However, the proxy chosen for the assessment of the overall degree of financial integration appears to be somewhat problematic, given that it is a purely quantitative measure of financial integration. It provides more information on the existence of capital mobility between countries and less information on price convergence on financial markets, respectively on the existence or non-existence of converging rates of return (yields) for different financial instruments. As a matter of fact, capital mobility is only one of two prerequisites of financial integration, the other being the convergence of yields for financial instruments (e.g. bonds) with the same maturity and risk.

The authors explain their preference for a quantity-based indicator to measure the overall level of financial integration by highlighting the disadvantages of price-based measures, which are briefly summarized in footnote. In any case, even if the sum of assets and liabilities to GDP is an indicator which has the advantage of simplicity, it is debatable whether it constitutes the best option for the aim of this analysis. Although used in several studies as a measure of financial integration, this indicator appears to be a more suitable measure of financial openness.

To conclude, a suggestion on the sample of countries chosen for this contribution seems worth making. The authors performed their analysis on a sample which includes 17 countries from emerging Europe and 11 countries from emerging Asia. As both groups of countries are very heterogeneous, it would have been very interesting to also run the regressions on subgroups of countries. Emerging Europe, for instance, could be divided in three subgroups: the new EU Members States, the candidate countries (Croatia, Macedonia and Turkey) and the potential candidate countries (Albania, Bosnia & Herzegovina, Montenegro and Serbia). For emerging Asia, three possible subgroups would be the newly industrialized countries (Hong-Kong, South Korea, Singapore and Taiwan), the middle and low income country members of ASEAN[1] (i.e. Indonesia, Malaysia, Philippines) as well as a subgroup of outliers (China, India).

10.3 Comments on Chap. 9

The chapter on "Sustainable Real Exchange Rates in the New Member States": Is FDI a mixed blessing? by Babecký, Bulíř and Šmídková proposes an empirical model of FDI-driven exchange rates to assess the linkages between FDI inflows and real exchange rates developments in the new Member States (excluding Malta and Cyprus) and in a group of three so-called "forerunners" (Greece, Portugal and Spain) for the period 1995–2013. The impact of FDI on the real exchange rate is modelled by using standard money- and goods equilibrium (IS-LM) schedules, a classical production function and the uncovered interest parity condition.

The contribution is based on the somewhat provocative as well as restrictive hypothesis that FDI can be a "pure blessing", "mixed blessing" or "no blessing" for an early euro adoption by the new EU Member States. As the latter requires nominal

[1]Established in 1967, ASEAN (Association of Southeast Asian Nations) is currently the most advanced integration framework in Asia.

convergence, including nominal exchange rate stability, the outcome will depend on the extent and speed of real exchange rate appreciation in the medium term. The authors argue that FDI inflows are the main driver of real exchange rate appreciation since traditional explanations, such as, a significant currency devaluations at the beginning of the transition process, the Balassa– Samuelson effect as well as the hypothesis of external wealth accumulation, cannot sufficiently explain the extent of the observed real exchange rate appreciation in the new EU Member States.

This chapter also provides a "financial crisis" scenario, which assesses the impact of a large decline in foreign demand on the trajectories of sustainable real exchange rates of the new Member States. In the stylized facts section, the authors fine-tune the grouping of the countries in the sample according to their exchange rate regime ("hard peggers" vs. "inflation targeters") and provide noteworthy details on the monetary strategies of individual countries (e.g. on Slovakia and Romania). Moreover, the contribution is complemented by an interesting discussion on the real exchange rate dynamics in the new Member States in which FDI inflows have been channeled predominantly into non-tradable sectors. However, the authors claim that the data and measurement difficulties to distinguish between tradable and non-tradable FDI inflows for the purpose of the sustainable real exchange rate model appear to be insurmountable.

It is worth mentioning that the authors calculate the sustainable level of external debt for each country by factoring in the ability to meet its financial obligations, instead of simply assuming a fixed level of external debt for all countries. This type of analysis is of particular interest at the current juncture, as the external debt of several new Member States will most likely increase substantially in the coming years.

One of the main contributions of this chapter is the concept "integration gain", i.e. net export gains and productivity improvements stemming from FDI inflows and resulting in real exchange rate appreciations. However, it is debatable whether "integration gain" is the most appropriate term for the net export gains, which the authors attribute to gains from financial integration. These gains are rather a corollary of financial liberalization and dismantling of internal and external capital controls in most of these countries in the mid-1990s. Consequently, the new Member States became important recipients of FDI well before joining the EU, though the accession perspective certainly led to further increases in the contribution of FDI to gross fixed capital formation in these countries.

The authors do not extend the discussion to the impact of other capital flows (e.g. portfolio investment or EU structural funds) on the real exchange rates of the countries in the sample. However, apart from substantial FDI inflows, all these countries have also benefited significantly from other capital inflows, especially pre-accession and structural funds. For instance, the new Member States received structural funds amounting to EUR 17.8 billion (2.1% of GDP) in 2007 (European Commission 2009).

In the policy implications section, the authors claim that the "forerunners did not attract additional FDI after euro adoption" due to a prolonged period of overvaluation and conclude that a similar scenario is likely to happen to the new Member States. However, it is worth exploring whether the loss of attractiveness of Greece,

Portugal and Spain for FDI inflows can be also attributed to other country-specific factors, such as the size of the economy, geographical location, quality of institutions, infrastructure and business environment. Furthermore, since exchange rate volatility appears to constitute rather a deterrent of FDI inflows, the adoption of the euro may actually spur further FDI inflows.

Finally, while the rationale of the "pure blessing" and "mixed blessing" hypotheses is plausible, the hypothesis that "FDI can be no blessing at all" is definitively too restrictive. It assumes that FDI inflows to non-tradable sectors leading to a worsening of the trade balance have only a negative impact on the ability of a country to adopt the euro.

Reference

European Commission (2009). *Five Years of an enlarged EU: Economic achievements and challenges, European Economy 1*, Economic and Financial Affairs DG.

Part IV
Integration, Openness and Growth: Did Accession Make a Difference?

Chapter 11
The Second Transition: Eastern Europe in Perspective

Stefania Fabrizio, Daniel Leigh, and Ashoka Mody

Abstract The countries of Eastern Europe have achieved two remarkable transitions in the short period of the last two decades: from plan to market and, then, in the run-up to and entry into the European Union, riding a wave of global trade and financial market integration. Focusing on the second transition, this paper reaches three conclusions. First, by several metrics, East European and East Asian growth performances have been about on par since the mid-1990s; both regions have far surpassed Latin American growth. Second, the mechanisms of growth in East Europe and East Asia have been very different. East Europe has relied on a distinctive – often discredited – model, embracing financial integration, with structural change to compensate for appreciating real exchange rates. In contrast, East Asia has contained further financial integration and maintained steady or depreciating real exchange rates. Third, the ongoing financial turbulence has dulled the sheen on East European performance but, thus far, has not obviously differentiated emerging market regions: rather, the hot spots in each region reflect individual country vulnerabilities. The paper, in closing, speculates on whether the East European growth model is sustainable and replicable.

11.1 Introduction

The recent setback notwithstanding, the group of Central and Eastern European (CEE) nations have emerged from decades under socialist planning as vibrant

---

S. Fabrizio
Strategy, Policy and Review Department, IMF, Washington, DC, USA
e-mail: SFABRIZIO@imf.org

D. Leigh
Research Department, IMF, Washington, DC, USA

A. Mody
European Department, IMF, Washington, DC, USA

F. Keereman and I. Szekely (eds.), *Five Years of an Enlarged EU*,
DOI 10.1007/978-3-642-12516-4_11,

market economies within the fold of the European Union (EU). This impressive transformation occurred in less than two decades, and within that short time span, there were, in turn, two distinct transitions – the first from planned to market systems and a second that achieved increasing economic sophistication riding on the wave of globalization. The paper argues that this achievement, particularly in the second transition, was the result of an economic development model that has no recent precedent. Indeed, to the extent that the Central and Eastern European approach to growth and structural transformation had been attempted in the post-World War II period, it stood largely discredited. For these reasons, the paper offers a broader comparative commentary on the economic achievements and growth strategy of two other groups of emerging market economies, those in Latin America and, especially, in East Asia.

It is the case that even as this paper is being written, a global shock of a substantial magnitude is propagating through the world economy. The CEE economies are being subjected to a severe test. Some countries, in particular, had placed themselves in a more vulnerable situation than others and they are likely to suffer substantial contraction. However, as of this writing, it is not evident that the CEE economies as a group will ultimately be impacted more so than other regions. As the global crisis continues to unfold, countries in all regions are feeling the pressure, with specific countries in those regions under particular stress. Within Central and Eastern Europe and elsewhere, country efforts will need to complement global initiatives to cushion the shock and help preserve the gains achieved.

And the CEE gains before the crisis hit were substantial. Consider a metric of the accomplishments. The GDP per capita (in PPS terms) of each of the ten Central and Eastern European countries we consider is measured as a ratio of the GDP per capita of the EU-15 (the first fifteen members of the European Union). We start the story in 1995, by when the turmoil from the first transition was largely complete and all countries had passed beyond their lowest output point following the break from communism (Fischer and Sahay 2004). Figure 11.1 shows the subsequent gains through 2003, they year before eight of the ten countries (i.e., all other than Bulgaria and Romania) entered the EU. Although, the starting points of the countries varied widely – from a low of 30% for a number of countries to about 70% for the Czech Republic and Slovenia – all countries gained on the more affluent EU-15. Recall, this phase included the emerging market crises from Mexico to Russia, the last of which in particular hurt some of the CEE economies. In the second phase, with the entry of eight countries in the EU and strengthening prospects of Bulgarian and Romanian entry, the climb continued and was about as strong in the further catch up and about as broad-based. Particularly impressive was the increase achieved by the Czech Republic from its already high per capita income; in contrast, Hungary, a star of previous years, made only modest gains.

To place this achievement in perspective, we compare it with the gains made by Latin American and East Asian economies over the same period. Here we benchmark the per capita income to the United States per capita income, taking simple

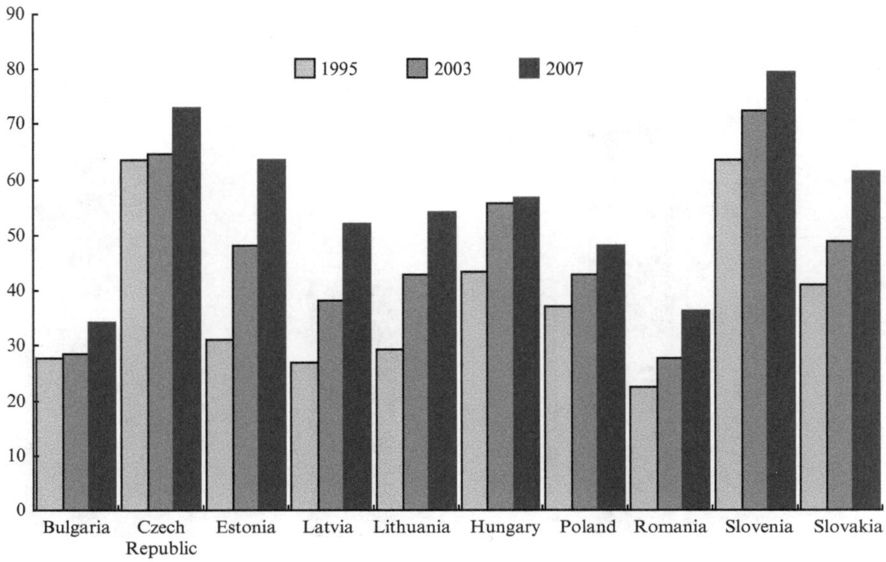

Fig. 11.1 Central and Eastern Europe: GDP per capita as percent of EU-15 GDP per capita, 1995–2007
Notes: GDP in PPS per habitant; Data for Romania are available starting in 1999
Source: Eurostat

averages of the countries in each group (Fig. 11.2).[1] Clearly, there is variation, often significant variation, within each group and so the picture we portray does not do justice to individual achievements within each region. Nevertheless, the comparative trends are revealing. The CEE economies had an average per capita income ratio relative to the U.S. per capita income of 29% in 1995, which increased by 12% points to 41% in 2007. The Latin American experience is a clear contrast. The average per capita GDP relative to the United States has remained below 25% since 1995. The ratio actually fell during the crisis years from 1995 to 2003 and in the next 4 years merely regained the 1995 level. Thus, it was not just the 1980s that were a lost decade for the Latin America but despite efforts at macroeconomic stabilization and more openness, Latin America has failed to gain any significant ground now for almost 30 years (though as Zettelmeyer 2006, suggests the variation within Latin America may be higher than in other regions, masking significant differences across countries). The East Asian economies made rather more progress. Recall also that East Asia economies had experienced exceptional growth for several years prior to 1995, some from the 1970s and, as such, their scope for

[1]Unless otherwise stated, the group of Latin American countries includes Argentina, Brazil, Chile, Colombia, Mexico, Perú, and Venezuela, and the group of East Asia countries includes China, Hong Kong, Indonesia, Korea, Malaysia Philippines, Singapore, Taiwan, and Thailand.

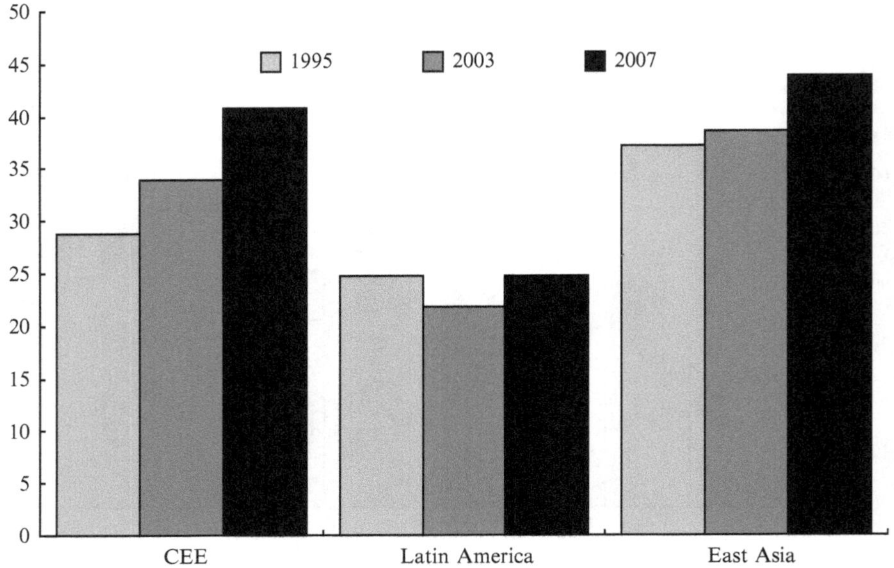

Fig. 11.2 GDP per capita as a share of US GDP, major emerging market regions, 1995–2007
Source: IMF WEO Database

further growth was more restricted. The crisis years definitely slowed down East Asia, not surprising since countries in the region were at the epicenter of the turmoil during 1997–1998. Thereafter, East Asian economies resumed their catch up process (Fig. 11.2).

The questions of interest then are: did development and growth strategies vary across these regions and, if so, what do they tell us about the trade-offs that policymakers have made? This paper's thesis is that the CEE nations have embraced the opportunities of globalization – along with its potential downsides and risks – more so than any other region. This approach distinguishes their growth achievements, the mechanisms of growth, and the structural transformation witnessed. Two features of the policy approach are particularly relevant. First, international financial integration has been a central aspect of the growth strategy. That integration has contributed to sustained inflows of capital, including not only foreign direct investment but also bank lending and portfolio flows. The counterpart of these flows has been a sometimes large current account deficit. Second, with capital inflows, real exchange rates have been allowed to appreciate. But the commitment to trade openness has remained unwavering, as countries' external trade has become an increasing share of their GDP. In turn, maintaining competitiveness has required a transformation of the product structure and quality.[2]

[2]The CEE countries also participate in the European labor market, which despite its current restrictions allows considerable and increasing mobility. Countries in other regions have more particular – historically and geographically determined – opportunities for benefiting from

This approach, combining real exchange rate appreciation and current account deficits, stood largely discredited. Indeed, the collapse of Latin American economies in the midst of the debt crisis of the 1980s is often attributed to just such a strategy. In the 1960s and 1970s, Latin America did grow rapidly, borrowing from abroad. But the Latin American economies failed to sustain their competitive ability and the debtors' loss of confidence led to their withdrawal and a severe crunch. Similarly, these factors also contributed to the East Asian crisis of 1997–1998. And, indeed, that risk remains in the CEE economies, and, as the global financial turbulence continues, the risk may be turning into a reality form some economies. A sharp contraction is ongoing especially in those countries that experienced the most heady growth rates. For these countries, there could be lasting consequences with a prolonged slowdown.

The contrast with East Asia is noteworthy. The East Asian growth miracle has been viewed through widely varying lenses, with some seeing the experience as evidence that markets do not by themselves deliver growth, and need to be "governed" by wise politicians and technocrats (Wade, 1990) and others insisting, however, on the primacy of the disciplines and opportunities afforded by international markets (World Bank, 1993). These debates have receded following the Asian crisis and the focus has shifted to how countries choose to interact with global markets. East Asia has once again attracted approval (Prasad et al. 2006, and Rodrik 2008). In broad terms, with some country variation, the East Asian approach has been an amalgam of reinforcing elements that include: relatively high savings rates (postponed consumption), a lid on currency appreciation, a modest pace of international financial integration, resulting in small current account deficits or even surpluses and growing international reserves. Thus, while East Asia has continued its engagement in international trade, it has done so with depreciation of the real effective exchange rate (unlike in the Central and Eastern Europe) but accompanied with structural transformation in its export structure (as in Central and Eastern Europe).[3] Moreover, East Asia has moved in the direction of self-insurance through reserve accumulation rather than in international risk sharing through greater financial integration and more reliance on international capital for intertemporal consumption smoothing.

This paper does not attempt a normative evaluation of the different approaches to engagement with globalization. Rather, the rest of the paper documents the features of the growth strategy and the growth outcomes in Central and Eastern Europe, Latin America, and East Asia. The next section focuses on Central and Eastern Europe. It describes the increasing reliance of all countries in this region on international trade and financial markets, accompanied by the strengthening of domestic institutions. While the extent to which any one country has proceeded

international labor mobility. The complexity of this issue and the limited data preclude analysis in this paper.

[3]Rodrik (2008) argues that an undervalued real exchange rate compensates for institutional weaknesses, which would otherwise thwart the growth of the tradeables sector necessary for overall growth.

in a particular direction differs, the overall similarity of the thrust is striking. This is followed by a comparative perspective across the three regions of interest. Here the differences are striking. To assess the outcomes from these strategies, the next section reports on the growth outcomes resulting from their differing development strategies, reporting a descriptive analysis of growth accelerations and the findings of growth regressions. A concluding section speculates on the sustainability and replicability of the CEE growth model.

11.2 Openness and Institutions in the Central and Eastern Europe

The degree of trade openness has increased steadily in all countries, with the exception of Romania, where it appears to have stalled in recent years (Fig. 11.3). In 1995, the ratio of trade (exports plus imports) to GDP was less than 100% for 5 of the 10 countries we consider. By 2007, there were only two such countries, Poland and Romania. Clearly, many of the CEE countries are small and it is to be expected that they will be open to trade. What is remarkable is the continued and substantial increase in trading relationships. In this regard, the CEE countries have been riding an international wave of globalization, wherein trade has, in

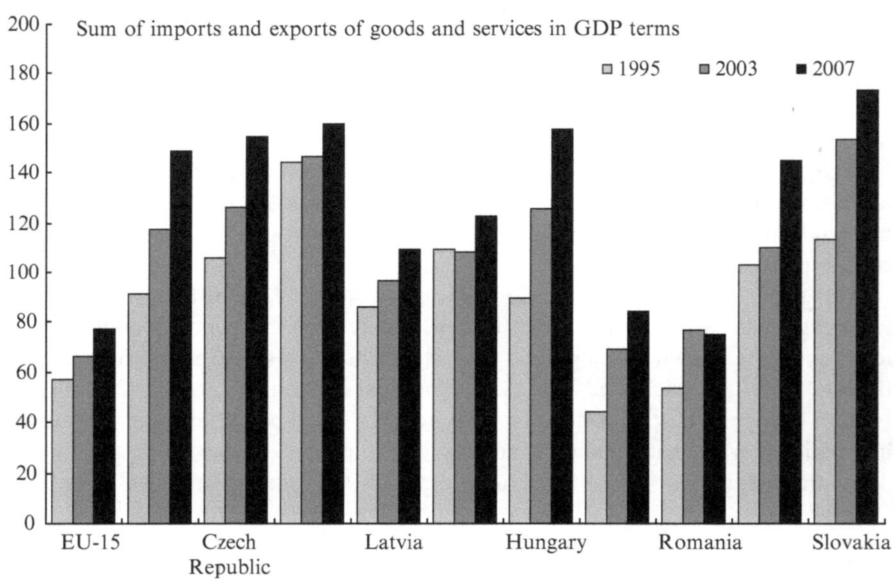

Fig. 11.3 Central and Eastern Europe: trade openness trends, 1995–2007
Notes: Data for Romania are available starting in 1998
Source: Eurostat

general, grown faster than production. Within Europe, even the more advanced economies have participated to an increasing degree in international trade. Thus, the trade to GDP ratio of the EU-15 increased by almost 20% points from just under 60% in 1995 to just under 80% in 2007. Nine of the 10 CEE countries increased their ratios by more than 20%; only Estonia, which was already highly open in 1995, experienced a somewhat smaller increase in the trade-to-GDP ratio.[4]

The rapid increase of the trade-to-GDP ratios in the CEE economies is also seen in their increased market shares (shares of their exports in world exports). Again, the timing and the extent vary by country but in all cases the gains are significant (Fig. 11.3). Note, as we discuss below, this is a key factor differentiating Central and Eastern Europe from the other regions: the increase in market shares was achieved even while the exchange rates were appreciating significantly. The appreciation is typically attributed to the so-called Balassa-Samuelson effect. While the size of this effect remains controversial, there is a more basic ongoing process. The dual processes of catch up in per capita incomes and the integration into Europe has meant that prices in the CEE countries have also been catching up with European price levels. Fighting this process of real exchange rate appreciation would risk negating also the gains from the convergence and integration process (Fig. 11.4).

The implication, therefore, is that the combination of increased market shares with appreciation of the real exchange rate has required a substantial transformation of the economy (see also European Commission 2003, for documentation of the transformation of the economic structure of these countries). While there are many facets of this transformation, we focus here on the structure of exports. Two findings (detailed in Fabrizio et al. 2006) are a rise in the product quality and an increased technological content of the exports. These trends are summarized in Fig. 11.5.[5] The quality of a product is proxied by the unit value of the country's exports relative to the average unit value of world's exports of the same product. For the country, then, we aggregate these unit values over finely defined products to obtain an aggregate unit value ratio. A rise in this ratio implies that the country's unit values are rising faster than that of the world. This is what we see for most countries. Figure 11.5 reports the logarithm of the unit value ratios and, as such, a value of zero implies that the country's product quality is at the same level as the world exports. Of the CEE countries, Latvia and Lithuania are just above the world level in 2004 (the most recent year for which disaggregated data comparable across countries is available). These countries also did not experience a significant rise in their unit value ratios or in the high- and medium-tech component of their exports. Thus, much of their increased export share in world trade has reflected a catch up process from under representation in global trade; it is possible that changes are occurring at a finer level that we are not able to capture.

[4]Here, as elsewhere in the paper, we have not explored the implications of the geographical distribution of trade. As documented by Hermann and Winkler (2009), the CEE continue to trade heavily in Europe, while the East Asian and Latin American economies rely to a much greater extent on the United States. These differences could eventually have implications for growth.

[5]This figure does not include Bulgaria and Romania; the next draft will attempt to incorporate them.

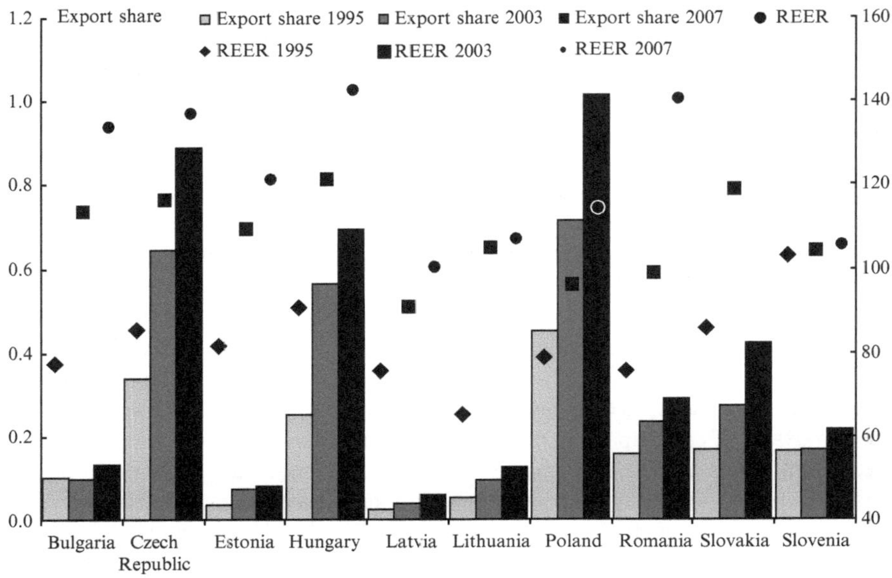

Fig. 11.4 Central and Eastern Europe: world market shares and real exchange rate trends, 1995–2007
Source: IMF WEO Database

Looking ahead, they, nevertheless, face the challenge of moving beyond a phase in which gains have been relatively easy. For the rest, the changes have been substantial, both in terms of product quality and in product structure. The gains have been principally in "medium-high" technology products, as the share of the low and medium-low products has declined. At the same time, many of these products are differentiated, such that product quality is valued more so than in standardized products that are bought principally for the most competitive price (for details see Fabrizio et al. 2006).

In parallel to their trade integration, the CEE countries have proceeded rapidly towards financial integration (European Commission 2009). Entry into the EU has been accompanied by liberalization of their capital accounts. This has been accompanied by extensive capital inflows and outflows. While the countries have been mainly recipients of capital from abroad (mainly from advanced European countries and, especially in the early phase in the form of foreign direct investment), they have more fundamentally placed themselves in a network of capital flow transactions in the region. Foreign banks that have established subsidiaries and branches in Central and Eastern Europe have been conduits of foreign capital for extensive lending to domestic businesses and households. As they have been integrated into European markets, sovereigns and corporates have borrowed on international capital markets at increasing lower spreads. Before the onset of the recent financial turbulence, Lithuania was paying virtually no risk premium over the rates charged to the German sovereign. While, in retrospect, some might argue

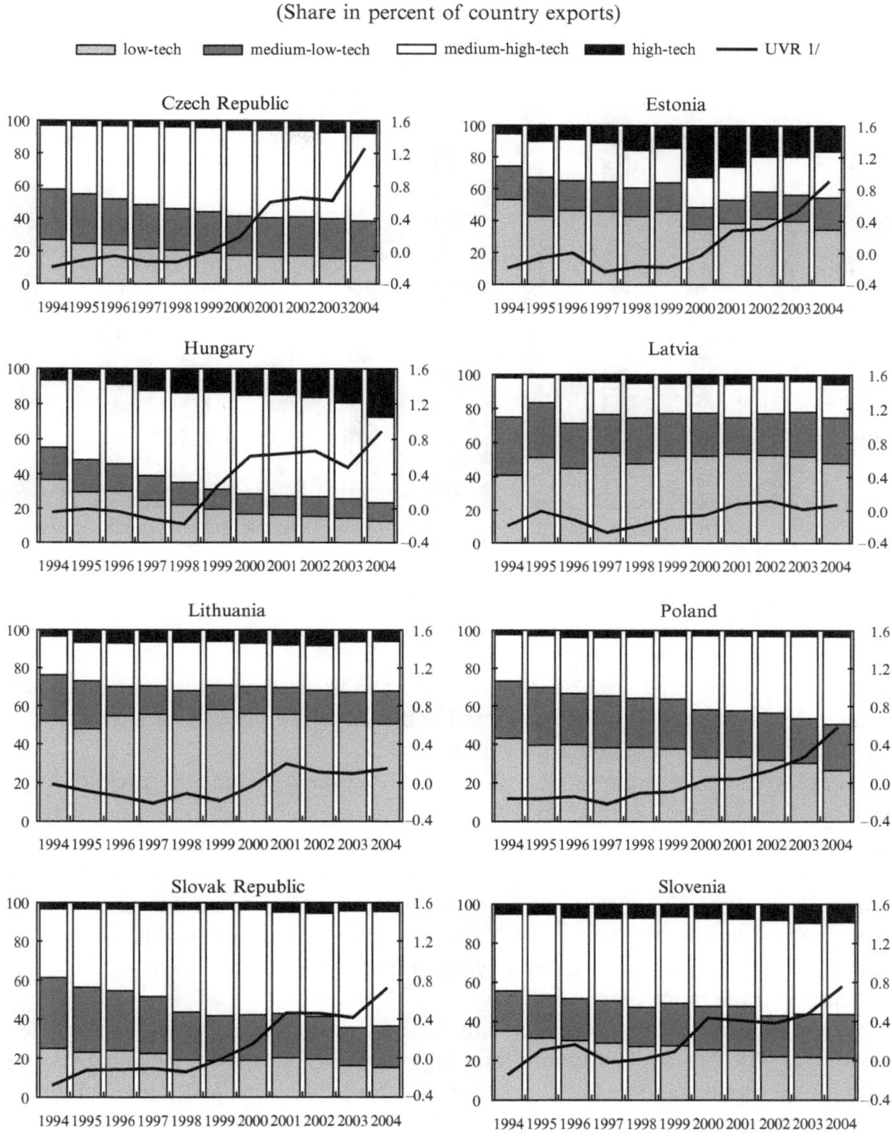

Fig. 11.5 Central and Eastern Europe: structural transformation of exports, 1994–2004
Notes: UVR is the unit value of a country's exports divided by the unit value of world exports. Expressed in logarithm so that value of zero means country unit value equals world unit value
Source: UN Comtrade

that the markets were being imprudent in pricing risk, financial integration has allowed access to substantial capital inflows. At the same time, many countries in Central and Eastern Europe (along with other countries at or below their income

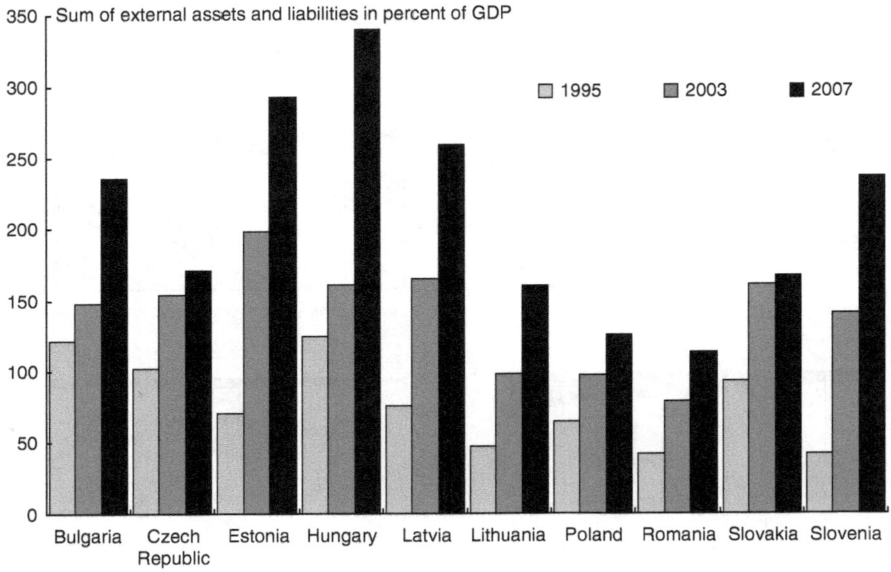

Fig. 11.6 Central and Eastern Europe: trends in financial integration, 1995–2007
Source: National Central Banks

levels in other regions) are also exporters of capital. As their firms have acquired greater financial strength and managerial self-confidence, they have expanded by moving into neighboring countries and beyond.

These trends are summarized in Fig. 11.6, where financial integration is measured as the sum of external assets and external liabilities as a ratio of GDP (analogous to exports plus imports as a share of GDP). The increase in financial integration is sharp everywhere. From less than 100% in the mid-1990s, the financial integration ratio has increased to above 200% in a number of countries in just over a decade. While the metrics are not strictly comparable, this increase by about 100% points in many cases is considerably larger than the 20–40% points increase in trade ratios discussed above.

Finally, openness has been accompanied by institutional strengthening (see Roland 2005). Strong institutions are important to sustaining the engagement with global product and financial markets and also in supporting efficient outcomes from that engagement. The extent to which this complementarity has played out in the CEE economies is not easy to identify precisely. Fischer and Sahay (2004) do conclude that institutional strengthening in these economies has been key to their growth process (as do Schadler et al. 2006). The examination of the role of institutions in Central and Eastern Europe requires further thought. Fischer and Sahay (2004) use a broad measure of institutions to include the development of central banks, treasuries, tax systems, commercial law, and, more broadly, the development of the market economy through measures such as privatization. Their analysis then focuses on the variation in such measures within the group of

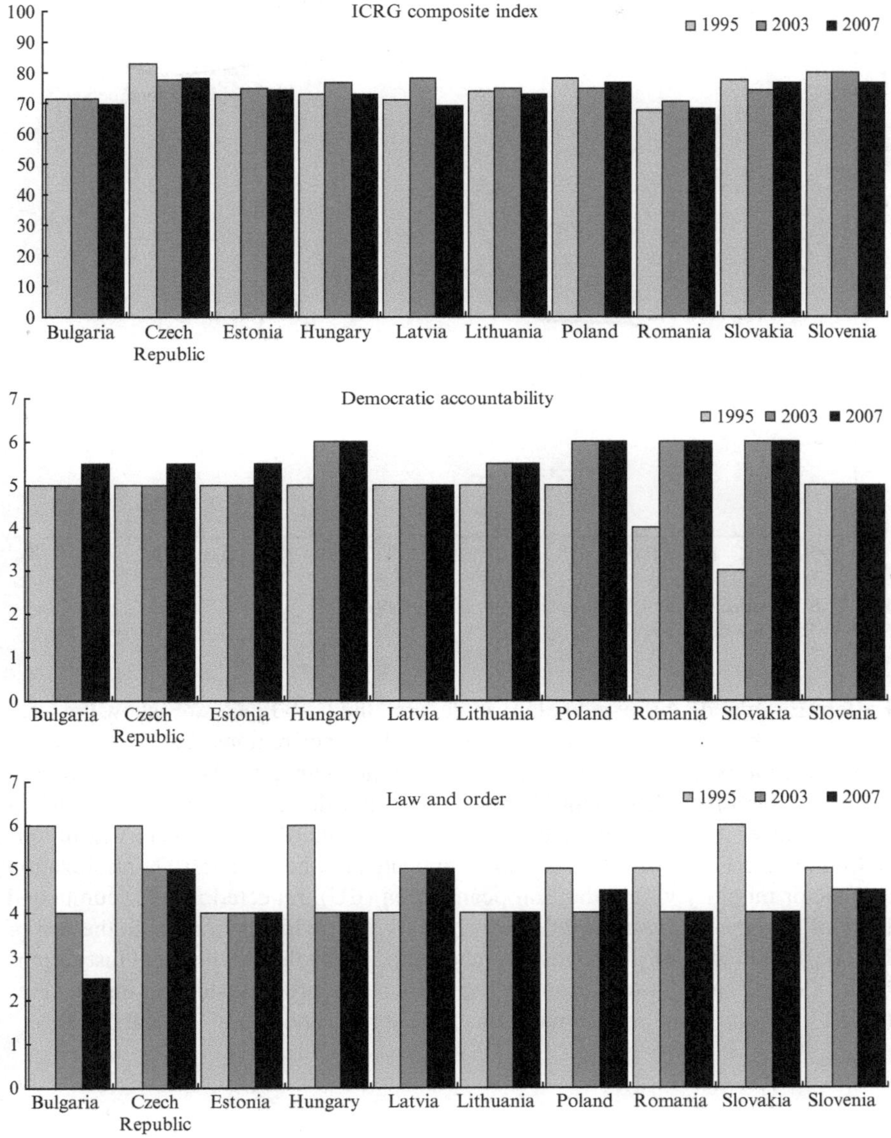

Fig. 11.7 Central and Eastern Europe: trends in institutional strength, 1995–2007
Source: International Country Risk Guide

transition economies. If instead, a comparison is sought across European emerging economies and other regions, then it is necessary to use other indices for which comparable cross-country data is available. The Fig. 11.7 reports the governance indicators of the International Country Risk Guide (ICRG). This aggregate measure does not show large changes over time within particular countries in Central and

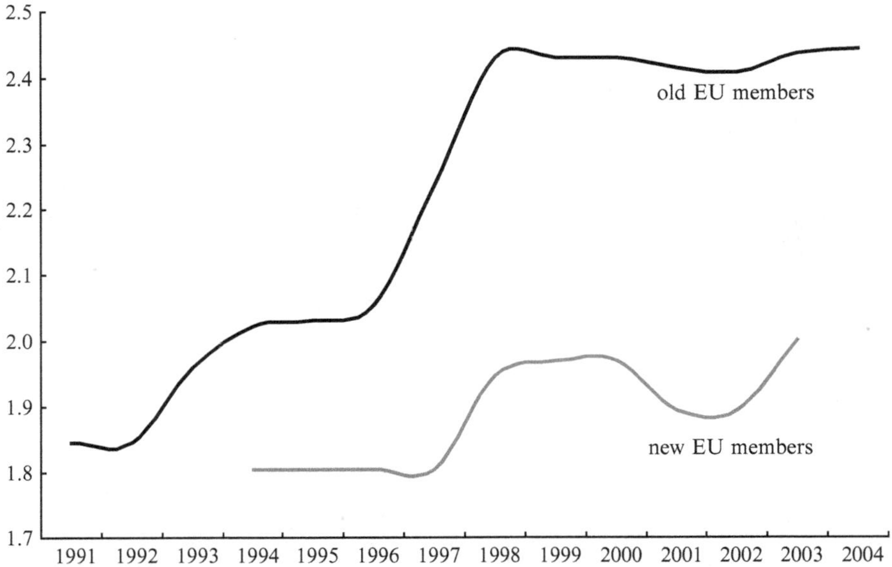

Fig. 11.8 Average value of fiscal institutions index, 1991–2004
Source: Fabrizio and Mody (2008)

Eastern Europe. As discussed below, in general, the ICRG measures show the CEE averages to be generally higher than that for the other regions; but, interestingly, over time, the other regions have caught up in the aggregate, there are subcomponents in which the CEE countries have apparently declined, and others in which they are lower than emerging markets in other regions. The analysis of institutions in Central and Eastern Europe is also complicated by the regulatory harmonization and factor mobility within the European Union (EU), reflected in its accumulated body of law, the *acquis communautaire*. Clearly, by reducing borders to the rest of Europe, these regulatory changes played an important role. On the fiscal institutions front, Central and Eastern Europe has also made progress to varying degrees (Fig. 11.8), with some occasional setbacks (Fabrizio and Mody 2006 and 2008).

11.3 Emerging Market Regions in Perspective

In this section, we follow the same sequence, using the same metrics, to place the CEE achievements in perspective. In summary, we conclude that Central and Eastern Europe has moved faster with respect to trade integration (despite their real exchange rate appreciation), have moved decisively faster in terms of financial integration, and about on par (when judged by a variety of metrics) with respect to institutional development. Given our focus here on Central and Eastern Europe, we do not examine the inter-country differences for Latin America and East Asia, except to point out where the inclusion in the East Asian averages of Hong Kong and Singapore, two city states premised on external links, misrepresents the more general tendencies in that region. Because we do not discuss, individual country experiences in the other regions, readers may justifiably question some of our general characterizations.

Consider, first, the trends in trade openness. For the CEE countries, the increase in openness at the country level reported in the previous section is seen in the steady rise for the region as a whole (Fig. 11.9). East Asia's trade openness has followed a similar track (this chart excludes Hong Kong and Singapore, which are very open by this measure and further raise East Asian estimated openness).

The contrast with Latin America is striking. Unlike for Central and Eastern Europe and East Asia, where openness has been upwards of 100%, that for Latin America is closer to 50%. As we have cautioned above, these regional comparisons need to be interpreted with care. Some of the Latin American countries, e.g., Brazil, are large and it is to be expected that trade will play a smaller role in large countries. Nevertheless, even the increase over time in Latin America's openness index has been lackluster. These trends are mirrored in export shares (Fig. 11.10). Starting from a low base of just above 1½% of world exports in 1995, the CEE share approached 4% in 2007. East Asia was an exporting powerhouse already in 1995 but nevertheless increased its share of the world market by about 3% points by 2007 to almost 20%. The Latin American world share, in contrast, remained in a narrow range between 4 and 5%. It is possible to interpret the data as suggesting that there was some modest increase in Latin America's share between 1995 and 2000 but that it is remained stable since then, while Central and Eastern Europe and East Asia have continued to gain ground.

The juxtaposition of these trends in export shares against real exchange rate trends highlights an important difference between Central and Eastern Europe and East Asia. In Central and Eastern Europe, as noted above, the real exchange rate has steadily appreciated but despite that export shares have also increased. East Asia's real exchange rate, in contrast, has trended down, although since 2004 the downtrend may have partially reversed. Thus, East Asian gain in market share has at least in part been helped by favorable exchange rate movements. The Latin American real exchange rate has, along with its export share, remained relatively flat.

These trends are linked to those in financial integration and current account developments. Here the differentiation between Central and Eastern Europe and East Asia sharpens. The CEE openness ratio increased from about 75% in 1995 to about 225% in 2007, a threefold increase. Though East Asia was also trending up in the 1990s, following the crisis in the later part of the decade, that trend came to an abrupt stop. In this regard, East Asia and Latin America are closer to each other, in level and even trend. Further, in Abiad et al. (2008) we argue that financial integration in Europe has been associated with a downhill flow of capital from rich to poor countries.[6] This has meant that the CEE economies have run current account deficits reflecting the inflow of capital (Fig. 11.11). The East Asian

[6]Hermann and Winkler (2009) provide further details regarding trade developments across the CEE and East Asia.

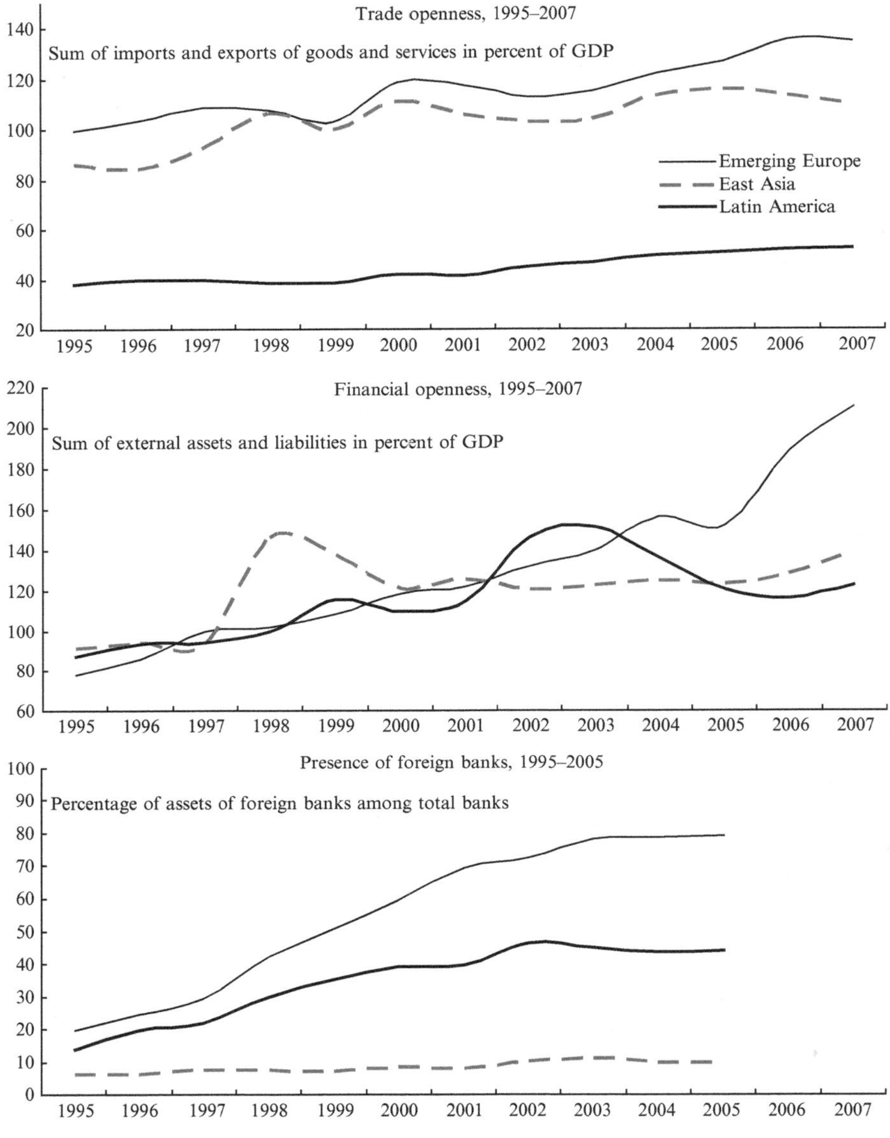

Fig. 11.9 Regional trends in trade and financial openness, 1995–2007
Source: IMF

economies, as is well known, have run surpluses in recent years. Thus, the East Asian economies while restricting their further international financial engagement also began to self insure by running surpluses and accumulating reserves. While the CEE economies have been able to supplement domestic savings with foreign savings, allowing consumption to rise in anticipation of future income growth.

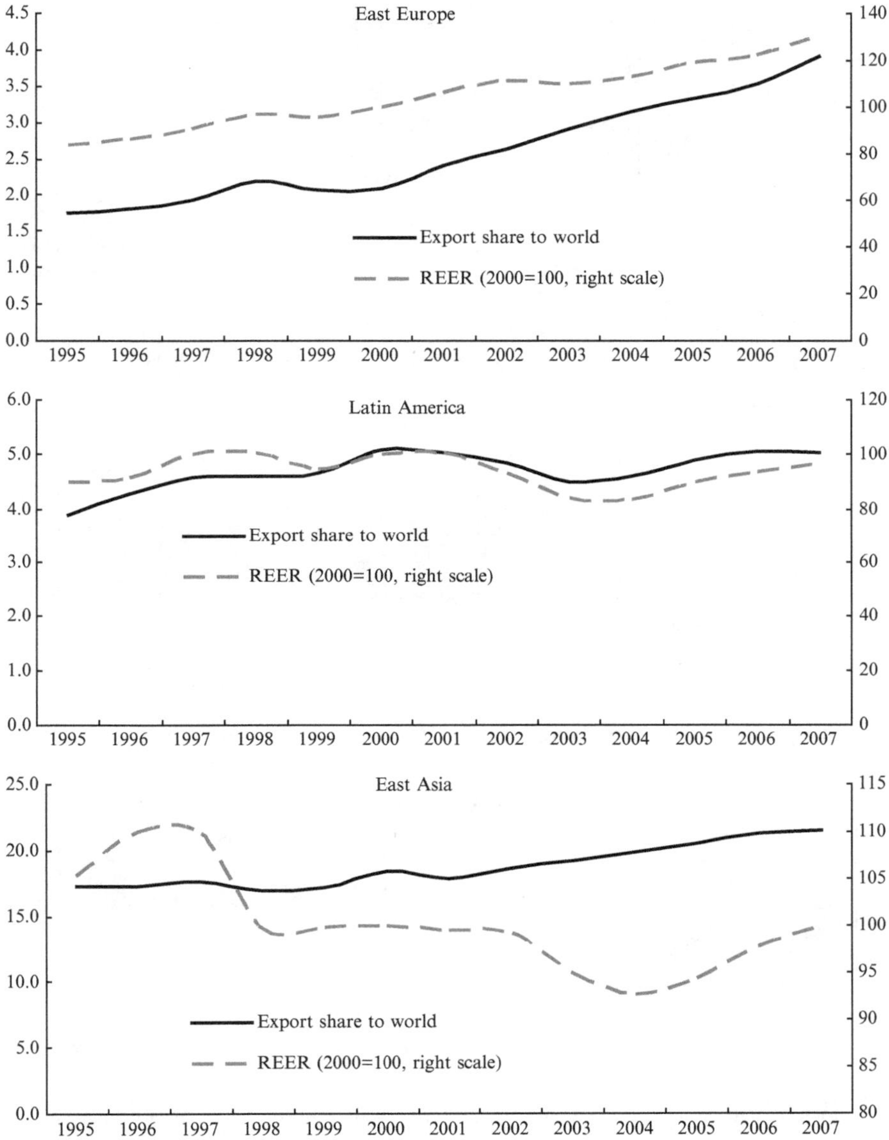

Fig. 11.10 Regional trends in exports shares and real effective exchange rates 1995–2007
Source: IMF, DOT and INS

In this regard, as with financial integration, Latin America has tended to be more like East Asia, with a greater tendency over time to self insure.

Finally, we once again see that the CEE emphasis on trade and financial openness has been supported by strong institutions (Fig. 11.12). Here, there are

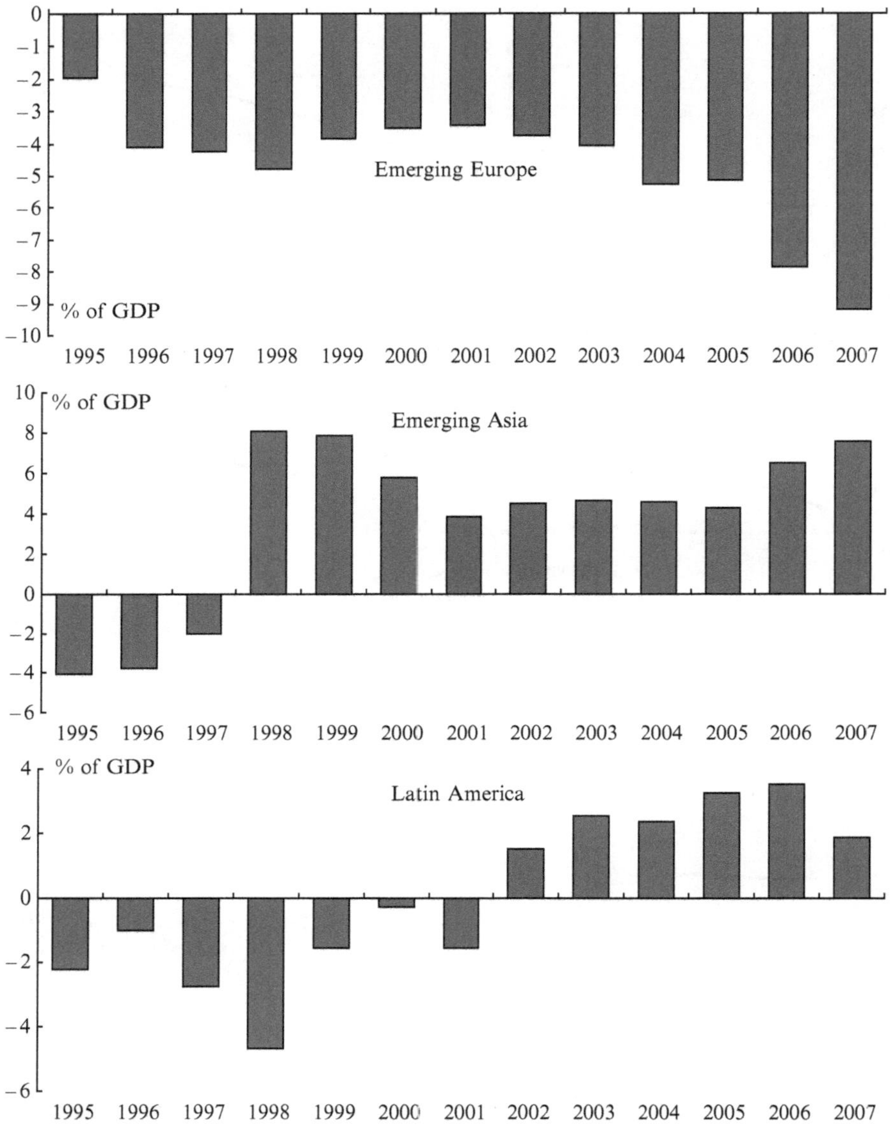

Fig. 11.11 Current account trends, 1995–2007
Source: IMF

three observations, which require further analysis and reflection. First, in the aggregate ICRG measure, Central and Eastern Europe have overall led the other regions. In the most recent years, though, the others have caught up and the small fall in Central and Eastern Europe reflects a downgrading of Latvia by the CEEC.

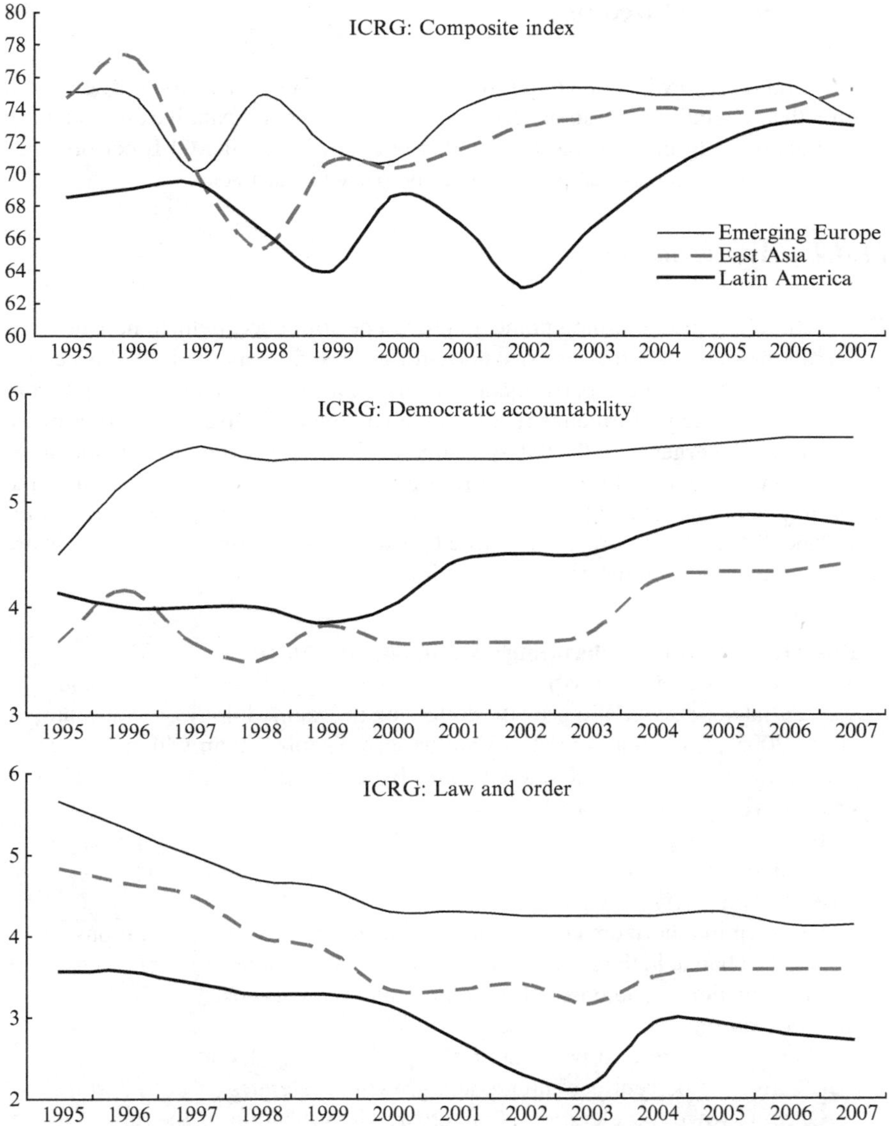

Fig. 11.12 Regional trends in institutional strengthening, 1995–2007
Source: International Country Risk Guide (2008) and authors' estimates

Second, the one area in which Central and Eastern Europe have both led and improved their performance is "democratic accountability," though again by this measure, the others have also caught up. Finally, in terms of "law and order," all are thought to have declined in effectiveness.

11.4 Growth Outcomes

These trends can now be related to growth outcomes. This section reports new work on growth accelerations and some results also from earlier comparative cross-country growth analysis. In general, the picture that emerges is that the CEE performance in recent years is impressive, but it is about on par with East Asia.

11.4.1 Accelerations

This section focuses on turning points in growth performance, defined here as rapid accelerations in growth that are sustained for at least 5 years. Note that accelerations refer to the absolute performance of the country itself and is distinct from convergence, or the performance relative to other countries, discussed earlier in the paper. The convergence reflected typically did reflect acceleration; while most accelerations ongoing before the most recent crisis will end, convergence in some cases may continue. Box 11.1 details the criteria for assessing growth "accelerations" and Table 11.1 reports the identified growth acceleration episodes. These are broadly consistent with the episodes identified by Hausmann et al. (2005).

Box 11.1 Growth Accelerations: Methodology and Data

The key feature of a growth takeoff is a both a high *level* of growth and a substantial *acceleration* in growth. Following the methodology of Hausmann et al. (2005), growth accelerations are defined as episodes in which the real per capita PPS GDP growth rate increases by at least 2% points, and in which growth averages at least 3.5% per year over a 5-year horizon.[7]

Formally, let growth rate $g_{t,t+n}$ denote the growth rate of GDP per capita (y) at time t over horizon n, where:

$g_{t,t+i} = \ln(y_{t+i}) - \ln(y_t)$, $i=1, \ldots, n$.

Let the initial horizon, i.e. the minimum length of growth accelerations, be N, and the change in the growth rate at time t be Δg_t, where $\Delta g_t = g_{t,t+n} - g_{t-n,t}$

Identification of the onset of growth accelerations is based on the following two criteria:

(1) $g_{t,t+n} \geq Z$ percent per annum, i.e., growth is rapid; and

(2) $\Delta g_t \geq Y$ percent per annum, i.e., growth accelerates.

Once a growth acceleration is underway, identification of the end of the acceleration is based on the following two criteria:

(3) $g_{t,t+n} \leq X \rightarrow$ growth for the following N-year period dips below X percent per annum;

(4) $g_{t+1,t+2} \leq W \rightarrow$ annual growth for the following year dips below W percent per annum.

(continued)

[7]The algorithm for identifying growth accelerations was generously provided by Jeromin Zettelmeyer and Jean Salvati.

The parameters used for the analysis are $N = 5$; $Z = 3.5$; $Y = 2$; $X = 2$; $W = 3$. Relaxing the thresholds for identifying growth takeoffs produces a larger number of accelerations.

Table 11.1 Growth acceleration episodes, by region

Region	Country	Year	Growth before	Growth after	Difference in growth	Duration
Emerging Europe	Bulgaria	1998	−3.8	5.1	8.9	9
	Czech Republic	2000	1.1	4.4	3.2	7
	Estonia	1992	−6.5	3.5	10.0	15
	Hungary	1995	−2.1	3.8	5.9	12
	Latvia	1994	−12.1	3.8	15.9	13
	Lithuania	1996	−8.8	3.5	12.3	11
	Poland	1991	−1.7	4.4	6.1	16
	Romania	1999	−0.1	4.9	5.0	8
	Slovak Republic	1993	−6.5	4.8	11.3	14
	Slovenia	1995	−0.5	4.3	4.8	12
East Asia Pacific	Cambodia	1999	0.9	4.7	3.8	8
	China, P.R.	1976	1.5	4.6	3.0	31
	Hong Kong SAR	1968	5.8	8.7	2.8	26
	Hong Kong SAR	1999	−0.5	3.5	4.0	8
	Indonesia	1965	−0.9	3.9	4.8	31
	Indonesia	2002	−1.5	4.2	5.7	5
	Korea	1965	3.7	8.2	4.5	42
	Lao People's Dem. Rep	1991	1.0	4.0	3.0	16
	Malaysia	1969	3.1	5.3	2.2	15
	Malaysia	1989	1.6	5.6	4.0	8
	Mongolia	2000	1.8	4.1	2.4	7
	Papua New Guinea	1969	1.8	4.3	2.5	4
	Papua New Guinea	1988	0.6	5.0	4.4	6
	Singapore	1965	7.1	10.7	3.6	32
	Thailand	1975	2.6	5.5	2.9	21
	Thailand	2001	−0.4	4.8	5.2	6
	Vietnam	1989	2.1	4.3	2.2	18
Latin America	Argentina	1966	1.2	3.5	2.3	5
	Argentina	1989	−3.8	6.5	10.3	8
	Argentina	2002	−4.3	7.5	11.8	5
	Bolivia	1971	−1.9	3.6	5.5	5
	Brazil	1966	2.0	6.2	4.3	11
	Chile	1975	−2.8	5.2	8.0	5
	Chile	1985	−1.6	4.2	5.8	13
	Colombia	1967	1.2	4.0	2.8	12
	Colombia	2002	−0.8	4.0	4.8	5
	Costa Rica	2002	1.8	4.4	2.6	5
	Dominican Republic	1967	−0.8	5.1	5.9	8
	Dominican Republic	1991	0.0	4.5	4.5	16
	Ecuador	1968	1.9	6.6	4.7	10

(*continued*)

Table 11.1 (continued)

Region	Country	Year	Growth before	Growth after	Difference in growth	Duration
	Guatemala	1967	2.0	4.0	2.0	13
	Haiti	1975	−0.2	3.7	3.9	5
	Haiti	1989	−2.7	3.7	6.4	9
	Honduras	1974	0.5	4.0	3.6	5
	Jamaica	1967	2.9	6.7	3.8	5
	Jamaica	1985	−0.9	4.4	5.3	5
	Mexico	1995	−0.4	4.0	4.4	5
	Panama	1975	1.9	4.8	2.8	7
	Panama	2001	1.1	4.2	3.1	6
	Paraguay	1973	2.5	5.2	2.6	8
	Peru	1990	−4.0	4.2	8.2	5
	Peru	2001	0.3	4.7	4.4	6
	Trinidad and Tobago	1971	0.7	5.5	4.8	11
	Trinidad and Tobago	1994	−0.6	4.0	4.6	13
	Uruguay	1974	1.0	4.2	3.3	6
	Uruguay	1991	2.1	4.2	2.1	7
	Venezuela, Rep. Bol.	2002	−3.4	5.5	8.9	5

Notes: Table reports growth during 5-year period before start of acceleration, growth during first 5 years of acceleration episode, and the difference in growth

The regions included in the analysis include: (1) a global sample comprising all countries with a peak population of more than one million; (2) Central and Eastern Europe; (3) East Asia and Pacific (Cambodia, China, Hong Kong, Indonesia, Korea, Lao, Malaysia, Mongolia, Papua New Guinea, Philippines, Singapore, Thailand, and Vietnam); and (4) Latin America (Argentina, Bolivia, Brazil, Chile, Colombia, Costa Rica, Dominican Republic, Ecuador, El Salvador, Guatemala, Haiti, Honduras, Jamaica, Mexico, Nicaragua, Panama, Paraguay, Peru, Trinidad and Tobago, Uruguay, and Venezuela). Since $N = 5$, the earliest and latest years for start of growth acceleration are 1965 and 2002, respectively.

There were a large number of growth accelerations in Central and Eastern Europe in the past 15 years. In the original Hausmann et al. (2005) article, which introduced this concept of accelerations, there were only two CEE accelerations because their data stopped in 1997. Table 11.2 reports the estimated (unconditional) probability of growth acceleration. The probability is defined as the number of growth acceleration episodes divided by the number of country-years in which an episode could have occurred. For the global sample, the average probability is found to be 4%, implying that a typical country would have a chance of about 33% of experiencing a growth takeoff in a given decade. In Central and Eastern Europe, the estimated probability is higher, at about 7% per year, somewhat higher than that in East Asia and Latin America. However, the table also suggests that the longevity of growth spurts has been greatest in East Asia, averaging 15 years,

Table 11.2 Frequency of growth accelerations, by region

Region	Frequency (percent)	Avg. duration	Episodes	Observations
All	4.0	9	157	3956
Central and Eastern Europe	6.9	12	10	144
East Asia Pacific	4.4	15	20	457
Latin America	4.3	8	30	698
Memo items				
Middle East North Africa	3.5	9	14	395
South Saharan Africa	3.9	7	50	1270

Notes: Table reports number of growth episodes divided by number of observations in each region

compared with 12 years for Central and Eastern Europe, and 8 years for Latin America.[8]

Table 11.3 examines what variables are correlated with the start of growth accelerations. The table reports the average change in the value of a given variable during the first 5 years of growth acceleration. It also reports whether the change is significantly different from zero.[9] The general trends reported in the previous section are amply confirmed for the growth acceleration episodes.

- Growth accelerations in Central and Eastern Europe have many standard features, such as increases in private investment, declines in inflation, and improvements in the terms of trade.
- While trade openness – increased exports and imports – are associated with growth accelerations, in Central and Eastern Europe, stepped-up imports are more salient, consistent with their increased current account deficits during accelerations. The difference with the other two regions is clear.
- Another key difference is the significant appreciation in real exchange rate within Central and Eastern Europe, which contrasts with depreciation during the growth accelerations in East Asia.
- Financial openness and the presence of foreign banks also more reliably predict growth accelerations in Central and Eastern Europe.[10]

[8]The analysis is based on data up to end-2007. The takeoff episodes under way as of 2007 may have been interrupted by the recent financial crisis. However, because the methodology for identifying the start and end of growth takeoffs is based on 5-year periods, it will not be possible to confirm whether an acceleration episode ended in 2007 until data for 2012 are available.

[9]The timing of the growth acceleration is taken to be the 3-year period centered on the dates listed in Table 11.1. A 3-year window reduces the risk of narrowly missing the timing of acceleration.

[10]The presence of foreign banks is measured as the percentage of foreign banks in total bank assets, and is taken from Claessens et al. (2008). In related work, Hermann and Winkler (2009) find evidence that the presence of foreign banks contributes to explaining the difference between the current account balances of emerging Asia and CEE countries. De-facto financial openness is measured as the sum of external assets and liabilities in percent of GDP. De-jure financial openness is measured using an updated version of the widely-used Chinn and Ito (2006) capital-account-openness index.

Table 11.3 Correlates of growth accelerations (change during first 5 years)

Region	All	CEEC	EAP	LAC
Macroeconomic circumstances				
Investment/GDP	1.865***	3.147**	3.197***	2.293***
Exports/GDP	0.70	4.26	4.79	1.85
Imports/GDP	1.49	7.141***	1.64	0.73
REER (increase = appreciation)	−3.86	21.94***	−20.55*	0.22
Inflation	−86.08***	−118.5**	−17.82	−61.92
Terms of trade	4.115**	6.807***	4.70	6.954*
CA deficit/GDP	−0.749*	3.618**	−1.45	−1.21
Political circumstances				
Polity IV: composite	0.28	0.963*	−0.26	0.48
Polity IV: executive constraints	0.121*	0.296*	−0.03	0.313*
ICRGComposite index	6.626***	6.262**	5.682**	7.900***
ICRG: democratic accountability	0.405***	0.594**	−0.21	0.529***
EU integration index		0.220***		
Economic liberalization				
Trade openness	7.485***	8.360*	25.21***	5.053***
Financial openness (de facto)	27.66***	33.05***	1.45	14.88*
Financial openness (de jure)	0.228***	1.165***	0.15	0.28
Presence of foreign banks	16.06***	40.92***	18.38***	−2.88
Private credit/GDP	2.850***	0.88	2.51	2.359**
EBRD – large scale privatn.		0.975***		
EBRD – small scale privatn.		0.764***		
EBRD – enterprise restruct.		0.605***		
EBRD – price liberalization		0.369***		
EBRD – trade and forex		0.665***		
EBRD – competition policy		0.543***		
EBRD – banking reform		0.765***		
EBRD – securities markets		0.889***		
EBRD – overall infrastr.		0.937***		

Notes: Statistical significance at the 1%, 5%, and 10% level denoted by ***, **, and *, respectively. The abbreviation "CEEC" refers to Central and Eastern European Countries, "EAP" refers to East Asia and Pacific countries, and "LAC" refers to Latin American countries

- Increasing democratic accountability and institutional quality, as measured by widely-used indicators, play a particularly important role in CEE growth accelerations.[11]

[11]The Polity IV database has been widely used by researchers as a source of data on political-institutional features (Center for International Development and Conflict Management 2007). The Polity IV composite index ranks countries' political institutions on a 21-point scale, with higher values corresponding to greater degree of democracy than autocracy. The Polity IV executive constraints sub-index measures the extent of institutionalized constraints on the decision-making powers of chief executives, and ranges from 0 to 10 with a higher score indicating less de facto operational independence (and more accountability) of the country's chief executive.

- Finally, the process of integration with the European Union (EU) – measured by an index capturing membership application, negotiation, accession, ERM-II entry, and Euro adoption – is a statistically significant predictor of growth accelerations.[12] Furthermore, a regression analysis suggests that EU integration has predictive power for growth accelerations that goes beyond that contained in standard indicators of institutional quality and economic liberalization (not reported here).

11.4.2 Traditional Growth Analysis

In more conventional growth studies (Schadler et al. 2006 and Abiad et al. 2008), we reach several conclusions that underline the achievements of Central and Eastern Europe while also offering cautionary lessons. First, total factor productivity growth has played a significantly more important role in Central and Eastern Europe during recent years than is the case in East Asia; in Latin America, total factor productivity has either been flat or even tended to decline. Second, some of the gains achieved by Central and Eastern Europe were related to exogenous factors. The Baltic nations, in particular, started with low initial per capita incomes allowing for more scope for catch up. Throughout the CEE region, relatively low population growth rates have also helped in achieving per capita income gains. Third, policy institutional development has helped Central and Eastern Europe: but here the picture is mixed. The Baltic countries, in particular, have benefited from small governments, trade openness, advances in education, and institutional development. The Central European economies also benefit from trade openness and enjoy the educational and institutional advantages but their larger government size, the cross-country regressions suggest, pulls their growth down. Finally, a key advantage that the CEE economies enjoy is access to foreign capital. Abiad et al. (2008) show that in Central and Eastern Europe, the downward flow of capital has been associated with more rapid income convergence. While all in Central and Eastern Europe have benefited from this process, those with lower income gained more.

In sum, while the advantages vis-à-vis Latin America are clear, the mix of factors vis-à-vis East Asia do not give Central and Eastern Europe a decisive advantage. While openness and institutional development have complemented each other to give Central and Eastern Europe a strong boost, important challenges lie ahead. As the Baltic nations made further progress, the easy catch up possibilities will be increasingly exhausted. For the Central European economies, the challenges are also likely to come from fiscal challenges. Achieving leaner governments will imply making difficult choices on expenditure priorities and greater efficiency of public service

[12]Following Danninger and Jaumotte (2008), the index measures the degree of European integration, and is built as a score (from 0 to 1) for achieving different stages of the formal integration process, namely 0.2 points each for EU membership application, initiation of negotiation for EU membership, EU accession, entry into ERM II, and euro adoption.

delivery; this, in turn, will allow lowering tax rates increasingly necessitated by international tax competition. Not least, the very openness of Central and Eastern Europe, especially financial openness, exposes them to a reversal of capital of flows. Even if sudden stops in capital flows do not materialize, Blanchard (2006) has cautioned that continued real exchange rate appreciation may yet produce new tests of competitiveness.

11.5 Financial Turbulence: A Test of the Economic Model?

The ongoing financial turbulence has put the CEE model to test. Current accounts are shrinking and growth is slowing rapidly. Some economies are contracting. In most countries, economic convergence is likely to be set back in the short run. But a bigger risk is that the reinforcing relationship between capital inflows and growth on which the CEE model is based could break down. This would reaffirm the view of some that the model is inherently unstable, either because capital flows are fickle or because the incentives of policymakers, firms, and households ultimately generates behavior that proves inimical to the success of the model. Keen observers remain concerned that Eastern Europe, with its current account deficits and elevated international financial exposure, will prove to be particularly vulnerable to ongoing developments. Thus, Paul Krugman has written on his blog (October 31, 2008):

> Eastern Europe 2008 = East Asia 1997. The key to the Asian crisis – and of Argentina's collapse in 2002 – was the way domestic players leveraged themselves up with foreign-currency loans. When the capital inflows dried up, and the Asian currencies plunged, these debts suddenly became a much bigger burden, decimating balance sheets and causing a downward spiral of deleveraging. And here we go again.

Our perspective on the prognosis is as follows. The world has been subject to a massive shock. The waves from this shock have continued to extend their reach, including in their fold a wider range of financial instruments and markets and a broader range of countries. With the announcement that Chinese exports had fallen on a year-on-year basis in November, the crisis had clearly delivered a blow to Asia. Growth forecasts for 2009 and 2010 continue to be marked down – the process is ongoing and the results are not known. Within the context of this broad correlated shock, markets have differentiated countries. Our reading of the data is that the country differentiation is greater than regional differentiation. In turn, the country differentiation reflects specific policies and vulnerabilities that are being spotlighted and, possibly, amplified by the global shock.

If we examine indicators measuring financial stress, such as stock prices, sovereign bond spreads, and exchange rates, systematic singling out of Central and Eastern Europe does not appear to have occurred. In particular, while Central and Eastern European countries appear to have experienced greater financial stress as measured by stock price indexes, they have, as a group, been less

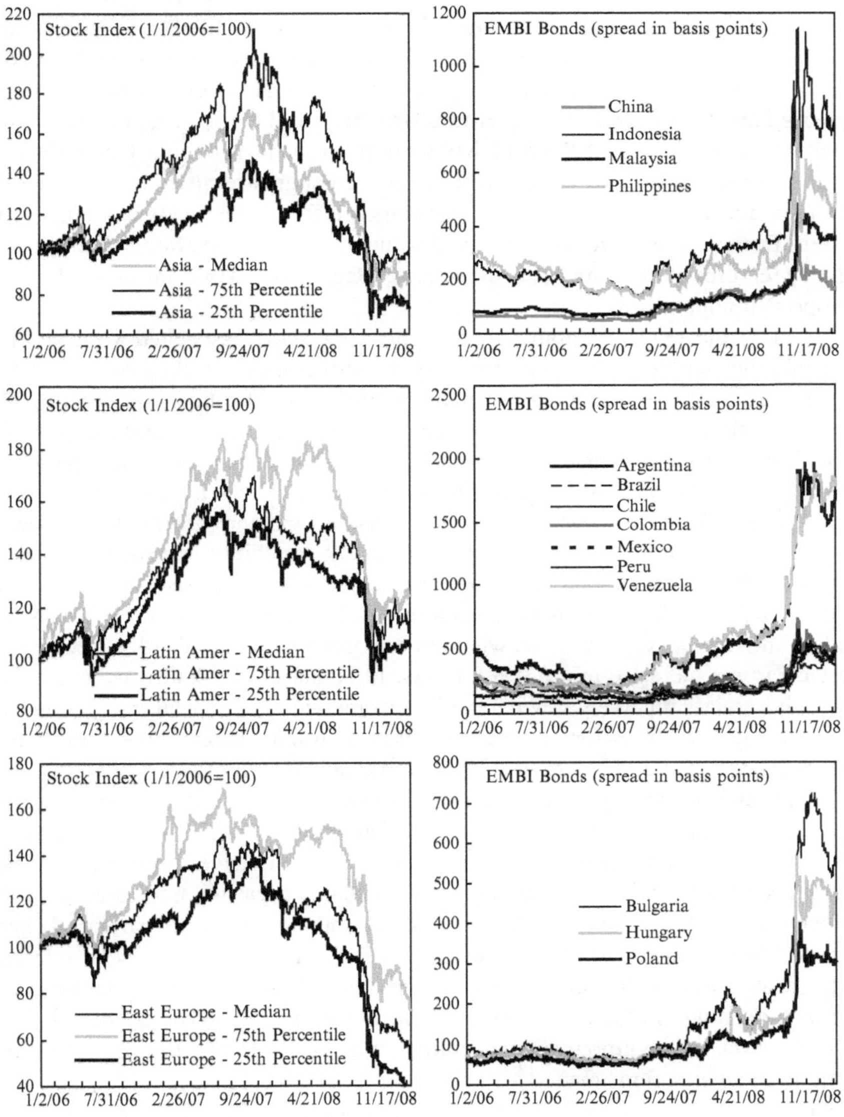

Fig. 11.13 Financial stress.
Note: figure reports data from 1 January 2006 to 16 December 2008
Source: Thomson Financial/Reuters/DataStream

severely hit based on sovereign bond spreads. To illustrate this point, Fig. 11.13 shows the median stock price index (bordered by the 25th and 75th percentile indices) with January 1 2006 as the base, and the EMBI sovereign bond spread. Relative to its peak, the median stock-price index fell 57% for Central and Eastern Europe, 31% for Latin America, and 47% for the Asian countries in our sample. However, the data on sovereign bond spreads – available only for a few countries – suggests a more favorable performance for Central and Eastern Europe. Limited though the data are, they suggest that sovereign bond spreads increased less for Central and Eastern Europe than for the other regions. While the correlated risks across the world have raised spreads in Central and Eastern Europe, these have gone up elsewhere also. Luengnaruemitchai and Schadler (2007) in analysis before the recent crisis argued that the spreads in Central and Eastern Europe were lower not only in absolute terms but also after controlling for country features explaining bond spreads. Average spreads in Central and Eastern Europe still appear low.

As such, the evidence points to particular hot spots associated with specific vulnerabilities within each region. Hungary had difficulties in rolling over its public debt and asked the IMF and the international community for financial support. The markets' early focus on Hungary reflected chronic budget deficits and rising public debt. While these have come under greater control in the past few years, the recent history of missed targets will require sustained effort to rebuild a reputation for fiscal discipline. In this sense, the stress on Hungarian bond and currency markets reflected markets' traditional concern with sovereign policy credibility and long-term fiscal sustainability. Latvia with its large current account deficits has also sought external financial support. The Latvian story is more clearly tied to the specific CEE growth model. The Latvian case was one where that model was pushed hard, exceeding by most measures the appropriate speed limits. In Abiad et al. (2008), we argue that although Latvia's relatively low per capita income and its financial integration into Europe created the basis for running a significant current account deficit, the actual deficits in 2006 and 2007 were well above those norms.

Countries in other regions are facing their own stresses. Asian economies have, for such an eventuality, built up significant foreign exchange reserves. But as the crisis has spread, and their short-term growth prospects have dimmed, countries within Asia have faced differing degrees of financial pressure associated with the rollover of private international debt. Indonesia and Korea have experienced sharp currency depreciation and are continuing to lose foreign exchange reserves. While policy responses have helped mitigate the pressures, these examples further emphasize that, even within the context of a global shock, markets have not been guided by perceptions of common regional vulnerabilities but have thus far been more subtle in the distinctions made.[13]

The fallout from the financial tensions will continue. The deleveraging of the financial sector can be expected to interact with a weakening global economy, creating a financial-accelerator-like process. The intensity of this process will depend, however, in significant part on the wisdom and the international coordination of the policies adopted. As such, the test of the CEE model will continue to unfold. Our analysis offers some grounds for hope. The strength of institutions

---

[13]Particularities of countries include their relationships to international banks of varying strengths and vulnerabilities.

developed over the past 15 years or so should provide considerable flexibility and buffers to absorb the shocks.

11.6 Conclusions

Looking across the regions, the role of trade openness stands out as a central element of the growth process. East Asia has harnessed the potential of such openness over a long period of time to reinforce and renew its growth and the CEE experience of the last 15 years confirms that association. The use of cross-country regressions to infer causal effect of trade openness on growth has often been questioned (see Rodriguez and Rodrik 2000). It is possible, and indeed, likely that the causation works both ways, but what is clear is that over any medium-term spell, growth and trade openness are strongly associated with each other. Openness brings ideas and competition – competition not just to local producers of goods and services, but competition also in the political arena, helping challenge constituencies favoring the status quo. The continued lag in trade openness remains an important distinguishing feature of Latin America. As Zettlemeyer (2006) notes, the reduction of tariff barriers has helped; but, possibly non-tariff regulatory barriers have held back a more dynamic relationship with international markets.[14]

Seen over an extended period of the past half century, East Asia's performance remains remarkable for the strength and persistence of its growth. The most successful of the economies of this region have been consistently able to renew themselves, overcoming their own growth bottlenecks and adapting to the changing international environment. In this perspective, the CEE achievements, while clearly impressive, are more recent and the ability of their approach to deliver sustained increases in standards of living remains to proven.

As such, the major achievement of Central and Eastern Europe – an achievement of interest to analysts of the development and growth process but more so to policymakers in the region who must sake to preserve it – is the harnessing of market forces in the context of rapid globalization and alongside an unequivocal commitment to open domestic democratic processes. As this paper has argued, the CEE economies have gone farther in using the potential of global markets than other regions. This has been so especially with regard to financial openness where the continued push towards increased financial integration has been remarkable not only for its strength but also because the others have turned their back on it just as Central and Eastern Europe have pushed forward. In doing so, they were able to give their populations an earlier consumption dividend from this growth and integration process than has typically been possible in prior growth episodes.

[14]There are other, some would argue more important, factors that have held back Latin American growth, including a heavier reliance on natural resources, deeper inequalities, and a political and economic interaction that generates greater volatility (Zettelmeyer 2006) reviews the many strands of these discussions.

To the extent that this model has been successful, some would argue that it is not replicable. The CEE economies – despite the trauma of the first transition from central planning – emerged with a distinguishing depth of human capital. Moreover, as they transitioned from their former isolation, they found themselves in the midst of thriving product and financial markets. And, the embrace into the EU, through its emphasis on regulatory harmonization, strengthened institutional structures and, by reducing the barrier of "borders," reinforced their integration into European markets. Testing these propositions is no easy task, and we do not attempt it here. Nevertheless, in recent work, we have argued that this experience may well provide some valuable lessons for the opportunities that will arise as nations become more financially integrated (Abiad et al. 2008).

Looking ahead, Central and Eastern Europe face three challenges. The first is from financial integration itself. The longer the global turbulence continues, the more the CEE model will be tested. It is already clear that the Baltic nations are facing a severe pull back in their growth rates. The IMF forecast published in April 2009 was that real GDP in Estonia, Latvia, and Lithuania, would experience an average contraction of about 11% in 2009. This is not completely surprising: they were growing at a pace that was perhaps in any case not sustainable. The retrenchment of external capital has ensured a more rapid curtailment than many had expected. The test of the model will lie in whether the Baltics or other countries in the region face prolonged output losses. If that were to happen, concerns from prior developmental experiences to accelerate growth with foreign capital will be reinforced. This test is going to be a severe one to the extent that it occurs in the context of a broader global and systemic retrenchment of financial markets. In that sense, a reading of the ongoing experience will need to distinguish between large exogenous global shocks and unsustainable debt structures that in the past have triggered emerging market crises.

Beyond the immediate concerns, there remains the challenge of generating continuing productivity growth. Some part of the achievement in this regard may well have been easy pickings as capital and labor were more productively deployed. But clearly, the shifts in production structure and quality are evidence that a more fundamental transformation has also occurred. The question is: can this continue? And, if not, will the relentless appreciation of the real exchange rate (as prices and wages move towards levels of advanced European nations) undermine competitiveness. That this is no idle speculation has been emphasized by Blanchard (2006) in his review of the Portuguese experience. Entry into the euro area allowed the Portuguese economy to attract foreign capital and grow rapidly. But a failure to strengthen internal sources of productivity abruptly changed the dynamic. From large current account deficits and high growth, Portugal went to continued large external deficits and low growth. Blanchard warns that when placed in this setting of external deficits and low growth, the policy options are limited and returning to the more virtuous growth cycle is difficult.

And, that highlights the final challenge. While the forces of globalization can be usefully harnessed to achieve long-term growth, domestic policies must keep pace to productively participate in that potential but also to guard against adverse developments. Going forward, the task becomes harder as political constituencies are more effectively able to pursue their self interest. Nowhere is this more of an issue than in the allocation of budgetary resources, which in turn reflects broader policy priorities. The nature of institutional development that Central and Eastern Europe is now embarked on is subtler and more complex than the more basic institutions of governance and property rights that they successfully established. Creating checks and balances in a complex democracy that allows for the expression of many voices while ensuring the public good is not just the next challenge, it is a continuing one.[15]

Acknowledgments The authors are grateful for generous comments to Tassos Belessiotis, Ryszard *Rapacki,* István P. Székely, and to several participants at the workshop organized by Directorate-General for Economic and Financial Affairs (DG ECFIN) of the European Commission on "Five years of an enlarged EU – a positive-sum game," Brussels on 13 and 14 November 2008. Susan Becker provided valuable research assistance.

References

Abiad, A., Leigh, D., & Mody, A. (2008). International finance, capital mobility, and income convergence. International Monetary Fund, mimeo.

Blanchard, O. (2006). *Adjustment within the euro: The difficult case of Portugal.* Cambridge, MA: Massachusetts Institute of Technology, Mimeo.

Center for International Development and Conflict Management. (2007*). Polity IV project: Political regime characteristics and transitions, 1800–2007.*http://www.systemicpeace.org/polity/polity4.htm

Chinn, M., & Ito, H. (2006). What matters for financial development? Capital controls, institutions, and interactions. *Journal of Development Economics, 81*(1), 163–192.

Claessens, S., Van Horen, N., Gurcanlar, T., & Sapiain, J. M. (2008). *Foreign bank presence in developing countries 1995–2006: Data and trends.* Washington: World Bank.

Danninger, S., & Jaumotte, F. (2008). Divergence of current account balances across emerging economies. *IMF World Economic Outlook,* September 2008.

European Commission (2003). European competition report, 2003. *European Commission Staff Working Document,* SEC(2003)1299.

European Commission (2009). Five years of an enlarged EU – Economic achievements and challenges. *European economy,* 1/2009.

Fabrizio, S., Igan, D., & Mody, A. (2006). *The dynamics of product quality and international competitiveness.* IMF Working Paper, No. 07/97. Washington, DC: International Monetary Fund.

Fabrizio, S., & Mody, A. (2006). Can budget institutions counteract political indiscipline? *Economic Policy, 21*, 689–739.

Fabrizio, S., & Mody, A. (2008). *Breaking the impediments to budgetary reforms: Evidence from Europe.* IMF Working Paper, No. 08/82. Washington, DC: International Monetary Fund.

Fischer, S., & Sahay, R. (2004). Transition economies: The role of institutions and initial conditions. *Festschrift in honor of Guillermo Calvo,* April 15–16, 2004. Washington, DC: International Monetary Fund.

Hausmann, R., Pritchett, L., & Rodrik, D. (2005). Growth accelerations. *Journal of Economic Growth, 10*(4), 303–329.

[15]For an application of these ideas to budgetary institutions, see Fabrizio and Mody (2006, 2008).

Hermann, S., & Winkler, A. (2009). Real convergence, financial markets, and the current account – emerging Europe versus emerging Asia. In F. Keereman & I. Szekely (Eds.), *Five years of an enlarged EU*. Heidelberg: Springer.

Luengnaruemitchai, P., & Schadler, S. (2007). *Do economists' and financial markets' perspectives on the New Members of the EU differ*? IMF Working Paper, No.07/65. Washington, DC: International Monetary Fund.

Prasad, E., Rajan, R., & Subramanian, A. (2006). Patterns of international capital flows and their implications for economic development. Presented at the symposium *"The new economic geography: Effects and policy implications*". Jackson Hole, Wyoming: The Federal Reserve Bank of Kansas City. Retrieved August 24–26, 2006, from http://www.kc.frb.org/PUBLICAT/SYMPOS/2006/sym06prg.htm

Rodriguez, F., & Rodrik, D. (2000). Trade policy and economic growth: A skeptic's guide to the cross-national evidence. In B. Bernanke & K.S. Rogoff (Eds.), *Macroeconomics annual 2000*. Cambridge, MA: MIT Press for NBER, 2001.

Rodrik, D. (2008). *The real exchange rate and economic growth*. Cambridge, MA: John F. Kennedy School of Government, Harvard University.

Roland, G. (2005). After enlargement: Institutional achievements and prospects in the new Member States. Proceedings of the 3rd ECB conference The new EU Member States: convergence and stability. Frankfurt: European Central Bank. pp. 35–58.

Schadler, S., Mody, A., Abiad, A., & Leigh, L. (2006). *Growth in the central and eastern European countries of the European Union*. IMF Occasional Paper, No. 252. Washington, DC: International Monetary Fund.

Wade, R. (1990). *Governing the market*. Princeton: Princeton University Press.

World Bank. (1993). *The making of the east Asia miracle: Economic growth and economic policy*. Oxford: Oxford University Press.

Zettelmeyer, J. (2006). *Growth and reforms in Latin America: A survey of facts and arguments*. IMF Working Paper, No. 06/210. Washington, DC: International Monetary Fund.

Chapter 12
An Evaluation of the EU's Fifth Enlargement with Special Focus on Bulgaria and Romania

Fritz Breuss

Abstract The fifth EU enlargement in 2004 and 2007 not only extended the Single European Market, but it also led to the enlargement of the euro zone, which since 2009, encompasses 16 out of 27 EU Member States. Moreover, the Schengen area has also been expanded to include 25 European countries (22 EU Member States). A first evaluation shows that the new member countries have already been able to benefit noticeably from their participation in the single market (SM), despite being not yet fully integrated labour markets. However, the international financial crisis also shadows onto the economies of the new Member States. After an ex post evaluation, the possible future integration effects of EU's 2007 enlargement by Bulgaria and Romania are simulated with a simple macro-economic integration model able to encompass as many of the theoretically predicted integration effects as possible. The direct integration effects of Bulgaria and Romania spill-over to the old Member States, including Austria and the ten new Member States of the 2004 EU enlargement. The pattern of the integration effects is qualitatively similar to those of EU's 2004 enlargement by ten new Member States. Bulgaria and Romania gain much more from EU accession than the incumbents, in the proportion of 20:1. In the medium-run up to 2020, Bulgaria and Romania can expect a sizable overall integration gain, amounting to an additional 1/2% point real GDP growth per annum. Among the incumbent EU Member States, Austria will gain somewhat more (+0.05%) than the average of EU-15 (+0.02%) and the ten new EU Member States (+0.01%), which joined the EU in 2004.

F. Breuss
Vienna University of Economics and Business, Austria

F. Keereman and I. Szekely (eds.), *Five Years of an Enlarged EU*,
DOI 10.1007/978-3-642-12516-4_12, © Springer-Verlag Berlin Heidelberg 2010

12.1 Introduction

EU enlargement is progressing. With the entry of Bulgaria and Romania in 2007 the EU has completed its fifth enlargement which started in 2004 with the accession of ten new members. The EU will enlarge further by absorbing the countries of the Western Balkans (starting with Croatia) and later may be also Turkey will become a member of the EU. EU-27 with 492 million inhabitants is the largest regional economic integration area, forming a specific kind of regional integration agreement with economic and institutional integration, ranging from a customs union to the SM, and is being extending step by step towards an economic and monetary union (EMU) with a single currency – the euro.

The fifth EU enlargement was dominated by political motives, whereas the preceding enlargements served essentially economic interests to enlarge the single (or internal) market and to create a monetary unification with a single currency. The founding fathers of the European Integration process, however, wanted to create structures to secure sustainable political stability in Europe after the catastrophe of the Second World War. The reason why the fifth EU enlargement was such a grand project was the fact that with it – starting with the breakdown of communism in 1989 – the political separation of Europe was finally ended. Whether this important step of European unification – a step of historic dimension – will pay off finally in economic terms cannot yet be answered definitively. Due to the large gaps in income levels between East and West this integration step will entail economic adjustments. For many entrepreneurs – primarily in the old EU Member States – the enlargement of the SM opened up great chances to expand their business. However, the advantages of free movement of capital and hence the great chances for foreign direct investments in the new "emerging markets" are contrasted by the disadvantages of the new Member States resulting from the still transitionally closed labour markets for their work force in the majority of the old Member States.

Nevertheless a first evaluation of 5 years of an enlarged EU shows that the expectations of integration effects – primarily in the new Member States – have been fulfilled. The economies of nearly all new Member States expand faster than before being integrated in the SM of the EU. The participation in EU's customs union fostered intra-EU trade. The next step is the full participation in EMU with the takeover of the Euro. Four new Member States (Slovenia in 2007, Malta and Cyprus in 2008, Slovakia in 2009) are already member of the Euro area. The enlargement of the Schengen area in December 21, 2007 by 9 out of 12 new Member States was a further important step of integration. Even Switzerland takes part in the Schengen process as of December 12, 2008. The other new EU Member States will follow later: Cyprus in 2009, Bulgaria and Romania in 2011. Schengen and the Euro are two visible and concrete integration steps which can be directly "felt" by the citizens and are positively associated with EU integration. This helps to improve the pro-EU mood of the population, which presently is not so good in many EU Member States. The international financial crises which unfolded in earnest mid-year 2008 pushed the industrialized world into recession in 2009/

2010. This will also have negative spill-overs to the new EU Member States, although their performance is still better than in the old EU Member States.

A first empirical evaluation of 5 years of an enlarged EU is made in the next section. In Sect. 12.3 we develop a generalized unified theory which is able to capture most of the theoretical integration effects one expects from enlarging an existing Union. The hitherto and the expected future integration effects are then demonstrated in the case of Bulgaria's and Romania's EU integration. Sect. 12.5 presents the results of this integration models for Bulgaria and Romania as well as the spill-overs to Austria, old and the new EU Member States. Conclusions are drawn in Sect. 12.6.

12.2 Experiences with the EU's Fifth Enlargement in 2004 and 2007

The fifth EU enlargement in 2004 and 2007 not only extended the Single European Market, but it also lead to the enlargement of, the euro zone, which since 2009, encompasses 16 out of 27 EU Member States. Moreover, the Schengen area has also been expanded to include 22 Member States. The new member countries have already been able to benefit noticeably from their participation in the SM, despite being not yet fully integrated labour markets and a still not completed SM for Services (Breuss et al. 2008). The more the EU Member States can trade with each other without trade barriers within the SM the more they are protected against the perils of globalization (Breuss 2008b). Enlarging the SM therefore extends also this valuable shield. On the other hand one could argue that the bigger the share of intra-EU trade in total trade due to enlargement (presently, it amounts already to nearly 2/3 of total trade of EU Member States) the less interested the EU might be in an early finalization of the Doha Round (Breuss 2008a).

With the completion of its fifth enlargement in 2007 the EU increased the number of its members from 25 to 27. However, like in the preceding enlargement steps (1995 and 2004) only small countries entered the EU. In 2004 EU's population increased by 19%, in 2007 by only 6%, GDP (at PPS) increased by 9% and 2% respectively. Intra-EU trade increased by 11% and 1 × 1/2%, respectively.

A first evaluation leads to the following conclusions (Breuss 2007c, 2009):

- The majority of the new Member States have grown faster in the period since 2004 than in the previous 5 years. Slovakia (+4.7%), Romania (+3.7%) and Czech Republic (+3%) as well as Poland (+2.4%) exhibited a higher average annual growth rate of real GDP than the 12 new Member States on average (+2.1%). Bulgaria performed like the average. Hungary (−1.2%) was the only country with declining average growth rates and hence was the only loser of enlargement so far.

The economy of EU-27 on average grew faster by 0.1% point than before 2004, whereas EU-15's GDP growth rate was slightly less (by 0.1%). This growth bonus of 0.2% points matches with the expectations in previous studies on the integration effects of the fifth EU enlargement (e.g. Breuss 2002).

The international financial and economic crisis spilled also over to the new EU Member States in Eastern Europe. Although they did not cause the crisis they nevertheless were hurt much harder than the old EU Member States. In its Autumn 2009 Economic Forecast the European Commisssion (2009) sees the three Baltic states Estonia (real GDP −13.7%), Latvia (−18.0%) and Lithuania (−18.1%) in a deep recession (or even depression) in 2009, lasting already over 3 years (2008–2010). With the exception of Poland (+1.2%) all new 12 EU Member States are in a more or less deep recession in 2009. Since autumn 2009, however, in most countries a slight recovery is under way. The deep recession in Eastern Europe in 2009 results for the first time in a slightly worse overall economic performance in the 12 new EU Member States (real GDP −4.4% on average) than in the old Member States (−4.1%).

- The last EU enlargement, however, also contributed to a statistical "impoverishment" of the enlarged EU. As a consequence of the enlargement, the average GDP per capita was reduced by nearly 11% points. Therefore, the completion of one of the Lisbon targets – the closing of the income gap vis-à-vis the USA – is getting more difficult than before. After EU enlargement, the income gap vis-à-vis the USA has increased to 51% points from 35% points between the USA and EU 15. We need a long period of catching-up in the new Member States with permanently high growth rates in order to eliminate this difference.
- Other macro variables exhibited a mixed picture. The situation of the labour market has improved in most new Member States, their unemployment rates decreased. Inflation could be largely subdued. With the exception of Hungary, the budgetary consolidation process succeeded in all new Member States.
- The new EU Member States expanded their trade with the old EU Member States. Even more trade was created between themselves. Also the old EU Member States redirected their trade flows towards the new Member States (intra EU trade creation), a process at the expense of intra-EU-15 trade (intra-EU trade diversion).
- In spite of the brisk trade activities since 2004 it seems as if the old EU Member States could exploit their comparative advantages much better than the new Member States. This is reflected in the improvement of the trade and current account balances with the new Member States. Many new Member States, however, generated high deficits in both balances with the old Member States. Only the more advanced five Central and Eastern European countries, primarily neighbours of Austria, performed relatively better.
- Since their opening-up in 1989 and more so after the EU enlargement in 2004 and 2007, the new market economies in Eastern Europe developed into an important emerging market for companies in Western Europe. In particularly countries like Austria, but also Germany with long-lasting traditional relations with the Central and Eastern European countries took advantage from this new situation. The Netherlands, Austria and Germany are the most prominent foreign

direct investors in the Central and Eastern European countries. Those new Member States which privatized early on and to a large degree in the transition attracted the biggest share of FDI inflows.

- With the exception of Slovenia, Malta, Cyprus and Slovakia, the new Member States are not yet ready to become full members of the EMU. They have to wait and try to comply with the Maastricht convergence criteria. In most of the new Member States, either the inflation rate (and/or the long-term interest rate) is too high, or the budget deficit is not in conformity with the criteria. The latter is particularly true for Hungary.

12.3 A Stylized Generalized Unified Theory of EU Enlargement

The theory of regional economic integration has to deal with geographically discriminatory trade policy issues and is regulated in different types of Regional Integration Agreements (RIAs)[1], ranging from Free Trade Agreements (FTAs) to Custom Unions (CUs) and in the case of the EU it is a SM and partly also an EMU. Starting with the seminal work on CUs by Viner (1950), the theory of RIAs evolved along the lines of the new trade theory and was sometimes ahead of the political reality of RIAs, sometimes behind them. In the meantime the economic (and institutional) integration of the EU has come to its maximum possible level of an EMU with a single currency. Whereas most of the world-wide existing RIAs can be analyzed with Viner's theory of CUs or maybe with the theoretical extensions and generalizations of his followers (e.g. Corden 1972; Lloyd 1982; Kennan and Riezman 1990) the evaluation of EU's economic integration effects requires much more ingredients of modern trade theory. This is even more the case if one wants to analyze EU's enlargement which – as a special case – is the integration of two kinds of economies, a bloc of high-income countries (the old EU-15) with a bloc of medium- to low-income (mostly transitional) economies (the ten new Member States which acceded the EU in 2004 and Bulgaria and Romania who became EU

[1]Regional Integration Agreements which are also called Regional Trade Agreements (RTAs) or free trade areas (FTAs) are preferential agreements and in principle inconsistent with the GATT's most favored nations (MFN) principle. Sluggish or no progress in the Doha Development Round has accelerated further the rush to forge Regional Trade Agreements. The total number of (at the WTO) notified preferential agreements in force is currently 170, while a further considerable number is under negotiations/proposal stage (see Crawford and Fiorentino 2005, p. 1). Pascal Lamy (see: http://www.wto.org/english/news_e/sppl_e/sppl53_e.htm), Director-General of the WTO forecasted recently that by 2010 around 400 of such agreements could be active, increasing the complicated web of incoherent rules, coined by Professor Bhagwati (1995) a "spaghetti bowl" of twisted rules of origin. Whereas the trade purists condemn bilateral "spaghetti bowls" as second or third best welfare solutions to liberalizing world trade, Baldwin (2006B) takes them as political facts and as "building blocs on the path to global free trade". For a description of EU's spaghetii bowl, see Breuss (2007b), p. 649.

members in 2007). In this case of integration of unevenly high developed countries factors movements might dominate the trade effects.

Due to the complexity of EU's integration (enlargement in particular) one dreams of finding a "Grand Unified Theory" (GUT) like in theoretical physics.[2] In the case of regional economic integration, Baldwin and Venables (1995) recommended such a GUT for the case of a (fictitious) country entering a Regional Integration Agreement and by Kohler (2004) for the case of an incumbent country (Germany) if the EU is enlarging. In this section we present a stylized GUT of EU's enlargement. Based on this insights, we build a simple model of EU's fifth enlargement encompassing as many of the integration effects predicted by the GUT as possible.

In the following we study the welfare change in an open economy – in our case for a small country – joining the EU.

Following Baldwin and Venables (1995, p. 1691) suppose that the welfare of a representative consumer in the new EU Member State at the time of acceding the EU can be represented by an indirect utility function $V(p + t, n, E)$, where p is the vector of border prices, t is a vector of trade costs including the tariff equivalent of import barriers (NTBs like border controls), n is a vector of the number of product varieties available in each industry, and the scalar E is total spending on consumption. Expenditure of a new EU Member State is equal to the sum of factor income, profits, and rent from trade barriers that accrues to domestic agents (including the government), minus investment plus income out of the EU budget under the title of structural funds transfers: $E = wL + rK + X[(p + t) - a(w, r, x)] + \alpha t m - I + SF$. Total factor income is $wL + rK$, where L and K are the country's supply of labour and capital and w and r are factor prices. The third term on the right hand side is total profit. It is the inner product of the economy's production vector X and the gap between domestic prices and average costs, $a(w, r, x)$, where average cost in each sector depends on factor prices and production per firm in that sector, x. Domestically accruing trade rents amount to αtm, where m is the net import vector (positive elements indicate imports) and α is a diagonal matrix that measures the proportion of the wedge t that creates income for domestic agents; $\alpha = 1$ for a tariff or other barrier with domestically captured rent (DCR) and $\alpha = 0$ for a barrier where no trade rent is captured domestically (non-DCR). For example, t may represent real trade costs or a quota or voluntary export restraints (VER) under which foreigners capture the quota rents or in the case of integrating into the SM the trade costs of border control. Finally, I denotes investment and SF net income from structural funds transfers out of the EU budget.

[2]Theoretical physicists are searching for a unified theory that unifies three "fundamental" gauge symmetries: hypercharge, the weak force, and quantum chromo dynamics. So far, physicists have been able to merge electromagnetism and the weak nuclear force into the electroweak force, and work is being done to merge electroweak and quantum chromo dynamics into a QCD-electroweak interaction. Beyond grand unification, there is also speculation that it may be possible to merge gravity with the other three gauge symmetries into a "Theory of Everything" (THE); see: http://en.wikipedia.org/wiki/Grand_unification_theory).

By totally differentiating $V(p+t, n, E)$ and dividing through by the marginal utility of expenditure V_E Baldwin and Venables (1995, p. 1601 and Appendix A) derive an equation (here slightly extended) of welfare change which can be interpreted as a stylized GUT for a new EU Member State in the process of EU enlargement[3]:

$$\begin{aligned} dV/V_E = {} & \alpha t\, dm - md[t - \alpha t] - m\, dp \\ & + [p + t - a]\, dX - xa_x\, dx + (V_n/V_E)\, dn \\ & + (\tilde{r}/\rho - 1)\, dI \\ & + dSF \end{aligned} \tag{12.1}$$

A GUT of enlargement should be able to explain at least three major effects of regional integration: *allocation of resources* (static "trade effects", "scale effects"), *accumulation or growth effects* and *location effects*[4] inclusive *factor movements.* Equation (12.1) involves the following integration effects:

12.3.1 Trade Effects

The first row includes static welfare effects of models with *perfect competition*. The first term is the "trade volume" effect. The trade volume changes subject to the wedge created by DCR trade barriers, αt. The second term is the "trade cost" effect, measuring the change in costs generated by changes in the non-DCR elements of trade barriers. The third is the "terms of trade" effect. The last effect occurs only if the acceding country is a large country having the possibility to influence world trade prices. In the case of EU's enlargement 2007 (as in those of 2004) only small countries joined the EU, which means that the third term is zero[5]. Prior to EU

[3]Kohler (2004) derives a similar welfare equation for a single incumbent EU country, in particular for Germany.

[4]Location effects are discussed by Baldwin and Venables (1995, pp. 1616 ff.) in the context of the insights of models of "economic geography", pioneered by Krugman (1991). This model category also considers factor movements from one location to the other, from the "periphery" to the "centre" or vice versa.

[5]Baldwin and Venables (1995, pp 1604–1605) discuss in the context of a Regional Integration Agreement with "large" countries the case of three countries, in which countries one and two form the Regional Integration Agreement and country three remains outside. The members of the Regional Integration Agreement can influence the terms of trade, and hence, the third term of (12.1) becomes relevant. The theoretical analysis of three-country problems (with three goods) becomes easily intractable or delivers ambiguous results (Lloyd, 1982). The Kemp–Wan theorem (Kemp and Wan, 1976) gives a powerful and beautiful answer to the question what configuration of trade policy (towards non-members) would result in a necessarily welfare improving Custom Union. The Kemp–Wan theorem gained further attraction in alternative interpretations (Richardson, 1995) and extensions of free trade areas (Ohyama 2004; Bond et al. 2004).

accession, candidate countries of the 2004 and 2007 enlargement already abolished tariffs in trade with the old EU Member States in the context of the asymmetric liberalization process of the Europe Agreements (EAs). After EU accession the new Member States entered the Custom Union of the EU and now participate in EU's SM program. That meant, on the one hand, adjustments of the national external tariff to EU's CET (Common External Tariff) and the abolishment of border controls. Hence, the remaining trade costs were eliminated. Interpreted with (12.1), in the pre-accession period (with $\alpha = 1$) the reduction of tariffs (t) contributed negatively to welfare (first term), whereas after accession (with $\alpha = 0$) the elimination of border controls and hence reduction of trade costs (t) contributed positively to welfare (second term).

Euro's pro-trade effect: The experience with the existing Euro area so far shows that the introduction of the Euro additionally reduces transaction costs and hence stimulates intra-euro-area trade in the range between 5 and 15% (with 9% the best estimate), depending on the method of gravity model estimates (for a critical survey, see Baldwin 2006a). New research suggests, however, that reduced transaction costs were not primarily responsible for the pro-trade effect of the introduction of the Euro, arguing instead that it was caused by the export of new goods to Euro zone economies. The mechanism driving this is seen in a reduction in the fixed cost of introducing new goods into Euro zone markets (for such arguments, see Baldwin 2006a, p. 87). Applying the "Casella effect" (see footnote 6) to the introduction of the Euro one finds a small country bonus: on average the Euro has led to improvement of small Euro area countries relative export performance by 3–9% (Badinger and Breuss 2008b). One can expect that the same mechanism will play a role when the new Member States of EU's 2004 and 2007 enlargement will join the Euro zone (first estimates forecast an increase of 5% intra-euro-area trade in the new EU Member States; Belke and Spies 2007).

12.3.2 Scale Effects

The three terms in the second row capture theoretical predictions of models with increasing returns to scale and *imperfect competition*. The first term is the "output" effect, arising if there is a change in output in industries where price differs from average cost. The second term is the "scale" effect, which gives the value of changes in average costs induced by changes in firm scale[6]. The third terms gives "variety" effects which may arise when the number of differentiated consumer products changes, like in trade models with Dixit–Stiglitz type utility functions and ingredients of the theory of monopolistic competition (Grossman and Helpman 1991).

---

[6]A special case is the "Casella effect". It implies that in case of trade bloc enlargement the gains from enlarging the bloc fall disproportionately on small countries, because – if economies of scale imply that firms located in large countries enjoy lower costs – the entrance of new members diminishes the importance of the domestic market and improves the small countries' relative competitiveness (Casella 1996). Empirically, the "Casella effect" cannot be generally verified (Badinger and Breuss 2006).

12.3.3 Accumulation Effects

The term in the third row captures what is also called the "growth" effect of regional integration. It implies that a change in investment is instantaneously costly, but it also augments the capital stock with a social rate of return $\tilde{r}$. Discounting this at a social discount rate ρ gives the present value $\tilde{r}/\rho$, and a change in investment has a first-order welfare effect if this ratio differs from one.

12.3.4 Net EU Budget Receiver Effects

The term of the fourth row indicates the welfare improvement of being a net receivers vis à vis the EU budget. All countries of the fifth EU enlargement were poor countries and therefore eligible for high structural funds transfers out of the EU budget.

12.3.5 Location or Globalisation Effects

A stylized GUT of a country joining the EU should also capture effects of "globalisation" or factor movements. Integration of rich and poor countries under the conditions of the rules of the SM (free movement of capital and labour, besides free movement of goods and services) induces huge factor flows: FDI from the old to the new EU Member States because of expected higher rents in the "emerging markets" of Eastern Europe and labour from the new to the old Member States because of the huge wage differential in the order of up to 1:10. Such factor movement and its welfare implications are only indirectly captured in (12.1). FDI inflows in the acceding country may renew the capital stock and hence increase investment (third row). Labour emigration leads to a welfare loss ("migration loss") in the sender country and to a welfare gain ("immigration surplus") in the recipient country (the old EU Member States). In the context of (12.1) labour migration could be only interpreted if one assumes wage differentials in the expenditure equation E, which would induce migration. In the special case of EU enlargement it might well be that the effects of factor movements dominate the trade effects.

12.4 A Model-Based Evaluation of Bulgaria's and Romania's Accession to the EU

In what follows, we assume that the direct integration effects of the 2007 EU enlargement – i.e. the participation in the SM – occur only in the acceding countries Bulgaria and Romania. The old EU (EU-15), the new Member States of the 2004

EU enlargement (EU-10[7]) and Austria are affected only indirectly via spill-overs from Bulgaria and Romania. Hence, we work with a prototype model approach for the case of three countries and two trade blocs. We model the integration effects explicitly for Bulgaria and Romania, using a simple macro-model approach with no sectoral break-down like in computable general equilibrium (CGE) models. Most of the econometrically estimated equations are reduced form equations, capturing the essential linkages of integration channels (Appendix A in Breuss 2009).

12.4.1 Implementing the Theoretical Integration Effects

On the basis of the stylized GUT of (12.1) we explain the integration effects considered in our simple model and the channels of interactions. However, contrary to the theoretical ambitions laid down in (12.1) which explain changes in welfare due to regional integration for a new member of a Regional Integration Agreement we aim at explaining the changes in real GDP as the final "welfare" measure due to the EU accession of Bulgaria and Romania. Most of the integration effects modelled target directly the accumulation or growth effects of enlargement and do not consider static trade effects and its implications of trade creation and trade diversion.

12.4.1.1 Trade Effects

Static Welfare Effects[8]

A separate CGE analysis of the enlargement of EU's customs union in 2004 and 2007 is executed by applying the GTAP 6 CGE model (Dimaranan 2006) with 12 countries/regions, 3 sectors and 5 factors of productions using a data base for 2001 (Table 12.1). The EU-27 Custom Union was simulated by eliminating all remaining tariff barriers between the Member States and considering the adjustment of national external tariffs to the Common External Tariff of the EU. Prior to 2004 and 2007 the EU-15 Custom Union already existed. Therefore only tariffs on trade between the countries of the EU-10, Bulgaria and Romania on the one hand and

[7]EU-10 includes the Czech Republic, Cyprus, Estonia, Hungary, Latvia, Lithuania, Malta, Poland, Slovakia and Slovenia. The integration effects of EU's 2004 enlargement for the old and new Member States were estimated with model simulations in Breuss (2002).

[8]Only in this static welfare analysis using the GTAP 6 CGE model we distinguish between welfare and GDP effects. In the GTAP model, economic welfare is derived from the allocation of national income between consumption, government consumption and savings. Welfare is then decomposed leading to the following welfare contributions: (1) endowment contributions to welfare from changes in primary production factors; (2) technical efficiency in using the production factors, and (3) allocative efficiency.

Table 12.1 Trade effects of EU's enlarged customs union (incl. Turkey) as of 2004 and 2007

Trade with	Austria	EU14	EU-10	BG	RO	TR	CA	WF	GDP
	Bilateral trade (%-change compared to baseline = EU-15 CU)						In % of GDP, change		%-change
Austria	–	−0.63	7.26	28.02	15.56	−0.87	−0.02	0.06	0.01
OMS – AT	−0.25	−0.26	4.26	38.21	14.43	−0.49	0.01	0.01	0.00
EU-10	4.97	4.60	10.78	0.66	−0.46	20.84	−0.70	0.22	0.24
Bulgaria	4.66	13.06	37.58	–	−7.26	8.95	−2.82	1.10	1.19
Romania	3.53	4.37	39.12	−17.67	–	0.22	−3.02	0.65	0.65
Croatia	−1.88	−1.77	30.48	−4.29	30.97	19.24	−0.10	0.22	0.04
Albania	0.08	−0.03	−0.38	−17.50	24.06	8.50	0.03	−0.02	−0.01
Turkey	1.93	2.67	30.15	−17.50	43.81	–	−0.17	0.19	0.08
EFTA	−0.06	−0.12	1.72	17.91	13.72	−2.77	0.02	−0.01	0.00
Rest Europe	−1.45	−1.28	15.42	−7.37	19.60	17.49	−0.11	0.10	0.01
NAFTA	0.20	0.01	4.84	−5.78	12.93	1.03	0.01	0.00	0.00
RoW	0.06	−0.08	1.07	−15.66	−1.41	6.21	0.02	0.00	0.00
Total	0.26	0.06	4.90	12.43	10.16	2.39	0.00	0.00	–

Notes BG = Bulgaria, RO = Romania; TR = Turkey, EFTA = Switzerland and Rest-EFTA; Rest Europe = Russia and Rest Eastern Europe; NAFTA = North American Free Trade Agreement, RoW = Rest of the World; CA = current account; WF = Welfare; GDP = real GDP
Source: Own simulations with the GTAP 6 model with 12 countries/regions, 3 sectors (food, manufacturing and services) and 5 factors of production (land, unskilled labour, skilled labour, capital and natural resources); data base for 2001

those for trade between EU-10, Bulgaria and Romania with EU-15 (incl. the customs union with Turkey) on the other hand had to be eliminated; in addition EU's CET had to be adopted by the newcomers. The calculated trade, welfare and GDP effects are to be interpreted as long-run deviations from the base line, which is the Custom Union of EU-15 (inclusive Turkey).

The main winners of the EU-27 Custom Union are the new ten Member States of EU's 2004 enlargement, Bulgaria and Romania of EU's 2007 enlargement and partly also Turkey. Trade creation in intra-trade between the EU-10 states increased by 10.8%, welfare and real GDP increased by 0.2%. Even bigger welfare and GDP effects resulted for Bulgaria and Romania which could stimulated their trade with EU-10 considerably. Austria also profited from additional trade creation with the new Member States and a slight welfare gain of 0.06% of GDP. The remaining Member States of EU-15 increased its trade with the group of EU-10 by 4 × ¼% and even more with Bulgaria and Romania. However, welfare and GDP did not change. EU's 2004 enlargement led to a considerable trade diversion from the old EU Member States to the new ones. Austria's trade with the other old Member States declined to the same amount as trade among the old Member States. If one extends this exercise and considers the trade cost reduction by eliminating border controls (SM entry effect) – assuming bilateral reduction of trade costs equivalent to a 2.5% tariff reduction – augments the results of the Custom Union exercise slightly, but does not change the qualitative results of changes in the pattern of regional trade flows.

Is then the progressing EU enlargement consistent with the Kemp–Wan theorem? This would imply that trade with non EU Custom Union countries remained unchanged and would not hamper third country's welfare. Although our analysis is not directly suitable to evaluate the Kemp–Wan theorem, one conclusion can be drawn from the fifth EU enlargement: trade of the old Member States (excluding Austria) with the rest of the world (RoW) declined slightly whereas those of Austria's and EU-10's trade with the RoW increased. As the decline of the old Member States' trade (excluding Austria) is nearly zero implying no welfare changes in RoW, but welfare increases in the enlarged EU's Custom Union one could conclude that this approximately satisfies the Kemp–Wan propositions.

Dynamic or Growth Effects of Trade (Trade and Productivity Links)

In our simple enlargement model for Bulgaria and Romania we consider the growth-enhancing effect of the opening up of both countries (for the explicitly estimated equations, see Appendix A in Breuss 2009). In line with the insights of Frankel and Romer (1999) on the links between trade and productivity (for an industry perspective, see Badinger and Breuss 2008a), surveyed by Lewer and Van den Berg (2003) we model directly the link between the change of openness (measured by export (X) plus import (M) shares of GDP) and productivity growth in the productivity equation (PR). Via implementing PR as a proxy for total factor productivity in our GDP equation (Y) we are able to capture the trade effect on growth for Bulgaria and Romania. The shares of exports are explained by the usual income (weighted GDP growth of the partner countries in EU-15, Austria and EU-10) and relative price (real exchange rate) effects plus an EU enlargement or scale effect in the export equation. The EU enlargement effect is captured by a dummy for the increasing size of the EU from 6 over 9 to 10, 15, 25 and 27 (ENLCTR). In this way we can also capture the opening-up of the EU in its trade with the CEECs via the EAs since 2000, already prior to EU accession in 2007. The import share equation (M) explains imports with the usual income (instead of its own GDP growth, the export share variable X is used) and relative price (real exchange rate-REER) effects. Additionally, a dummy (INT) captures the effects of the opening-up of trade with the EU via the asymmetric trade liberalization of the EAs prior to EU accession in 2007.

12.4.1.2 Other Effects

Scale and Imperfect Competition Effects

As we deal only with a simple aggregate or macro model for Bulgaria and Romania we capture only one effect of imperfect competition of the second row of (12.1). We model mark-up pricing in our price equation (P). We assume that after participating in EU's SM price competition increases and hence, reduces the market power of incumbent firms in Bulgaria and Romania. This pricing behaviour can be detected empirically in the old EU Member States after creating the

SM in 1993 (Badinger 2007). This reduces the mark-up on unit labour costs and hence dampens inflation.

Accumulation Effects

Only one accumulation or growth effect via the capital augmenting effect of real gross fixed investment is predicted theoretically in the third row of (12.1). However, the equation does not explain how investments are induced. In our investment equation (I) we explicitly try to explain changes in investment by FDI inflows (FDI) and by transfers out of the EU budget (here we use only the structural funds transfers in % of GDP – the variable COH) for improving the infrastructure. Via the GDP equation additional investments stimulate real GDP. With this modelling approach we combine the effects of the third and fourth row of (12.1). Besides the growth enhancing effect of trade opening (X + M) we also consider the positive link of changes of research and development for GDP growth. Hence, we consider the primary message of the new endogenous growth theory of trade (e.g. Romer 1990; Grossman and Helpman 1991). Changes in the share of research and development in GDP (R&D) stimulate productivity and via the GDP equation also GDP growth.

From the hitherto existing practical experience with the SM program we know that newcomers in the SM experienced a striking productivity shock in the first adjustment phase. We implement such a transitional shock exogenously into our productivity equation (PR) by adjusting the residual accordingly (Table 12.2).

Location or Globalisation Effects

Integration of unevenly developed economies induce stark factor movements which may dominate trade effects. In the case of EU enlargement one can speak of a "mini-globalisation" as a subset of the world-wide globalisation.

1. *"Migration effects"*: According to Borjas (1995) migration of labour may lead to an "immigration surplus" – i.e. a welfare gain – in the recipient country and – as a mirror image – one must conclude that it leads to a "migration loss" or welfare loss in the country from which labour emigrates. We model these effects in the equation for employment (E) and in those for the unemployment rate (U) in a reduced form. In both cases changes in the labour force via migration have a positive (negative) impact on the respective variables in the host (sender) countries of migrants. As in the case of EU's 2004 enlargement, transitional arrangements[9] concerning the free movement of labour were negotiated in the

[9]The exact transitional provisions fort he free movements for workers in the case of the 2004 enlargement can be found on the homepage of the European Commission: http://ec.europa.eu/social/main.jsp?catId=507&langId=en and in the case of the 2007 enlargement: http://ec.europa.eu/social/main.jsp?catId=508&langId=en.

Table 12.2 Model inputs for simulating integration effects

Scenarios	Integration effects	Pre-accession period 2000–2006	EU membership 2007–2020
		Inputs in the models for Bulgaria and Romania	
1	Trade effects	Exports (X): since 2004 EU25 instead of EU-15 Imports (M): since 2000 more openness due to EAs liberalization (same inputs in BG and RO)	Exports (X): since 2007 EU27 instead of EU-15 Imports (M): since 2007 additional openness due participation in EU's CU and single market in BG and RO
2	Investment effects of FDI	FDI inflows: since 2000 2% of GDP more in BG (+½% in RO)	FDI inflows: after 2007 petering out of this process
3	Investment effects of structural funds transfers	SF transfers: no input	SF transfers: since 2007 ½% of GDP more with declining tendency
4	Productivity stimulating R&D	R&D: no input	R&D: since 2007 0.1% of GDP (BG) and 0.25% of GDP (RO) higher
5	Mark-up pricing	MUP: no input	MUP: since 2007 5% lower mark-ups with declining tendency in BG and RO
6	Exogenous productivity shock	PR: no input	PR: since 2007–2010 an increase in productivity by ½% in BG and 1% in RO with declining tendency
		Inputs in the models for Bulgaria, Romania and in Austria, EU-15 and EU-10	
7	Migration effects	LS: no input	LS: since 2014 1% of labour force migrates from BG (−36,000) and RO (−92,000) to AT (20%), to EU-15 (70%) and to EU-10 (10%)

Notes: SF = structural funds transfers out of the EU budget; EAs = Europe Agreements; LS = labour supply; MUP = mark-up index; PR = labour productivity; R&D = expenditures on research and development model inputs refer to an integration scenario in comparison with a baseline scenario without EU integration (for the detailed model inputs, see Appendix B Breuss 2009)

accession treaties with Bulgaria and Romania. We assume that only after 7 years, i.e. from 2014 onwards labour can freely migrate from Bulgaria and Romania to EU-15, EU-10 and Austria.

2. *FDI flows:* The opening-up of Eastern Europe created a new region of "emerging markets" nearby the western European countries. Statistical data by the Austrian National Bank show that the return on equity (RoE) of FDIs in Eastern Europe increased much faster and they are higher than those achieved in the old EU countries since 1989 (Altzinger 2006; Fuchs 2006). FDI inflows in Bulgaria and Romania help to improve investment (our investment equation I) and hence stimulate GDP growth. The FDI net outflows of the EU-15 and that of Austria are modelled explicitly as determined by the weighted GDP growth in the partner countries of the enlarged EU.

Euro Participation Effects

The stylized GUT of enlargement is not able to capture the more complex effects involved if an EU member participates in the EMU. As we discussed earlier, however, we can – due to reduced transaction costs – expect similar pro-trade effects in the new EU Member States when introducing the Euro. In order to take account of the possible macro-economic effects of the Euro zone participation we estimated a Taylor rule for Bulgaria and Romania explaining the setting of the short-term interest rates (RS). In case of a future Euro zone participation – which requires the fulfilment of the Maastricht convergence criteria – one could substitute the national Taylor rule in Bulgaria and Romania by the ECB's Taylor rule, which explains monetary policy for the Euro zone. The long-term interest rates, which are also a determinant of GDP growth, are linked to the change in the short-term interest rates. Euro area participation may also imply additional economic adjustment mechanisms: a reduction of exchange rate uncertainty; more general efficiency and, hence an increase of total factor productivity (growth effects); but also fiscal restraints could dampen aggregate demand when the Stability and Growth Pact rules (SGP; see Breuss 2007a) have to be met. A first positive overall perspective is the outcome of macro-model simulations in the case of Slovenia's entry into the Euro zone on January 1, 2007 Neck and Weyerstrass (2007).

Models for Bulgaria and Romania

In addition to the explicit implementation of all of the possible integration effects, the macro models for Bulgaria and Romania are closed by explaining GDP growth (Y) with the usual economic variables (productivity, investment, employment, unemployment) as well as the policy variables (fiscal and monetary policy stance). GDP growth then is linked with the unemployment rate (inverted Okun's law), the latter with wage bargaining (Phillips curve). The budget balance is also connected with the overall economic development and the latter determines the public debt dynamics. For Bulgaria and Romania – two transition economies – we explicitly model the Balassa–Samuelson effect by explaining the real effective exchange rate (REER) by the gap of GDP per capita relative to EU-15. A catching-up equation calculates the adjustment process in GDP per capita relative to those of EU-15.

Models for EU-15, EU-10 and Austria

According to our philosophy we consider only the indirect integration effects on the old EU Member States. The trade relations of EU-15 with Bulgaria (0.2% of total exports) and Romania (0.6%) and those of the EU-10 (0.4% and 1.6% respectively) and even those of Austria (0.5% and 1.5% respectively) are just too small to expect a considerable direct integration impact on the old EU Member States. Therefore we model only spill-overs from Bulgaria and Romania to the old EU Member States via GDP equations with weighted GDP growth's of Bulgaria and Romania as explanatory variables.

As already mentioned, we also model net FDI outflows (FDINET) from the EU-15 and from Austria as determined by GDP growth in the partner countries, and hence also in Bulgaria and Romania. In the case of Austria we also explain the declining wage share (functional income distribution – the variable LQ) by increased net FDI outflows (most of which are connected with the new opportunities in the new emerging markets of the new EU Member States). This reduced form equation tries to capture in a nutshell the strong link between changes in product prices and that of factor prices predicted by the Stolper–Samuelson theorem in the case of trade liberalization. Accordingly, one can expect that after opening-up of the markets of Eastern Europe due to the trade liberalization with the EAs, the relative factor prices (rental price to wages) of the capital-abundant countries of the old EU-15 (and hence also that of Austria) increased (resulting in a decline in the wage share) whereas the relative factor prices of the labour-abundant countries in the new EU Member States in Eastern Europe must have decreased (Breuss 2007d). Hand in hand with the income distribution effect of trade liberalization, the accelerating net FDI outflows from Austria into the new EU Member States enforced the pressure on the wage shares. An auxiliary equation calculates Austria's income performance relative to that of EU-15.

12.4.1.3 Model Inputs

The integration effects in Bulgaria and Romania are simulated by considering seven scenarios (Table 12.2). We have to differentiate between a pre-accession phase and the EU membership phase proper. The integration process into the EU starts with a pre-accession phase in which the candidate countries are supported with several financial aids (ISPA, SAPARD, etc.) out of the EU budget. Trade integration already takes place before becoming an EU member. Trade between the old EU and the CEECs was already liberalized via the EAs in an asymmetric manner. Tariffs on EU's imports from Bulgaria and Romania were abolished already in 1997, while the tariffs on imports from the EU in the latter countries were eliminated in 2002. Being an EU candidate country makes these economies attractive and secure for FDIs. With EU accession the new members are participating in the Custom Union of the EU implying an adjustment of their national tariffs to EU's Common External Tariff.

Prior to EU accession the import tariffs in Romania (19%) were higher than in Bulgaria (12%), whereas EU's CET was around 6%. Also the tariffs for agricultural products were much higher in both countries than in the EU. Besides becoming a member of the Custom Union of the EU the newcomers enter the SM what implies a productivity shock and more competition and, therefore, a dampening effect on prices. The new Member States have better access to the research framework programs of the EU and – because they are poor countries – are eligible to receive structural funds transfers out of the EU budget.

The exact quantitative inputs used in the simulations of the seven integration scenarios are collected in Appendix B of Breuss (2009). In some cases the inputs are the same in both countries, in others we differentiate between Bulgaria and Romania. Ex ante, one never knows the intensity of the adjustments shocks (e.g. in labour productivity) and one can only speculate about the length or the timing of the shocks. In principle, the quantification of our inputs are calibrated according to past experiences with the enlargement of EU's SM.

12.5 Integration Effects of EU's 2007 Enlargement

Ahead of EU's fifth enlargement in 2004 a vast variety of studies were undertaken with the whole range of models available – multi- and single countries CGE models or world and single countries macro models. The great attraction to carry out such studies was founded in the novelty of the problem. Past EU enlargements primarily dealt with the integration of industrial countries with comparable levels of development (although Greece, Portugal and Spain lagged somewhat behind the old EU Member States). The eastern enlargement of the EU posed several challenges. The formerly communist and planned economies firstly had to qualify as an EU candidate country according to the Copenhagen criteria (the countries had to transform to democracies, market economies and they had to adjust their legal system to EU's acquis communautaire). Secondly, after the systemic transformation these countries had to catch-up to the EU's income levels and to reorient their trade relations from the former CMEA to the EU. The EU supported this process by liberalizing trade relations with the CEECs in the EAs.

Most of the model simulation studies ahead of the EU's 2004 enlargement resulted in an asymmetric but win–win outcome (for an overview of the results, see European Commission 2006). On average, both the old EU-15 Member States and the newly acceding countries can expect positive welfare and GDP gains. However, the gains of the new Member States will be much higher than those of the old EU-15 on average, sometimes at the proportion of 10:1 (Breuss 2002). Within the old EU-15 Member States those countries with more intensive trade relations already before accession (like Austria and Germany) can also expect higher welfare gains than those countries at the periphery of the EU (like Portugal and Spain) which do no trade much with the CEECs. The latter might even lose in the enlargement game.

In the case of the 2007 enlargement by Bulgaria and Romania we can expect a similar pattern as in the 2004 enlargement[10]. The newcomers will gain the most,

[10]One of the lasting problems in connection with the 2007 enlargement is corruption. The unsuccessful fight against corruption forced the European Commission to cancel financial aid in the case of Bulgaria. On 26 November 2008, Bulgaria lost 220 million Euro of pre-accession funding after the European Commission confirmed its July decision to bar two agencies from handling Phare money. This came after the European Commission adopted a decision to suspend roughly 500 million Euros of EU funding when it released its monitoring report on Bulgaria on

Austria will profit more from spill-overs than EU-15 and the ten new EU Member States, which joined the EU in 2004 (EU-10).

12.5.1 Bulgaria and Romania

For the new EU Member States we fully modelled the expected integration effects of entering EU's SM. The macro-economic effects for some major variables are shown in Table 12.3. The overall results (all seven scenarios combined) exhibit the following features:

1. Due to our input calibration the overall effects in both countries are quite similar.
2. The integration effects started already in the pre-accession period. Preparation for accession resulted already in a higher average annual growth of real GDP of 0.3% in Bulgaria and 0.2% in Romania.
3. The integration effects started to accelerate with joining the EU in 2007. Calculated until 2020 we expect an average annual growth effect of real GDP of 0.6% in both countries. Cumulative real GDP gain from 2000 to 2020 will have reached some 9% points.
4. Due to the need to adjust the efficiency of the economy to the challenge of the SM, labour productivity will increase by around 1/2% point per year after 2007.
5. More competition in the SM leads to a deceleration of inflation – more in Romania than in Bulgaria.
6. In accordance with the predictions of the Balassa-Samuelson hypothesis, both countries will appreciate their currencies in real terms during the catching-up process.
7. The income gap vis-à-vis EU-15 will be steadily closing – on average by around 3% points per annum between 2007 and 2020.
8. Like in other less developed countries joining the EU (e.g. Greece, Portugal and Spain) we can expect that the current account balance will further deteriorate in Bulgaria and Romania as imports increase much faster than exports. Bulgaria starts with a current account deficit of 14% of GDP in 2007, Romania with a 12% deficit.
9. The policy variables – budget balance, debt to GDP ratio, as well as interest rates (with the exception of Romania) – are not very much affected by joining the EU.
10. Due to higher GDP growth, the unemployment rate declines.

---

23 July 2008. Similar problems still exist in Romania. However, so far the European Commission only warned Romania because of the shortcomings in judicial reforms and the fight against corruption (see EurActiv: http://www.euractiv.com/en/enlargement). Transparency International in its 2008 Corruption Perception Index ranks Romania in place 70 and Bulgaria in 72 (http://www.transparency.org/news_room/in_focus/2008/cpi2008). The economic impact of the lasting corruption practice in both new EU Member States cannot be quantified properly but will probably have a negative impact on FDI inflows and internal economic efficiency.

Table 12.3 Direct integration effects of EU's 2007 enlargement in Bulgaria and Romania

Integration effects	Scale	Pre-accession period 2000–2006		EU membership 2007–2020	
		Bulgaria	Romania	Bulgaria	Romania
GDP, real	%	+0.3	+0.2	+0.6	+0.6
GDP, real	C%	+1.8	+1.2	+9.2	+8.9
GDP, real (incl. migration)	%	+0.3	+0.2	+0.5	+0.6
Investment quota (% GDP)	%	+1.5	+0.5	+0.7	+0.6
Labour productivity (PR)	%	+0.3	+0.2	+0.4	+0.5
Employment (E)	%	+0.0	+0.0	+0.3	+0.1
Wages, nominal (W)	%	+0.3	+0.1	+0.3	−0.2
Inflation rate (P)	%	+0.0	−0.0	−0.2	−0.6
Unit labour costs (ULC)	%	+0.1	−0.1	−0.2	−0.8
Unemployment rate (U)	%	−0.4	−0.0	−2.8	−0.4
Budget balance (% GDP)	%	+0.1	+0.0	+0.3	+0.1
Public debt (% GDP)	%	−0.1	−0.0	−0.2	+0.1
Interest rate, short-term	%	+0.1	+0.2	+0.2	+2.0
Interest rate, long-term	%	+0.0	+0.1	+0.0	+1.9
Exports[a] (% GDP)	%	+1.3	+1.5	+4.6	+3.5
Imports[a] (% GDP)	%	+3.2	+2.9	+12.9	+10.1
Real effective exchange rate	%	+0.1	+0.1	+0.4	+1.0
Wage share (LQ) (% GDP)	%	+0.0	+0.0	+0.6	+0.2
GDP p.c. relative to EU-15	%	+0.2	+0.2	+3.3	+3.1

Notes: The direct integration effects are without migration effects; % = annual average growth rate in % or average annual change in % of GDP; C% = cumulated deviations from the baseline in % points

Source: Own simulations with the integration models of Appendix A (Breuss 2009)

[a]Goods and services

If one breaks down the overall GDP effects into the *seven integration scenarios* (Table 12.2 and Appendix B in Breuss 2009) one recognises the following features:

1. Contrary to the postulates of some of the literature of the endogenous growth theory (e.g. Romer 1990; Rivera-Batiz and Romer 1991) and in accordance with empirical results of the past EU integration experiences (Badinger 2005), the growth effects of integration are only short-lived. EU integration means a temporary shock to the level of GDP, which translates into a jump in GDP growth rates but does not lead to a permanent steady-state increase of growth. This pattern is replicated here in the case of Bulgaria and Romania in Fig. 12.1.
2. The biggest GDP growth shock stems from the exogenous productivity shock (scenario six). As we do not know ex ante how strong this shock might be and how long it will last, we calibrated it as such that it is somehow similar in both countries, with a slightly stronger impact in Romania because the productivity performance was weaker than in Bulgaria ahead of EU accession. Anyway, we distributed the shock only over the period 2007–2010 and made sure that it dies away later on.
3. Of course, in the case of the productivity shock one could also consider larger or smaller impact on the economies. Here, we assumed only modest shocks.

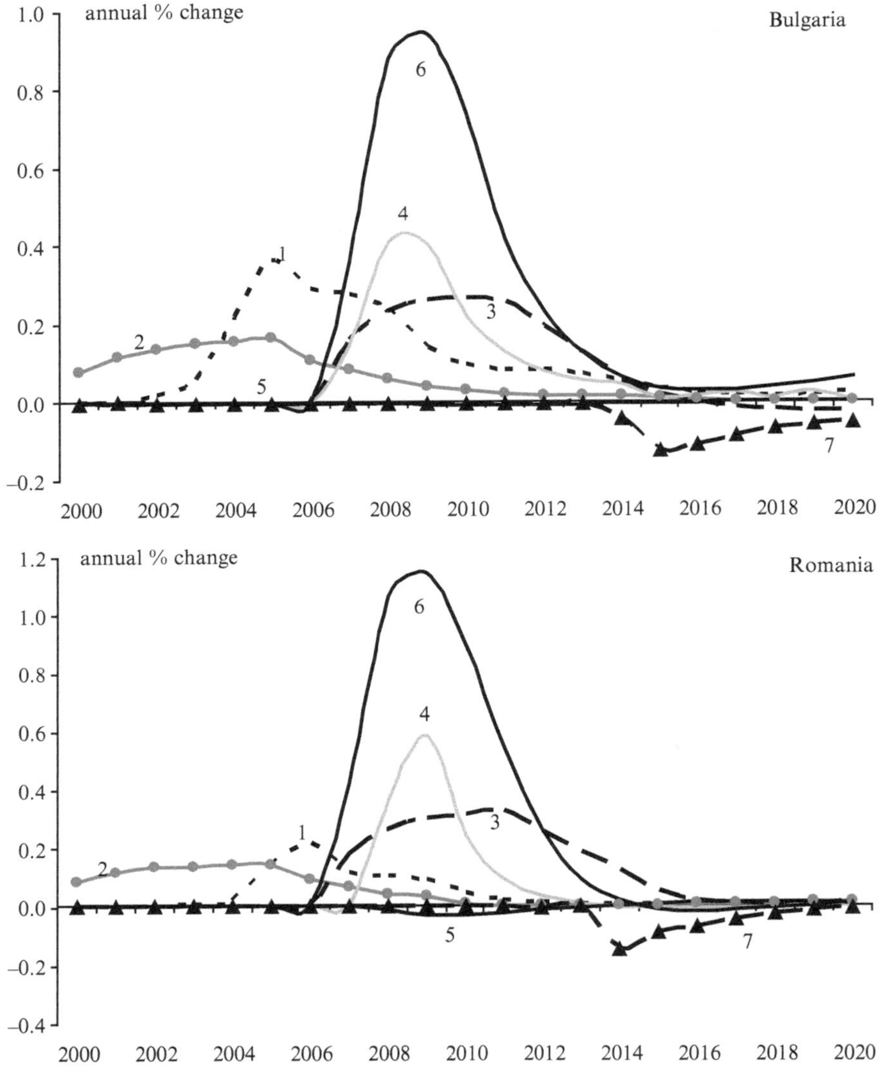

Fig. 12.1 Short-term growth impact effects of 2007 EU's enlargement in Bulgaria and Romania: real GDP effects of seven scenarios. Notes: Scenarios: 1 = trade effects, 2 = investment effect of FDI, 3 = investment effect of structural funds, 4 = productivity effect of R&D, 5 = mark-up pricing; 6 = exogenous productivity adjustment shock, 7 = migration effect
Source: Author's own calculations

4. The trade induced GDP growth effect (via higher productivity growth) peters out relatively fast after EU accession.
5. The mark-up pricing behaviour has no impact on GDP.
6. As expected, migration exerts a negative effect on GDP ("migration loss"), starting with 2014 when the EU opens its labour markets completely. The

simulation exercise of scenario seven is only a tentative one, maybe considering a too strong migration effect when assuming that 1% of the labour force in both countries could emigrate in each year, starting in 2014.

Figure 12.2 shows the resulting long-run cumulative level effects of GDP for the seven integration scenarios in both countries. Again, the assumed (exogenous) productivity jump is the single strongest integration effect.

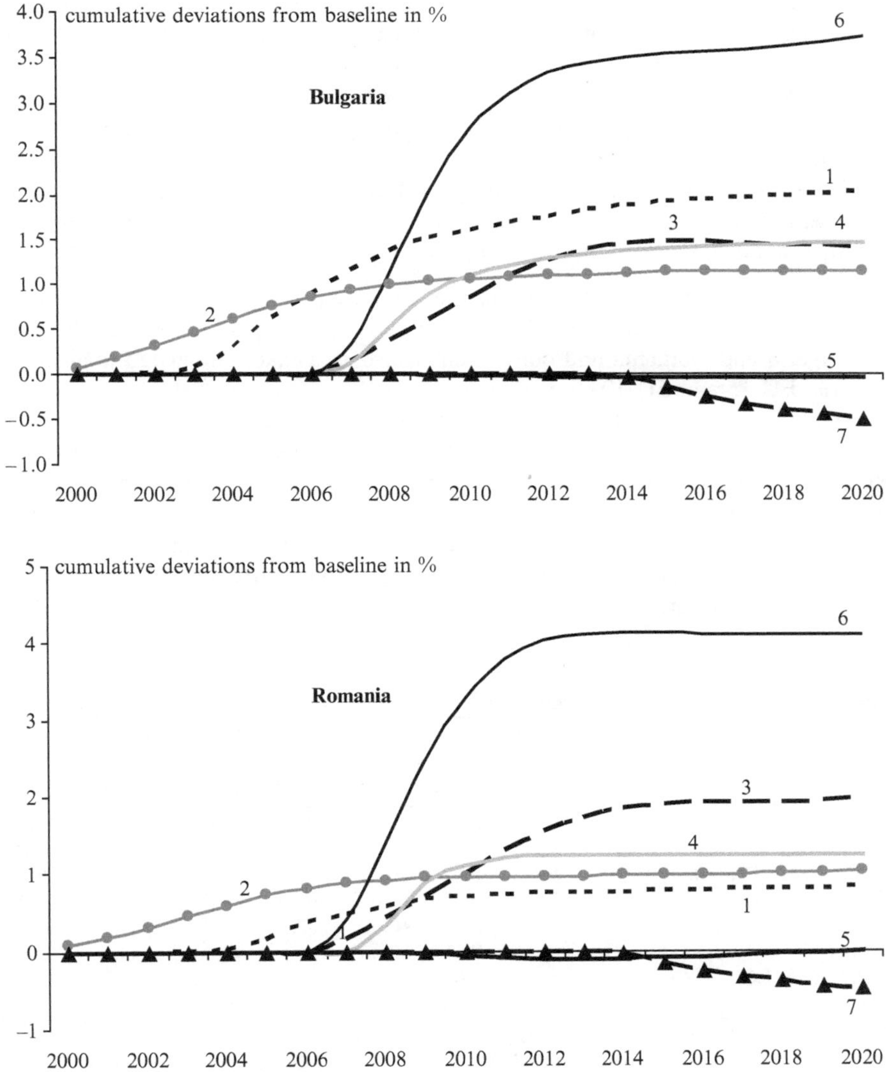

Fig. 12.2 Cumulative long-run effects of 2007 EU's enlargement in Bulgaria and Romania: real GDP effects of seven scenarios. Notes: Scenarios: 1 = trade effects, 2 = investment effect of FDI, 3 = investment effect of structural funds, 4 = productivity effect of R&D, 5 = mark-up pricing; 6 = exogenous productivity adjustment shock, 7 = migration effect
Source: Author's own calculations

12.5.2 Spill-Overs to Austria, Old and New Member States

As mentioned earlier the old EU Member States are affected by the accession of Bulgaria and Romania only indirectly via trade spill-overs and factor movements (FDI outflows and labour immigration). The results, collected in Table 12.4, exhibit the following features:

1. *Austria*, which on average trades more with Bulgaria and Romania than with the old and new Member States can also expect somewhat higher GDP gains: 0.03% additional annual GDP growth in the period 2007–2020, compared to 0.01% in EU-15 and EU-10, respectively.
2. Derived from the slightly positive GDP effects, we also get more improvement in the labour market and net FDI outflows.
3. The further process of EU's "mini-globalisation" by an ongoing enlargement towards lower-income countries implies a further (slight) deterioration of Austria's income distribution, i.e. a shrinking wage share.

As already mentioned before, we cannot expect a permanent increase of steady-state GDP growth. Instead, we foresee a temporary jump in GDP growth rates in Bulgaria and Romania and consequently also in a much alleviated manner in Austria, EU-15 and EU-10 (Fig. 12.3).

The long-run level effects of the cumulated real GDP due to EU' 2007 enlargement are depicted in Fig. 12.4. Calibrated as such that both countries, Bulgaria and Romania can expect similar long-run GDP effects, we see Bulgaria slightly ahead in the cumulated GDP in 2020. Figure 12.4 nicely shows that also EU's 2007 enlargement may be a win–win situation. The gains in Bulgaria and Romania are relative to Austria are in the order of 20:1. The integration effects for Austria, EU-15 and EU-10 are shown in Fig. 12.5.

Table 12.4 Indirect integration effects[a] of EU's 2007 enlargement in Austria, EU-15 and EU-10

Integration effects	Scale	Pre-accession period 2000–2006			EU membership BG, RO 2007–2020		
		Austria	EU-15	EU-10	Austria	EU-15	EU-10
GDP, real	%	+0.03	+0.00	+0.00	+0.03	+0.01	+0.01
GDP, real	C%	+0.10	+0.02	+0.01	+0.50	+0.18	+0.10
GDP, real (incl. migration)	%	+0.03	+0.00	+0.00	+0.05	+0.02	+0.01
Employment (E)	%	+0.00	+0.00	+0.00	+0.00	+0.01	+0.00
Unemployment rate (U)	%	−0.01	+0.00	+0.00	−0.03	−0.09	−0.01
FDInet (% GDP)	%	+0.01	+0.00	–	+0.04	+0.01	–
Wage share (LQ)	%	−0.03	–	–	−0.10	–	–
GDP per capita. relative to EU-15	%	+0.03	–	–	+0.33	–	–

Notes: Indirect integration effects are without migration effects; % = annual average growth rate in % or average annual change in % of GDP; C% = cumulated deviations from the baseline in % points
Source: Own simulations with the integration models of Appendix A (Breuss 2009)

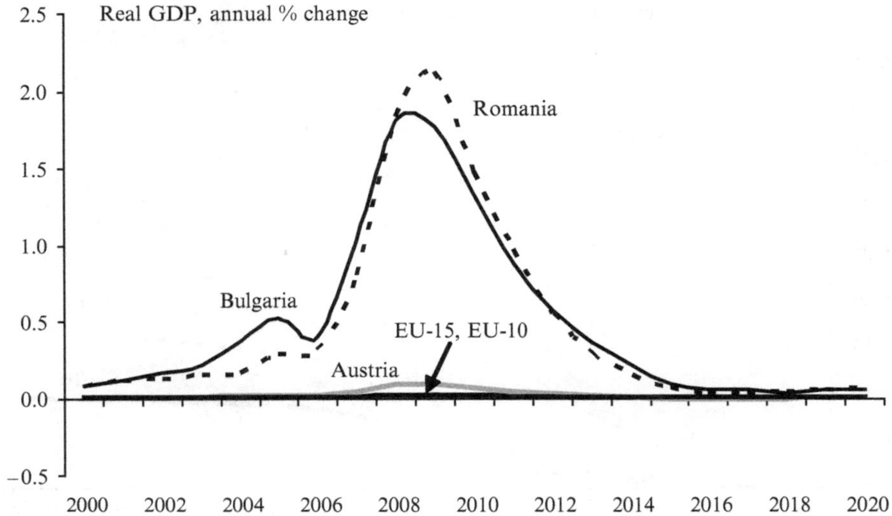

Fig. 12.3 Short-term overall integration effects: Bulgaria, Romania, Austria, old and the other new Member States
Source: Author's own calculations

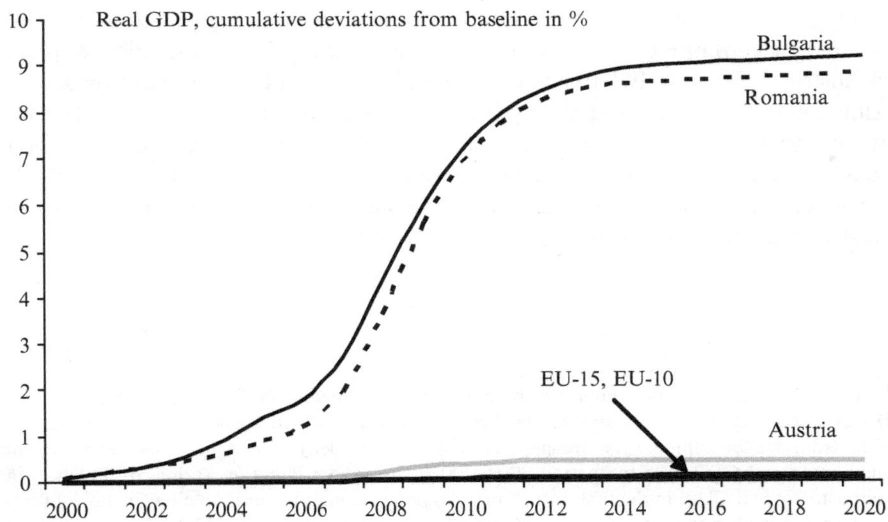

Fig. 12.4 Long-run overall integration effects of EU's 2007 enlargement: Bulgaria, Romania, Austria, old and the other new Member States
Source: Author's own calculations

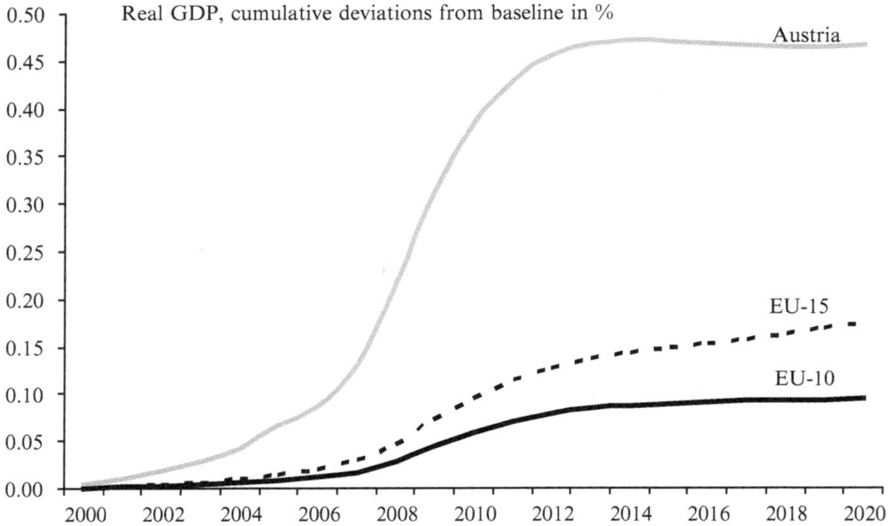

Fig. 12.5 Long-run overall integration effects of EU's 2007 enlargement: Austria, old and new Member States
Source: Author's own calculations

Finally, we show the results of the assumed migration that starts in 2014 (scenario seven) in Fig. 12.6. As expected, we replicate the "immigration surplus" in Austria, EU-15 and EU-10 and the "migration loss" in Bulgaria and Romania.[11] Although, for only demonstrative purposes we assumed that starting in 2014. We assume that 1% of the labour force of Bulgaria and Romania will leave their countries each year and migrate to Austria, EU-15 or EU-10. The GDP effects are small: −0.07% real GDP p.a. in Bulgaria and −0.05% in Romania; +0.03% in Austria and practically zero in EU-15 and EU-10.

[11]In a study on the economic impact of migration flows following the 2004 enlargement process D'Auria et al. (2008) achieve similar results: those countries which opened their labour markets right from the beginning (like Ireland, the UK and Sweden) gained the most measured in cumulative real GDP over the period 2004–2007. The sender countries (primarily Poland), in contrast, lost real GDP. In the first 4 years of enlargement roughly 1 million citizens moved from the 10 new Member States to the 15 old Member States. The UK received 532,000 persons, Ireland 162,000, Germany 96,000, Spain 67,000, Italy 32,000 and Austria 26,000. In Ireland the cumulative real GDP increase (+4.2%) was highest, followed by UK (+1%) and Austria (+0.4%). In the other old Member States the "immigration surplus" amounted to around +0.1% or less. In the sender countries the largest GDP loss was exhibited in Latvia (−3.5%), Lithuania (−4.7%) and Poland and Slovakia (each −2.1%). In the remaining new Member States the "migration loss" was less pronounced (see D'Auria et al. 2008, p.18).

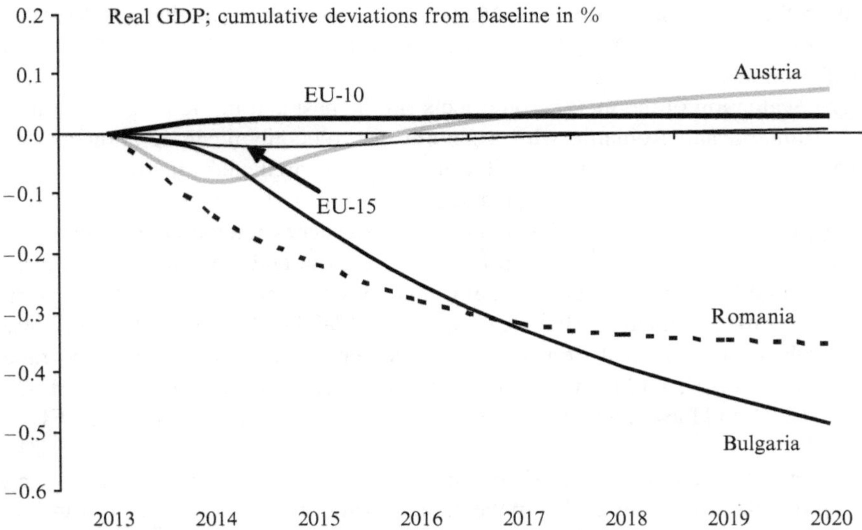

Fig. 12.6 Migration effects of EU's 2007 enlargement: Bulgaria, Romania, Austria, old and the other new Member States. Notes: Assumption: after the end of the 7 year transitional arrangement concerning the free movement of labour, migration starts in 2014, amounting to 1% of labour force leaving Bulgaria and Romania for the host countries with the following shares: Austria (20%), EU-15 (70%) and EU-10 (10%)
Source: Author's own calculations

12.6 Conclusions

A first evaluation of the grand fifth EU enlargement lead to the following basic findings:

- In most of the new Member States the economy grew faster since 2004 or 2007 than before.
- The recent enlargement statistically resulted in an "impoverishment" of the enlarged EU, i.e. the average GDP per capita decreased.
- The new Member States increased trade with the old Member States, but even more trade was created with each other. Also the EU-15 countries redirected their trade flows towards the new Member States at the cost of reducing intra-EU trade.
- The old EU Member States could exploit much better their comparative advantages than the new Member States theirs. This is reflected in a continuous improvement of the trade and current account balances of the old EU Member States with the new ones. As a mirror image, the current account balances of the new Member States with the old ones deteriorated.

- With the exception of Slovenia, Malta, Cyprus and Slovakia, the new Member States are not yet ready to fully participate in EMU, either because of too high inflation rates or too big public deficits.
- The evaluation of the integration effects (in the past and in the long-run future) of Bulgaria and Romania with a simple macro-economic integration model, trying to encompass as many of the theoretically predicted integration effects possible, leads to the following results:
- Bulgaria and Romania gain much more from EU accession than the incumbents, by the proportion of 20:1. Up up to 2020, Bulgaria and Romania can expect a considerable overall integration gain, amounting to an additional 1/2% point GDP growth annually. The incumbent EU Member States will profit only slightly from this latest step of EU enlargement. Due to more intensive trade relations, Austria will gain somewhat more (+0.05%) than the average of EU-15 (+0.02%) and the ten new EU Member States (+0.01%) which joined the EU in 2004.
- The prototype model presented and applied here for Bulgaria and Romania may in principle also be applicable in the case of further EU enlargements toward the countries of the Western Balkan (e.g. Croatia) and Turkey.

References

Altzinger, W. (5–6 May 2006). *On the earnings of Austrian affiliations in the new EU member countries.* Paper presented at the Annual Meeting of the Austrian Economic Association, NOeG 2006, Vienna.

Badinger, H. (2005). Growth effects of economic integration: evidence from the EU member states. *Weltwirtschaftliches Archiv, 141*(1), 50–78.

Badinger, H. (2007). Has the EU's single market programme fostered competition? Testing for a decrease in mark-up ratios in EU industries. *Oxford Bulletin of Economics and Statistics, 69*(4), 497–519.

Badinger, H., & Breuss, F. (2006). Country size and the gains from trade bloc enlargement: an empirical assessment for the European Community. *Review of International Economics, 14*(4), 615–631.

Badinger, H., & Breuss, F. (2008a). Trade and productivity: an industry perspective. *Empirica, 35*(2), 213–231.

Badinger, H., & Breuss, F. (2008b). Country size and the trade effects of the euro. Review of World Economics (Weltwirtschaftliches Archiv), 145(2), 207–223.

Baldwin, R. (2006a). *In or out: does it matter? An evidence-based analysis of the euro's trade effects.* London: Centre for Economic Policy Research (CEPR). 2006.

Baldwin, R. (August 2006b). *Multilateralising regionalism: spaghetti bowls as building blocs on the path to global free trade.* CEPR, Discussion Paper, No. 5775, London.

Baldwin, R., & Venables, A. J. (1995). Regional economic integration. In G. M. Grossman & K. Rogoff (Eds.), *Handbook of international economics* (Vol. III, pp. 1597–1644). Amsterdam, Lausanne, New York, Oxford, Shannon, Tokyo: Elsevier Science B.V.

Belke, A., & Spies, J. (18–19 May 2007). *Enlarging the EMU to the east: what effects on trade?* Paper presented at the Annual Meeting of the Austrian Economic Association (NOeG 2007), Klagenfurt University.

Bhagwati, J. N. (1995). U.S. trade policy: the infatuation with free trade areas. In J. N. Bhagwati & A. O. Krueger (Eds.), *The fangerous drift to preferential trade agreements* (pp. 1–18). Washington, DC: The AEI Press.

Bond, E. W., Riezman, R. G., & Syropoulos, C. (2004). A strategic and welfare theoretic analysis of free trade areas. *Journal of International Economics, 64*(1), 1–27.

Borjas, G. J. (1995). The economic benefits from immigration. *The Journal of Economic Perspectives, 9*(2), 3–22.

Breuss, F. (2002). Benefits and dangers of EU enlargement. *Empirica, 29*(3), 245–274.

Breuss, F. (Ed.). (2007a). *The stability and growth pact: experiences and future aspects.* Wien, New York: Springer.

Breuss, F. (2007b). Erweiterungs- und nachbarschaftspolitik der EU. *WIFO-Monatsberichte, 8* (2007), 641–660.

Breuss, F. (2007c). Erfahrungen mit der fünfte EU-erweiterung. *WIFO-Monatsberichte, 12*(2007), 933–950.

Breuss, F. (2007d). *Globalization, EU enlargement and income distribution.* WIFO Working Papers, No. 296, June 2007 and FIW Working Papers, No. 008, http://www.fiw.ac.at.

Breuss, F. (2008a). Die Zukunft Europas. *Beitrag zum Außenwirtschaftsleitbild des Bundesministeriums für Wirtschaft und Arbeit* (BMWA), Wien, Mai.

Breuss, F. (2008b). EU und Globalisierung. *Wirtschaftspolitische Blätter*, 55. Jg., 3/2008, 561–578.

Breuss, F. (2009). An evaluation of the EU's fifth enlargement: with special focus on Bulgaria and Romania. *European Economy, Economic Papers, 361.*

Breuss, F., Fink, G., & Griller, S. (Eds.). (2008). *Services liberalisation in the internal market.* Wien, New York: Springer-Verlag.

Casella, A. (1996). Large countries, small countries and the enlargement of trade blocs. *European Economic Review, 40*(2), 389–415.

Corden, M. W. (1972). Economies of scale and customs union theory. *Journal of Political Economy, 80*(3), 465–475. Part 1.

Crawford, J.-A., & Fiorentino, R.V. (2005). *The changing landscape of regional trade agreements.* Discussion Paper, No. 8, Geneva: World Trade Organization.

D'Auria, F., Mc Morrow, K., Pichelmann, K. (2008). Economic impact of migration flows following the 2004 EU enlargement process: a model based analysis. *European Economy, Economic Papers, 349.*

Dimaranan, B. V. (Ed.). (2006). *Global trade, assistance, and production: the GTAP 6 data base. Center for global trade analysis.* West Lafayette, IN: Purdue University.

European Commission (2006). *Enlargement, two years after: an economic evaluation.* European Commission, European Economy, Occasional Papers, No. 24, Brussels.

European Commission (2009). European economic forecast: autumn 2009, *European Economy* 10/2009.

Frankel, J. A., & Romer, D. (1999). Does trade cause growth? *The American Economic Review, 89*(3), 279–399.

Fuchs, M. (2006). Österreich als aktiver Investor in der globalisierten Wirtschaft: Zahlungsbilanz im Jahr 2005. *Statistiken Q3/06, Oesterreichische Nationalbank* (OeNB), Wien.

Grossman, G., & Helpman, E. (1991). *Innovation and growth in the world economy.* Cambridge, MA: MIT.

Kemp, M., & Wan, H. Y. (1976). An elementary proposition concerning the formation of customs unions. *Journal of International Economics, 6*(1), 95–97.

Kennan, J., & Riezman, R. (1990). Optimal tariff equilibria with customs unions. *Canadian Journal of Economics, 23*(1), 70–83.

Kohler, W. (2004). Eastern enlargement of the EU: a comprehensive welfare assessment. *Journal of Policy Modeling, 26*(7), 865–888.

Krugman, P. R. (1991). *Geography and trade.* Cambridge, MA: MIT.

Lewer, J. J., & Van den Berg, H. (2003). How large is international trade's effect on economic growth. *Journal of Economic Surveys, 17*(3), 363–396.

Lloyd, P. J. (1982). 3×3 theory of customs unions. *Journal of International Economics, 12*, 41–46.

Neck, R. &. Weyerstrass, K. (18–19 May 2007). *Macroeconomic effects of Slovenia's euro area integration*. Paper presented at the Annual Meeting of the Austrian Economic Association, NOeG 2007, Klagenfurt University.

Ohyama, M. (2004). *Free trade agreements and economic welfare: beyond the Kemp–Wan theorem*. Keio University, KUMQRP Discussion Paper Series, DP2003-11, February.

Richardson, M. (1995). On the interpretation of the Kemp/Wan theorem. *Oxford Economic Papers, New Series, 47*(4), 696–703.

Rivera-Batiz, L. A., & Romer, P. M. (1991). Economic integration and endogenous growth. *The Quarterly Journal of Economics, CVI*(2), 531–555.

Romer, P. M. (1990). Endogenous technological change. *Journal of Political Economy, 98*(5), S71–S102. Part II.

Viner, J. (1950). *The customs union issue*. New York: Carnegie Endowment for International Peace.

Chapter 13
Comments on Chapters 11 and 12

Ryszard Rapacki

Abstract The contributions by Leigh et al. and Breuss differ in scope and focus. While the former relies mostly on 'back casting' and provides a broad comparative perspective on economic growth in transition and emerging economies, the latter looks forward and focuses on two particular countries, offering a useful analytical framework to study the impact of EU enlargement. The Comments suggest possible extensions and clarifications in the two chapters. The author however is fully convinced that they shed new light on the process of transition in Central and Eastern Europe and add to our understanding of the actual and potential effects the EU Eastern enlargement.

13.1 Introductory Remarks

The two contributions differ in scope and focus. In the first paper, Daniel Leigh and colleagues, in a very interesting comparative analysis, put the growth experience of Central and East European countries in a broader perspective by comparing these countries to emerging economies in East Asia and Latin America. The paper relies predominantly on "back casting" although some elements of prediction are also present.

The analysis by Fritz Breuss, on the other hand, looks forward as the model and the findings resulting from this model for Bulgaria and Romania focus on the possible future effects of EU membership.

R. Rapacki
Warsaw School of Economics, Warsaw, Poland
e-mail: rrapacki@sgh.waw.pl

F. Keereman and I. Szekely (eds.), *Five Years of an Enlarged EU*,
DOI 10.1007/978-3-642-12516-4_13, © Springer-Verlag Berlin Heidelberg 2010

13.2 Comments on Chap. 11

This chapter offers an insightful comparative perspective on economic growth trajectories and patterns of macroeconomic performance in three groups of emerging economies – in Central and Eastern Europe, East Asia and Latin America. It nicely blends the empirical analysis with theoretical discussion that is well-rooted in the mainstream growth theory and other relevant economic models. As a result, the paper sheds some new light on the most salient features and determinants of CEE transition economies' road from plan to market, highlighting the differences as well as similarities of their macroeconomic performance to the patterns established earlier in East Asia and Latin America.

Being very comprehensive in content and rich in inspiring conclusions the paper leaves not withstanding some space for possible extensions. In this regard, three remarks or suggestions concerning the role of institutions seem worth making.

Firstly, while addressing the issue of institutional determinants of economic development in the three groups of countries concerned it would be perhaps worthwhile referring to de Soto's (2002) book and his discussion on why capitalism succeeded in the West and failed in many other regions of the world including Latin America. According to de Soto, the most critical factor behind the diverging experience with market economy was the degree to which the economy was formalized and property rights were enforced.

Secondly, it could be interesting to include the "trust factor" or the social capital to the analysis, for example along the lines put forward by Fukuyama (1996). This might provide an additional differentiating factor between Latin America (low-trust societies) and East Asia (high-trust societies) on the one hand, and Central and Eastern Europe (low-but-rising trust societies?) as an explanatory variable of their diverging development patterns and macroeconomic performance.

Thirdly, it would be desirable to carry out further research to extend the scope of the paper and assess the relative explanatory power of the "EU factor" or "external anchor" as a driver of economic growth – in addition to the growth determinants discussed in the paper. There is empirical evidence, suggesting that the existence of an "external anchor", such as for example, the prospect of the EU membership can significantly accelerate the process of institutional reforms in the candidate countries (Rapacki et al. 2007). As shown, inter alia, in the EBRD's annual assessments (EBRD 2008), countries that were invited to join the European Union had initiated their reforms earlier, implemented them much more effectively and with greater commitment, and today are much more advanced in the reform process than other former centrally planned economies. Moreover, the use of "external anchors" can lead to different reform paths not only within the group of transition economies, but also in a much broader sample of countries. According to an IMF study (IMF 2002, p. 102), the quality of institutions in the new EU member states was, by 2002, higher on average than in other countries in the world at a comparable level of development. On the other hand, in the other transition economies, particularly CIS countries, the development of the institutional market infrastructure is slightly lower than in countries with a similar income levels.

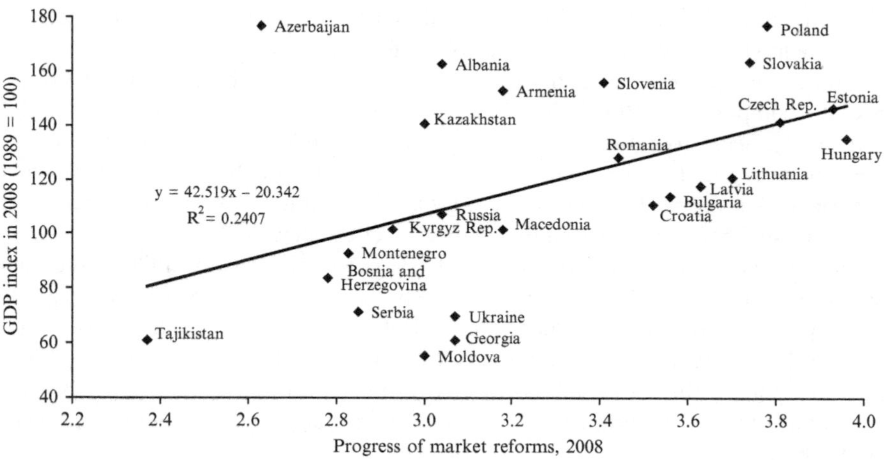

Fig. 13.1 The progress of structural reforms and economic growth in transition countries Notes: Transition countries excluding Belarus, Turkmenistan and Uzbekistan
Source: Rapacki (2009)

It should be also emphasized in this context that the progress of structural (or market) reforms was an important determinant of economic growth in transition countries. As Fig. 13.1 shows, countries that advanced more in the process of systemic transformation achieved faster GDP growth on average in 1990–2008 than those that were lagging behind. The positive correlation between these two variables is especially clear in CEE transition economies. By contrast in countries such as Moldova, Ukraine, Tajikistan, Serbia and Montenegro, the lack of major structural reforms contributed to negative GDP growth rates throughout the analyzed period.

In addition to these general suggestions to the authors, a number of minor remarks are worth making.

First, the full comparability of "acceleration episodes" in CEE countries with those in East Asia and Latin America is somewhat questionable. At least four to five episodes (out of eleven; see Table 11.1) in the former group of countries followed a "transformation recession" triggered by a systemic change or shock therapy (as e.g. in Poland). That is, the nature of growth accelerations in CEE might have been rather different ("extraordinary") from those in other regions as they were caused by a very specific institutional shock.

Second, the authors put all "acceleration episodes" into one basket, irrespective of their starting level and sign. Hence, two questions appear appropriate: (1) is there a difference between an acceleration from negative growth rates versus the one from positive growth levels, and similarly (2) is there a difference between an acceleration from low positive versus high positive growth levels (as in the case of e.g. Singapore)?

Third, does the "acceleration story" offer any lesson for a possible scale of subsequent slow downs (as e.g. nowadays in the Baltic states)?

Fourth, the paper does not discuss the possible factors behind the decline of an overall composite ICRG index in CEE countries between 2003 and 2007 (Fig. 11.7). Seen from a slightly different, i.e. geographical angle, later in the text the argument goes that the decline in question was brought about by adverse trends experienced in Latvia. In fact (see Fig. 11.7 again), as much as seven out of ten CEE countries suffered a backlash in this respect over the period 2003–2007.

Finally, while discussing the drivers of fast economic growth in CEE countries within the framework of the traditional growth theory, the authors ascribe a significant role, as a growth determinant, in the Baltic countries to small-governments. This has been only true however since the turn of the 1990s and the present decade – for most part of the 1990s the size of governments in those countries had been comparable to "big-government" economies in Central Europe (except for Slovakia after 2003).

13.3 Comments on Chap. 12

In his interesting contribution, Professor Breuss embarks on an econometric exercise aimed at quantifying possible future effects of the recent EU (2007) enlargement involving two new members – Bulgaria and Romania. While mostly sharing the logic of his approach and the pertinent conclusions, I believe that the following remarks are worth considering.

The first comment of general nature refers to the scope and coverage of the paper. As the study focuses on two particular countries only, it would be interesting to test how the inclusion of direct effects of the EU enlargement for other new member countries from Central and Eastern Europe change the results of the model.

Secondly, while discussing the opportunities and threats of the catching up process Professor Breuss addresses – among other issues – the problem of fiscal restraint, or the trade off between the real convergence and the nominal convergence, as a possible barrier (perhaps not so much for Bulgaria but definitely so for Romania) to an accelerated economic growth. The nominal convergence has to be achieved by the new EU members as they are bound to fulfill the Maastricht criteria to become eligible for the membership in the Economic and Monetary Union. In my view however, the trade off in question may be significantly alleviated if the "golden rule" of public finance is applied. The essence of the "golden rule" comes down to the postulate for the excess of public expenditure over revenue (the fiscal deficit, or more precisely, the borrowing requirement of the government) to be used for the financing of public investment. Thanks to such investment, particularly in infrastructure, positive externalities for the private sector arise and it is possible to sustain or even accelerate the rate of economic growth (real convergence), despite fiscal tightening (nominal convergence).

Finally, the paper does not provide an explicit explanation of the content of the "migration loss" notion – it is not clear if it encompasses remittances of Bulgarian and Romanian workers undertaking temporary or permanent jobs in other EU countries.

It is important to emphasize, however that despite the issues raised above, the paper offers an impressive analytical framework to study the impact of EU enlargement.

As a concluding remark it should be emphasized that both papers shed new light on the process of transition in Central and Eastern Europe and add to our understanding of the actual and potential effects of the EU Eastern enlargement. Similar to Rapacki and Próchniak (2009), they leave not doubt that the first 5 years of enlargement was a positive-sum game.

References

De Soto, H. (2002). *The mystery of capital. Why capitalism triumphs in the west and fails everywhere else*. Polish Edition: Fijorr Publishing.

EBRD (2008). Transition Report 2008. London.

Fukuyama, F. (1996). *Trust. The Social Virtues and the Creation of Prosperity*. London: Penguin Books.

IMF (2002). *World Economic Outlook 2002*, Washington, DC.

Rapacki, R. (Ed.). (2009). *Economic Growth in Transition Countries: Real Convergence or Divergence? (in Polish)*. Warsaw: PWE (Polish Economic Publishers).

Rapacki R. and M. Próchniak (2009). *The EU Enlargement and Economic Growth in the CEE New Member Countries*. European Economy, Economic Papers, No. 367, March 2009.

Rapacki, R., Z. Matkowski and M. Próchniak (2007). Economic Situation and the Progress of Market Reforms (chapter III). In D. Rosati (Ed.), *New Europe – Report on Transformation* (pp. 67–107). Krynica: Institute of Eastern Studies, XVII Economic Forum, 5–8 September.

Index

Kolibri 360 GmbH
Ferdinand-Jühlke-Straße 7
99095 Erfurt, Deutschland
produktsicherheit@kolibri360.de